DISARMING STRANGERS

PRINCETON STUDIES IN

INTERNATIONAL HISTORY AND POLITICS

Series Editors
Jack L. Snyder and Richard H. Ullman

DISARMING STRANGERS

NUCLEAR DIPLOMACY WITH NORTH KOREA

Leon V. Sigal

PRINCETON UNIVERSITY PRESS

PRINCETON, NEW JERSEY

COPYRIGHT © 1998 BY PRINCETON UNIVERSITY PRESS
PUBLISHED BY PRINCETON UNIVERSITY PRESS, 41 WILLIAM STREET,
PRINCETON, NEW JERSEY 08540
IN THE UNITED KINGDOM: PRINCETON UNIVERSITY PRESS,
CHICHESTER, WEST SUSSEX
ALL RIGHTS RESERVED

SIGAL, LEON V.
DISARMING STRANGERS : NUCLEAR DIPLOMACY WITH
NORTH KOREA / LEON V. SIGAL
P. CM. -- (PRINCETON STUDIES IN INTERNATIONAL HISTORY AND POLITICS)
INCLUDES BIBLIOGRAPHICAL REFERENCES AND INDEX.
ISBN 0-691-05797-4 (CL. : ALK. PAPER)
1. NUCLEAR NONPROLIFERATION.   2. UNITED STATES—
FOREIGN RELATIONS—KOREA (NORTH)
3. KOREA (NORTH)—FOREIGN RELATIONS—UNITED STATES.
4. DIPLOMACY. I. TITLE II. SERIES
JZ5675.S55   1997   327.1'747—DC21   97-24502   CIP

THIS BOOK HAS BEEN COMPOSED IN GALLIARD

PRINCETON UNIVERSITY PRESS BOOKS ARE PRINTED
ON ACID-FREE PAPER, AND MEET THE GUIDELINES FOR
PERMANENCE AND DURABILITY OF THE COMMITTEE ON
PRODUCTION GUIDELINES FOR BOOK LONGEVITY
OF THE COUNCIL ON LIBRARY RESOURCES

HTTP://PUP.PRINCETON.EDU

PRINTED IN THE UNITED STATES OF AMERICA

1   3   5   7   9   10   8   6   4   2

CONTENTS

Appendix II

PREFACE

I FIRST became interested in Korea when I joined the Editorial Board of the *New York Times* in June 1989. It was obvious that the end of the Cold War would greatly affect that divided land. I also knew from my experience in the United States government that the combustible combination of forward deployed forces on both sides of the Demilitarized Zone and our nuclear presence on the peninsula posed especially grave risks. One was that North Korea and South Korea would seek nuclear arms of their own. Another was that any crisis could get out of hand.

With that knowledge, and little else in mind, I wrote an editorial that appeared on June 25, 1990, urging the United States to "help the Koreas in from the cold" by coaxing them into military disengagement and diplomatic reengagement. "North Korea may accept international nuclear safeguards and is proposing new arms cuts," the editorial read. "These steps could ease the military confrontation on the peninsula and allow the U.S. to reduce its force of 45,000 troops in the South. And there would be no reason to keep U.S. nuclear weapons there." In a December 13, 1990, editorial I went further, urging diplomatic and economic ties with the North. My original draft recommended unilateral withdrawal of U.S. nuclear arms from the peninsula, but it was cut in last-minute editing.

I returned to the theme on February 4, 1991. "Washington could meet Pyongyang's concerns," I wrote, "by beginning to withdraw its nuclear weapons. It could also reduce the scale and frequency of military exercises in the area." Editorial page editor Jack Rosenthal let me have my say, as he would until he left the Editorial Board to run the magazine at the end of 1993.

After the December editorial, South Koreans, officials and former officials, began calling with invitations to lunch. A few Korea experts got in touch. The Asia Society invited me to a luncheon speech by Assistant Secretary of State Richard Solomon at the Waldorf Astoria. There I met Tony Namkung and we arranged to talk further. The South Korean ambassador to Washington invited me to lunch that April and a month later I met Ho Jong, a North Korean ambassador at the United Nations. I was soon in regular contact with American, South Korean, and North Korean officials, as well as a dozen experts on proliferation, in and out of government, and anyone knowledgeable about North Korea I could find, American, Japanese, and South Korean.

For the next six years I wrote some sixty editorials on nuclear diplomacy with North Korea—all but two that the *Times* ran on the subject. I was free to write what I wanted on all but two occasions, in June 1994 and in April 1995, when my editorials were rewritten or scrapped.

In the course of those six years I became intimately familiar with many of the nongovernmental contacts with North Korea, or Track II diplomacy. I thought the story was an important one that many people had misunderstood. When I left the *Times* I believed I was familiar enough with the details of U.S.–North Korean contacts to tell it right.

Little did I know. Only after long and repeated interviews with nearly all the American participants and quite a few South and North Koreans did I begin to realize how much of the history I thought I knew was wrong.

In trying to reconstruct the events of 1988 to 1995, I have benefited from the prior work of Mitchell Reiss, Michael Mazarr, and others. I also want to thank the many people in Washington, Seoul, and elsewhere whom I spoke to about the North Korean nuclear issue at one point or another from 1990 on: Gary Ackerman, Ahn Byung-joon, David Albright, Steven Aoki, Arima Tatsuo, Les Aspin, Bae Ho Hahn, Harry Barnes, Sandy Berger, Hans Blix, Stephen Bosworth, Robert Carlin, Ashton Carter, Dick Christenson, Gennady Chufrin, James Clapper, Marion Creekmore, Lynn Davis, James Delaney, Robert Einhorn, Steven Fetter, Thomas Finger, Stephen Flanigan, Steven Fleishman, Gary Foster, Leon Fuerth, Robert Gallucci, Robert Gates, Gong Ro-Myung, Donald Gregg, Vernon Guidry, Han Song Ryol, Han Sung Joo, Selig Harrison, Peter Hayes, Ho Jong, John Holum, Hyun Hong-Choo, Arnold Kanter, Charles Kartman, Spurgeon Keeny, Kim Dae Jung, Kim Kyung-Won, David Kyd, Anthony Lake, James Laney, Paul Leventhal, John Lewis, Stephen Linton, Thomas Longstreth, Winston Lord, Gary Luck, John McCain, Thomas McNamara, Gary Milhollin, Tony Namkung, Joseph Nye, Park Shun-Il, Park Soo-Gil, John Pike, Daniel Poneman, Nick Rasmussen, Roe Chang-hee, Roh Tae Woo, Jamie Rubin, Randy Rydell, Gary Samore, Brent Scowcroft, Larry Smith, Henry Sokolski, Stephen Solarz, Richard Solomon, Leonard Spector, Gordon Sullivan, Lynn Turk, Leonard Weiss, Frank Wisner, and Joel Wit, as well as two C.I.A. officials, two military officers, three Chinese officials, and two Japanese officials who must remain nameless. I interviewed many of them for this book.

I have tried as much as possible to get my sources to speak on the record, but when they did not, I have tried to identify them as fully as I could in the text. I am grateful to the dedicated public servants who took the time to confide in me, especially to those who do not share my conclusions.

I want to thank the Rockefeller Foundation, the W. Alton Jones Foundation, and the Social Science Research Council for their generous support, and especially Tom Graham, George Perkovich, and Ken Prewitt, without whom I could not have done this study. I also want to thank Richard Ullman, Bruce Cumings, and the editors at Princeton University Press, as well as Morton Halperin, Meredith Hyman, Judd Kahn, Michael McLean, Nicholas Rizopoulos, John Steinbruner, and others, who will have to remain nameless, for their comments and criticisms. Special thanks too to my wife, Meg, who was a tireless and supportive critic, and to my son, Jake, who will not have to worry about a nuclear North Korea.

New York City
31 July 1997

ABBREVIATIONS

A.C.D.A.	Arms Control and Disarmament Agency
C.I.A.	Central Intelligence Agency
DMZ	Demilitarized Zone (between North and South Korea)
D.P.R.K.	Democratic People's Republic of Korea (North Korea)
F.B.I.	Federal Bureau of Investigation
G.D.P.	gross domestic product
I.A.E.A.	International Atomic Energy Agency
INR	Bureau of Intelligence and Research, State Department
K.E.D.O.	Korean Energy Development Organization
LWR	light-water reactor
M.A.C.	Military Armistice Commission
M.F.N	Most Favored Nation
M.I.T.	Massachusetts Institute of Technology
MWe	megawatt
N.G.O.	non-governmental organization
N.N.S.C.	Neutral Nations Supervisory Commission
N.P.T.	Nonproliferation Treaty
N.S.C.	National Security Council
O.S.D.	Office of the Secretary of Defense
R.O.K.	Republic of Korea (South Korea)
SOPs	standard operating procedures
U.N.	United Nations
UNSCOM	United Nations Special Commission on Iraq

DISARMING STRANGERS

1

UNCOOPERATIVE AMERICA

*If you fight a war to preserve the N.P.T., that's like burning
a village in Vietnam to save it.
(Donald Gregg)*[1]

THE TROUBLE with American foreign policy since the end of the Cold War is that the United States has been unwilling to use military force, or so the prevailing orthodoxy goes. American influence abroad is said to have waned because its threats are no longer credible. Yet that orthodoxy ignores another source of foreign policy failure—American unwillingness to cooperate with strangers. In a number of recent cases the United States has tried threats to get its way when promises seemed more likely to succeed. Whether with Russia or Japan, with Cuba or the Palestinians, we have recoiled from giving cooperation a chance. We have also had difficulty making promises and keeping them.

That seems puzzling. Of course, cooperative strategies are not always appropriate for achieving American aims abroad. At times, too, conciliation alone will not suffice. It needs to be combined with coercion, or at least the threat of coercion. Yet a compelling case can be made for trying cooperation.

Cooperation works. It can succeed where coercion would fail. It is also cheap by comparison. Coercive measures like economic embargoes are costly to the sanctioner as well as to the sanctioned. The costs often fall disproportionately on sectors of the American economy with the political power to undo sanctions. For example, the grain embargo imposed on the Soviet Union in 1980 after its invasion of Afghanistan was lifted by President Reagan in 1982 under pressure from the farm lobby.

Military force is even more costly. The sacrifice of life and treasure give policy-makers pause. Yet they usually discount another substantial cost, erosion of public support for foreign involvement. A majority of the foreign policy establishment believes that the United States has less clout in the world today than it did a decade ago and wants it to play a much more assertive role abroad. The American public does not share that view.[2] Most Americans are much more amenable to other forms of overseas engagement, even foreign aid, than to military intervention.[3] For foreign policy-makers to define America's role in the world in military terms—to emphasize coercion instead of conciliation—may feed the fires of isolationism.

Cooperation, or "cooperative threat reduction" in the well-chosen words of Senators Sam Nunn (D-GA) and Richard Lugar (R-IN), is essential in meeting what many consider the most critical foreign policy challenge facing the United States today: stopping the spread of weapons of mass destruction. The growing integration of economies through direct foreign investment and trade has sped up the diffusion of technology useful in bomb-making. Acting alone, the United States cannot impede the flow of equipment and material that countries need to manufacture nuclear arms. It has to have help from other countries to deny proliferators vital supplies.

Denying them the means of bomb-making is inadequate by itself. Denial can buy time and provide early warning, but it cannot succeed forever. The interdiction of supply has to be supplemented by efforts to reduce demand. Unlike a strategy of pure denial, which threatens proliferators with economic and political isolation, convincing countries not to build the Bomb requires cooperating with them, however unsavory they may be. Countries that seek nuclear arms are insecure. Trying to isolate them or force them to forgo nuclear-arming could well backfire. They need reassurance to ease their insecurity.

A strategy of **diplomatic give-and-take** that combines reassurance with conditional reciprocity, promising inducements on the condition that potential proliferators accept nuclear restraints, might just persuade them to give up their quest. The strategy requires identifying allies inside the target state who have no interest in nuclear-arming, probing their willingness and ability to attain common ends, and then working with them.[4] Cooperative threat reduction may be especially difficult, yet all the more imperative, when the state in question has a history of egregious or seemingly irrational international behavior, when evidence of internal change is difficult to discern or deliberately obscured, and when contact with the country is so limited that potential allies within its political system are not easy to find.

Cooperative threat reduction has a long record of accomplishment. American reassurances and inducements have helped convince South Korea, Taiwan, Brazil, Argentina, South Africa, Ukraine, Belarus, and Kazakhstan to abandon nuclear-arming in recent years.[5] Only in Pakistan have inducements failed, although Pakistan has stopped just short of assembling deliverable warheads. Despite this history of accomplishment, the United States persists in choosing coercion instead of cooperation in trying to stop the spread of weapons of mass destruction.

The American effort to keep North Korea from acquiring nuclear arms is a case in point. In the end, the United States did reach an accord with the Democratic Peoples Republic of Korea (D.P.R.K.) which, if fully implemented, will leave Korea nuclear-free and begin to relax the military confrontation on the peninsula. That accord satisfied all of Washington's security requirements and at modest cost.

Yet the tortuous path that the United States took to reach an agreement is much less praiseworthy. After three years of failure after failure with coercive diplomacy, it finally tried cooperation and succeeded.

Nuclear diplomacy with North Korea is representative of a class of cases the United States is likely to face frequently after the Cold War. North Korea's nuclear program had to compete for attention with many other countries and problems, domestic as well as foreign. During the Cold War, any country or problem that touched on the Soviet-American conflict dominated the concern of policy-makers at the rank of assistant secretary and above. Now, without the framework of the Cold War to set priorities, they find it difficult to decide what to do with their scarce time and political capital. More than ever before, they jump from issue to issue, paying only intermittent attention to any of them. That makes them especially susceptible to the influence of their own predispositions and the domestic politics of the moment.

Putting together a deal with Pyongyang, despite the risks that nuclear-arming by North Korea posed to American interests in Asia, did not get the sustained attention it deserved from top officials until 1994. With Congress unwilling to spend money on foreign programs, policymakers were reluctant to expend time and political capital mustering support for any policy as unpromising as nuclear deal-making with North Korea. Threats seemed cheaper and more expedient than promises, at least in the political currency of Washington. Unfortunately, the strategy of coercion ran a significant risk of failure, even war.

A History of Failure

The standard American account of nuclear diplomacy with North Korea goes something like this: Despite having signed the nuclear Nonproliferation Treaty in December 1985, North Korea remained determined to develop nuclear arms. In an effort to reassure the North, the United States withdrew all its nuclear warheads from the Korean peninsula. Appeasement failed. North Korea signed an agreement with South Korea on December 31, 1991, pledging a nuclear-free peninsula, but refused to carry it out. It signed a nuclear safeguards agreement with the International Atomic Energy Agency, only to renege on inspections. The United States then adopted a strategy of threats and inducements, resuming Team Spirit military exercises with South Korea, while at the same time making numerous concessions, without success. North Korea kept denying full access to inspectors. When North Korea began removing spent fuel rods from the Yongbyon reactor in May 1994, the United Nations Security Council moved to impose sanctions. Only under duress, the standard account has it, did the D.P.R.K. relent. With sanctions about to enter into force, former President Jimmy Carter went to Pyongyang and won a pledge from Kim Il Sung to freeze the North's nuclear program. The D.P.R.K. signed the Agreed Framework with the United States on October 21, 1994, committing itself to give up nuclear-arming in return for replacement of its nuclear reactors, a supply of fuel oil, security guarantees, an end to the American economic embargo, and gradual diplomatic normalization—a deal that will take years to fulfill. "The Agreed Framework is the product of months of determined diplomacy and firm negotiation," Secretary of State Warren Christopher testified before the Senate Foreign Relations Committee. "We negotiated from a position of strength."[6] Senate Minority Leader Robert Dole drew a very different lesson, "It is always possible to get an agreement when you give enough away."[7]

The standard account is wrong.

Its major premise, that North Korea remained hell-bent on nuclear-arming, is open to question. Although that intention could not be ruled out, evidence of North Korean intentions was more ambiguous than the worst-case analysis suggested. To build bombs, it needed plutonium. The explosive ingredient for nuclear weapons, plutonium is produced by all nuclear reactors as a by-product of fission and deposited in the spent nuclear fuel. A country determined to make bombs would want to unload spent fuel rods from its nuclear reactor as soon as possible and reprocess them, extracting the plutonium from the rest of the nuclear waste. Yet North Korea has done no reprocessing since 1991. It also delayed discharging spent fuel, at least from the spring of 1993, when the I.A.E.A. expected the reactor to be refueled, until May 1994. While it resisted full international inspections, it did permit I.A.E.A. inspectors to verify that it was not removing spent fuel from the reactor or reprocessing it. The partial freeze was a sign that North Korea might be willing to give up nuclear-arming in return for American security assurances and political and economic benefits. But the D.P.R.K. was unwilling to give something away for nothing.

That posed a fundamental choice of how best to stop North Korea from nuclear-arming. Of course, it would have been preferable for the D.P.R.K. to live up to its obligations under the Nonproliferation Treaty. But what if it did not? What if it demanded inducements for complying? Vocal sentiment in the American foreign policy establishment, this book will demonstrate, overwhelmingly favored enforcing the treaty instead of offering inducements to North Korea. Many denounced inducements as appeasement. In their logic, making a deal meant yielding to nuclear blackmail. Yet appeasement of the weak by the strong promotes peaceful change. Appeasement, while it is a term of opprobrium around Washington, would have been wrong under two conditions, neither of them applicable: if North Korea had had unlimited ambitions and the means to pursue them, and if North Korea had been stronger and inducements would have further strengthened it at American expense.[8]

To other opponents of conciliation, offering inducements to North Korea for fulfilling its Nonproliferation Treaty obligations seems morally unconscionable. They ignore that the treaty itself embodies inducements for signing, most notably, help with nuclear power in return for forgoing nuclear-arming.

Those who opposed conciliation and instead wanted the treaty enforced assumed that if the United States bribed North Korea to refrain from nuclear-arming, it would set a dangerous precedent, undermining efforts to curb proliferation. Surely, a nuclear-armed North Korea would have set back the nonproliferation cause more than the precedent of inducing Pyongyang to disarm. Contrary to conventional wisdom, such inducements would not have set a dangerous precedent, inviting other countries to reap the benefits of bomb-making. The world is not full of nuclear-arming countries. Potential proliferators are few in number, none of them eager to start nuclear-arming for the primary purpose of being bought off. Indeed, the offer of benefits for North Korea to disarm would set no precedent at all. The United States has repeatedly used inducements in the past to get countries like South Korea and the ex-Soviet states to ban the bomb. Compelling North Korea to comply could prove more costly, and hardly more certain of success, than giving it what it wanted.

Instead of engaging in diplomatic give-and-take, however, Washington insisted that Pyongyang comply fully with the Nonproliferation Treaty as a *precondition* for negotiations and threatened it with economic sanctions, even air strikes, if it did not. The United States drew attention to North Korea's nuclear past and its nuclear potential and ignored its nuclear self-restraint. In an attempt to compel compliance, it adopted what became known as the carrot-and-stick policy. That policy was aptly characterized by one proponent: "To get a mule to move, you have to show it the carrot and hit it with a stick at the same time."[9] The mule may be struck repeatedly, but is fed the carrot only when it reaches the mule-driver's destination, if at all.

The metaphor was not lost on the D.P.R.K. In May 1993, just before high-level talks resumed in New York, North Korean negotiators asked an American visitor in Pyongyang, "What is the meaning of sticks and carrots?" One of them showed the visitor the entry in an old Merriam-Webster dictionary, which had a drawing of a donkey with a bunch of carrots dangling beyond its reach. Next to the donkey stood its master, stick in hand.[10]

Holding out the promise of talks as a reward for good behavior deprived the United States of a way to resolve its nuclear differences with North Korea. From 1988 until late 1993, even when the United States entered into talks, it did not negotiate. Diplomatic dialogue without give-and-take is a prescription for deadlock. As chapters 2–4 show, that is just what happened in five years of fitful talks between the United States and North Korea. Worse yet, the few promises Washington did make were not always carried out, often because it was dependent on others, South Korea and the I.A.E.A., to fulfill them.

Like a porcupine encountering an eagle, North Korea bristled at American threats. It followed a strategy of **tit-for-tat**, reciprocating American gestures of cooperation and retaliating when the United States reneged on its promises. (The interaction is summarized in chapter 5. Readers may also want to refer to the chart in appendix I.) As the D.P.R.K. repeatedly said, "It is the disposition and will of our people and army to answer dialogue with dialogue and strength with strength."[11] The vicious cycle of renege and reprisal came perilously close to spiraling out of control in June 1994, provoking a war neither side wanted. That such a tit-for-tat pattern emerges from the history of nuclear diplomacy from 1988 to 1995 may seem surprising to most observers, who have concluded that North Korea alone was the culprit, breaking its non-nuclear pledges and trying desperately to keep on building bombs.

It took three years of failed attempts at coercive diplomacy before Washington finally began cooperating with Pyongyang in the summer of 1994. Even then, the breakthrough came as the result of a private initiative—Track II diplomacy by former President Jimmy Carter. Chapter 6 describes how Carter, backed by a handful of nongovernmental organizations, overturned American policy by undercutting the sanctions strategy and revived chances for a diplomatic deal. Yet his efforts were widely disparaged, even by some top officials of the Clinton Administration.

President Bill Clinton, to his credit, took advantage of the Carter initiative to change course and engage in diplomatic give-and-take. He was bitterly assailed for doing so. In the face of severe criticism, with little support from the foreign policy establishment, the administration eventually got North Korea to agree to halt and roll back its nuclear arms program in return for gradual normalization of political and economic relations, construction of replacement reactors to generate nuclear power, and a supply of heavy fuel oil in the interim (see chapter 7). The agreement could be the start of a fundamental transformation on the Korean peninsula, ending the Cold War confrontation there.

The Clinton Administration, belatedly, claimed success for its negotiating strategy, but it attributed much of that success to coercive diplomacy. Officials still do today. That claim is dubious. Coercion had only led to North Korean recalcitrance, raising the risk of war. By publicly disavowing the sanctions strategy and trying cooperation, Jimmy Carter opened the way to a settlement. Even before he did so, that strategy had become a dangerous bluff. Sanctions might have spurred North Korean bomb-making; they could not prevent it. Even a total trade embargo could not have kept North Korea from making nuclear arms since it already had whatever it needed to make them. Denying it oil might eventually have caused its economy to collapse, but this prospect worried South Korea, Japan, and China, which would have to suffer the consequences—mass migration, instability, and possibly war. They were unwilling to enforce sanctions stringent enough to strangle North Korea.

The threat of military force was no more credible than sanctions. If North Korea had nuclear arms or enough plutonium to make them, U.S. intelligence had no idea where they were, and air strikes could not target what could not be found. Even striking the reactor at Yongbyon risked spewing radiation on Japan. That left the option of conquering North Korea, but for good reason, neither the United States nor South Korea wanted to take that risk, especially with a potentially nuclear-armed North. Economic sanctions and military force were empty threats.

North Korea was not about to be bluffed. Nor was it about to comply first and hope to reap the benefits later. Only when Washington satisfied its concerns did Pyongyang relent. A strategy of cooperative security, not coercive diplomacy, accounts for the success of diplomacy in Korea.

The cost of cooperative threat reduction on the Korean peninsula is comparatively modest. The total price of replacing the nuclear reactors, plus the supply of oil, is reckoned to be $5 billion, almost all of it borne by South Korea, Japan, and others. The U.S. contribution is about $30 million a year, which Congress has balked at financing. In contrast, the direct operating cost of maintaining the current American troop presence in Korea is $2.5 billion *a year* and the costs of stationing U.S. forces there instead of at home is another $800–900 million.[12] The costs of retaining forces to meet a Korean contingency runs into the tens of billions of dollars. Team Spirit joint military exercises in 1993 cost the Pentagon $900 million.[13] Stationing a carrier battle group in the Sea of Japan could run around $900 million a year in operating and maintenance costs alone—$1.8 billion a year if the cost of procuring the ships and aircraft and paying for manpower are taken into account.[14] A precautionary buildup in South Korea in the event of sanctions would have cost the Pentagon "a few hundred million dollars a year," according to the estimate of the Secretary of Defense. The costs of a war on the Korean peninsula would be prohibitive—as many as one million military and civilian casualties, including 80,000 to 100,000 American lives lost, and $100 billion, by one worst-case U.S. military estimate cited in Congressional testimony.[15]

Why the United States found it so difficult to cooperate with North Korea and nearly stumbled into war is initially a story of failure—the failure of the Bush and Clinton Administrations to get the policy right, the failure of President Clinton to get the politics right, and the failure of much of the intelligence community to get the assessments right. Not only the American government was at fault. South Korea and Japan failed to come to terms with their neighbor. International institutions failed as well, particularly the International Atomic Energy Agency, which seemed more concerned about having North Korea strictly abide by its safeguards agreement than about inducing it to abandon nuclear-arming. Nuclear diplomacy with North Korea is also a story of failure of most American experts on Korea and nonproliferation, who opposed conciliation and instead promoted reckless alternatives, and failure of much of the press, which misinterpreted events and misled readers. Above all, it was a failure of an American foreign policy establishment that discouraged cooperation at every turn.

For too long U.S. policy toward North Korea was muscle-bound and brain-dead. The question is why. The answer begins with uncertainty about North Korea's intentions and capabilities.

Shared Uncertainty, Shared Certitude

North Korea could have been on Mars for all that the United States knew about it. It was a faraway land of unknowns and unknowables explored mostly by space probes, in this case, spy satellites. Few Americans had ever visited North Korea or talked to a North Korean, not to mention its leaders. In their efforts to get to know one another, it was not clear whether North Korea or the United States was more of a hermit kingdom.

For American policy-makers as well as much of the foreign policy establishment, North Korea was a blank screen on which to project their own predispositions and prejudices. "The arguments in Washington were largely projections by Americans with strong views about how they thought it would react," one highly placed Clinton Administration official recalls. "Nobody knows what's going on in North Korea. Nobody knows who decides things there."[16]

North Korea's history of bizarre and brutal behavior and its highly adversarial style of bargaining sowed uncertainty about what it was doing and how best to respond. Its habit of floating concessions on a sea of threats and vituperation alarmed and dismayed even those who favored conciliation. A pragmatic and prudent response to uncertainty would have been to treat estimates of North Korean nuclear capabilities and intentions as rough guesses rather than facts, to probe North Korean intentions through diplomatic give-and-take and avoid running a high risk of war. The response, instead, was worst-case assessments and rash policies—threats of economic coercion, even armed force.

Why were policy-makers and the people who tried to influence them so unwilling to countenance negotiating with North Korea before reaching for their guns? Efforts to deal with North Korea's nuclear-arming were impeded by four beliefs that were widely shared in the foreign policy establishment. These beliefs, or shared images, informed the politics of nuclear diplomacy both in and out of the American government.[17]

A key belief, or shared image, is that proliferation is just too difficult to prevent—that once a nation decides to build the Bomb, it cannot be persuaded to stop. Top officials, who already have plenty to do, are unwilling to tackle problems deemed too daunting. Without their sustained involvement, officials who have day-to-day responsibility for preventing proliferation are often marginalized and find it difficult to implement workable strategies, especially ones that require inducements rather than threats and exact economic and domestic political costs. The belief that proliferation is unstoppable is an article of faith to so-called realists, who assume that all states seek military security in preference to any other value and that nuclear-arming makes states secure. This belief is bolstered by pessimistic assumptions about the ease of building the Bomb because of the diffusion of nuclear know-how and nuclear technology and material. The belief persists despite the fact that the number of nuclear-armed states remains far lower than was widely predicted in the 1960s and despite recent successes in persuading countries to dismantle their nuclear programs.

A second shared image is that North Korea was a "rogue" state, the last redoubt of Stalinist-style communism, motivated to build bombs by hostility to the outside world. Much of North Korea's own behavior reinforced its image as an archetypal rogue: its 1950 aggression that led to a brutal war, its acts of terrorism including the 1983 bombing in Rangoon that barely missed South Korean President Chun Doo Hwan but killed seventeen members of his entourage, its internal regimentation, its dogmatism and harsh diatribes against the United States and South Korea, and its bizarre bargaining and brinkmanship. Although it had ceased acts of terrorism and muted its anti-American rhetoric by 1988, the image of a communist rogue state ruled by a latter-day Genghis Khan was difficult to shake. That image inspired officials to fill in the blanks about North Korea. They treated it as an outcast, implacable and inimical, with a master plan to deceive the world and acquire nuclear arms. That made it an easy target for demonization. Belief in this image also blinded observers, including much of the U.S. intelligence community, to contrary evidence of Pyongyang's efforts to accommodate Washington. It led many to conclude that the only way to stop North Korea's bomb program was to compel the collapse of the communist regime in Pyongyang.

A third shared image is that the main proliferation menace comes from rogue states like North Korea, Iran, and Iraq. Russia, China, Israel, India, and Pakistan are not considered rogue states. Yet some of them pose even greater proliferation risks by stimulating their neighbors to acquire nuclear arms and serving as sources for nuclear know-how and technology. Moreover, even if U.S. intelligence estimates were correct, as of 1995 North Korea may have amassed a bomb's worth or two of nuclear material. Iran had none and would not be able to produce a bomb on its own for at least seven years—five years for Russia to build a reactor at Bushehr begun by West Germany, plus at least two more years to generate a bomb's worth of plutonium from the reactor's spent fuel and fabricate it into a warhead.[18] By comparison, Russia had 24,000 warheads and enough nuclear material—plutonium and highly enriched uranium—to make tens of thousands more. With corruption rife, loosening controls especially at Russia's civilian nuclear installations, there is a serious risk that weapons-grade material could be smuggled out and end up in, say, Iran. Yet some in Congress, outraged at Russia for its reactor sale to Iran, tried to cut off aid for dismantling Russian warheads and controlling the extracted nuclear material.

The fourth and most pernicious belief is that the way to get states to abandon their nuclear ambitions is to demonize them as outlaws and force them to disarm—**the crime-and-punishment approach** to preventing proliferation. Yet there is no global sheriff to enforce international law and it is difficult to round up a posse to mete out punishment. When Washington has tried this approach, as it did with North Korea, coercion and threats proved counterproductive. Instead of discouraging insecure states from nuclear-arming, this strategy may give them more of a reason to do just that. Even those who reject demonization believe that cooperation cannot work and that coercion is the only way to disarm potential proliferators. It is rooted in their belief that America's influence in the world rests ultimately on its weapons and not on its wealth or its ideas.

Especially for those who view the world as a Hobbesian war of all against all with little prospect of cooperation and who believe that the unilateral display of muscle is the surest strategy for the United States to get its way in the world, the necessity for cooperation is a difficult lesson to absorb. Failure to absorb it has impeded nonproliferation efforts with North Korea and will continue to do so with Iran and others.

These **shared images of nuclear diplomacy** shaped the politics of dealing with North Korea within the American government. Primitive realism took the place of pragmatism.

That led officials to certain conclusions about North Korea's intent to develop nuclear arms and the dim prospects for dissuading it. Their mind-set made them inattentive to contrary evidence and disinclined to probe North Korean motives. In particular, it led them to ignore the question why, if North Korea was determined to acquire a nuclear arsenal and had the means to do so, did it not just go ahead and build bombs? Why did it instead delay unloading spent nuclear fuel from its reactor, stop reprocessing plutonium, and invite I.A.E.A. inspectors into its nuclear facilities to verify that it had?

The same shared images of nuclear diplomacy also informed most of those in the foreign policy establishment and Congress who took an active part in the public discourse on North Korea. These beliefs became important domestic political impediments to deal-making with North Korea.

The Politics of Diplomatic Paralysis

It used to be axiomatic around Washington that politics stops at the water's edge. Like most Washington axioms, the notion that foreign policy was insulated from domestic politics never could withstand close scrutiny. In nuclear diplomacy with North Korea, it was demonstrably false. Time and again, domestic politics prompted the Bush and the Clinton Administrations to adopt a posture of toughness and inhibited them from making anything like acceptable offers to North Korea. The result was diplomatic deadlock, and worse, a crisis that nearly got out of hand.

The politics of confrontation was of a narrow sort. The American public was largely inattentive; when polled, it was sharply divided over going to war to prevent North Korea from making nuclear arms. The pressures that put both administrations in uncompromising positions came from members of Congress and the foreign policy establishment, including nongovernmental and academic experts on nuclear and Korean affairs. Chapters 9 and 10 will explore some reasons for that.

Few in Congress or the foreign policy establishment believed that a diplomatic solution was possible. Far fewer were willing to defend deal-making in public. More outspoken members favored economic and military pressure on North Korea. Their views registered with special force because they were routinely quoted in the news. Chapter 8 will examine why. Institutional changes in Congress and the electoral process also favored the outspoken. These institutional changes, while tightening up party lines and intensifying partisanship, privileged those members of Congress who stood out in the crowd instead of going along with it. The way to stand out in a cast of hawks was to advocate force.

Senior officials in the Bush and the Clinton Administrations were themselves skeptical that diplomacy could succeed. Given the doubt and hostility in Congress and in the foreign policy establishment, both administrations were loath to try. Until the spring of 1993, they sought to avoid talks. When they did negotiate, they shied away from tabling specific offers. When they did make proposals, they cloaked concessions in threats. When they made promises, they did not always keep them.

Both administrations were particularly vulnerable to hard-line pressure on the North Korean nuclear issue. President Bush's failed attempt to appease Iraq was an Achilles heel that, some administration officials feared, Democrats and right-wing Republicans were eager to exploit. The Clinton Administration, accused of vacillation and weakness from its inception, felt similarly constrained. Yet war posed much greater political risks for a president who was elected on a platform of domestic renewal and a commander-in-chief who had troubled relations with the armed forces.

Most senior officials did not try to discern North Korea's motives, difficult as that may have been, or to design probes of its intentions. Doubtful about striking a nuclear deal and knowing that other influential Americans thought likewise, top officials in both administrations were attentive to domestic politics and closed-minded about what North Korea was saying and doing. That led to a number of rude surprises. It very nearly led to war.

PART I

COERCION FAILS

2

THE BUSH DEADLOCK MACHINE

Finding the truth about the North's nuclear program is an
example of how what we "know" sometimes leads us away
from what we need to learn.
(Robert Carlin)[1]

MOST SENIOR officials in the Bush Administration, including National Security Adviser Brent Scowcroft, his deputy and later C.I.A. Director Robert Gates, Secretary of State James Baker, Secretary of Defense Dick Cheney, and Undersecretary of Defense Paul Wolfowitz, shared the belief that nuclear diplomacy with North Korea could not succeed. Domestic politics, in particular, vocal hostility to dealing with North Korea in Congress and the foreign policy establishment reinforced their reluctance to try.

When the United States offered security assurances, North Korea responded in kind. Yet the Bush Administration did not learn from the experience. After that brief flirtation with conciliation, it opted for coercion. Wary of trying to satisfy Pyongyang's wants in return for halting and rolling back its nuclear arms program, Washington did not attempt to engage in diplomatic give-and-take. Instead, it adopted the crime-and-punishment approach, precipitating a crisis.

The administration used the International Atomic Energy Agency to police the North's nuclear program and tried to use the U.N. Security Council to enforce compliance with the nuclear Nonproliferation Treaty. North Korea was told to live up to its obligations under the treaty, or else. Although the crime-and-punishment approach did not preclude concessions—prosecutors, after all, do plea bargain—it was more compatible with parole, or time off for good behavior. Only when North Korea complied fully with the Nonproliferation Treaty would the United States consider cooperating with it.

The Bush Administration encouraged the I.A.E.A. to get tough with North Korea. It also pressed South Korea to hold up economic and other ties until Seoul secured intrusive nuclear inspections in talks with Pyongyang. That left the United States hostage to an I.A.E.A. and a South Korea whose own internal politics led them at times to adopt even more prosecutorial postures.

The I.A.E.A.'s role is often misunderstood. Because all nuclear reactors produce plutonium as a by-product of nuclear fission, it is essential to safeguard nuclear power plants and other nuclear facilities against misuse for bomb-making. The I.A.E.A. performs its safeguards mission in two main ways: by monitoring these facilities with surveillance cameras, radiation detection gear, and occasional inspections, and sealing off critical areas to impede diversion of nuclear material; and by material accountancy, carefully weighing and measuring the flow of nuclear material in and out of declared facilities to detect any diversion. Safeguards require the consent and cooperation of the host country.

The agency has little ability to detect, let alone monitor, undeclared nuclear facilities on its own. It has to rely on member nations to detect clandestine sites and share intelligence with it.

An offspring of the Nonproliferation Treaty, the I.A.E.A. has often been caught in a contradiction embedded in that treaty between promoting nuclear power and preventing nuclear-arming. At the time of its founding, many member nations regarded intrusive inspections as an infringement on their sovereignty and resisted empowering the agency with that right. Countries that contribute significant shares of the agency's financial support, like Japan and Germany, have balked at paying for tighter safeguards. As a United Nations agency, the I.A.E.A. has a diverse governing board, including some countries that have nuclear arms ambitions of their own, or American allies that regard a viable threat of proliferation as a justification for their own nuclear-arming.

As a consequence, the agency did not always place the highest priority on nuclear safeguards. Its regular budget was one indication of that. It allocated only about one-third to its safeguards mission, nearly all of it in countries that pose no real risk of proliferation. It spent considerably more on technical assistance for civilian nuclear efforts. North Korea was itself getting about $250,000 a year in such aid.

Another indication of the agency's priorities was its lackadaisical initial response to North Korea's joining the Nonproliferation Treaty. The North had eighteen months from the time it signed the treaty on December 12, 1985, to conclude a safeguards accord with the I.A.E.A. The agency mistakenly sent Pyongyang a type-66 draft agreement intended to cover individual sites rather than a type-153 appropriate for a party to the treaty. It was not until June 1987 that the I.A.E.A. got around to sending the correct agreement. The agency then allowed the December 1988 deadline for North Korea's reply to pass without taking action.[2]

By 1990 the I.A.E.A. began transforming itself in ways that were not anticipated in North Korea and only dimly appreciated by top American policy-makers. Under fire for failing to detect Iraq's bomb program, it was determined to redeem its reputation. The agency asserted its right to conduct special inspections at undeclared nuclear sites, instituted more timely reporting requirements for constructing or modifying nuclear facilities, introduced new techniques for taking radiation samples and analyzing them, and adopted new internal procedures for using intelligence from member states to police suspected violations.[3] It was also determined to lay down the law in North Korea, out of fear that any flexibility in implementing safeguards would create an unfortunate precedent for other would-be proliferators. That put it on a collision course with Pyongyang, which wanted something in return for granting inspectors greater access.

South Korea also had difficulty dealing with North Korea. South and North Korea were creatures of a World War II ceasefire and the ensuing Cold War. Each based its legitimacy on being the antithesis and antagonist of the other. South Korea was non-communist and anti-communist. North Korea, though frequently referred to as the last Stalinist state, was hardly a model of Marxist-Leninist orthodoxy. It had refused to join COMECON, the Soviet trading bloc. It talked about self-reliance, which was its way of saying that it was no "puppet" of the Japanese or the Americans or anyone else. It was willing to cooperate with outsiders, but on its own terms, and its ideology of *juche* was flexible enough to accommodate various forms of economic experimentation, even dependence on South Korea for nuclear power.

The issue of North-South relations was a vital and delicate one in South Korean politics. This led Seoul to try to control all contact with Pyongyang and avoid the impression it was following Washington's lead. It also led Seoul to blow hot and cold about talks between Washington and Pyongyang—warming up whenever the talks sputtered and turning cool whenever they made headway.

Under the Roh Tae Woo government dominated by ex-generals, South Korea did create an opening for relations with North Korea under its so-called "Northern policy," but that policy was primarily aimed at taking advantage of the end of the Cold War to forge ties with the North's allies. Roh's successor, Kim Young Sam, who took office a month after Bill Clinton, was the nation's first freely elected civilian president. Having won just 40 percent of the vote, he was acutely sensitive to hard-line opposition in Seoul's press and foreign policy establishment, especially the holdovers from years of military rule who filled the bureaucracy.

Actions by the I.A.E.A. and the R.O.K. led a mistrustful Pyongyang to conclude that Washington was refusing to deal or reneging on past promises. Pyongyang, in turn, retaliated.

Dealing with Korean Insecurities

No country has been the target of more American nuclear threats than North Korea—at least seven since 1945.[4] Even when the United States refrained from expressly menacing the North, its military presence posed an existential nuclear threat. For over thirty years, beginning in 1957, the United States deployed nuclear arms in South Korea. It also conducted numerous military exercises with nuclear-capable artillery and fighter-bombers on the Korean peninsula and carrier aircraft just off-shore.[5]

Insecurity fed by the American nuclear threat may have spurred North Korea to try to develop nuclear arms in the early 1960s. In 1963 it asked the Soviet Union for help in building the bomb. In 1964 Soviet and North Korean experts, some of them Soviet-trained, set up a nuclear research facility at Yongbyon. In 1965 the Soviet Union supplied North Korea with a small 2–4 megawatt research reactor. It also helped the North mine its own uranium. China helped as well. Although the Soviet Union and China did not provide North Korea the bomb-making technology it needed, they did not do enough to restrain their client either.

Clear signs of nuclear-arming by South Korea in the early 1970s coincided with a step-up in North Korea's nuclear arms program. The United States denied South Korea the means to pursue its nuclear arms ambitions by persuading France to cancel plans to equip it with reprocessing facilities, convincing Canada to call off a reactor deal, and getting Belgium to back away from supplying the South with a nuclear fuel fabrication facility.[6] Washington also induced Seoul to ratify the Nonproliferation Treaty in 1975, which it had signed in 1968, with offers of security assurances, dropping plans to withdraw some of its troops from Korea and reiterating its nuclear guarantee. Nevertheless, in early 1975 American intelligence analysts concluded, "South Korea was moving rapidly to acquire materials, equipment and expertise that would enable it to build nuclear weapons."[7] Seoul's nuclear program prompted President Jimmy Carter to offer still more reassurance, calling off a planned troop withdrawal in 1978 and reaffirming the U.S. nuclear pledge in 1979.[8] Still, South Korea kept its bomb-making option open.

North Korea's security continued to erode as the South outpaced the North militarily throughout the 1970s and the North could not count on its sometime allies, the Soviet Union and China. Ever since the 1970s, some U.S. intelligence assessments have concluded that South Korea has the edge, especially in the air, and could repulse a North Korean attack even without throwing U.S. forces into the balance.[9] To South Korea, the American military presence may have seemed like in-surance against attack. To North Korea, it looked like a threat. By the 1990s, some North Korean officials were seeing the American troop presence in a new light, as a restraint on South Korea and a counter-weight against Japan, Russia, and China.

Public accounts still dwell on North Korea's million-man army and its massive concentrations of forward-deployed artillery and tanks, but the vaunted million-man army is largely a fiction. It has not conducted large-scale tank or combined arms exercises in years. Of the estimated 1.1 million North Koreans under arms, about 923,000 are in the army. A half million of them are either soldier-workers engaged in civil construction, North Korea's equivalent of the U.S. Army Corps of Engineers, or paramilitary troops, in units that train irregularly and are not combat-ready. North Korea has some 3,950 tanks, nearly double that of South Korea, but many are obsolescent. The North could field some 600 combat aircraft, but many of them are older models, no match for South Korea's modern fighters.[10] That leaves the North's ground forces and lines of supply vulnerable to attack from the air.

Forward deployment, instead of showing North Korea's aggressive intent, may be its way to compensate for qualitative inferiority. That puts it in a position to strike first should war appear imminent, before allied air power can blunt an attack and interdict its long lines of supply, as occurred during the Korean War. "They don't want to be all strung out the way they were the last time," says General James R. Clapper, Jr., Director of the Defense Intelligence Agency from 1991 until 1994 and former intelligence chief in the Korea and Pacific commands. "They think the best defense is a good offense." So precarious is the military balance from Pyongyang's vantage point that every time a large-scale exercise takes place in South Korea, the North has to mobilize its forces, at considerable expense. "That's why," says Clapper, "they go nuts at Team Spirit."[11]

Under these conditions, a surprise attack by the North could not be ruled out. Nor could a devastating artillery barrage on parts of Seoul, within range of the North's front lines.

North Korea's increasing insecurity did not prompt it to undertake a crash program to build the bomb. Instead, it proceeded by fits and starts. It built a small (1,000-kilowatt) research reactor in the mid-1950s, followed by a 2–4 megawatt research reactor, which went operational in 1967. In 1977 the Soviet Union, with U.S. encouragement, persuaded North Korea to place that reactor under international safeguards, only to have South Korea resume its nuclear program. North Korea's interest in nuclear-arming first became manifest after it began construction of a 5-MWe reactor at Yongbyon in 1979. The reactor became operational in January 1986. Moderated by graphite and fueled by natural uranium, both of which North Korea has in ample supply, it had a low burn-up rate especially well suited for generating an exceptionally high proportion of plutonium-239, the critical ingredient of nuclear arms, in its spent fuel. In December 1985, as international concern about North Korea's nuclear ambitions intensified, the Soviet Union induced the D.P.R.K. to sign the Nonproliferation Treaty with a promise of four nuclear power reactors, a promise it never fulfilled. In 1985 the North also began construction of a 50-MWe gas-graphite reactor at Yongbyon and later a 200-MWe gas-graphite reactor at Taechon.

In 1988 U.S. intelligence detected construction at Yongbyon of what it later concluded was a reprocessing plant to extract plutonium-239 from spent reactor fuel. When fully operational, the plant was assessed to have the capacity to reprocess spent fuel from all three North Korean reactors—yielding 30 bombs' worth of plutonium a year.

In the spring of 1989 the Yongbyon reactor was shut down for 71 days, another 30 days or so in 1990, and about 50 days in 1991, which eventually led U.S. intelligence to suspect that spent fuel had been removed for bomb-making.[12] North Korea reprocessed spent fuel in 1989, 1990, and 1991, according to I.A.E.A. analysis. How much plutonium it produced became a matter of considerable contention. In 1991, however, the D.P.R.K. began negotiating a safeguards agreement with the International Atomic Energy Agency and an agreement with South Korea to ban the possession, basing, and manufacture of nuclear arms, including a ban on reprocessing.

This brief chronology suggests why most experts in and out of government could regard North Korea as a principal threat to the nonproliferation regime. Yet it also prompts a fundamental question: if North Korea was so intent on acquiring a nuclear arsenal, why would it negotiate a safeguards agreement that would open Yongbyon to international inspection? Why consider a ban on reprocessing? Why not just go ahead and build bombs?

One possibility is that by the late 1980s, the North Korean leadership saw a potentially far graver threat to its survival, one that nuclear arms could not forestall—economic stagnation. In the 1950s and 1960s North Koreans had managed to make communism work and the North's economy outperformed the South's. By the 1970s, however, South Korea had caught up and surpassed it. In the 1980s, while the South's growth was accelerating, the North's slowed to a crawl, under 2 percent a year, compounding the hardship of sustaining its defense effort. By 1993 South Korea's GDP was $300 billion a year; North Korea's $21 billion. In per capita terms the gap was $9,200 to $1,000. (South Korea's population was 44.9 million, nearly double North Korea's 23.9 million.) With the collapse of the Soviet empire and the economic transformation of China, the North's supply of imported oil at subsidized prices was sharply curtailed, impeding the mining of coal, its principal energy source. Oil imports from the Soviet Union dropped to 40,000 tons in 1991 from 440,000 tons in 1990 and coal production fell 6.5 percent. Starting in 1990, North Korea's GDP contracted—falling 3.7 percent in 1990, another 5.2 percent in 1991, and 5 percent in 1992—making its high level of military spending unsustainable, even for a command economy. Foreign trade, always limited in this most autarkic of economies, plummeted to $2.6 billion in 1992. (By comparison, South Korea's two-way trade with the United States alone was $32 billion that year.) As the North's exports were cut in half, its foreign debt ballooned, slowing imports of much-needed capital equipment.[13]

At the same time the D.P.R.K. faced increasing political isolation. South Korea played host to the 1988 Olympic games, with North Korea's allies, the Soviet Union and China, both in attendance. South Korea secured separate seating for the two Koreas at the United Nations on September 17, 1991, over the North's objections. It also established diplomatic relations with all of North Korea's onetime allies, including the Soviet Union on September 30, 1990, and China on August 24, 1992.

By the late 1980s, North Korea was in a parlous position militarily, economically, and politically. That led observers to different conclusions. Many feared it might lash out against its neighbors. A few hoped it might reach out and accommodate them.

At the time the fears seemed more justified than the hopes. In retrospect it seems possible that North Korea's acceptance of a U.N. seat of its own was a sign—albeit one not easy to discern, given its hostile rhetoric and its limited contact with outsiders—that it was fundamentally changing course. Two American analysts thought so at the time. Robert Carlin and John Merrill of the State Department's Bureau of Intelligence and Research (INR) saw the North's acceptance of dual seating at the United Nations, along with the decision to seek diplomatic relations with Japan, as "major policy shifts with long-term implications, not just tactical maneuvering." They also saw that the North's idea of confederation as an interim step to unification opened the way for it to deal with the government in the South "as a legitimate negotiating partner." Engaging the United States in talks, they argued, "has seemingly become more important than the withdrawal of U.S. troops" from Korea, a long-standing D.P.R.K. demand. Pyongyang had learned to regard its allies as unreliable: "The experience of the mid-1950s, when Kim Il Sung had to stave off joint Sino-Soviet attempts to overthrow him, only reinforced the leadership's conviction that outside powers, even nominally fraternal ones, could not be trusted."[14] Now the D.P.R.K. was reaching out to its foes in order to improve its economic, political, and military position.

In 1990, as chapter 6 will show in more detail, North Korean officials were telling a few American visitors that the D.P.R.K.'s longtime leader Kim Il Sung had made three watershed decisions. Siding with pragmatists in Pyongyang who sought both a limited opening to Western investment and trade to stimulate economic growth and a relaxation of the armed confrontation to reduce the country's defense burden, Kim began partially opening up his autarkic economy to the outside world. Inter-Korean trade, for instance, surged from $18.8 million in 1989 to $174 million in 1992, before tapering off as the nuclear crisis overheated.[15] Second, Kim opted to normalize relations with the United States, the one country that could restrain the military threat from South Korea and open doors to the rest of the world, politically and economically. The hope was that the United States would become a broker and guarantor of peace on the Korean peninsula and encourage investment and trade from South Korea and Japan. Third, instead of trying to delegitimate and destabilize South Korea or pursuing its long-stated aim of unifying the peninsula, the North was prepared to coexist with the South.

This was not the first time that the North moved to open its economy; it had tried and failed in the late 1960s and early 1980s. Nor was this the first time it had sought detente with the South; in 1979 and in 1984 it tried and failed, then reverted to extreme hostility. Nor was this the first time it had sought engagement with the United States; it tried and failed in the late 1970s and again in the mid-1980s.[16]

While North Korea was reaching out to the United States and Japan, South Korea was pursuing its "Northern policy," trying to isolate the North and leave itself free to deal with Pyongyang on its own terms. Neither North nor South could quite bring itself to cooperate with the other, and even a policy of live and let live was still susceptible to the pull of the past—a fratricidal war in which three million Koreans died.

To the South, the North's continued existence represented a challenge to its own legitimacy and sense of self. For Washington to be dealing with Pyongyang while it looked on gave Seoul fits of dependency and status anxiety. It worried that its own favored position with Washington would somehow be diminished.

Worse yet, an American policy of engagement with the North might prop up the communist regime and perpetuate the division of Korea. That aroused Korean nationalism on both the left and the right. It helped sustain the deeply held belief on the left that the United States was keeping Korea divided to justify its troop presence on the peninsula. It aroused fears on the right that America's purpose was to prevent the emergence of a powerful Korea. The left nurtured the hope that North and South Korea, left on their own, would gradually reconcile and grow together. Seoul's hawks, who thrived in the climate of pervasive mistrust, feared reconciliation. Preferring collapse to cooperation, they hoped to strangle North Korea's economy, topple the communist regime, and unify their divided land by absorbing the North, German-style. Economic implosion, however, could trigger military explosion.

Little of this was appreciated in Washington in 1988 when the North Korean nuclear program first became an issue.

North Korea Reciprocates for U.S. Security Assurances

American security assurances were needed to convince an insecure North Korea to abandon nuclear-arming. These assurances took nuclear forms: withdrawal of all American nuclear warheads from the Korean peninsula and suspension of Team Spirit, the large military exercise conducted annually with South Korea. When the Bush Administration unilaterally provided these assurances, North Korea reciprocated, putting the brakes on bomb-making.

In 1988, the last year of Ronald Reagan's presidency, American reconnaissance satellites first detected what turned out to be a North Korean reprocessing plant under construction near the 5-MWe reactor at Yongbyon. The discovery led Washington to get Moscow and Beijing to press Pyongyang to sign a safeguards agreement with the I.A.E.A., opening its nuclear sites to inspection. Yet traditional sphere-of-influence diplomacy made little headway beyond that.

On October 31, 1988, the Reagan Administration quietly opened a direct diplomatic dialogue with North Korea in Beijing. Some eighteen meetings between the political counselors in the two sides' embassies took place from 1988 through 1991. Yet this point of contact meant little in Washington. "Anything that came through the Beijing channel was almost instantly dismissed," says a State Department official.[17] The nuclear issue was raised only perfunctorily in this venue. Washington instead continued to pursue the issue indirectly through Moscow and Beijing.

At the time of the first exchanges in Beijing, the United States adopted a so-called "five-point policy," allowing travel to North Korea and unofficial visits by academic, cultural, and athletic groups and commercial exports of food, clothing, and medical supplies on a case-by-case basis, but setting five preconditions for improving government-to-government relations. North Korea had to soften its anti-American rhetoric, provide credible assurances that it had ceased its support of terrorism, account for or repatriate the remains of over eight thousand Americans missing in action during the Korean War, engage in a dialogue with South Korea, and put its nuclear activities under I.A.E.A. safeguards.[18] Washington's message to Pyongyang was you go first.

Two years later the Bush Administration took the initiative. A blast detected at Yongbyon led U.S. intelligence to conclude that North Korea was testing high explosives that could be used to detonate a nuclear device. During a visit to Washington in early June 1990 South Korean President Roh Tae Woo made that assessment public. Instead of using the disclosure to start a confrontation, the White House tried to reassure Pyongyang: "The United States reaffirms that it is not a threat to North Korean security, and we seek to improve relations with that country." North Korea's actions would determine "the pace and scope" of relations.[19]

En route to Washington, Roh had stopped off in San Francisco for a meeting with Soviet President Mikhail Gorbachev, a capstone of his Northern policy. According to a South Korean spokesman, Roh told Gorbachev, "We do not seek military superiority over North Korea, and we have no intention to attack North Korea."[20]

Having helped arrange the June 4 Roh-Gorbachev meeting, Richard Solomon, assistant secretary of state for East Asian and Pacific affairs, and Donald Gregg, ambassador to South Korea, who had been C.I.A. chief at station in Seoul in 1973–75 and Vice President Bush's national security aide in the 1980s, worked with South Korea to try to expand the opening with North Korea. In the course of 1990 the Bush Administration eased the American embargo under the Trading with the Enemy Act by authorizing $1.2 billion in exports to North Korea, mostly food and medical supplies.[21] In October 1990 Solomon publicly indicated satisfaction with North Korea's response to the five-point policy by setting a single precondition, not five, for improving relations: the North would have to sign a safeguards agreement with the I.A.E.A.

While South Korea was wooing Russia, North Korea was reaching out to Japan. In September Shin Kanemaru, a backroom power broker and dealmaker in Japan's ruling Labor Democratic Party, met with Kim Il Sung, to discuss normalization. Japan's Foreign Ministry was surprised by Pyongyang's desire for diplomatic relations in view of its unremittingly hostile rhetoric toward Tokyo. It was also concerned that Kanemaru had gone too far to accommodate Kim and resentful that a politician had acted as go-between instead of deferring to diplomats. South Korea was even more resentful. It was bad enough that North Korea was trying to break out of its diplomatic isolation. Even worse, Japan was helping. Worst of all, the North was demanding war reparations from Japan, which would reduce Seoul's economic leverage over Pyongyang. With help from the Japanese Foreign Ministry, Seoul succeeded in reining in Kanemaru. It insisted that he condition normalization on I.A.E.A. inspections, prior consultation with Seoul, and North-South negotiations. That put Japanese relations with North Korea on hold. Having seen Japan's willingness to defer to South Korea, North Korea directed its attention to improving relations with the United States.

Some American officials were preparing to respond. In the spring of 1991 Assistant Secretary of State Solomon chaired an interagency review on North Korea. The product of that review, NSR-28, framed three options. One was to stay the course, with some limited exchanges, some easing of travel restrictions, and other modest inducements while urging the North to sign a safeguards agreement with the I.A.E.A. A second was engagement including direct dialogue with the D.P.R.K., moves toward diplomatic relations, reduction of joint U.S.-R.O.K. military exercises, assurances against U.S. nuclear use, and withdrawal of U.S. nuclear warheads from Korea. A third was coercion, using diplomatic, economic, and military means. There was agreement within the administration that the current policy was inadequate and that option three, coercion, was premature. The fight came over the scope of engagement.[22] Opposition to engagement was spearheaded by Deputy National Security Adviser Robert Gates, who played on doubts that it would be reciprocated. Inertia triumphed for the moment. What officials called, appropriately, "the modest initiative" became administration policy. "We laid in place a game plan," says Solomon, "but we didn't have enough bureaucratic support here. We couldn't do anything with it until President Bush decided to withdraw the nuclear arms from the South."[23]

The nuclear withdrawal provided the critically needed impetus for North Korea to curtail its bomb-building. The Bush Administration had originally considered withdrawing some U.S. land-based tactical nuclear warheads from Europe in 1990. Short-range nuclear arms based in West Germany which were capable only of striking East Germany and Czechoslovakia made little strategic sense with Germany on the verge of unifying and Czechoslovakia in the midst of peaceful revolution. Pressure was mounting in Germany to rid the country of all nuclear arms. General Colin Powell, chairman of the Joint Chiefs of Staff, ordered a Joint Staff study that recommended removing the nuclear artillery.[24] In early May, as an inducement for Moscow to acquiesce to German unification, Robert Blackwill and Philip Zelikow of the National Security Council staff proposed withdrawing all but the air-delivered warheads from Europe and asking Moscow to reciprocate. They also proposed negotiating the global elimination of nuclear artillery and short-range missiles with the Soviet Union. When Europeanists in the State Department objected, fearing it would feed popular pressure in Germany to withdraw all nuclear arms, the proposal was changed to avoid any detailed offer to negotiate and instead withdraw the nuclear artillery shells unilaterally.[25] The withdrawal was scheduled for August 2, 1990, but the plan was shelved when Iraq invaded Kuwait.[26]

The nuclear withdrawal was revived and extended to Korea that fall. Ambassador Donald Gregg had been discussing it with General Robert RisCassi, the American commander-in-chief in Korea, and with Kim Chong Whi, President Roh's national security adviser. "I felt that if we had nuclear questions that could be raised about us in the South," says Gregg, "we would be much less able to cope with nuclear questions in the North." In October 1990 Gregg cabled Solomon with RisCassi's and Kim's approval to withdraw the American arms. Gregg worried about trouble from anti-nuclear activists in South Korea: "They could see that the removal of these damned things was not a step toward withdrawal, but really a step that could make things operate more effectively in the future."[27] General Powell also renewed the fight that fall, but was opposed by the service chiefs and by Secretary of Defense Dick Cheney.[28]

The idea of a nuclear withdrawal from South Korea received some public support in *New York Times* editorials on December 13, 1990, and February 4, 1991, and more importantly in a mid-February report of a nongovernmental study group that included General John Vessey, a retired U.S. commander in Korea and chairman of the Joint Chiefs of Staff; Gaston Sigur, assistant secretary of State for Asia and the Pacific in the Reagan Administration and author of the "five-point" policy; Kim Kyung-Won, once South Korea's ambassador to the United States; and Han Sung Joo, a Berkeley-educated professor at Korea University who was soon to be South Korea's foreign minister.[29] Yet the warhead withdrawal was also opposed across the political spectrum—from prominent conservatives[30] to former Carter Administration official and *New York Times* columnist Leslie Gelb, who contended that the way to deal with "the next renegade state" was to cut off all trade until it lived up to its obligations under the Nonproliferation Treaty.[31]

Although President Roh had gone along with the warhead withdrawal in 1990, he now resisted it vigorously.[32] In White House meetings on July 2–3, 1991, Roh won President Bush's assent that South Korea, not the United States, would play "a leading role" in any future negotiations with North Korea on nuclear matters. He also got a joint communique stipulating that North Korean acceptance of inspections "cannot be linked with any other issues," a reference to the withdrawal of U.S. nuclear arms in Korea.[33] Although that wording left open the possibility of removing the arms unilaterally, Roh wrung a pledge from Secretary of State Baker of "full consultation" before any withdrawal.[34]

Undersecretary of Defense Paul Wolfowitz held that consultation with South Korea's national security adviser Kim Chong Whi in Honolulu on August 7–8, 1991. The meeting was unannounced, but on August 9 an English-language daily, *Korea Herald*, citing "many analysts," said that "U.S. nuclear arms may be pulled out" as a way "to encourage the North to completely give up its plan to produce nuclear arms."[35]

The article made no mention of Seoul's grudging acceptance of a ban on reprocessing, also pressed upon it by Washington at the consultations in order to induce Pyongyang to do likewise.[36] Whether or not to seek a ban on reprocessing in South Korea occasioned a "huge" fight, recalls a senior U.S. official, that "pitted the deacons of the I.A.E.A. church who did not want to do anything to imply that I.A.E.A. compliance was insufficient" against officials who wanted to prevent the production of plutonium.[37] Just how resistant South Korea was to banning reprocessing became apparent in 1992 when it sought reprocessing technology from Canada and the United States. The United States turned down the bid and convinced Canada to do likewise. It would not be the last time that South Korea tried.[38]

When the nuclear withdrawal from Korea finally came, it was subsumed in a much wider context. That was important in the view of some senior officials. "We wanted to remove the weapons from the Korean peninsula as a move to get the North Koreans to change their attitude," says one, "but we didn't want to do it as a signal that we were withdrawing from Korea."[39] After informal discussions with National Security Adviser Scowcroft at his summer retreat in Kennebunkport, Maine, during the last week of August, President Bush on September 5, 1991, asked his advisers for "some new ideas on nuclear disarmament." The ideas he had in mind included the most sweeping unilateral cuts in nuclear arms ever.[40] Except for air-delivered arms in Europe, all tactical nuclear warheads based on land overseas or on board aircraft carriers and other ships would be redeployed to storage sites in the United States or dismantled. Strategic nuclear warheads on long-range ballistic missiles were not affected, but nuclear-armed strategic bombers were taken off alert.

The worldwide withdrawal was primarily intended to induce Moscow to follow suit, in order to tighten control over its vast nuclear stockpile in the immediate aftermath of the August coup against President Mikhail Gorbachev. There were "practical considerations" as well. "The Navy really wanted to take them off ships," says a top official. "But they were reluctant to take that step [on their own]." Yet the step was easier for senior administration officials, among them General Powell, National Security Adviser Brent Scowcroft and Undersecretary of State Arnold Kanter, who believed that tactical nuclear arms were not worth the risks they posed to their possessors. As a top Bush aide put it, "They did not confer any great military advantage. The implication of tactical nu-clear weapons was that this was a useful military weapon and I didn't see any reason to perpetuate that. I'm not for the use of nuclear weapons."[41]

On September 27, 1991, President Bush announced the nuclear withdrawal. His statement covered some forty W-33 artillery shells based in South Korea and others on ships offshore, but it was not ex-plicit about air-delivered weapons there, saying only that warheads for European-based fighter-bombers would not be withdrawn. His top-se-cret directive did specify the removal of some sixty B-61 gravity bombs for U.S. F-16s at Kunsan Air Force Base in South Korea. That was added inducement for North Korea to sign and implement the safeguards agreement it had negotiated with the I.A.E.A. in July.[42]

Opponents in Seoul and the Pentagon tried unsuccessfully to block withdrawal of the gravity bombs. On October 12 Don Oberdorfer of the *Washington Post*, a diplomatic correspondent with extensive experi-ence covering Korea, reported that Seoul was not consulted and had had "only minimal advance notice" of the Bush announcement.[43] He was misled by his sources. On October 23 national security adviser Kim Chong Whi went a step further. He told North Korea that acceptance of inspections should precede the nuclear withdrawal and disclosed that to the press.[44]

The withdrawal went ahead. On December 18, 1991, President Roh announced in a nationally televised address, "As I speak, there do not exist any nuclear weapons whatsoever, anywhere in the Republic of Korea."[45] The D.P.R.K. nevertheless insisted on confirmation from the United States. President Bush found an artful way to circumvent long-standing U.S. policy neither to confirm nor to deny the presence of nu-clear arms overseas. He replied to a question at a news conference in Seoul in early January, "[I] heard what Roh said and I'm not about to argue with him." He added, "To any who doubted his declaration, South Korea, with full support of the United States, has offered to open to inspection all of its civilian and military installations, including U.S. facilities."[46]

A related form of nuclear reassurance was cancellation of the 1992 Team Spirit exercises held every year since 1976 by the U.S. and R.O.K. armed forces. To the U.S. command in Korea, Team Spirit was just a routine readiness measure. To North Korea, Team Spirit posed a nuclear threat because U.S. nuclear-capable forces had taken part in the past. Since the mid-1980s, some American officials had been suggesting that Team Spirit was needlessly provocative and expensive and that canceling it "would get us something politically."[47] Ambassador Gregg had dis-cussed the possibility of cancellation with the American commander in Korea, General Robert RisCassi, the previous fall. It was clear to Gregg "how much the North hated Team Spirit. Whenever we ran it, they would go to a higher state of alert. It was an absolutely Pavlovian reaction."[48] Nor was Team Spirit required for readiness. "With the advent of computer simulation," says a high-ranking military officer with command experience in Korea, "you could train the same without all the great expense and wasted effort of putting all these people in the field." While it is being run, he adds, Team Spirit reduces preparedness for attack: "You pull people out of the front lines to run these large exercises, which weakens your front, so there's a lot of downside for readiness."[49]

South Korea opposed cancellation. It preferred to use the exercise to pressure North Korea into instituting North-South nuclear inspections. On October 30, 1991, South Korea's Defense Ministry released a white paper trumpeting the pressure strategy. North Korea's nuclear effort, it said, "must be stopped at any cost."[50] The Joint Chiefs of Staff opposed cancellation, partly because the South did and partly because they saw the North's demand that Team Spirit be canceled while it was free to run exercises as "an unbalanced proposal."[51]

Defense Secretary Cheney was inclined to favor suspension for budgetary reasons.[52] Transporting sizable troop contingents to South Korea made it the costliest exercise the Pentagon ran. To placate Seoul, Cheney took a tougher line at annual security consultations a month later. On November 11, 1991, he announced a delay in a scheduled withdrawal of six thousand U.S. troops from the South "until the danger and uncertainties surrounding the North Korean nuclear program and security in the region have been thoroughly addressed."[53] He also endorsed plans to enlarge other military exercises to make up for Team Spirit. Disclosure of the enlarged exercises was accompanied by a not very subtle warning to the North Koreans. General Colin Powell, Chairman of the Joint Chiefs of Staff, told reporters on background: "If they missed Desert Storm, this is a chance to catch a re-run."[54]

By the time President Bush visited Seoul on January 6, 1992, South Korea had relented. On December 16 Deputy Prime Minister Choe Ho Chung said "progress" in North-South "contacts relating to nuclear issues" could lead Seoul to cancel Team Spirit.[55] On January 7 the R.O.K. Defense Ministry finally announced the suspension of Team Spirit, but warned, "If, as feared by some, the North is found to be intent only on using intra-Korean accords to play political games, without any real interest in implementing them, Team Spirit exercises can be resumed at any time."[56]

American nuclear reassurances had the desired effect on North Korea. "Normally, you would expect it to be pocketed since we had not negotiated this with them," says Richard Solomon. "Instead it led to reciprocal acts by them."[57] On November 25, 1991, the D.P.R.K. announced it would sign its safeguards accord "if the United States begins the withdrawal of nuclear weapons from South Korea," a leap forward from its previous position that the U.S. had to eliminate its nuclear threat. The North also called for "D.P.R.K.-U.S. negotiations to discuss simultaneous inspections and removing the nuclear threat against us."[58]

On December 13, 1991, it concluded the first of two historic accords with South Korea, an Agreement on Reconciliation, Nonaggression, and Exchanges and Cooperation.

On December 31 it concluded a Joint Declaration on the Denuclearization of the Korean Peninsula agreeing not to "test, produce, receive, possess, store, deploy, or use nuclear weapons." Going beyond its obligations under the Nonproliferation Treaty, it pledged not to "possess facilities for nuclear reprocessing and enrichment." It also accepted inspections to be worked out by a Joint Nuclear Control Commission.

On January 7, 1992, the day that South Korea announced cancellation of Team Spirit, a D.P.R.K. Foreign Ministry spokesman announced its intention to sign a safeguards agreement with the I.A.E.A. "in the near future," citing U.S. statements "through various channels" welcoming "the South Korean authorities' declaration that there are no nuclear weapons in South Korea."[59] On January 30, 1992, North Korea signed its nuclear safeguards accord.

Most important of all, to make nuclear arms it is necessary to remove spent fuel from a nuclear reactor and reprocess it, extracting the plutonium. *Pyongyang halted the reprocessing of spent fuel. It also delayed removing spent nuclear fuel* from its reactor until May 1994, more than a year after the I.A.E.A. expected it to defuel. For the next year and a half, *North Korea allowed the I.A.E.A. to verify* that it was neither reprocessing nor defueling, even while it was impeding I.A.E.A. efforts to get at its nuclear past. Since 1991 it never resumed reprocessing, according to U.S. intelligence and I.A.E.A. assessments.[60] Having taken these steps, Pyongyang had reason to conclude that nuclear diplomacy might pay off.

"One Meeting Means One Meeting"

The Bush Administration did not wait to find out whether reassurance and reciprocity would work. Having made the decisions to withdraw all the nuclear warheads from Korea and to suspend Team Spirit exercises, it moved to adopt the crime-and-punishment approach, pressing North Korea to allow nuclear inspections and holding out talks as a reward for compliance with its demands.

The administration remained deeply divided over cooperating with

North Korea. Shared images of nuclear diplomacy clouded official perceptions. Many were wedded to what John Merrill of INR calls the "essentialist" view that the "North Korean behavior is fixed and all of a piece" and that "it is in the *nature* of the North Korean 'beast' to behave as it does."[61] Those who favored cooperation had won a series of skirmishes but they were about to lose a major battle, foreclosing diplomatic give-and-take for the last year of the Bush Administration and putting the United States on a collision course with North Korea.

The counterattack on cooperation was publicly launched in a column by Jim Hoagland in the *Washington Post* on October 24, 1991. It reflected the view of officials who favored a shift in strategy, "a new, more vigorous form of coercive diplomacy," including a financial embargo by Japan, to keep North Korea from making a bomb. Citing satellite photographs of smoking chimneys at the suspected reprocessing plant at Yongbyon, "the consensus of atomic detectives" was that the plant will be completed within six to twelve months and that North Korea could produce "a crude but effective nuclear weapon by 1995."[62]

Exhibit A for the prosecution was "Building 500," as U.S. analysts dubbed it. In late 1991 U.S. satellite photography had discovered North Korean workers digging trenches in the frozen earth and laying pipes between Building 500 and the reprocessing plant. Some concluded that the North intended to remove nuclear waste, containing plutonium, and secrete it there without the knowledge of international inspectors.[63]

Some began openly advocating force.[64] On September 27, 1991, the very day that President Bush was announcing the U.S. nuclear withdrawal, South Korea's Defense Minister Lee Jong Koo suggested a commando raid against North Korea's nuclear installations if it did not allow inspections.[65] The option of attacking the Yongbyon site, if the North should shut down the reactor and attempt to remove spent fuel for reprocessing, was endorsed by Defense Minister Lee at the Security Consultative Meeting with Defense Secretary Cheney in November 1991.

The chief stumbling block to coercive diplomacy became apparent at once. When Secretary of State James Baker tried to line up regional support at an Asia-Pacific Economic Cooperation meeting in Seoul in mid-November 1991, he met open opposition from China's Foreign Minister Qian Qichen. In what would become a recurring refrain, Qian insisted that "dialogue," not pressure, was the way to deal with the D.P.R.K.[66]

If coercion had its opponents overseas, cooperation faced political opposition closer to home, where it counted. When the idea of direct dialogue with North Korea leading to gradual normalization was advanced by Assistant Secretary of State Solomon and Undersecretary of

State Kanter, it ran into fierce resistance from National Security Adviser Scowcroft, his ex-deputy, now Director of Central Intelligence Gates, and from Undersecretary of Defense Wolfowitz.[67] Says one top official, "I was on the reluctant side. The talks were really a State Department initiative. I was skeptical of their utility at this time. This was a time of reevaluation in South Korea of where they were and where they were going, and they were getting a little flaky." Shared images of nuclear diplomacy informed his objection to talks: "I was worried about the North getting messages that we weren't trying to send . . . that we were thinking about withdrawing and that we were trying to prepare the ground. I'm more profoundly skeptical of North Korea than of any other country—both how they think, which I don't understand, and the series of bizarre things they have done. I don't think we can afford to take a chance of any misconstruing of where we are and our determination that they can't get away with anything." He wanted to "convey to them a sense that there is no way out."[68] According to another senior official, "The basic assumption in the intelligence community and in Defense was that these people are liars, they dug tunnels and you couldn't trust any agreement that you reached with them. Even if they let us in Yongbyon you wouldn't see anything."[69]

Bureaucratic opposition was fortified by highly placed resistance in Seoul and in Congress. Representative Stephen Solarz, a Democrat and chairman of the House Subcommittee on Asian and Pacific Affairs, who had first visited Pyongyang in 1980, was pivotal. During a trip to Pyongyang in December 1991 he talked to Kim Il Sung about the North's nuclear program, said to be the first Westerner to do so. "What's the use of a few nuclear weapons?" Kim Il Sung told him. "In 10,000 years' time we couldn't have as many nuclear weapons as you. Assume that we are producing nuclear weapons and have one or two nuclear weapons. What's the point? They'd be useless. If we fire them, they will kill the Korean people."[70]

On his return from Pyongyang, Solarz stopped off in Seoul to confer with President Roh Tae Woo. Roh, who wanted to take the lead in negotiating with the North, opposed direct American dialogue with North Korea on the nuclear issue. Solarz, who had ambitions to become Secretary of State in the next Democratic administration, became a convert, and an outspoken opponent of a diplomatic deal. As a result of his meeting with Kim Il Sung, he told reporters in Seoul after seeing Roh, "I came to the unmistakable conclusion that North Korea seems more interested in avoiding a satisfactory resolution to the nuclear problem than in facilitating one."[71]

With a leading Democrat and South Korea's president both opposed, deal-making with North Korea faced an uphill struggle. It could also antagonize right-wing Republicans, some of whom were considering a campaign to deny Bush the renomination for president. Opponents picked up South Korean arguments against engaging in direct talks, that doing so would be regarded as a sign of weakness and an opportunity to drive a wedge between Washington and Seoul.

During President Bush's visit in early January 1992, Seoul renewed its assault on direct dialogue between Washington and Pyongyang. South Korea's ambassador to the United States, Hyun Hong-Choo, noted in a briefing for reporters, "We think that as Koreans, we can read their minds a little better."[72] In the South Koreans' view, no foreigner could ever really understand the North. The Americans assured President Roh that "we weren't going to get out in front of them," says Charles Kartman, then director of Korean affairs in the State Department. "Words were said at an authoritative level that if it ever came down to choosing between failure on the nuclear issue or harming our alliance with the R.O.K., we would rather fail on the nuclear issue."[73]

"Our internal problems," says Kartman, "were much greater than the problems we perceived in satisfying South Korean sensitivities." Chief among them were the shared images of nuclear diplomacy. "There was a belief in a monolithic North Korea," he notes, "whose motives were hard to read but could be characterized as getting something for nothing. There was very little readiness to believe in North Korean willingness to cooperate with the I.A.E.A." Moreover, the proponents of diplomatic give-and-take had largely exhausted their political capital obtaining nuclear reassurances for the North. "To the extent that we thought that there were other things the North Koreans were interested in," says Kartman, "they were largely lumped together in the vague notion of normalization."[74]

With little domestic support for a negotiated solution and well-entrenched opposition, it was difficult to overturn the policy of coercive diplomacy. The fight came over "whether to use the N-word," says a senior official.[75] A divided administration, in the words of another senior official, reached "a classic bureaucratic compromise," to hold one high-level meeting with North Korea, no more, and to use that meeting, not to begin diplomatic dialogue, but to restate its requirements for any future talks.

The high-level talk took place on January 22, 1992, in New York. Representing the United States was Arnold Kanter, undersecretary of state for political affairs. Heading the D.P.R.K. delegation was Kim Yong Sun, secretary for international affairs of the Korean Workers' Party and a candidate-member of the Politburo. The three-hour formal session consisted of sequential monologues more than the give-and-take of diplomatic dialogue. Kanter, says a participant in the talks, "was on a very tight leash."[76]

His main message was one of nuclear reassurance. The United States, he emphasized, posed no threat to North Korea. All American nuclear arms, he noted, had been withdrawn from Korea. He invited the North to see for itself by carrying out the North-South denuclearization accord and inspecting U.S. bases in the South. He read a version of a "negative security assurance" given to all signatories in good standing of the Nonproliferation Treaty, that the United States would refrain from using or threatening to use nuclear arms against them.* That pledge would apply to North Korea once it fulfilled its obligations under the treaty.

In more general terms Kanter also sketched the economic miracle transforming the Pacific Rim and framed a choice for North Korea: join the international community and reap the benefits by cooperating on nuclear and other issues of concern, or else face increasing isolation and fall further behind economically. Kanter was "firm" about the need for North Korea to implement its safeguards agreement with the I.A.E.A. and institute bilateral inspections with the South, but he was under strict instructions "to be very vague" about future benefits. The nuclear issue, the United States was insisting, had to be settled first, on its own terms. It was not about to offer specific diplomatic and economic rewards in return for an end to nuclear-arming by North Korea. Kanter "had plenty of help in the room," other agency representatives who would assure his strict adherence to the approved talking points.[77]

Kim Yong Sun replied with set speeches of his own, demanding the cessation of U.S. threats and withdrawal of nuclear arms from the South. He did say the North was prepared to have American troops remain on the Korean peninsula, even after unification. He proposed cooperating to meet the primary threat to the region, Japan, an idea Kanter vehemently rejected. "It was very clear," says a senior official, "that they were trying to find common ground with us."[78] Both in the formal talks and in nearly an hour of informal conversation over drinks in a restaurant afterward, Kanter rebuffed repeated efforts by Kim to obtain a joint

* The difficulty was that the negative security assurance announced by Secretary of State Cyrus Vance to the U.N. Special Session on Disarmament on June 12, 1978, says, "The United States will not use nuclear weapons against any non-nuclear weapons state party to the N.P.T. . . . except in the case of an attack on the U.S., its territories or armed forces, or its allies, by such a state allied to a nuclear weapons state, or associated with a nuclear weapons state in carrying out or sustaining the attack." The exception applied to members of the Warsaw Pact and, of course, to North Korea, then allied with the Soviet Union and China. On April 5, 1995, Secretary of State Christopher, trying to win indefinite extension of the Nonproliferation Treaty, announced a modified version of the 1978 formula which made exception only for an attack "carried out or sustained by such a non-nuclear-weapon state *in association or alliance with* a nuclear-weapon state." A nuclear free North Korea would be subject to U.S. nuclear threat only if it and China together attacked South Korea, not if it did so on its own. Stated U.S. policy has since been further qualified, leaving a loophole for nuclear use if the United States or an ally is attacked with chemical or biological weapons. North Korea has chemical weapons.

communique marking the meeting or to commit the United States to further high-level talks. "He never said we're prepared to normalize relations," says a senior administration official who favored saying so. "But it was implicit that we prepared to start a process of negotiation."[79]

Charles Kartman has a less generous assessment. "The United States Government was transfixed by a preconception of what these talks were about—North Korea's nuclear security. This is why two things dominated discussions of what we would put on the table. One of those was nuclear weapons deployments and the other was the negative security assurance." Those favoring diplomatic give-and-take, Kartman included, put much less weight on political and economic normalization. To North Korea, political and economic relations were a source of security. Without such ties to the United States, it would remain insecure. "Basically," Kartman says, "I think we had it wrong. We were going down the wrong road for a long time."[80]

The Bush Administration set two preconditions for resuming high-level talks with North Korea, I.A.E.A. inspections and progress toward bilateral inspections with South Korea. In Pyongyang's view, it was being asked to give up its bargaining chip first, and only then would the United States talk about quid pro quos. In Washington's view, the United States was not about to pay for North Korea to do what it had already agreed to do by signing the Nonproliferation Treaty. "North Korea's compliance with pre-existing obligations was not and should have been a bargaining chip. You cannot sell that horse twice," says a senior official who served in the Bush and Clinton Administrations. "It is a horrible precedent if legally binding obligations can be designated mere bargaining chips." Reminded that North Korea had always insisted on reciprocity from Washington as the price of its adherence to the treaty, the official replied, "But I don't care what they said."[81]

Those who favored diplomatic give-and-take with the North lost, and gave up the fight. From January 1992 on, the Bush Administration ignored North Korean efforts at accommodation. It interpreted North Korea's refusal to comply with subsequent I.A.E.A. demands as evidence of duplicity and recalcitrance, not as a bargaining tactic to get something in return for giving up nuclear-arming. The United States refused to be drawn into negotiations, a stance it would maintain for the ensuing year and for the same reason—skepticism about the likelihood of success and fear of the domestic political repercussions of failure.

Washington's refusal to negotiate or to commit itself to gradual diplomatic or economic ties prompted Pyongyang to delay the start of I.A.E.A. inspections until spring, pending ratification of the safeguards agreement by its Supreme People's Assembly. Washington had yet to learn that in dealing with Pyongyang, it would not get something for nothing.

Bush Administration policy has been described as one of "carrots and sticks." It did proffer carrots: the nuclear withdrawal, cancellation of Team Spirit, acceptance by Seoul of a ban on reprocessing, and a single high-level talk. And it received plenty in return: a ban on reprocessing, a delay in refueling, and the safeguards agreement. Yet it soon reverted to a policy of pure stick: coercive diplomacy to secure access for I.A.E.A. and R.O.K. inspectors, using inspections to curtail Pyongyang's nuclear program while counting on North Korea's economic decline and growing political isolation to compel it to yield. One official characterized policy at the time as "putting the North in a vise, smiling all the while, and offering it a way out."[82] The administration, Undersecretary of State Kanter later said, took a "hard line, refusing to offer any specific inducements or incentives to the D.P.R.K. or even to hold political-level meetings with North Korean officials to try to work out a solution."[83]

In effect, the Bush Administration held out high-level talks as a reward for good behavior. That may have made sense for the first visible diplomatic meeting between the United States and North Korea since the Korean War. After all, the regime in Pyongyang did want legitimation from Washington and a high-level meeting provided a measure of that. Yet further high-level talks would have lent little additional legitimacy to the regime. Why reject the means of probing the North's nuclear intentions, possibly leading to a resolution of the dispute?

Three other meetings were held with D.P.R.K. representatives in 1992, one in late September in New York by a State Department official on the Korea desk, another in November in Washington by a senior U.S. intelligence official, and a third in December when Senator Robert Smith (R-NH) went to Pyongyang. The purpose was to urge North Korea to comply with the I.A.E.A., not to negotiate.

The Clinton Administration continued to treat high-level talks as a reward rather than a path to a negotiated settlement. One consequence was that the January 1992 session was the last to be held until June 1993. As Kanter replied after Kim Yong Sun repeatedly wrote to him that summer trying to resume high-level talks, "One meeting meant one meeting."[84]

Ignoring the North's Offer

The standard American account asserts that North Korea was pursuing a strategy of "cheat and retreat" throughout 1992, while the United States and the I.A.E.A. were tightening the screws and forcing it to comply. Yet the pattern of events is open to a very different interpretation, that North Korea was engaged in show-and-tell, revealing enough to demonstrate willingness to make a deal while withholding enough to retain its bargaining leverage.

On March 14, 1992, North Korea agreed provisionally to establish a Joint Nuclear Control Commission with the South to monitor the 1991 joint denuclearization accord. On April 10 the North Korean Supreme People's Assembly ratified the safeguards agreement with the I.A.E.A. Once it did, Pyongyang was surprisingly forthcoming about its nuclear program. On May 4 it gave the I.A.E.A. a 150-page declaration inventorying its nuclear material and equipment, a response more prompt and detailed than was required under its safeguards agreement. It disclosed some of what a determined proliferator should have wanted to hide. In addition to three reactors, its declared inventory confirmed construction of a reprocessing plant, somewhat disingenuously described as a radio-chemical laboratory. North Korea's most surprising disclosure was that it had reprocessed some 90 grams of plutonium in the past.

American intelligence had been unaware of the reprocessing. North Korea's declaration prompted a reassessment that the North may have removed enough spent fuel to extract one or two bombs' worth of plutonium. "It was only in hindsight," says a U.S. official, "that people went back and said in 1989, when there was this hundred-day outage, that must have been when they removed spent fuel."[85]

I.A.E.A. Director-General Hans Blix made an official visit to North Korea on May 11–16, 1992. He accepted an invitation to tour the reprocessing plant at Yongbyon, which he found to be still under construction and far from fully equipped. He was told the I.A.E.A. could "visit" any site it wanted to, even those not on the list of declared nuclear facilities subject to inspection. Pyongyang even showed some of its nuclear installations on national television, which could be picked up abroad.

An ad hoc inspection was scheduled for the end of May to verify the North's initial declaration. Once that audit established a baseline for the North's nuclear facilities and materials, the I.A.E.A. could then institute routine inspections. The D.P.R.K., in the words of a senior State Department official, was now moving "faster than anyone believed possible" but "slower than we would like" on I.A.E.A. safeguards.[86]

Having engaged in a little show-and-tell, North Korea invited the I.A.E.A. and the United States to pay to see more. Its invitation was ignored.

During Blix's May visit, North Korean officials asked him for help in acquiring new light-water reactors and supplying them with nuclear fuel in return for abandoning reprocessing.[87] On June 1 North Korea repeated the proposal in a meeting with American diplomats in Beijing.[88] Only a member in good standing of the Nonproliferation Treaty was entitled to such help. That was an opening for the United States to negotiate with North Korea about replacing its gas-graphite reactors in return for a ban on nuclear-arming.

The Bush Administration, determined to pursue the crime-and-punishment approach, dismissed the idea out of hand. "If I had seen it," recalls a senior administration official, "it wouldn't have rung any bells. I would have said, 'This is wacko. Where is this coming from?'"[89] "All that people cared about in 1992 was to see that the North would successfully implement its safeguards agreement," says a State Department official.[90] "It was a piece of extraneous information," says another. "It went in one ear and out the other."[91] There was no interagency deliberation and no reply. The request for new reactors received so little attention that when the North revived it in July 1994, it came as a complete surprise to U.S. negotiators, including the two quoted here, who served in both the Bush and Clinton Administrations.[92]

Charles Kartman, director of Korean affairs at the State Department, says he found the proposal "interesting" because "the North Koreans had contracted with the Soviets to build LWRs, so there was at least some grounding in their own economic planning." Very few officials understood that, says Kartman, and those who did were low down in the bureaucracy. "We heard about the LWR gambit with enormous skepticism." It was inconceivable to officials, including Kartman, that the North Koreans "would substitute the LWRs for peaceful purposes for a nuclear program that had military purposes." Moreover, "There was very little readiness to believe in North Korean willingness to cooperate with the I.A.E.A." In Kartman's view, officials reacted the way they did "because we didn't have enough knowledge about North Korea and because it flew against everyone's prejudice."[93]

Instead of interpreting North Korea's revelations and its offer of more to come as opening gambits in nuclear diplomacy, nonproliferation experts outside the government took their cue from the I.A.E.A. and from professional pessimists in American intelligence and fed doubts about North Korean disclosures. The failure of U.S. intelligence to uncover the Iraqi nuclear program was on everyone's mind.

The campaign was foreshadowed by Director of Central Intelligence Gates as the I.A.E.A. neared agreement with the D.P.R.K. on procedures for its first inspection. He made headlines on February 25 by telling the House Foreign Affairs Committee, in response to questions by Representative Solarz, that North Korea was "a few months to a couple of years" from having an atomic bomb. As the *New York Times* pointed out in an editorial five days later, however, that differed from the prepared statement cleared by the intelligence community, which represented their agreed judgment. It read, "*Even after North Korea accumu-*

lates enough plutonium, making a device would require several additional steps that could require months or even years."[94] The North Koreans, Gates added, "had a deception plan for hiding their nuclear capabilities," a theme that was replayed in days to come. Toby Gati, director of INR, later called Gates's replies "the absolute worst-case analysis."[95] An INR analyst recalls, "Our view has always been that there is not enough information about the history of that reactor and the reprocessing to do anything more than put an upper bound on the amount of material they may have reprocessed. That's a very fuzzy estimate."[96]

North Korean misdeeds were embellished in subsequent disclosures to the press. Large trucks were sighted "hauling things away" from the reprocessing plant, "a U.S. official" told the *Washington Post*.[97] By the time the safeguards agreement came into force, Gates was telling journalists North Korea was "close, perhaps very close to having a nuclear-weapons capability," implying more than a crude device or two.[98] Others in the C.I.A. who favored the worst-case assessment, like Gordon Oehler, the National Intelligence Officer for Science Technology and Proliferation, fed fears in the expert community and the news media.[99] South Korean intelligence even trotted out a North Korean defector, an ex-diplomat in Africa with no nuclear know-how, to say that he was "convinced" the North had underground nuclear facilities.[100]

The campaign succeeded. Nongovernmental experts ignored the D.P.R.K. invitation to nuclear diplomacy and spoke only of doubt, delay, and deception. "The plot thickens," Leonard Spector of the Carnegie Endowment for International Peace told a *Washington Post* reporter. "There is apparently a third reactor we didn't know about. So of course you start to think, 'What else is there we don't know about?'"[101] Gary Milhollin, director of the Wisconsin Project on Nuclear Arms Control, argued in an op-ed that "U.S. intelligence analysts" think North Korea now has enough plutonium for "six to eight atomic bombs" but Hans Blix "is loath to believe it." So were other U.S. intelligence analysts, but that did not dissuade Milhollin. The North Koreans, he continued, "have told incredible stories about their nuclear past. They say the small reactor didn't work when they started it up in 1987, so they have run it only sporadically. This contradicts U.S. observations, which shows continuous operation at high power." The "observations" were suppositions, a matter of considerable controversy in the intelligence community, but for Milhollin they were facts. Calling their "monster" reprocessing plant a "laboratory," the North Koreans "assure Mr. Blix that it is not ready to operate. But North Korea probably wouldn't have built it without a successful prototype, and U.S. analysts fear that the prototype, still hidden, could already have extracted enough plutonium for bombs." If I.A.E.A. inspectors "believe the North Koreans," concluded Milhollin pointedly, "they may face another Iraq."[102]

North Korea's proposal to curtail bomb-making in return for replacement reactors was scarcely mentioned. Instead, the experts called for search and seizure of North Korea's hidden nuclear assets. Congressman Solarz shared their conclusion: the U.S. had to "insist on the right of the I.A.E.A. to conduct challenge inspections" and to secure that same right for South Korea.[103]

Faced with such pressures, at least partly self-generated, and blinded by shared images of nuclear diplomacy, the Bush Administration chose to ignore the North Korean offer and instead step up its demands for I.A.E.A. and North-South inspections.

Witnesses for the Prosecution

Having adopted the crime-and-punishment approach, behind the scenes the administration was urging the I.A.E.A. to tighten up its monitoring procedures and pressing South Korea to insist on elaborate and intrusive inspections of its own—inspections so demanding that, as one senior U.S. official put it, "if the North accepted them, the South might have to reconsider."[104] One arms controller who was intimately involved adds, "To anyone who had an arms control background, these inspections were totally unworkable, totally unacceptable."[105] A State Department official recalls, "We couldn't decide what the hell we meant. I would go over to D.O.D. and ask, 'Do you really mean that if they engage in these bilateral inspections, you will open the bases in the South?' and they would say, 'We're not so sure about that.'"[106] "The South Koreans were spun up by us," says a State Department analyst. "The view was that the I.A.E.A. was a weak reed and you needed to make up for that by a rigorous South inspection regime. This technical perspective ignores the ups and downs of North-South relations or what an inspection means to a Korean: an inspection has a script and the purpose is to stage a show and not to lose face."[107] The I.A.E.A. also bridled at the thought that South Korean inspections were needed because the I.A.E.A.'s were not rigorous enough for Washington.

Washington leaned on Seoul to give priority to inspections and to delay other North-South ties until it obtained them. The Roh Administration, which wanted to expand trade with the North, did not conceal its resentment. Foreign Minister Lee Sang Ok put it bluntly, "Forestalling dialogue over [the] nuclear controversy is not an effective method."[108]

Inspections seemed to confirm the worst suspicions. In their second ad hoc inspection at Yongbyon in July 1992, I.A.E.A. inspectors took smear samples at glove boxes used for handling nuclear material. Subsequent analysis revealed an "anomaly" in the North's initial declaration to the I.A.E.A. The D.P.R.K. claimed it had separated about 90 grams of plutonium in spring 1990, but the analysis showed that reprocessing had occurred on three separate occasions—in 1989, 1990, and 1991—and involved different batches of irradiated material.* It reached no firm conclusion about the amount of plutonium extracted.

The reprocessing could have had an innocent explanation. "They may have been converting a small amount of plutonium to oxide to show to the inspectors," says a Pentagon official. "You can't make a bomb out of oxide."[109] Yet many took it as conclusive evidence of North Korean deception. "Once we discovered they had not made an accurate declaration, all of our energies focused on the I.A.E.A. process, which meant building a coalition to put pressure on North Korea to comply with its obligations," says a senior U.S. proliferation specialist who was involved in the issue from 1988 on. "The interesting question is whether we missed an opportunity in mid-1992 to head this off."[110]

Another inspection in September led to "a prototype standoff," says a State Department official who dealt with the I.A.E.A. During earlier visits inspectors had been too interested in the reprocessing plant to get around to the suspected waste sites, but by now they had "a new attitude" and were interested in "all sorts of anomalies." Eventually the North relented and let the inspectors go to one of the waste sites. They were met by a military officer who said there was nothing new there, but some construction was "patently new." Earth had been bulldozed around one building. It had had two stories above ground a few months ago; now it had one. The inspectors were allowed to take radiological measurements, but no samples, and left without visiting the second site.[111] Unbeknownst as yet to the inspectors, U.S. intelligence satellites had detected North Korean efforts to bury pipes connecting the reprocessing plant to the waste site.

The administration further toughened its stance once the I.A.E.A. detected the discrepancies in the North's initial declaration. To the American ambassador in Seoul, Donald Gregg, the I.A.E.A. was "a bunch of wild-haired proctologists running around North Korea asking the North Koreans to submit to all kinds of indignities without telling

* The different levels of americium-240 and 241 isotopes in the samples was one telltale, suggesting spent fuel had been removed from the reactor on three separate occasions. When plutonium is extracted from spent fuel, so is americium, which decays rapidly, in effect serving as an "atomic clock," allowing analysts to determine when the spent fuel was removed. The ratio of plutonium-239 to 240 isotopes is another telltale.

them how it was going to benefit them."¹¹² Gregg's view was decidedly in the minority.

Already by June the administration's attention was turning to the fall election.¹¹³ President Bush was anxious to keep the Republican right in the fold and he was not about to hand hawkish Democrats an issue. Moreover, polls were registering public disenchantment with his preoccupation with foreign policy, so the less said on the subject the better. Any official proposing to overturn the policy of coercive diplomacy and negotiate with North Korea faced an uphill battle. No one was willing to try. "They were expecting follow-up from us," says a State Department official. "No decisions were being made on our side. We were getting ready for elections. Everything was in neutral."¹¹⁴ The opening for talks passed by default. Worse was yet to come.

Interregnum Politics: No One Stands Up to Team Spirit

To military officers, troops that do not drill are cannon fodder. To be combat-ready, U.S. and R.O.K. forces in Korea conducted various exercises to practice reinforcing their positions in the South and repelling an invasion from the North. By far the most provocative was Team Spirit.

When the annual Team Spirit exercise was called off for 1992, it was not canceled for good, but Defense Secretary Cheney began beefing up other exercises precisely for that eventuality. In August 1992 the first such exercise, Focus Lens, was run—with more troops than Team Spirit. "Essentially what happened is we reloaded Team Spirit into August," recalls a State Department Korea hand. "We had one helluva big exercise."¹¹⁵

That was more than enough to satisfy military requirements, but it did not placate the South Korean high command. To Koreans in the South and North alike, Team Spirit had acquired a symbolic significance far beyond its military meaning. During the summer of 1992 Defense Ministry officials in Seoul began publicly suggesting that resumption of Team Spirit in 1993 was a foregone conclusion. When the R.O.K. military requested the start of joint planning for the exercise, it won the endorsement of General RisCassi, who, as the commander-in-chief in Korea, commands the South Korean as well as the American forces there. RisCassi, a sophisticated and cerebral officer, knew Team Spirit was not essential to ensure force readiness, but he did not want to pick a fight with R.O.K. officers under his command.

Team Spirit was an instrument of coercive diplomacy, a way to put pressure on the North to accept intrusive mutual nuclear inspections with the South. "I never believed that Team Spirit was an effective training mechanism for the forces," says a senior military officer with command experience in Korea. "It in fact became a diplomatic tool."[116] That was also the view of a top Bush Administration official: "I was always in favor of going forward with Team Spirit on the grounds that we had to convince the North that there was no way out for them and that we weren't weakening in our determination."[117] Pyongyang was resisting such inspections, while allowing the I.A.E.A. limited access and seeking to negotiate on outstanding nuclear issues with the United States.

To hard-liners in Seoul, Team Spirit had a different political purpose altogether. Impending presidential elections were likely to replace Roh, an ex-general, with a civilian. Team Spirit would restrain too rapid a rapprochement with North Korea, which had the potential to reduce the defense budget, and with it, the privileged status of the armed forces. Confrontation with the North could also inhibit consolidation of civilian control of the military. "The North and the South," says a State Department Korea specialist, "were destined for a train wreck and both wanted to have it."[118]

Team Spirit was the final act of a "triple whammy," says an experienced State Department Korea-watcher, an orchestrated counterattack by Seoul's hawks "to put the brakes on" talks with the North.[119] "In late August the R.O.K. came and told us," says another State Department Korea hand, "that President Roh Tae Woo is coming to the end of his term. He's not in a position to make any long-term commitments. We're going to slow the dialogue because he's a lame duck."[120] In mid-September the South Korean chief negotiator at the North-South political talks, Lee Dong Bok, refused to table a proposal on reuniting divided families approved by President Roh because he deemed it too accommodating. That effectively shut down the talks a month after they had begun. In late September the National Security Planning Agency, formerly the K.C.I.A., "ginned up a spy scandal," adds a veteran Korea-watcher. It announced a massive roundup of a North Korean spy ring in the South. Among those arrested were some opposition politicians. The roundup was well timed. Using the spy scandal as pretext, the hawks succeeded in canceling a visit to the North by South Korea's deputy prime minister to discuss inter-Korean economic cooperation. He was reciprocating a July visit to Seoul by Kim Dal Hyon, a cousin of Kim Jong Il believed to be a key economic reformer in the North. The North Koreans "read it quite correctly as sabotage."[121]

At the end of September Kenneth Quinones, a Korea desk officer at the State Department, had a long meeting with North Korean representatives in New York to try to undo the damage. "Everything he did," says a State Department official, "was aimed at reassuring them that if they would remain calm, we could move ahead and restore momentum in talks with the South."[122]

The issue of Team Spirit came to a head, as it always had, just before the annual U.S.-R.O.K. Security Consultative Meeting. One was scheduled for October 8, 1992, in Washington. When Seoul submitted a draft communique to be issued after the meeting, it sparked an interagency struggle in Washington. Seoul's proposed language said that Team Spirit would resume "unless there is significant progress toward completing the bilateral [North-South] inspection regime." The State Department Korea desk, believing that resumption of Team Spirit was "on the top of the North's list" of concerns, vigorously opposed the decision. It succeeded in softening the communique language. It also tried to delay preparations in order to buy time for the I.A.E.A. to work something out with North Korea. Yet Defense Secretary Cheney looked favorably on resuming the exercises. Because Team Spirit had arisen in military channels, says a State Department Korea hand, the Department of Defense "had the hammer on the issue" within the U.S. government.[123] "The advantages of using Team Spirit as a club appealed to many people, and the advantages of satisfying R.O.K. demands that we use a club was obvious," says Charles Kartman, the State Department country director for Korea. He and other Korea hands in the State Department argued that "we didn't need the club. It was inherent. To make it explicit would lead to some sort of reaction" from North Korea. That was "understood by a relatively few people and those few people were unable to persuade the others." Kartman and his colleagues lost. "People were looking for clubs and not for solutions. That was the mind-set here," Kartman explains. "The voice of caution was rather low level."[124] One higher-level official who opposed Team Spirit, the U.S. ambassador to South Korea, Donald Gregg, says he was not told in advance of the decision.[125] While the issue had been debated in Seoul for months, it was resolved in Washington, as it usually is, at the last minute, leaving him in the dark until it was too late. After the October 8 meeting, the U.S. and the R.O.K. announced preparations for Team Spirit in March 1993.

North Korea reacted sharply to the communique, calling resumption of Team Spirit "a criminal act" intended to "put the brakes on North-South relations and drive the North-South dialogue to a crisis" and "casting dark shadows on the U.S.-D.P.R.K. relations which are showing signs of improvement."[126] At a North-South meeting on October 22 to work out nuclear inspections, the North demanded that the South cancel the exercise or else it would cancel the talks.[127] The same day, the chief D.P.R.K. delegate to the North-South Joint Economic Cooperation and Exchange Committee issued a statement warning that the North-South dialogue could not proceed "while a large-scale thermonuclear war rehearsal is conducted."[128] On November 13 Choe U Jin, North Korea's chief delegate to the Joint Nuclear Control Commission talks with the

South passed along a warning that the North might disrupt I.A.E.A. inspections if Team Spirit were held.[129] Choe pressed for cancellation of the exercise at the Commission meeting on November 27. As the starting date for the exercises neared, North Korea warned it would "suspend the peace process" if Team Spirit went ahead.[130] In January, working-level U.S. representatives met again with the North Koreans in New York. "It was a long meeting," says an American participant, "and the whole focus was, if you guys start Team Spirit, we will respond with drastic measures."[131]

Pyongyang's repeated warnings were ignored. American officials were inclined to dismiss what Pyongyang said in public as propaganda, so few top policy-makers bothered to read the full texts of the North's public statements. Shared images of nuclear diplomacy may explain why they ignored the private warnings or viewed them as the bluster of a rogue state that was feeling the pinch of the crime-and-punishment approach.

To reverse the decision, senior State Department officials would have had to insist on an interagency review. That meant intervening on a military matter, taking issue with an ally, and overturning the administration's policy of coercive diplomacy. Given the battle lines within the government, the prospects for stopping Team Spirit were uncertain at best. No official at the level of assistant secretary or above was prepared to try. The issue did not formally arise until the fall. By then, President Bush's reelection was in doubt. Senior officials were not looking for a new policy; they were looking for new jobs. The outgoing Bush Administration was content to leave the initiative to its successor, and policy floated in a political void.

On January 25, five days after Bill Clinton was sworn in as President of the United States and just one month before the Kim Young Sam Administration took office, South Korea's Defense Ministry announced that Team Spirit would step off in mid-March. Some 120,000 troops would take part, including 50,000 Americans. So would three B-1 bombers, once configured exclusively for nuclear missions.[132]

Stopping Team Spirit once plans were set in motion was more difficult than saying no in the first place. For one thing, neither new president wanted to look soft on defense. Kim Young Sam, like Bill Clinton, was a domestic reformer who did not want to make waves overseas. Even more important, both were suspect in military circles. Kim was intent on purging the senior military ranks and did not want to pick another fight with the armed forces. He also was beholden to hard-liners for winning the presidency. He was not about to take the lead and call off Team Spirit just days before it was scheduled to start.

The incoming Clinton Administration took quite a while to get organized. By the time it did, it was being accused of weakness and vacillation at home and abroad. With little faith that North Korea could be dissuaded from getting bombs, top-ranking officials were not eager to take charge of negotiating a nuclear deal with North Korea—or take the blame if talks failed. With few senior officials confirmed by the Senate by late spring, policy was mostly left to lower levels, dominated by holdovers from the Bush Administration. "We were on auto-pilot," says a Defense Department official.[133] Cancellation of Team Spirit became a casualty of interregnum politics, and so, for a while, did nuclear diplomacy with North Korea.

Senior Clinton Administration officials in the Pentagon did not regard Team Spirit as militarily essential. They worried about an adverse North Korean reaction, but that worry was outweighed by the likely adverse South Korean reaction to cancellation and the resulting political fallout in Washington.

Upon taking office, Secretary of Defense Les Aspin was briefed by General Powell and the Joint Staff on places where pending military contingencies could cause trouble. Korea ranked high on the list. "We were concerned about the proliferation aspect and we were concerned about the war-stimulating aspect," says a senior participant. Aspin asked how much preparedness would be sacrificed by deferring Team Spirit, and his aides did look at alternatives to holding Team Spirit that March. Gary Luck, who had taken over from RisCassi as the commander-in-chief in Korea, was flexible about the need for Team Spirit, so long as he was able to run some joint exercises. "We do have military needs that need to be met," he told the civilians, but "there are lots of ways to skin this cat."[134] Powell, however, insisted that exercises not be held hostage to North Korean threats. When the new government in Seoul gave the go-ahead, the Clinton Administration allowed the exercises to proceed.[135] "As their first big decision in office, they were not going to do something that appeared to undercut the strong position that the previous administration had taken and, in particular, upset our allies," says one official. "The feeling was, they signed the goddamn safeguards agreement. We're not going to pay them to implement it."[136]

The new administration also continued its predecessor's policy of using the I.A.E.A. to pry open access to North Korea's nuclear facilities, in an effort to constrain its nuclear program without offering anything in return.

There was also a shakeup at the I.A.E.A., says a State Department expert, which led to a "period of confrontation." Those in the safeguards division who had been "dealing with member states as if they were colleagues instead of potential proliferators were all swept out." They were replaced by a new team, headed by Demetrios Pericos, whom one American official calls a "junkyard dog" for his zeal in uncovering Iraq's nuclear program after the Persian Gulf War.[137]

The I.A.E.A. began carefully building a case for prosecuting North Korea for noncompliance with the Nonproliferation Treaty. In its November ad hoc inspection the agency asked North Korea to clear up discrepancies in its initial declaration. It was trying to find out whether the reactor had ever been refueled, which would have allowed several bombs' worth of plutonium to be removed for reprocessing. Dissatisfied with the reply, the I.A.E.A. asked to sample the reactor fuel, but the refueling machine at Yongbyon was broken. "No one had done the technical analysis," says a Defense Department official. "From what was known about isotope ratios in doing the nondestructive analysis, it was thought that at the time the I.A.E.A. requested the inspection, it could tell the difference between a refueling and a nonrefueling scenario." By February 1993 it was believed that the nuclear fuel was too old to do a nondestructive analysis. That was found to be untrue in July 1993, this official says, when experts at Los Alamos discovered that the fuel still "could have told you everything you needed to know."[138]

The I.A.E.A. was in no mood to wait to do nondestructive analysis of the spent fuel when the North refueled its reactor. Instead, it chose another, less conclusive way to find out whether the reactor had ever been refueled. It asked to take samples at two nuclear waste sites at Yongbyon. When the North refused, Director-General Blix on February 9, 1993, requested a special inspection of the waste sites. The I.A.E.A. had conducted only two special inspections in the past—in Romania and in Sweden.

North Korea rejected the request as an infringement of its sovereignty. While inspectors were in the reprocessing plant, protested the D.P.R.K. Minister of Atomic Energy in a February 22 note to the I.A.E.A., they "searched every nook and corner of rooms with instruments like a policeman searching the house of a suspected criminal, not as guests who came at the invitation of the host."[139] On February 25 the I.A.E.A. Board of Governors took the unprecedented step of setting a one-month deadline for access to the waste sites and warned of "further measures" by the U.N. Security Council if North Korea failed to comply.

If North Korea might have been willing to trade away its nuclear bargaining chips in high-level talks with the United States, it was not about to let the I.A.E.A. whittle away that leverage without getting something in return. Nor was it about to yield to a threat to resume Team Spirit.

American unwillingness to offer North Korea inducements for nuclear compliance and the resumption of Team Spirit had predictably perverse consequences. To those in North Korea who hoped to bargain away its nuclear program, this seems to have been a recipe for stalemate, and worse. It temporarily sidetracked once-promising careers of some officials who had promoted the opening to the West, among them, Kanter's interlocutor, Kim Yong Sun, who was removed from the Politburo by year's end.[140] It also led to the first of several acts of brinkmanship by Pyongyang.

On March 8, 1993, Team Spirit began and President Kim Il Sung ordered North Korean forces placed on "semi-war alert status." On March 12 Pyongyang gave the world ninety days' notice of its intent to withdraw from the Nonproliferation Treaty.

Most experts outside the government mistook North Korea's intent to withdraw as irreversible. "If not," wondered nonproliferation expert Gary Milhollin, "why take the political heat?"[141] Yet the D.P.R.K.'s official statement on its withdrawal implied it would reconsider when the United States "stops its nuclear threats," meaning Team Spirit, and "the I.A.E.A. secretariat returns to its principle of independence and impartiality," referring to special inspections.[142] The public statement passed virtually unremarked.

North Korea's abrupt turnabout sparked a small firestorm in Washington and Seoul. Secretary of State Warren Christopher told a Defense Appropriations Subcommittee he might favor an oil embargo on North Korea. Not to be out-muscled, subcommittee chairman John Murtha (D-PA) said "military action" might be necessary.[143] In Seoul the North's actions triggered a high-level alert of forces. In the National Assembly several legislators called on the government to resume nuclear-arming, prompting Foreign Minister Han Sung Joo to disown any intent to do so, "Under no circumstances will we consider going nuclear ourselves" because it "would legitimize the North Korean nuclear program and perhaps provoke Japan to reconsider one of its own."[144]

There were scattered counsels of restraint. An editorial in the *New York Times* on March 12, the day of the North Korean announcement, noted that Team Spirit, sought by military hard-liners in the previous government in Seoul, was unnecessary and called for bilateral talks between Washington and Pyongyang to break the current impasse and cool off the hotheads in both Koreas.[145] On March 21 Robert Manning, an adviser on Asia at the State Department during the Bush Administration, and Leonard Spector, an expert on nonproliferation at the Carnegie Endowment, wrote an op-ed questioning whether coercion would work and recommended striking a deal with North Korea.[146]

By then Washington and Seoul had taken a cautious stance. On March 16 President Clinton noted that North Korea still had time to "reverse its decision, and I hope [it] will do so," the U.S. political counselor in Beijing met with his North Korean counterpart, and Seoul went ahead with repatriation of a North Korean soldier held captive in the South since the Korean War.[147]

Clinton's cautiousness came under immediate fire. "The central issue," insisted an editorial in the *Wall Street Journal*, "is not how to get Pyongyang back into the multilateral fold, but how to deal with a very real threat."[148] To David Kay, a former I.A.E.A. official, waiting for a "change of heart" in Pyongyang was the "failed logic" that had kept inspectors out of North Korea for eight years after it signed the Nonproliferation Treaty. Instead, he urged the U.N. Security Council to prepare to "implement—under Chapter VII of the U.N. Charter, which it used to institute effective inspections in Iraq—an inspection regime with far greater powers than the normal I.A.E.A. safeguard visits."[149] Kay's worst suspicions were widely shared, that North Korea, caught in the act of bomb-making, was now abandoning the Nonproliferation Treaty to make still more bombs and that coercion was the appropriate response—even if, as in the case of Iraq, that took a war.

Washington, having tried to ease North Korean concern about the American nuclear threat, misread the response that it got from Pyongyang. Uncertain about North Korea's nuclear intentions and capabilities, it fell back on shared images of nuclear diplomacy and adopted the crime-and-punishment approach. The United States ignored North Korea's entreaties to engage in further diplomatic give-and-take, and instead tried to compel it to comply with the Nonproliferation Treaty without offering anything in return. That put the two countries on a downhill slide to confrontation and crisis.

3

THE CLINTON ADMINISTRATION TIES
ITSELF IN KNOTS

The processes of government have sometimes been described
as a struggle for power among those holding public
office. . . . There is another struggle of far more consequence,
the effort to diffuse or avoid responsibility. Power gravitates
to those who are willing to make decisions and live with the
results, simply because there are so many who readily yield to
the intrepid few who take their duties seriously.
(Dean Rusk)[1]

THE CLINTON Administration inherited a failing North Korea
policy from the Bush Administration. It compounded its trou-
bles by making two mistakes at the very outset. It embraced ends
that could not be attained with certainty anytime soon, if ever, and it
adopted means that were doomed to fail.

The administration's initial aim was no nuclear weapon in North
Korea. That became its avowed aim on November 7, 1993, when President Clinton, in an appearance on *Meet the Press,* said that "North Korea
cannot be allowed to develop a nuclear bomb." Yet, by the time Clinton
spoke, some say misspoke, officials were trying to give priority to a more
ascertainable, more urgent, and more achievable aim: to keep North
Korea from producing more plutonium for bomb-making. By that time,
too, a draft National Intelligence Estimate was circulating in the government putting the odds at a "better than even chance" that North Korea
already had one or two nuclear bombs. Perhaps so, but it was difficult to
know for sure.

The means that the administration threatened to employ, economic
sanctions, were unlikely to achieve either aim. Even a total embargo
could not have prevented North Korea from nuclear-arming since it already had what it required to make more bombs and did not need any
imports from abroad. Conceivably, a total embargo could have caused
economic collapse in the North, but collapse might have set off mass
flight, even war. For fear of just such instability, neighboring China,
South Korea, Russia, and Japan, who had frontline responsibility for enforcing a tight embargo, did not want to impose one. Without their full

backing, the president would have to settle for the appearance of sanctions. Once he did that, he would leave himself open to being outhawked by his domestic opponents. Worse yet, he would greatly increase the risk of war, a problem for a politician who had been assailed for having avoided the draft during the Vietnam War. By comparison, a diplomatic probe of North Korean intentions, offering specific inducements on the condition that Pyongyang take verifiable steps to end its bomb-making, might have postponed a confrontation, leaving him no worse off and possibly attaining his aims. It was a more tenable political course than the alternatives—sanctions, air strikes, and all-out war.

Officials are supposed to be experts in policy; presidents, experts in politics. President Clinton's initial misjudgments were political. By publicly stating his aim was to deny North Korea even one nuclear warhead, he defined the problem in a way that defied solution. To address it, he adopted a posture, not a policy—a tough stance that would ultimately force him either to back down or to run an excessive risk of war. His choice of ends and means were the luxury of an opposition party. Out of power without responsibility for results, Republicans could afford to demand the impossible and insist on rash means that could succeed only at intolerable cost, if at all. The president could not.

Deal-making with North Korea looked like a sure loser to some top Clinton Administration officials. Instead of redefining ends and means, for most of their first year in office they tried to avoid tough choices. Nuclear diplomacy was the subject of only three Principals' Committee meetings in all of 1993. "We had a gaping void at the top of the bureaucracy," says a State Department official.[2] With no one at the top in charge, American diplomatic strategy was one of drift punctuated by spasms of zigzagging. "Among the top issues that might have grabbed the attention of the administration as being suited to some sort of strategic consideration, was Korea given any special place?" reflects one highly placed official. "Typically at the bottom. And this was at radical variance with what I think were the geopolitical and military realities." The resulting policy "was a series of ad hoc improvisations without any organizing concept."[3]

National Security Adviser Anthony Lake, for one, seemed reluctant to put together a diplomatic deal that North Korea might find acceptable. Lake saw himself more as a policy broker than a policy entrepreneur in this case. He was "working very hard to frame consensus positions" and accommodate "differences of view among various departments," says a top official. "If there were not consensus positions, we were going to get torn apart because we were under extraordinary pressure from the outside on these issues, not just from the right, but also from moderates like Brent [Scowcroft] and Arnie [Kanter] who were calling for extraordinary military actions."[4] Given the pivotal position of the N.S.C. staff in the foreign policy process, that ensured bureaucratic inertia. Secretary of State Warren Christopher, who was acutely sensitive to hawkish pressures, also steered clear of seizing the diplomatic initiative. Secretary of Defense Les Aspin, never in the President's inner circle, was already becoming the odd man out.

The issue devolved to the lower ranks. Assistant Secretary of Defense for Nuclear Security and Counterproliferation Ashton Carter made a grab for the issue in March 1993, but he was not confirmed by the Senate until June and lacked the authority to act. That spring, with high-level talks in the offing, the State Department was assigned responsibility for conducting nuclear diplomacy with North Korea. Undersecretary of State for Politico-Military Affairs Lynn Davis and Undersecretary for Political Affairs Peter Tarnoff did not take charge. Nor did the Assistant Secretary of State for East Asian and Pacific Affairs, Winston Lord. The official who "had the action" was Assistant Secretary of State for Politico-Military Affairs Robert Gallucci.

Gallucci, at age forty-eight, had spent twenty years working on nonproliferation in the Arms Control and Disarmament Agency and State Department. Having served in the intelligence community and dealt with the I.A.E.A., he knew their strengths and weaknesses. Not a member of the club, he was a technical expert in a department where geographic expertise counted, a member of the civil service in a department dominated by the Foreign Service, and a specialist in a department that rewarded generalists.

In the arcane arena of arms control, nonproliferation lacked the sex appeal of strategic arms talks with the Soviets. Despite the lip service paid to it, preventing the spread of nuclear arms was usually subordinated to maintaining good relations with countries like South Africa, Pakistan, India, Israel, or even Iraq. Having taught international relations before entering the government, Gallucci was thinking about returning to academic life and spending more time with his children.

His academic background may have made him more willing to listen to outsiders than most bureaucrats are. He was unusual in another way as well: he preferred doing something rather than being somebody. He was a risk-taker in a bureaucracy that promotes those who shun responsibility, who go along to get along, covering their rears all the way. His career got a spectacular boost when, in the aftermath of the Persian Gulf War, with the I.A.E.A. in ill repute, the United Nations set up a rival Special Commission (UNSCOM) to uncover and dismantle Iraq's program to manufacture weapons of mass destruction. As the ranking American in UNSCOM, Gallucci led an inspection team that was held hostage by Iraqi troops outside the Ministry of Defense. With a sheaf of

incriminating documents inside his coat pocket, Gallucci coolly negotiated the release of his team.

The choice of Gallucci to conduct nuclear diplomacy with North
Korea had two main consequences. As an assistant secretary, he lacked
the bureaucratic clout to put together the makings of a deal. Indeed, for
much of 1993 he had no one-on-one meetings with Secretary of State
Christopher. Lacking authority within the State Department, he had to
clear initiatives with Davis, who was cool to diplomatic give-and-take
with North Korea, or with Tarnoff, who had many other concerns. He
smoothed one potential source of friction, with the Bureau of East Asian
and Pacific Affairs, by establishing good working relations with a deputy
assistant secretary in that bureau and his deputy on the negotiating
team, Thomas Hubbard. To muster interagency support, Gallucci
would have to forge alliances with the National Security Council staff
and the Defense Department.

The second consequence of choosing Gallucci was to reinforce the
impression, both in and out of government, that proliferation was *the*
issue, not relations between the two Koreas or broader security and political concerns in East Asia. Issues have different faces for senior officials, Congress, and the press, and North Korea's withdrawal from the
Nonproliferation Treaty had already cast the nuclear face into the glare
of public exposure, relegating North-South and regional aspects into
the shadows. Spotlighting proliferation also brought different actors to
the fore—the I.A.E.A. and technical experts in the policy-making and
intelligence agencies, who were committed to the crime-and-punishment approach.

Critics would later argue that, had the Bureau of East Asian and
Pacific Affairs under Assistant Secretary of State Winston Lord seized
the issue the way it had under Richard Solomon during the Bush Administration, the nonnuclear aspects would have had a higher priority.
Perhaps so, but the bureau's interest in maintaining good relations with
ally South Korea might have inhibited direct dealings with longtime foe
North Korea, impeding nuclear diplomacy.

Coaxing North Korea Partway Back into the Treaty

North Korea's signature on the Nonproliferation Treaty was the legal
basis for curtailing its bomb-making. The treaty limited the number of
lawful nuclear-weapons states to five: the United States, the Soviet
Union, Britain, France, and China. It also established the right of the
I.A.E.A. to inspect member states' nuclear activities and to gather evidence of suspected violations. The treaty was not self-enforcing—no

treaty is—but it did establish norms essential for rallying international opposition to nuclear-arming by North Korea. Trying to get North Korea to comply fully with the treaty was the major premise of any sound nonproliferation policy.

The administration was reluctant to spell out inducements for North Korea to comply. That left it no alternative but coercive diplomacy, trying to compel North Korean compliance by threatening economic sanctions. In seeking U.N. Security Council backing for sanctions, however, it had to convince China and others that it had tried diplomacy and failed. That required it to enter into negotiations with North Korea, precisely what Pyongyang had been trying to get Washington to do all along.

An appreciation of North Korea's insecurity might have led the administration to abandon coercive diplomacy. It did not. Instead, it pursued what it called "the step-by-step approach." By insisting that North Korea take the first step, it set preconditions for high-level talks. Only after the North complied fully with I.A.E.A. safeguards and resumed North-South talks would the United States engage in diplomatic give-and-take. Washington would not get very far going step by step.

There was little domestic political support for deal-making. Proliferation experts, following the I.A.E.A.'s lead, preferred to have North Korea renounce the treaty than to bribe it to comply. The very thought of accommodation with a hateful communist regime in Pyongyang also antagonized unilateralists on the right wing of the Republican Party, who distrust international cooperation and prefer the United States to go it alone in the world. They pushed strenuously to derail diplomacy and confront North Korea. Collapse, not cooperation, was their idea of how to deal with the North's nuclear program.

Amid such implacable opposition outside and skepticism inside, the Clinton Administration moved to resume talks with North Korea. Secretary of State Christopher, Secretary of Defense Aspin, and National Security Adviser Lake met with South Korean Foreign Minister Han Sung Joo in Washington on March 29, 1993. Afterward, Han said that they had reached a general understanding on a "stick-and-carrot" approach to the North Koreans: "The threat of sanctions plus certain face-saving inducements will help them comply." Han emphasized the need for carrots, arguing that "pressure alone will not work." A senior State Department official, told of Han's comments, said that Pyongyang "always had the kind of assurances" Seoul was talking about and that Washington had no plans to offer a more explicit quid pro quo.[5] That strongly implied a policy of all stick, no carrot.

Daniel Poneman, senior director for nonproliferation at the N.S.C., demurs. "Not being explicit does not equal no carrots. A whiff of carrot means a lot in the face of a forty-year embargo." He adds, "You might say that was not enough, and we reached the same view later, but the policy was always a two-track approach."[6] Yet North Korea was not about to settle for less than specific promises and intended to hold the United States to them. "We watched how you dealt with the Russians," said a senior North Korean at that time, referring to Washington's fitful cooperation with Moscow. "We will not let that happen to us."[7]

The day after South Korea's foreign minister met with senior U.S. officials, North Korea's Minister of Atomic Energy "categorically" rejected the I.A.E.A.'s demand for a special inspection, but invited consultations on "implementation of the safeguards agreement"—inspections at other than the nuclear waste sites.[8] On April 1 the I.A.E.A., in an unprecedented act, declared the D.P.R.K. in violation of its safeguards agreement. There were 28 ayes, but China voted no, along with Libya, while India, Pakistan, Syria, and Vietnam abstained. The I.A.E.A. referred the matter to the U.N. Security Council to enforce compliance. On April 8, in a move designed to avoid a veto by China, the Security Council president issued a statement urging further consultations between the I.A.E.A. and the D.P.R.K.

In what was to become a leitmotif of U.S. nuclear diplomacy, the I.A.E.A. vote and Security Council action stirred yearnings to romance China. It was a case of looking for love in all the wrong places. In a prescient column in the *Washington Post* of April 1, 1993, Jim Hoagland reported that on March 22 Assistant Secretary of State for Asian and Pacific Affairs William Clark, a Bush Administration holdover, had heard from Japanese officials that China might be willing to help with North Korea, but its price was renewal of its most-favored-nation (M.F.N.) trading status. Recalling that Bill Clinton had berated George Bush during the 1992 campaign for being soft on China, Hoagland wrote, "To get sanctions or other U.N. pressure applied to North Korea, America will have to avoid a Chinese veto in the Security Council. Will Beijing cooperate if Clinton attaches stringent human rights conditions to renewal of the preferential M.F.N. trading rules that helped China amass an $18 billion trade surplus with America last year?" Hoagland advised against relying on China: "Do not exaggerate China's influence or willingness to use what influence it possesses constructively in North Korea . . . Be the opposite, in short, of George Bush."[9] Hoagland's was a minority voice within the foreign policy establishment.

Tokyo had its own reasons for wanting Washington to renew most-favored-nation status for Beijing. It feared that promoting human rights in China would raise tensions in the region.

Beijing also had its own interests in keeping North Korea non-nuclear. It wanted to discourage Japan from nuclear-arming and prevent South Korea from eventually inheriting North Korea's nuclear program.

As Foreign Minister Qian Qichen put it in November 1991, "We do not want to see the existence of nuclear weapons on the Korean peninsula."[10] China disagreed with the United States over how best to achieve that aim. As a matter of principle, it had never exercised its veto in the Security Council. Yet, having suffered from a U.S.-led embargo in the past, Beijing was opposed to economic sanctions.[11] Whether it vetoed a Security Council resolution or abstained, it was unwilling to enforce an oil embargo or other stringent sanctions for fear of destabilizing its next-door neighbor. China was also sensitive about control of its border with North Korea, which resembles the one between the United States and Mexico. Smuggling runs rampant, often with the connivance of local authorities, who benefit both politically and financially from the profitable cross-border traffic in goods and currency. With ethnic Koreans in substantial numbers on both sides of the border, it could become a convenient escape route for those fleeing deprivation in North Korea in the event of an economic embargo. The central government was struggling with newly assertive regional authorities throughout China. Trying to enforce sanctions could embarrass Beijing, or worse, set off local unrest.[12]

The Clinton Administration tried to exploit China's reluctance to face up to sanctions by getting Beijing to press Pyongyang. "The threat of sanctions," says a top official in the administration, "moved the Chinese to help lean on the North Koreans because the Chinese didn't want to go through that."[13] Just how hard Beijing leaned on Pyongyang is open to question. When the Clinton Administration sought unconditional renewal of M.F.N. in early June, it would cite its need for China's help with North Korea as a public justification. Such help was not, in fact, a motive for the administration's decision.[14] For its part, Beijing emphasized the limits of its influence in Pyongyang and never linked its stance toward the North with M.F.N.[15] It did lend tacit political support to American efforts by abstaining on U.N. Security Council resolutions and by helping to draft statements for the Council president urging North Korean compliance. It reportedly showed its displeasure in March by turning down a request by Kim Jong Il to see Deng Xiaoping during a visit to Beijing. Kim canceled the visit. In turn, a high-level Chinese visit to Pyongyang on April 15, on the occasion of Kim Il Sung's birthday, was canceled, the D.P.R.K. briefly sealed its border with China and North Korean guards had fired on the Chinese.[16] China also was unwilling to bail out the North Korean economy. At the same time, China offered the North an alternative to nuclear-arming, reaffirming their solidarity and reassuring it about the Sino-Korean alliance. The Chinese also kept telling Washington, in effect, "Forget about us. Talk to Pyongyang."

"To some extent the diplomatic effort was forced on us by tactical considerations," says a U.S. official. "The only way we could build a consensus at the U.N. Security Council to impose sanctions was to demonstrate that the North Koreans were unwilling to make a deal."[17] Yet the Chinese would not be easy to convince. They remained in close contact with North Korea, putting them in a good position to judge which side was impeding a deal and leaving the North Koreans unconvinced of China's willingness to impose sanctions.

While much of Washington was wondering whether or not China would back sanctions, few considered resolving the dispute through direct talks with North Korea. In a public statement on April 6 that received only cursory notice, the D.P.R.K. Foreign Ministry elaborated its position. It accused "some officials of the I.A.E.A. secretariat and some member nations" of "deliberately ignoring our reasonable proposal and patient efforts to seek a negotiated settlement of the problem." Even after declaring its intent to withdraw from the Nonproliferation Treaty, the statement pointed out, Pyongyang was prepared to let the I.A.E.A. monitor its nuclear installations to prevent any diversion of nuclear material to bomb-making: "We made it clear that we were ready to fulfill our commitments under the [safeguards] agreement." The "so-called 'nuclear problem,'" how much plutonium it may have reprocessed in the past, was "not a problem between our country and the I.A.E.A." but "between us and the United States," and should not be raised "in the U.N. arena" but "resolved through negotiations between the D.P.R.K. and the United States."[18] North Korea was telling the United States, "Forget about China. Let's make a deal."

Later that month, a North Korean ambassador to the United Nations, Ho Jong, telephoned Kenneth Quinones of the State Department's Korea desk. Quinones, without authorization, took the initiative and spoke to Ho. Their conversation led to working-level talks in New York. "Even before Ho Jong called, we were already engaged internally in how to approach the North," says a State Department official. "There was a consensus for talking."[19] Perhaps, but that consensus did not extend to what to tell North Korea. Nor were the North Koreans of much help. It was difficult, says a senior official, to pluck "the nuggets of reason" from "the ocean of vitriol" spewing out of Pyongyang.[20]

Defense Secretary Aspin had set up a North Korean task force chaired by Assistant Secretary Ashton Carter in an attempt to wrest control of the issue from the State Department. "It was both a help to them and a worry to them," says Carter.[21] Its first product was a March 1993 position paper for the National Security Council drafted by Philip Zelikow and other Bush Administration holdovers who worked for Carter. Carter "wanted the military options taken very seriously," says a Defense

Department official, and Zelikow's paper did. "It was very pessimistic about the prospects for negotiations," the official says. "It was basically looking at what to do when negotiations failed." The paper recommended an attack on North Korea's nuclear facilities. "If they started to take the spent fuel out of the reactor, we would have an opportunity. Once it was out of the reactor, that opportunity was gone."[22] The draft "appalled" others in Carter's office and reinforced doubts about the military options. "It was so rosy. The probability of war was very high and saying that it wasn't was just irresponsible."[23] Top Pentagon officials were briefed on the conclusions but the paper was closely held and not distributed interagency for fear that its disclosure could be dangerously provocative, at home and abroad. "I was very worried about leaks," says Carter, "and their effect on the actual situation."[24]

What would become a key difference between Defense and State first surfaced in a paper drafted for Carter by Steven Fetter, another member of his staff: whether the top priority should be special inspections to get at the nuclear past or inspections to impede further bomb-making. "The State Department's highest priority seemed to be the integrity of the [nonproliferation] regime," says a Defense Department official. "The Pentagon's highest priority was no bomb. That later became no more bombs."[25] Very soon after he became involved in March 1993, Thomas Hubbard began attending meetings of the Pentagon task force. "Ash Carter was saying, 'Hey, you guys are all wrong. It's not special inspections. It's the fuel rods.' We were buffeted back here [in the State Department] on whether our principal objective ought to be the procedural one of following the safeguards agreement in all its terms or whether the objective ought to be a freeze, getting them to do something about those fuel rods."[26] That difference in priority underlay the difference between the crime-and-punishment approach and diplomatic give-and-take.

The Pentagon task force reported to Defense Secretary Aspin and Deputy Secretary William Perry in early May. "The trap for us was an inspected bomb program," says Ashton Carter. That widely shared concern prompted the first conclusion of the task force: "Simply restoring North Korea to the N.P.T. and the I.A.E.A. is necessary but not sufficient." The second conclusion disputed the State Department's priorities: "Pinning down the details of North Korea's past reprocessing is not as important as stopping further reprocessing." A third conclusion disputed State's policy preference: "We are skeptical about the ultimate effectiveness and desirability of using economic sanctions as a stick if initial diplomatic efforts fail." A final conclusion was the most contentious of all: "A failure to contain the North Korean nuclear program would pose a threat to the vital interest of the United States." A vital interest is one for which the United States would be willing to wage war. Wary of "the new crowd," the Joint Staff dissented.[27]

As the Clinton Administration moved to resume high-level talks, the idea that North Korea could be persuaded to reconsider its withdrawal from the Nonproliferation Treaty encountered a storm of skepticism. "It's not going to happen," said one intelligence source.[28] "There is no credible evidence that I am aware of that the North is using the nuclear program as a bargaining chip," said a senior analyst. "North Korea has shown it wants to maintain this program and it is willing to pay a price to do that."[29] North Korea "is not yet ready—and perhaps never will be—either to abandon its bomb or to start serious exchanges with Seoul," asserted Aidan Foster-Carter, a Korea specialist at Leeds University. Far from welcoming economic engagement, its leaders fear "plague-bearing mosquitoes, fatally infecting a regime founded on an absolute quarantine against the outside world."[30]

At least two observers publicly dissented. Michael Mazarr, senior fellow at the Center for Strategic and International Studies, thought the North Koreans' "frustration" with the stalled talks was one motive for threatening to abrogate the Nonproliferation Treaty. The reasoning went, "Why not provoke a crisis because we're not getting any economic or political benefits out of this?"[31] Selig Harrison of the Carnegie Endowment for International Peace argued, "The way to deal with the North is to hold out the promise of clearly defined, carefully calibrated rewards linked to specific concessions on the part of Pyongyang. Pressure alone merely strengthens the hard-liners."[32]

Hawks in Seoul could not have disagreed more. In an op-ed in the *Far Eastern Economic Review*, Ahn Byung Joon, professor of international relations at Yonsei University, threw down the gauntlet, "It must be made absolutely clear to the rulers in Pyongyang that all necessary means will be taken to prevent North Korea from acquiring a nuclear capability."[33] The phrase, "all necessary means," is a customary euphemism for all-out force, including the use of nuclear weapons.

More encouraging phrases came from North Korea. If there are talks, said Ho Jong, "there will be some compromises."[34] North Korea could retain some nuclear leverage by remaining partially in and partially out of the Nonproliferation Treaty. It was ready to allow inspections in order to inhibit removal and reprocessing of spent fuel—checking seals for signs of tampering, reloading film and batteries in cameras, and other routine maintenance of its monitoring equipment at Yongbyon— but not much else. On April 22 the I.A.E.A. reluctantly accepted North Korea's offer "in order not to lose the continued validity of safeguards information."[35] That became known as *"continuity of safeguards."* Later on, I.A.E.A. officials would wrongly accuse the United States of inventing this term.

The I.A.E.A. also expected to observe the refueling of the reactor during its May inspection, but no refueling took place. The spent fuel then had four or five bombs' worth of plutonium. Removing it from the reactor was a necessary first step to reprocessing it and extracting the plutonium for bombs. *That North Korea did not refuel at this time was evidence that it was in no hurry to make more bombs.* "If you're hell-bent on making bombs," says a Defense Department official, "you should have refueled quickly."[36] Instead of calling attention to North Korea's restraint, officials in the I.A.E.A. and the U.S. government publicly expressed fear that it would divert spent fuel to bomb-making in the future.[37] The prevailing view, says Assistant Secretary of Defense Ashton Carter, who shared it, was, "They were playing for time, trying to figure out some way to keep this program going."[38]

On April 22, the day the I.A.E.A. acquiesced to limited inspections, Washington agreed to reopen high-level talks. The only inducement it was prepared to offer North Korea for not abandoning the Nonproliferation Treaty was more talks. There was no interagency agreement on anything else, not even suspension of Team Spirit.[39]

Instead, the administration remained fixated on Beijing. "The consensus is that China is the key to solving the North Korea crisis," said a senior government official, who expressed concern about "how much influence that gives Beijing and how it affects our China policy."[40] China still favored dialogue, not sanctions. On May 11, one month before North Korea's withdrawal from the Nonproliferation Treaty was due to take effect, the U.N. Security Council enacted a resolution calling on the D.P.R.K. to "reaffirm" its commitment to the Nonproliferation Treaty and "comply with its safeguards agreement." The vote was 13–0. China abstained, along with Pakistan.

On May 12, after two working-level meetings in Beijing held at North Korea's request, Robert Gallucci, chosen to head the American delegation at the high-level talks, saw "some indications that they are trying to resolve this." Others had doubts. North Korea is "not going to say, gosh, this is all a misunderstanding," warned one senior official.[41] On May 17 U.S. and D.P.R.K. representatives met at the United Nations and agreed to resume high-level talks on June 2. One official said, "We give it all about a 25 to 35 percent chance of success."[42]

Congressional antagonism to cooperation with North Korea made that prediction seem wildly optimistic. When negotiator Gallucci outlined the administration's approach at a May 26 hearing, several senators warned against rewarding North Korea for noncompliance. "We want to avoid that. We are insisting," said Gallucci, "that we resolve this issue on its merits, before we talk about other issues."[43] That did not allay sena-torial suspicions. "Are we prepared to make any concessions? For exam-ple, is Team Spirit a potential concession?" asked Frank Murkowski (R-AK). "Or have we established a policy that suggests this issue has to stand on the merits of proliferation, [that] it's not a matter of conces-sions?" Gallucci gave ground, saying that he would "speak to," not sat-isfy, a North Korean demand to cancel Team Spirit. Moderates joined in the spine-stiffening. Senator Richard Lugar (R-IN) wondered whether the President was going to prepare the American people for tougher measures to come. "The alarm bell really needs to ring," he said. "This is serious business."[44]

With his Congressional corset firmly in place, Gallucci met First Vice Minister of Foreign Affairs Kang Sok Ju in New York. Kang began by reciting from a prepared text. "The D.P.R.K. is not East Germany," he began, according to an American diplomat who was present. "We are not going to collapse. You cannot strangle us."[45] Instead of a return to the Nonproliferation Treaty, Kang proposed establishing a regional safeguards arrangement, like the one between Brazil and Argentina, and expressed the desire for "a quid pro quo." He received two of sorts: more high-level talks and a joint statement, the first ever between the two countries.

"Let's walk down this road together," Gallucci told the North Kore-ans.[46] Try, as he did, to sound accommodating, he was initially "hamstrung," says a member of the U.S. delegation. "He had virtually nothing to give." Even a reiteration of the security assurance that Un-dersecretary of State Kanter had given the North on January 22, 1992, was held in reserve. Later Gallucci recessed the talks and returned to Washington for authority to cancel Team Spirit. "It was a trump card he never had to play," adds the delegation member.[47] "I had a couple of other carrots in my bag," says Gallucci, "but I was prepared to reach into it only if the North Koreans were more forthcoming on inspections. They were willing to allow what the I.A.E.A. needed for monitoring diversion of spent fuel but nothing that involved the past."[48]

"What struck me in that round was their stubbornness," says Thomas Hubbard, deputy secretary of state for East Asian and Pacific affairs and the number two man on the U.S. delegation. The North Koreans even dropped hints that "maybe they had nuclear weapons." Others had a different recollection, of tough talk on both sides. "Everyone on the American delegation was gung-ho to sock it to these sons-of-bitches," recalls another delegation member. Yet glimmers of hope soon emerged. "We thought we detected that they might let the I.A.E.A. in if we didn't call them ad hoc and routine inspections," says Hubbard. "I felt confident that if we played around with words, we'd get what we wanted." A colleague recalls, "After a day or two, people came back and said, 'You know, their position is not that crazy. Maybe there's something there.'" An epiphany of sorts came the third night when the American delegation met over dinner. "For the first two days we were at a real loss, floundering around. . . . We were very dejected because we couldn't figure out how to get out of this." During dinner, Robert Carlin of INR recalled that North Korea, in its statement announcing its intent to renounce the Nonproliferation Treaty, had hinted at conditions for remaining in the treaty, conditions that might serve as the basis for a deal. Charles Kartman, director of Korean affairs at the State Department, told Carlin to draft talking points for the next day's negotiating session quoting that and subsequent North Korean statements. Gallucci recited them word for word. "It was as if an electric current ran through the North Korean delegation. A day later Kang started from the premise that they could go back into the N.P.T."[49]

Paying close attention to North Korea's words seemed to work. On June 11, 1993, one day before its withdrawal from the treaty was due to take effect, North Korea "decided unilaterally to suspend" that fateful step "as long as it considers necessary" while talks continued. The United States, in a unilateral statement, drew three "red lines." It "would regard additional reprocessing, any break in the continuity of I.A.E.A. safeguards or a withdrawal from the N.P.T. as harmful and inconsistent with our efforts to resolve the nuclear issue through dialogue."[50]

The two sides agreed to a set of principles for resolving their differences, among them, "assurances against the threat and use of force, including nuclear weapons" and "peace and security in a nuclear-free Korean peninsula, including impartial application of full-scope safeguards, mutual respect for each other's sovereignty, and noninterference in each other's internal affairs."[51] Many of the principles were drawn verbatim from the U.N. Charter and other international documents. "It was language that no one could possibly take exception to," says one of the drafters. Yet during interagency deliberations an N.S.C. staff member did: "'You can't say that.' We said it's in the U.N. charter, which incidentally we signed."[52]

There was hard bargaining over special inspections. "Kang would just go berserk when we said special inspections," says an American delegate, "but Washington had an anchor in us, saying you've got to put that in."[53] The disagreement was finessed with the phrase, "full-scope safeguards," a diplomatic term of art for ad hoc, routine, and special inspections. Nevertheless, to one Korea-watcher who was sympathetic to deal-making, whether the North would ever accept special inspections remained difficult to gauge, but "most of the evidence was negative.

Some of them were looking for a way to move, but they themselves did not seem clear on what to do."[54]

The principles were codified in a joint statement, the first ever between the United States and the D.P.R.K. (Text in appendix II.) To Kang, that was "really a turning point in our bilateral relations."[55] To U.S. officials, the joint statement was, in the words of one, "a holding action."[56] It kept North Korea in the Nonproliferation Treaty and it kept the United States at the negotiating table.

Not everyone reacted with relief at the result. The fact of the joint statement, even more than its contents, infuriated Seoul. "We didn't realize how much the South Koreans would scream," says a State Department official.[57] "The 'ROKs' thought we were certain to fail," says a delegation member. "They were very laid back until they got wind of a joint statement from the North Korean side. Then my telephone started ringing at 4 a.m."

American hawks could not conceal their dismay. *Washington Post* columnist Lally Weymouth, daughter of *Post* publisher Katherine Graham, carped, "Although a *New York Times* editorial congratulated the Clinton Administration for 'deft diplomacy,' it's hard to see why."[58] Frank Gaffney, a right-wing gadfly who worked on nonproliferation in the Reagan Administration Pentagon, was up in arms. "On June 11 North Korea took another major step toward the acquisition of nuclear arms," contended Gaffney. Instead of diplomacy, he proposed a doubling of U.S. forces in Korea, suspension of South Korea's trade links and Japan's flow of funds to the North, and covert operations to enforce an embargo to compel inspections.[59]

Having caught the world's attention by threatening to renounce the Nonproliferation Treaty, North Korea finally achieved its long-sought aim of high-level talks with the United States. Getting the United States to negotiate in earnest would take months more.

The Reactor Deal Redux

Washington was still intent on using the I.A.E.A. to rein in the North's nuclear program without having to concede anything in return. Pyongyang was equally determined to exploit its "unique status," partly in and partly out of the Nonproliferation Treaty, to wrest a deal out of Washington. With Washington reluctant to engage in give-and-take, negotiations proceeded inconclusively, and the strategy of forcing North Korea to open access kept running into a closed door.

Pyongyang was allowing I.A.E.A. monitoring in order to confirm what American intelligence was seeing for itself, that the Yongbyon reactor was still running and the reprocessing plant was not—evidence that the North was not removing spent fuel or producing more pluto-nium.[60] Pyongyang was also willing to let inspectors do the routine maintenance necessary to keep I.A.E.A. monitoring equipment in work-ing order. But it drew the line at more intrusive inspections that could have helped the I.A.E.A. ascertain how much plutonium may have been produced in the past. Whenever the agency tried to cross that line, it was rebuffed, provoking a new confrontation. North Korea insisted that the I.A.E.A. could gain unimpeded access to its nuclear facilities and to its nuclear past only as part of a larger deal with the United States. It had the makings of a deal to propose.

In May and June the United States, concerned that the I.A.E.A. might not regain access to the facilities at Yongbyon, began preparing an alternative, training the South Koreans to conduct inspections under the North-South denuclearization accord of 1991. "We went to Korea twice to pump them up for this," says one Pentagon participant.[61] In North-South talks on implementing the 1991 accord, Washington also urged Seoul to make its proposal more negotiable by dropping demands for short-notice challenge inspections and focusing on the main con-cern—diversion of spent fuel and reprocessing.

While pursuing the crime-and-punishment approach, Washington showed its indisposition to deal-making that June when it kept Israel from offering inducements to North Korea not to export missiles. Israeli suspicions about Pyongyang's role in missile proliferation had surfaced in 1991. Israel concluded that North Korea was selling SCUD-C mis-siles to Syria and had contracted to help construct a SCUD-C produc-tion line there.[62] The SCUD-C could hurl a one-ton warhead 400 kilo-meters, far enough to reach much of Israel from Syria. In October 1991 a North Korean cargo ship believed bound for Syria with SCUD-Cs and missile-manufacturing technology on board reportedly turned back after Israel threatened to intercept it. In February 1992 Israel alerted U.S. intelligence to another North Korean missile shipment bound for Syria and asked to have the ship intercepted. The U.S. Navy began tracking it, but this time the bluff failed and the ship reached port. Some civilians in the Pentagon favored boarding on the high seas, an act of war. The Navy and State Department were opposed. "What are we sup-posed to do," wondered one State Department official, "occupy every country involved in proliferation?"[63]

In 1993 Israel tried a different tack. This time, the impetus was an Iranian bid to purchase 150 Rodong-1 missiles, under development by North Korea. In January Israel opened talks in Pyongyang to establish diplomatic relations and provide $1 billion in investment and technical assistance to induce it to call off the sale. "Israel is the 'carrot' in the carrot-and-stick policy that the United States is employing against

North Korea," said Ben-Ami Shilloni, an East Asia specialist at Hebrew University.[64] Yet the United States was not about to dispense carrots, even Israeli ones, to North Korea. On June 14 Foreign Minister Shimon Peres met with Secretary of State Warren Christopher and South Korean Foreign Minister Han Sung Joo to discuss his pending visit to Pyongyang. Both objected. Instead of sending Peres to Pyongyang, the Israelis sent Eitan Bentsur, deputy director of the Foreign Ministry, who had conducted the January talks in Pyongyang, to meet with the North Koreans in Beijing. Israel did provide some technical assistance, but suspended all contacts after the United States expressed its displeasure.[65] A senior official sums up the American view, "A rogue negotiation by a third country on missiles would not necessarily have helped solve the nuclear problem."[66]

Israel had acted on the assumption that North Korea, desperate for hard currency and oil, was selling missiles for purely commercial reasons and could be bought off. A reasonable inference from the incident was that if deal-making made sense to an Israel directly threatened by missile proliferation, it was worthy of American consideration. North Korea had a deal in mind, one it had initially broached a year ago, to trade in its bomb-making for new nuclear reactors.

Replacement reactors may have appealed to technocrats in the D.P.R.K. Ministry of Atomic Energy. They also symbolized an end to the American economic embargo imposed under the Trading with the Enemy Act and other laws.* More important, they provided a fitting quid pro quo for allowing intrusive I.A.E.A. inspections because reactor technology was available only to members in good standing of the Nonproliferation Treaty. They also afforded appropriate political cover for accepting a ban on reprocessing: if the D.P.R.K., with its faith in self-reliance, could depend on outsiders for nuclear reactors, it could also rely on them for a supply of low-enriched uranium, not usable for bombs, to fuel the reactors. It would have no need for reprocessing to extract plutonium for reactor fuel.

High-level talks were set to resume on July 14. The prologue was not propitious. A sudden barrage of not-so-subtle nuclear threats reminded Pyongyang of a major motive for nuclear-arming. President Clinton, in Tokyo for a meeting of the Group of Seven industrial powers, drew attention to fears that Japan might feel "compelled to become a nuclear

* In addition to the Trading with the Enemy Act of 1950, other legal impediments to commerce with the D.P.R.K. include the Export Administration Act, the Trade Act of 1974 on Most Favored Nation, the Arms Export Control Act setting sanctions on missile proliferators, and the Anti-Terrorism and Arms Export Amendments Act of 1989 barring certain transactions for any state designated a "terrorist country." The Foreign Assistance Act bars aid to "any communist country" and "any country which engages in gross violations of internationally recognized human rights," and obliges U.S. officials to oppose World Bank or I.M.F. loans.

power."[67] Since 1967 Japan had adhered to three nonnuclear principles, not to possess, produce, or permit nuclear arms on its territory, but it was now objecting to G-7 endorsement of unlimited extension of the Nonproliferation Treaty when it came up for review in 1995. Foreign Minister Kabun Muto, trying to ease apprehensions that Japan was abandoning the three nonnuclear principles, only fed the fears: "I think there should be more national debate, so that we can have more consensus within this country." South Korea's reaction was appropriately blunt: "I don't think that's the right way to respond to the North Korean nuclear issue, and I simply don't understand why Japan takes that position," South Korean Foreign Minister Han Sung Joo told a reporter. "It only arouses concern that Japan is not fully committed to staying non-nuclear."[68]

President Clinton's next stop was South Korea. In a visit to the demilitarized zone, he tried to reassure Tokyo and Seoul about the American nuclear guarantee with a display of toughness. He succeeded in reminding North Koreans of the nuclear threat: "When you examine the nature of the American security commitment to Korea, to Japan, to this region, it is pointless for them to try to develop nuclear weapons, because if they ever use them it would be the end of their country."[69] Pyongyang's reaction was swift. "If anyone dares to provoke us," it warned, "we will immediately show him in practice what our bold decision is."[70]

In this charged atmosphere, high-level talks resumed on July 14. On the third morning North Korea tabled a proposal to replace its gas-graphite reactors with light-water ones. "That had been bruited in the past," says delegation member Thomas Hubbard. "Somebody once said we ought to be ready for that." Almost nobody in Washington was. The delegation had come to the talks prepared to address inspections and security assurances. "They threw us a curve ball." Gallucci and Hubbard went off to lunch with their North Korean counterparts, Kang Sok Ju and Kim Gye Gwan. "Kang really worked hard to convince us that this was a major change in North Korea's approach to the world," recalls Hubbard. "He told us it had Kim Jong Il's blessing and was designed to open up North Korea." The two Americans were impressed. "We came back from the lunch saying this was something we should work with."[71] They knew that no nuclear reactor was proliferation-proof: all reactors generate plutonium, the main ingredient of bombs, as a by-product of fission. Still, light-water reactors were less proliferation-prone than gas-graphite ones—especially if North Korea had to depend on imports of nuclear fuel. Most important of all, they knew no reactor could be supplied to any country that was not a member in good standing of the Nonproliferation Treaty, which meant North Korea would have to accept full inspections.

Domestic politics all but precluded a direct deal with the United States for the reactors. Administration officials assumed Congress would object to paying for reactors or to transferring American nuclear technology to North Korea. When Gallucci sought authorization from Undersecretary of State Peter Tarnoff and Undersecretary of Defense Frank Wisner to commit the United States to obtain replacement reactors from a third country, he was turned down. "They were very cautious," Gallucci recalls. "They wanted to make sure that we didn't do anything in the agreed statement that would have us bite down on this hook and end up on the line for a few billion dollars' worth of nuclear equipment for North Korea. We thought this was such a good deal that if it was up to us, we would have leaned forward."[72]

Without a commitment on replacement reactors, it proved difficult for the Americans to convince the North Koreans to accept ad hoc and routine inspections, never mind special inspections. A heat wave had hit Geneva and it was hotter at the negotiating table. At one point, Hubbard recalls, "Kang rolled up his sleeves and pant legs and went at it hammer and tongs." At another point, he and Gallucci were grappling with Kang Sok Ju and Kim Gye Gwan in the North Korean mission "faces red, practically shouting, when the North Korean wives walked in with McDonald's cheeseburgers."[73] They all laughed at the incongruity.

The talks managed to yield another agreed statement on July 19, 1993, but instead of issuing it jointly, the United States, bowing to South Korean objections, insisted that the two sides separately issue identical statements. The United States pledged to consider ways to replace North Korea's reactors: "As part of a final resolution of the nuclear issue, and on a premise that a solution to the provision of light-water-moderated reactors (LWRs) is achievable, the United States is prepared to support the introduction of LWRs and to explore with the D.P.R.K. ways in which the LWRs can be obtained."[74] The North Koreans translated the word "premise"—*chunje* in Korean—as "precondition," and took it to mean that the United States would obtain a commitment from others to provide the light-water reactors before the third round. Hubbard, who negotiated the statement with the North Koreans, says, "We never could figure out what they meant by 'on a premise.'"[75]

To the Americans it was not a formal offer of new reactors, just a commitment to negotiate, and it elicited a commitment to negotiate in return. The D.P.R.K. promised to begin consultations with the I.A.E.A. "on outstanding safeguards and other issues as soon as possible" and to "begin" North-South talks as soon as possible on bilateral issues, "including the nuclear issue." The North was once again prepared to allow inspections for the continuity of safeguards, impeding any diversion of nuclear fuel to bomb-making, but it stopped well short of allowing full inspections by the I.A.E.A. or any inspections by the South. They agreed to meet in two months to discuss "outstanding matters relating to the nuclear issue" and "to lay the basis for improving relations overall."

In a unilateral statement intended to put pressure on North Korea, Gallucci declared that the United States "would not expect to begin a third round of U.S. talks with the D.P.R.K. until serious discussions with the I.A.E.A. and R.O.K. are underway."[76] The unilateral statement was not binding on North Korea but it did tie the United States to the I.A.E.A. and the R.O.K., with unfortunate consequences.

Gallucci carefully characterized the accord as "a small but significant step." Others were less charitable. "They're staying in the [nonprolifera- tion] regime and becoming a nuclear-weapons power at the same time," said Thomas Cochran of the liberal-minded National Resources Defense Council. "Pretty neat trick."[77]

Nonproliferation experts across the political spectrum were increas- ingly impatient with what they saw as flaunting of the Nonproliferation Treaty and defiance of the I.A.E.A. by North Korea. Many wanted Pyongyang punished for noncompliance, not rewarded for coming part- way back into the Nonproliferation Treaty fold, and especially not with replacement reactors. Taking their cue from the I.A.E.A., most outside experts seemed more worried about preserving the integrity of the agency's inspection procedures than about preventing proliferation. They were also preoccupied with how much plutonium Pyongyang had already produced instead of how to keep it from producing more.

A very few outside experts dissented. In their view the future was more critical than the past. Urging the United States to defer any dead- line for special inspections, Spurgeon Keeny, president of the Arms Control Association, put it succinctly: "Whether the true figure is mea- sured in grams or is enough for a few weapons is important, but far less important than whether North Korea will be able to develop a substan- tial nuclear weapon program in the future."[78] The main lesson Michael Mazarr drew from the situation was that living with ambiguity about North Korea's nuclear past for a while was a tolerable price to pay for halting more bomb-making. Mazarr drew two other lessons as well, that it was essential for the United States to follow through on its diplomatic commitments and that pressure would exacerbate Pyongyang's para- noia, accelerate its bomb-making, and raise regional tensions.[79] Doug Bandow of the Cato Institute also questioned whether coercive nonpro- liferation would work: "The West should avoid taking precipitous ac- tion," he contended. He advocated diplomacy, starting with "a commit- ment by Washington to establish diplomatic ties and end the economic embargo against Pyongyang" if it fulfills its obligations to the I.A.E.A.[80] It was just such a commitment that Washington was unwilling to make.

Empty Threats

The Clinton Administration was under pressure to make a very different sort of commitment. Mounting impatience was prompting calls for economic sanctions and armed force. "Rather than trying to appease one of the last remaining Stalinist dictatorships in the world," wrote Larry DiRita of the Heritage Foundation, President Clinton should set a deadline for North Korea to allow international inspections, or else impose sanctions and consider "destroying military headquarters, ballistic missile launch sites, or command and control facilities."[81] Former Congressman Stephen Solarz, a Democrat, wanted to threaten "the kind of comprehensive sanctions against it that could bring about the collapse of the fragile North Korean economy." Acknowledging that this could lead to war, Solarz concluded, "However risky such a strategy may be, it would be far riskier to permit a rogue regime like North Korea to become a member of the nuclear club."[82] The *Economist* weighed in editorially: "North Korea has been given every diplomatic chance to do the right thing. It should now be given a deadline and told to honor its obligations—or expect to face undiplomatic sanctions." The *Economist* echoed most nonproliferation experts. "If North Korea is allowed to shrug off the new rules, then others with clandestine nuclear ambitions, such as Iran, will be emboldened to try." Its "defiance" also put a ban on nuclear tests at risk. "There is talk of asking the I.A.E.A. to verify a comprehensive test ban, if one can ever be negotiated."[83] The *Economist* neglected to mention that Britain opposed the ban. If coercion prompted North Korea to go nuclear, that would buttress the British case for continued testing.

The Clinton Administration engaged in some threatening talk of its own. In a September 21 speech in Washington, National Security Adviser Lake proclaimed a new policy of "enlargement" to expand the community of democratic, market-oriented nations. He warned against "backlash" states, like North Korea, that "sponsor terrorism and traffic in weapons of mass destruction and ballistic missile technology." Such states, he warned, face isolation, and if this did not inhibit them from aggressive actions, "we clearly must be prepared to strike back decisively and unilaterally."[84] Some of Lake's rhetoric was suggested by House Minority Leader Newt Gingrich (R-GA).[85]

Seoul, too, was a hotbed of impatience. Two days after the July 19 accord was announced, South and North Korea held the seventh meeting of the Joint Nuclear Control Commission, set up to implement the 1991 denuclearization accord. The South demanded that the North scrap the reprocessing plant at Yongbyon. Despite American pleas to ease its stand, the South insisted on challenge inspections. The North rejected them and instead suggested two rounds of I.A.E.A inspections to allay nuclear suspicions.[86] With Pyongyang not about to concede to Seoul what it was unwilling to give the I.A.E.A., North-South talks went nowhere fast.

Under harsh criticism from South Korean hawks, the Kim Administration began toughening its public stance. National security adviser Chung Jong-uk, a rival of Foreign Minister Han Sung Joo's since their days in academic life, began pushing a harder line, forcing Han to sound tougher in public. "Up to now we stuck to a conciliatory policy toward the North to avoid causing irritation," said Han, "but now we are considering a much stronger strategy."[87] President Kim Young Sam, who feared alienating the hard-liners, began publicly expressing fear that North Korea was just dragging out the talks while completing its nuclear program. One high-ranking South Korean official said diplomacy was almost exhausted: "We were showing a little impatience even before the U.S. government became impatient."[88]

The I.A.E.A. was making no more headway than the R.O.K. An August 3–10 inspection led to another standoff. The I.A.E.A. insisted North Korea obey the letter of the law and allow it to do what it wanted. On July 31 the North told the I.A.E.A. access would be limited to routine maintenance, such as replacing the video tapes and batteries. When the inspectors tried to cross that line, the North Koreans roughed them up. Inspectors felt physically intimidated, and one came down with a suspicious case of food poisoning. "The overall degree of access granted," the I.A.E.A. complained, "is still insufficient for the agency to discharge its responsibilities." Asked for the U.S. reaction, State Department spokesman Michael McCurry said, "This means progress is not being made."[89]

Privately, the I.A.E.A. was alarmed at discovering in August that in the reprocessing plant "the seal which gives access to the hot cells was broken," as an agency spokesman later put it, and another showed signs of tampering. The discovery was taken to be incontrovertible proof that further reprocessing was taking place.[90] It was not. The seal at the hot cell could have been damaged accidentally in the midst of ongoing construction, according to a government expert. Tampering with the other seal on the door, affixed by inspectors after verifying construction designs in the North's initial declaration to assure that pipes in the reprocessing plant could not siphon off plutonium for bombs, may have been an attempt to "tweak" the I.A.E.A., says a Pentagon official. The third seal remained in place, impeding access. To those with a Manichaean view of the North Koreans, any tampering was evidence that "they were rearranging the plumbing."[91] To Daniel Poneman, N.S.C. senior director for nonproliferation, "American policy was not Manichaean, but we did not have the luxury of assuming an innocent explanation."[92]

Publicly, the I.A.E.A. began pressing for wider access, insisting that inspections for the sole purpose of maintaining its monitoring equipment would not satisfy its concern that no diversion of nuclear material was occurring. The D.P.R.K. was prepared to accept inspections to maintain and replace the film and batteries, measures that could inhibit North Korea from removing and reprocessing more spent fuel. Washington was quietly urging the I.A.E.A. to agree.[93] Yet the agency was reluctant to settle for less than full-scope safeguards. As Director-General Blix would say during a mid-October visit to Seoul, "Safeguards are not anything you have a la carte, where a customer orders hors d'oeuvres and dessert. It is a whole menu."[94]

To expand its access, the I.A.E.A. resorted to brinkmanship. The monitoring cameras at Yongbyon ran out of film in September, leaving the North freer to divert spent fuel to bomb-making. That was partly the inspectors' own doing, says a Defense Department official. The cameras were capable of running at slower speed. "They set the cameras to run as fast as possible so that they could go back in. It was a game of chicken."[95] Once the film in the monitoring cameras was exhausted, the I.A.E.A. could insist on a thorough inspection of the reactor and reprocessing plant in order to assure that no diversion had taken place.

At the I.A.E.A.'s General Conference on September 27 Blix rejected "token safeguards measures" and warned members that the "area of noncompliance" was "widening."[96] They responded by voting 72–2 to urge North Korea to "cooperate immediately," but set no deadline. The D.P.R.K. thereupon suspended consultations with the agency.

On October 28 North Korea notified the agency it was willing to host an inspection for routine maintenance of the monitoring equipment, but it insisted that wider access would still depend on progress in talks with the United States.[97] On November 1 Blix told the U.N. General Assembly, "The area of noncompliance with the comprehensive safeguards has been widening. As a result, a number of verification measures of D.P.R.K.'s declared nuclear activities have become overdue and continuity of some safeguard-relevant data has been damaged."[98] He stopped short of saying that continuity had been *broken*, which would have required him to seek sanctions, derailing the U.S.-D.P.R.K. talks.

The General Assembly, by a vote of 140–1, called on the D.P.R.K. to cooperate with the I.A.E.A. Only the D.P.R.K. voted no, but there were nine abstentions. One abstainer was critical: China. The I.A.E.A.'s bluff was called. Without a credible threat of sanctions, it would have to accept less than its full program of inspections soon, or remain in the dark about what was going on at Yongbyon.

That same day Defense Secretary Les Aspin, en route to the annual Security Consultative Meeting in Seoul, stopped off in Tokyo to muster Japanese support for sanctions. His prime target was the flow of remittances from Koreans in Japan to their kin in North Korea, estimated to total $600 million a year, part of it the earnings of pachinko parlors. Some of that cash ended up in party coffers, notably those of the Socialists in Japan's ruling coalition. Fearful for the welfare of their families in North Korea, Koreans in Japan would not willingly comply with a ban on remittances and could circumvent it during visits to North Korea or China. The Japanese showed some inclination to curb high technology exports to North Korea but turned down Aspin on the remittances. As he acknowledged in a background briefing, "Both Japan and South Korea are concerned about allowing this to go on in a chronic, gnawing way, but no one really wants to move to sanctions yet."[99]

The likelihood that sanctions would prove politically provocative and economically ineffective was one major premise for deal-making. The risk of war was another. The armed services' reluctance to run that risk was also disclosed on Aspin's trip.

A meeting of U.S. and South Korean intelligence officials preceded the annual Security Consultative Meeting with South Korea. It was an occasion for the intelligence community to brief its assessment of the military balance in Korea. That threat briefing was used to highlight shortcomings that the Pentagon wanted South Korea to remedy, for instance, by buying Patriot antimissile batteries and counterbattery radars. It also documented that 70 percent of North Korea's forces had crept forward by now. The gradual forward deployment, which has been going on for over a decade, affected timely warning of an attack. The United States needed advanced warning to have time to transport reinforcements to Korea. An exhaustive set of warning indicators had been developed. "The problem with the warning process is that some of the indicators would stay present, sometimes for a month or more," says General James R. Clapper, Jr., Director of the Defense Intelligence Agency at the time. "You would then be inoculated and over a period of time become numb."[100] That still begs the larger question of whether North Korea could win a war by attacking with little or no warning. The assessment was that it could not.[101] Public disclosure of the threat briefing without providing the historical context could easily set off a war scare. Clapper says, "It's a function of having a freeze frame of a movie without having seen the last reel."

The prospect of sanctions made the military assessment more than a theoretical matter. While North Korea had never actually threatened to start a war if sanctions were imposed, the Pentagon had to be prepared for that possibility. Yet an overly dire assessment of war's likelihood risked becoming a self-fulfilling prophecy. The risk was increased by the precautions that the Pentagon would feel bound to take in the event of sanctions—the dispatch of substantial reinforcements that could easily be mistaken by North Korea as a prelude to war, triggering preemption. "The North Koreans are very sensitive about what threatens them. The paranoia has gotten worse as they've lost the Russians and the Chinese," says General Clapper. "Anything that we do, however defensive it looks, is offensive to them. That's why they don't even like to see logistical exercises."[102]

In the summer of 1993, the administration began planning a graduated campaign of coercive diplomacy, using sanctions and military deployments to pressure Pyongyang. The campaign of coercive diplomacy put the U.S. commander in Korea, General Gary Luck, in a predicament. "You've got to make your military moves so they don't drive our diplomatic actions," says a high-ranking officer. That required "playing our cards just right so that in the process of getting proliferation under control we didn't cause a ground war to be fought on the peninsula, a ground war which we thought we would win, but winning would come at great cost." Luck was asked, "What do you want to do in terms of reinforcements?" and he replied, "Time out. What are our diplomatic decisions going to be and then I can tell you what military moves to make. If you want to do a blockade or if you want to do sanctions, which they were calling an act of war, then prior to that, we need to take military and civilian actions to prepare ourselves."[103] Luck raised what some Pentagon civilians took to be a warning flag. "His position generally was," says a Defense Department official, "why are you stirring up all this trouble, boys, over some plutonium. You're threatening to start a war, and that's going to be a whole lot worse than any other alternative, so keep your priorities straight."[104] Washington was slow to heed his advice.

Just as sanctions encountered resistance in the Pentagon, so did air strikes and covert operations against North Korea's nuclear facilities. Air strikes had support among intrepid enthusiasts of air power, but the skeptics included members of the Joint Staff and senior civilians in the Defense Department. Among the armed services, on the Joint Staff, in the theater, and in the nuclear labs, recalls Assistant Secretary of Defense Ashton Carter, "The technical military facts were not very much in dispute. Different people had different representations of [what constituted] doing the job. Some people were more comfortable with a little more risk in the actual conduct of the operation."[105] Some Air Force officers contended that they had a high probability of destroying all the known nuclear sites without causing massive collateral damage or starting fires, spewing radioactivity across Japan. Others in the Pentagon, aware of air power's poor performance against Iraq's weapons of mass destruction, had their doubts, and speculation by intelligence analysts about clandestine sites in North Korean tunnels fueled them. As Air Force Chief of Staff Merrill McPeak told reporters at a breakfast backgrounder, "If you put them deep enough underground, we can't get down to it." Most important of all, bombers could not target what they could not locate. McPeak mused, "We can't find nuclear weapons now, except by going on a house-to-house search."[106]

Although air strikes were never ruled out, they were not a very attractive option. One reason was that the air options tended to expand in scope from a surgical strike on known nuclear sites to other suspect sites, to chemical and biological weapons facilities, to air defenses that guarded all of them, and to other military targets. The attitude was, says a Pentagon official, "while we're at it, why not get them all."[107] That was understandable because of the widespread belief in the Pentagon that air strikes were likely to trigger all-out war. One civilian privy to some of the plans says the planners "felt there would be a war but they were very optimistic the mission would be a success."[108] That sounds like a surgeon who tells the next of kin that the operation was a success but the patient died.

The military brass joined civilians in wanting the diplomats to solve the problem. This was a sea change from early 1993, when the chairman of the Joint Chiefs of Staff, Colin Powell, had favored the resumption of Team Spirit, lining up with opponents to a deal with North Korea. A key intervening event was the Clinton Administration's "bottom-up" review, which accepted the armed services' demands for a larger force structure than Powell and others thought they would be able to retain after the disappearance of the Soviet threat. With the Republicans poised to outbid the administration, the defense budget was pegged at Cold War levels, roughly $265 billion a year.

The North Korean threat was essential to the armed services' rationale for holding the line on the budget, a demanding and dubious requirement to meet two major regional contingencies, one shortly after the other, in the Persian Gulf and Korea. Once the administration had accepted the budgetary implications of the two-war requirement, however, the armed services had no interest in seeing the North Korean threat materialize.

They took steps to emphasize how costly a war could be. One planning estimate was chilling: 300,000 to 500,000 military casualties in the first ninety days of war.[109] It was the military's way of flashing a red light to the use of force in Korea.

That and other results of the Pentagon's studies were disclosed in a background briefing en route to Seoul by Aspin, identified misleadingly as "a top military officer on the trip." He drew attention to the forward deployment of North Korean forces near the demilitarized zone, putting them within artillery range of Seoul and in position to attack with little warning. "There is a very fine line between coercing North Korea to do what you want them to do, and provoking a tremendous disaster," the unnamed briefer cautioned. There is the prospect of "huge casualties if we make a misstep." Within days General Luck went on the record. "It is easy in Washington to regard this as just a chess game," he told the *New York Times*. "I keep reminding people that this is for real, and it's real scary."[110]

Hyperbolic reporting suggested that the North Korean buildup along the DMZ was recent, arousing public fears that war was imminent and prompting calls to dispatch American reinforcements. The briefing infuriated the White House. Yet within the administration, the Pentagon planners' conclusions strengthened the case for negotiating a way out of the impasse.

An Empty "Package Deal"

Talks with North Korea had resumed, unannounced, in August in New York. Two State Department officials, Kenneth Quinones of the office of Korean affairs and Gary Samore, director of the Office of Asian Proliferation, shuttled between Washington and New York to represent the United States.[111] In September Undersecretary of State Tarnoff upgraded the talks by naming Deputy Assistant Secretary of State Thomas Hubbard lead negotiator. The D.P.R.K. was represented by its United Nations delegates, Kim Jong Su and Ho Jong.

The two sides began working out conditions for resuming high-level talks. The North Koreans agreed to host inspectors for the purpose of assuring continuity of safeguards. In September the North told Hubbard to invite the South to Panmunjom the next week for working-level contacts leading to an exchange of special envoys. The United States, in turn, expressed willingness to consult South Korea about canceling Team Spirit.

What to do when high-level talks resumed was also being rethought. In September, when negotiator Gallucci visited Seoul, Foreign Minister Han Sung Joo suggested he abandon the "step-by-step approach," which required North Korea to satisfy American preconditions before the United

States would consider reciprocating. Han urged Gallucci to lay out a comprehensive package of quid pro quos, instead. Word of this suggestion reached the South Korean press, and through it, Pyongyang.[112]

In mid-October North Korea hosted Representative Gary Ackerman, who had succeeded Stephen Solarz as chairman of the House Subcommittee on Asian and Pacific Affairs. Kenneth Quinones of the State Department Korea desk accompanied Ackerman. The North allowed them to cross into North Korea through the DMZ, a shortcut denied American visitors for decades. In the course of the visit, Quinones was taken aside and told that the North Koreans had seen reports in the South Korean press about the comprehensive approach and were now ready to propose a package deal to him. Quinones objected to receiving an oral proposal, recalls a State Department official. He wanted it in writing. "No one would believe me," he told the North Koreans. He asked them to give him a "non-paper," a way to exchange ideas without the commitment implied in a formal negotiating proposal. His hosts were unfamiliar with this diplomatic nicety. "They howled. They thought that was hilarious."[113] Quinones's caution in having the North Koreans put the package deal on paper was not misplaced; he would later be wrongly accused of having inspired the North Korean initiative. In a bizarre postscript a year later, he was subjected to an F.B.I. investigation for his various encounters with North Korean diplomats in the United States.

The next morning Quinones was handed a detailed version of a package deal. It contained all the elements of what would become, eleven months hence, the Agreed Framework of October 21, 1994.

Instead of satisfying American preconditions as part of the step-by-step approach, the North was now proposing to lay out a road map, a sequencing of moves to be implemented reciprocally and simultaneously. Given the intense mutual distrust between the two sides, reciprocity was essential to build mutual confidence. Simultaneity would sidestep the irreconcilable dispute over who had to go first. "Hour after hour," says an American involved in the talks. "I would be required to read, 'when you have done A, we will do B.'" His North Korean counterpart would respond, "My instructions say if you mention preconditions, I am out of here."[114] By phasing in the moves, each side would retain some leverage in the form of unfulfilled promises to keep the other from reneging. Such an approach had an advantage for the Clinton Administration, which was having trouble making promises and keeping them. Without promises Washington lacked negotiating leverage, because its threats had not proven compelling. Now it would not have to give anything away without getting something in return. It could also retract its inducements if North Korea did not comply. To Washington, which had been reluctant to put its chips on the table, Pyongyang was saying: ante up now.

To ensure that its message did not get lost in the drumbeat of war in Washington and Seoul, Pyongyang also transmitted it through informal channels. Kim Yong Sun, who had been Kantor's interlocutor in the high-level talk of January 1992, discussed a version of the package with Peter Hayes of Nautilus Pacific Research on October 19. A report of the meeting was cabled to Washington, according to a State Department official who recalls reading it.[115] The report emphasized that if "the LWR issue were resolved successfully, then the D.P.R.K. would remain in the N.P.T." The North, Hayes noted, "does not care where the LWR technology comes from, whether it is American, Russian, South Korean. It fully understands that for the United States to provide technology, the export would entail clearing away political and legal barriers, which is the major reason why the LWR issue is so important." Washington was unmoved. "Once again, it made the point that LWRs are central, but once again, it did not send us off to design the architecture for an LWR project."[116] Selig Harrison of the Carnegie Endowment for International Peace and Kim Dae Jung, an opposition party leader and candidate for president of South Korea, also seem to have gotten wind of it.[117]

Then on November 11, in an official statement made public by the Foreign Ministry, Kang Sok Ju, head of the D.P.R.K. delegation to the high-level talks, insisted on "a clear distinction" between inspections to assure "continuity of safeguards," which it had already accepted and "might be expanded," and "full compliance with the safeguards agreement," which required "a package solution" in talks with the United States. He also drew attention to its curb on reprocessing: "We totally froze movement of nuclear material within the D.P.R.K."[118]

With the risks of coercion and the chances of cooperation increasingly obvious, the Clinton Administration began edging toward negotiating in earnest. In early October Defense Secretary Aspin convened a meeting to consider priorities—"a bull session" around "a big plate of donuts," according to one participant.[119] A catalyst for the discussion was a draft intelligence assessment then in preparation saying that North Korea could have a bomb or two, that construction of two new reactors was continuing with one near completion, and that a second production line was under construction at the reprocessing plant, doubling its capacity. While not necessarily accepting the assessment's conclusions, the Pentagon working group was gravitating to a policy first suggested in March and proposed to Defense Secretary Aspin in May: give priority to stopping further bomb-making by North Korea before trying to determine how many bombs, if any, it may have produced in the past. "There had been tension the whole year over how seriously to take all of the noise, all of these minor infractions which unfortunately we or the I.A.E.A. or the R.O.K. had said were important events," says a participant. "We were losing sight of our strategic purpose of no more weapons."[120] The group began to spell out what had to be done to dismantle the existing North Korean nuclear program and what access inspectors would need to satisfy its objectives, especially after the monitoring cameras had run out of film. The dominant view was that while special inspections should be deferred, ad hoc and routine inspections were required. The Pentagon also began to devalue the second priority. "The primacy of the dismantlement objective," says Assistant Secretary of Defense Ashton Carter, "seemed so obvious on the merits that it started us thinking about how valuable the special inspections were anyway."[121] U.S. experts concluded that special inspections were not the best way to get at North Korea's nuclear past.

At a mid-October Deputies' Committee meeting, negotiator Gallucci took the lead in moving in the same direction. Raising doubts whether the step-by-step approach was getting anywhere, he recommended adoption of the comprehensive approach. "Gallucci said this wouldn't work. The North Koreans have figured out that they have to do everything up front and we do nothing," recalls a participant.[122] Gallucci advocated canceling Team Spirit on the condition that North Korea allow the I.A.E.A. to complete the August inspection. Opposition came from the Joint Staff, which wanted to hold the North to the terms of the June 1993 agreed statement, requiring ad hoc, routine, and special inspections. Civilians in the Office of the Secretary of Defense were willing to cancel the exercise only if the D.P.R.K. accepted ad hoc and routine inspections for the duration of the negotiations.[123] "We were giving Bob a tough objective," recalls Ashton Carter, "but were not going to tell him how to go about achieving it."[124]

Gallucci also talked about reordering American objectives along the lines of recent thinking in the Pentagon. "I was aware, as was A.C.D.A., that we couldn't defend a deal that failed to deal with the past and Blix would never stand for it," he says. "But it was nuts to nail down the eight or two or no kilograms from the past and then have the North accumulate hundreds of kilograms in the future. That was technical arms control gone crazy."[125] Gallucci favored inspections for the purpose of continuity of safeguards, nothing more, but he was loath to negotiate with North Korea on behalf of the I.A.E.A. He said that "we shouldn't play matchmaker," recalls a Pentagon official.[126] The I.A.E.A., however, was demanding not only ad hoc and routine inspections, but also special inspections, which North Korea had repeatedly insisted was a matter for negotiation in high-level talks with the United States.

Seldom in the Clinton Administration was anything decided once and for all, and this meeting was no exception. "It was such a dysfunctional N.S.C. system at that time," says Assistant Secretary of Defense Ashton Carter, "that nothing could get done. There was almost an aversion to clarity because it binds one's hands. It used to drive me nuts. Everything was still up for grabs."[127] The Deputies' Committee did at least tacitly switch priorities. Special inspections of the waste sites, or whatever was needed to clear up the past, would be deferred to an eventual package deal. In return for suspension of Team Spirit in 1994, the North would be asked to resume talks with the South and to allow the August inspection to be completed and to assure access, acceptable to the I.A.E.A., for the purpose of preventing any future diversion of spent fuel to bomb-making.

The Clinton Administration was finally getting around to doing first things first, but it was not yet ready to say so in public. President Clinton himself set the tone. "North Korea cannot be allowed to develop a nuclear bomb," he told *Meet the Press* interviewers on November 7. "We have to be very firm about it."[128] The operative words should have been "nuclear program," not "nuclear bomb." Some officials dismiss the president's comment as a slip of the tongue. "This loose locution," says one, "should not be expected to bear the parsing it received."[129] Other officials say that the administration, in a month when the bodies of eighteen dead American servicemen were dragged through the streets of Somalia and a gang of toughs turned away the U.S.S. *Harlan County* from a dock in Haiti, could not resist the temptation to talk tough and offer little.

The hawks were in full cry. "The administration's response to North Korea's nuclear drive," wrote *Washington Post* columnist Charles Krauthammer on November 5, "has been all carrot and no stick. As an inducement to be nice, we have already given the North Koreans their first direct high-level talks with the United States. We have dangled diplomatic recognition. We are now dangling an offer to cancel joint U.S. military exercises with South Korea. These are gestures of weakness." Krauthammer was wrong on all counts but that did not slow him down: "Enough talk. The time has come for action."[130] He called for President Clinton to "get serious" and step up the pressure on North Korea by sending military reinforcements to the South and getting ready to impose tough economic sanctions against the North, even attacking its nuclear sites. Others were even more impetuous: "It's just a matter of time" before North Korea gets nuclear arms, warned Frank Gaffney, Jr., a Pentagon official in the Reagan Administration. He urged "military steps to neutralize those facilities that we know about." Even if a strike could not hit every site, it would still "disrupt" the nuclear program. "It is a question of risking going to war now, when U.S. military capabilities are still relatively strong and North Korean nuclear forces are minimal, if extant, rather than later when such advantageous conditions will almost surely not exist."[131] The *Economist* picked up the drum-beat. "At some point talking has got to stop," it declared in an editorial. "Faced with a chilling choice of risks—between a preemptive strike to cripple North Korea's nuclear program and waiting until its tough talk is backed up by nuclear threats—America would in the end be right to strike first."[132]

The chorus of war whoops was occasionally punctuated by counsels of patience. A November 3 editorial in the *Financial Times* argued that "tightening the international noose on what is already a pariah state would be at least as likely to result in greater instability as bring Pyongyang's paranoid leaders to their senses" and urged Washington "to negotiate with Pyongyang, rather than piling on more direct forms of pressure."[133] Dave McCurdy (D-OK), a member of the House Armed Services Committee, warned against sanctions and recommended "face-saving incentives" for inspections, specifically, an end to Team Spirit.[134]

In this overheated atmosphere the Principals' Committee of the National Security Council convened on November 15. Three options were on the table. One was the State Department's, a blend of the step-by-step and the comprehensive approaches. It was comprehensive in proposing that the United States offer political and economic inducements for North Korean compliance with its non-nuclear obligations, but it was two-phased: "Because Gallucci had told Congress [in March] he was going to do nuclear first, when State said it wanted to do everything, it meant in phases, first the nuclear and then the economic and political."[135]

The other two options were framed by civilians in the Office of the Secretary of Defense. One was to approach Kim Il Sung directly and say "everything we want to do for you and everything we want you to do for us," says one of its authors. "It was a waste to do this in diplomatic channels." The option was short of specifics on what the United States would do for North Korea: "We would suggest different possible structurings because there were lots of things that had potential support in the U.S. government and we didn't want to put one on the table, have them reject it and have things fall apart." The other problem was that as soon as the list of inducements expanded, so did the list of demands: "As soon as O.S.D. brought in non-nuclear chips on our side, there were people lined up to bring in non-nuclear chips on their side." The offer also had the flavor of an ultimatum: it was first set out in a memo under the heading, "Carry a Big Stick."[136]

The third option was a fallback position in the event that the second option was rejected, according to a Pentagon official, a last-ditch effort to delay sanctions and continue talks: "Let's not back ourselves completely into a corner. If we cannot achieve all of our goals in a comprehensive agreement, then we should be able to fall back to a freeze while we keep negotiating."[137]

The third option was opposed by everyone except its Pentagon proponents. The second option backtracked from Gallucci's March commitment to Congress. It also wrested the negotiations out of the hands of the State Department and turned them over to an outsider, undercutting Gallucci. "It was opposed by State," says the Defense Department official, "and Tony Lake killed it as a sign of weakness." The bureaucracy was told to lay out two options, a step-by-step approach and a package deal.

There was no agreement on the contents of the package. Secretary of State Christopher was worried about looking soft on North Korea. National Security Adviser Lake was skeptical, says a top official, about "putting carrots out there where they could be eaten without getting anything in return." The South Koreans' reaction to any American offer to the North was another reason for Lake's skepticism: "The more you rubbed their noses in it publicly, the worse off you were." Domestic politics was a less important consideration for Lake, says the official: "For sure you would get beaten up here." Gallucci had persuaded Lake of one thing, says the official, that stopping the North's nuclear program was the first priority: that "you cannot sacrifice the future on the alter of the past." But, he adds, "Bob wanted to show the North Koreans there was something in it for them. Not everyone in our government was thrilled with the conceptual approach."[138] Lake was still looking for consensus. It was difficult to find. Aware of South Korean sentiments, the Joint Chiefs of Staff did not want to call off Team Spirit, even though money for the exercises had already been cut from the Pentagon budget for the coming fiscal year. In the end the Chiefs relented—but on condition that Seoul announce the suspension. Diplomatic normalization remained to be resolved. "Working out the details," said one official, "will take a long time."[139]

In effect, the State Department option won: to accept a package deal in principle but to continue the step-by-step approach in practice, setting preconditions for a third round of high-level talks. The North Koreans, says a State Department official, had had "the expectation that by offering the comprehensive package, they could move up the date of the next round of high-level talks. We essentially said, wait a minute, if there's no credibility in your August agreement, why should we go forward and expect anything else from you?"[140] Once again, the United States was treating high-level talks as a reward for good behavior rather than a means to probe North Korean nuclear intentions and perhaps resolve the dispute. "We thought that it was a wonderful benefit to allow them to talk to us," says Deputy Assistant Secretary of State Thomas Hubbard. "The South kept saying the primary North Korean objective was to drive a wedge between us and the worst thing you can do is to meet with them at a higher level. We internalized that."[141]

In promulgating policy, Secretary of State Christopher obscured the shift toward diplomatic give-and-take by framing it in crime-and-punishment terms. "The United States is committed to a diplomatic solution," he said in a speech in Seattle. "If North Korea refuses the necessary inspections—and refuses to resume a dialogue with South Korea on nuclear issues—then we are prepared to recommend that the U.N. Security Council consider options other than negotiation."[142] Sticks were still easier to talk about in public than carrots.

Shared images of nuclear diplomacy still impeded deal-making with North Korea. Most vocal members of the foreign policy establishment remained committed to the crime-and-punishment approach in the belief that a communist rogue state like North Korea was not about to give up bomb-making. Diplomats who had direct dealings with North Korea became disabused of that belief. They began to sense the possibility of a deal. So did some senior officials. Yet, if they were no longer believers in the shared images themselves, they did not dare challenge the beliefs of others directly.

Instead, as the crime-and-punishment approach stirred fears of war, the proponents of diplomacy tried to capitalize on the profound pessimism. They cast the last-ditch offer as a political prerequisite for military action. "The only way we could keep this process alive inside with people who were nervous politically," says a Pentagon official, "was to argue that unless you went through the motions of diplomacy, you were going to get blamed for the war that ensued. You had to show that you had done everything you could. You had to convince the American public and the world that you had gone the last mile for peace—and what better way to do that than to go right to Kim Il Sung and lay it all out on the table."[143] Their first try failed, but once fear of impending war began to intensify, they would try again.

Seoul Gets the Shakes

The United States was ready to make another move in the step-by-step approach, one that would restrain further bomb-making in North Korea while deferring inspections to get at its nuclear past. Yet, having promoted the idea of comprehensive deal-making, South Korea began to have second thoughts. Hawkish pressures in Seoul put Foreign Minister Han on the defensive and led President Kim Young Sam to do an abrupt about-face.

On November 16, the day after the Principals' Committee meeting, U.S. negotiator Thomas Hubbard met with D.P.R.K. representatives in New York and formally accepted the idea of a package deal without specifying the contents. The commitment came in a reply by Gallucci to a letter from Deputy Foreign Minister Kang Sok Ju to address North Korea's concerns "*as* the nuclear issue was resolved," not after.[144]

That same day Arnold Kanter, undersecretary of state in the Bush Administration, told a Washington symposium on North Korea that the Clinton Administration, "in a reversal of longstanding U.S. policy," has "created at least the appearance that this North Korean stonewalling, far from imposing a cost or penalty, is being rewarded by continued American eagerness to negotiate further." Yet, Kanter acknowledged, "the Clinton Administration's approach presumably is based on the conviction that the 'hard line' taken by its predecessor was going nowhere." While the "payment of 'bribes' creates bad precedents" and could lead "would-be proliferators to conclude that an indigenous nuclear weapons program is the key that unlocks a treasure trove of economic and political benefits," he nevertheless concluded, "the North Koreans may insist on knowing—in relatively concrete terms—what's in it for them if they abandon their nuclear program."[145] That was the one thing neither the Bush nor the Clinton Administration had been willing to tell them. Another former official in the Bush Administration, Robert Manning, also presented a paper at the symposium calling for a package solution and went beyond Kanter to put contents into the package. So did Selig Harrison and Peter Hayes. It was the most powerful show of support for deal-making yet mustered. The little press attention it received dwelled almost exclusively on the need for sanctions.[146]

The hawks continued to dominate the public discourse. To *Post* columnist Charles Krauthammer, "Talk loudly and carry a big carrot" was the President's policy. "Letting other countries tell the United States what it cannot do is becoming a habit with Clinton." Dismissing regular inspections of declared nuclear sites as "a joke," he contended the choice by year's end will be "blockade or surrender."[147] No deal was good enough for proliferation expert Gary Milhollin of the Wisconsin Project, either: "If the worst thing that happens when you break the rules is that you get to negotiate, it's not much of a system." The only way to make North Korea behave was the crime-and-punishment approach: "[T]aking the North Koreans to the Security Council offers the best hope of a good solution, and it's the step that Mr. Clinton doesn't seem to want to take."[148]

The hawks' unstated premise was that stopping proliferation by Pyongyang required toppling North Korea's communist rulers. In the words of James Lilley, who had served as C.I.A. station chief and later as ambassador in Seoul and assistant secretary of defense, "Through these negotiations and carrots, you're helping the North Korean regime to survive. Over the next five years, it will develop its nuclear weapons potential and also be able to keep selling missiles to countries like Iran and Syria."[149]

Now it was South Korea's turn to narrow the diplomatic opening. Dependence on the United States in dealing with the North was kindling resentment in Seoul, even though domestic politics was keeping the South from dealing with the North on its own. Now the hawks began hurling accusations of appeasement at Foreign Minister Han for his advocacy of a comprehensive approach. According to Charles Kartman, deputy chief of mission in the U.S. embassy in Korea, the United States was unaware how politically isolated Han was becoming in Seoul.[150] Han's archrival, national security adviser Chung Jong-uk, was actively pushing a harder line. After negotiator Gallucci briefed Congress that suspension of Team Spirit was under consideration, a U.S. official disclosed that consultations with Seoul were underway on "whether to put more carrots on the table." Within the South Korean government, he contended, "The dominant view now is to encourage us to think of a creative solution."[151] That was a decidedly upbeat assessment.

The two obvious carrots were a beginning to diplomatic relations and an end to Team Spirit. South Korea began expressing strong reservations about both. On October 23 reporters in Seoul were told that South Korea was attaching two conditions to any suspension of Team Spirit, that the North accept an exchange of presidential envoys with the South and that it allow ad hoc and routine inspections. A week later Foreign Minister Han did not rule out improved ties between Washington and Pyongyang, but he insisted a third round of high-level talks, if held, should be limited to nuclear matters, adding, "Further talks between the United States and North Korea will be possible only when the nuclear problem is resolved."[152] That would rule out an offer of steps toward normalization as part of a package deal. On November 13 the Foreign Minister was utterly unaccommodating, "It is not yet the stage to consider the package deal insisted [on] by North Korea."[153] President Kim Young Sam also took advantage of a November 6 meeting with Japanese Prime Minister Morihiro Hosokowa to secure his pledge that "Japan will not normalize relations with Pyongyang unless the nuclear issues are resolved."[154]

Instead of carrots, South Korea's president began reaching for a stick: "I think perhaps it is about time we should consider the possibility of setting a deadline."[155] Opposition party members in the National Assembly again urged resumption of nuclear-arming.[156] Not to be outgunned, Defense Minister Kwon Young-hae refused to rule out a military attack on North Korea's nuclear installations. The North promptly canceled talks with the South.[157]

President Kim Young Sam was scheduled to meet President Clinton in Washington November 23, 1993. Despite the rumblings in Seoul, Foreign Minister Han managed to approve communique language opening the way to a comprehensive deal with North Korea. Yet President Kim was shaken by accusations that Washington had taken the lead in dealing with Pyongyang, leaving Seoul on the sidelines. He decided to show who was in charge and to do it in the most demonstrative way possible—in public at the White House with President Clinton at his side. "They needed to show that they were in the front of the train, not in back," says Gallucci. "That was okay with us as long as they headed the train in the right direction."[158] Yet, under pressure from hard-liners at home and encouraged by South Korea's ambassador to the United Nations, Yoo Chong-ha, during a stopover in New York, President Kim jammed on the brakes and tried to throw the train into reverse.

In a meeting with President Clinton, with Foreign Minister Han not in attendance, Kim abruptly objected to the phrase "comprehensive approach" and the offer to suspend Team Spirit. "Not only did jaws drop on the American side. Jaws also dropped on the Korean side," recalls a top official who was present. National Security Adviser Lake had been spending more time talking with his South Korean counterpart than he had with anyone else except the British, French, and Germans, adds the official, and thought "we had everything wired."[159] Kim also expressed dissatisfaction with the North's willingness to resume working-level talks in Panmunjom. Not about to meet the North halfway, he insisted on a meeting of presidential envoys in Seoul. He wanted the suspension of Team Spirit and the resumption of high-level talks conditioned on the exchange of envoys and "serious" North-South talks. "The critical thing was conditionality," says Deputy Assistant Secretary of State Thomas Hubbard, who negotiated the run-up to the summit. "Our conditionality was to agree to the modalities for the exchange of envoys, not to do it."[160]

At a White House press conference afterward with President Clinton, Kim went out of his way to sharpen the differences: "What we have agreed today—and I would very much want you to pay attention to the phrases we have used—is that we will make a thorough and broad effort to bring the issue to a final conclusion." That was "a matter of Korean semantics," says Gallucci. True, Pyongyang had been using the words "comprehensive approach," but the idea was originally Seoul's. Kim Young Sam's larger implication was the less comprehensive, the better. Addressing "speculation that if North Korea accepts I.A.E.A. inspections and dialogue with South Korea, then there will be concessions given to North Korea in return," he said, "I think this matter of suspending a Team Spirit exercise should be dealt with on its own."[161] Neither president mentioned normalizing relations with the North.

Foreign Minister Han sounded even less diplomatically inclined at his press conference later. "There are no packages. What North Korea is suggesting is to make them into packages, including the routine and ad hoc inspections. As far as we are concerned—that means both the Republic of Korea and the United States—these obligations are not negotiable and they cannot be put into any package. Any notion of packages can be considered only after all these basic obligations, plus progress in North-South Korean talks, have been fulfilled." Han made it clear that there had been no agreement on the contents of a package deal: "We haven't reached the stage where we can talk about such a deal, and much less what should be included in such a deal."[162]

At a White House background briefing minutes later, Daniel Poneman, N.S.C. senior director for nonproliferation, tried to narrow the distance between Washington and Seoul. Asked if the North Koreans could expect any benefits from the new approach, he replied, "We've told them we would be prepared to engage them on a broad range of issues. They would, of course, be at liberty to raise their own concerns, and I would presume that they would in some hope of having them satisfied."[163] He edged away from the U.S. commitment of November 16 to address North Korea's concerns.

Kim Young Sam's about-face was stunning. "We were completely blind-sided," says a Pentagon official. "That really locked us in. That accounts for the thrashing around in the coming months."[164] "President Kim's announcement took everyone by surprise," commented a former Korean diplomat later. "This is a perfect example of how the [Kim] Administration is conducting foreign policy by reacting to local headlines."[165] The same could be said of the Clinton Administration.

That evening, at a state dinner for Kim, National Security Adviser Lake worked out new instructions with his South Korean counterpart, Chung Jong-uk, for the working-level talks with the D.P.R.K. and handed them to negotiator Hubbard. "They represented a step backward," Hubbard recalls.[166] The United States and North Korea had been nearing agreement on announcing a date for the resumption of high-level talks and suspension of Team Spirit exercises once the D.P.R.K. and the I.A.E.A. agreed on inspections and working-level North-South talks resumed. Reneging on its previous position, the United States now said, "When the North Korean envoy visits Seoul for serious talks, he will be informed by the R.O.K. that Team Spirit will be suspended." After North-South talks began, "then there will be public confirmation of the suspension of Team Spirit and the United States will announce a date for the resumption of high-level talks."[167]

Once again Washington was insisting on preconditions for talks, this time at Seoul's behest, and tacitly threatening to resume Team Spirit if Pyongyang did not go along.

Hubbard flew to New York the next morning to meet with the North Koreans. "I did what any negotiator does. I tried to pitch it as a non-change," Hubbard recalls. The North Korean reaction to the American reversal was predictable. "They did not like it at all."[168] The D.P.R.K. representative, Ho Jong, complained that by giving Seoul "the prerogative to determine whether the D.P.R.K. envoy arrives in Seoul for serious talks" before announcing the third round of high-level talks, "This gives Seoul all the power to decide the pace of the U.S.-D.P.R.K. talks."[169] Washington should have been as concerned as Pyongyang was about that. It was an egregious example of alliance mismanagement.

North Korea's Foreign Ministry soon went public. "If the United States thinks pressure can work on the D.P.R.K.," a November 29 statement declared, it does "not yet know its dialogue partner." The statement cautioned South Korean authorities to be "mindful that their obstructions to the progress of D.P.R.K.-U.S. talks would precipitate their own destruction." Yet it ended on a promising note, "If the United States accepts the D.P.R.K.-proposed formula of a package solution, all problems related to the nuclear issue, including compliance with the safeguards agreement, will be solved and it will not take much time."[170] A December 1 statement from the D.P.R.K. Ministry of Atomic Energy was even more explicit. While Pyongyang would open its sites to the I.A.E.A. for continuity of safeguards, ad hoc and routine inspections "will be resolved one by one if further high-level talks will make progress and if further consultations with the agency will be held."[171]

The only reference to the North Korean statement in the American press came in a December 7 editorial in the *New York Times*, which also disclosed the two sides' negotiating positions:

> The present U.S. position is that before high-level talks resume, the North must first allow I.A.E.A. access to its nuclear sites and begin bilateral talks with South Korea. North Korea does not want to move first. Instead, it hopes to negotiate a package deal involving simultaneous concessions. How might such a deal unfold? First, just as I.A.E.A. inspectors are visiting the reactor at Yongbyon, North-South and high-level U.S.–North Korean negotiators would meet. The U.S. and South Korea would inform the North of cancellation of their Team Spirit military exercises. The U.S. could then propose a broader package deal.[172]

Yet the United States was still not ready to give much away in return for North Korean fulfillment of its Nonproliferation Treaty obligations. Before it was, the simmering crisis would boil over.

4

A "BETTER THAN EVEN" CHANCE OF

MISESTIMATION

> I used to imagine when the government took action that I
> found inexplicable, that it had information I didn't have. But
> when I had served in the government for some months I
> found that the issue was more complex: often the government
> does know something the people on the outside don't, but
> it's something that isn't so.
> *(Charles Frankel)*[1]

AN INTELLIGENCE estimate is an artifact that Washington treats like a fact. Its internal dissemination and its public disclosure can be used to dynamite existing policy.

A National Intelligence Estimate in late November 1993 concluded that North Korea already had one or two nuclear weapons and would never agree to give up its bomb program. The estimate was the product of hypervigilant imaginations in the American intelligence community. Its wide dissemination had two unintended consequences. It strengthened North Korea's bargaining position, and it nearly led to war.

In early December, within days of its completion, officials began selectively disclosing the estimate. Outside the government the estimate was explosive. Inside the government, it had a muffled impact. One reason for the official reception is that without much hard data the intelligence community was sharply divided about North Korea's nuclear past. Another is that the assessment did not point to a compelling policy conclusion. "I always found the differences more interesting than the conclusions the analysts reached," says a top administration official. "When analysts say you can't do it, as a policy-maker you ask, what does this mean in the real world? Do you throw up your hands and bomb or say the situation doesn't matter, or do you test the proposition with your hand on your wallet?"[2]

The sharp differences between the outsiders' and insiders' perspectives would bedevil nuclear diplomacy with North Korea in the months to come. To outsiders in Congress, in the foreign policy establishment, and especially in Seoul, the November estimate focused attention on the need for special inspections to ascertain how many nuclear weapons

North Korea already possessed, while casting doubt on North Korea's willingness ever to accept those inspections. The estimate also deepened belief among outsiders that North Korea was determined to make bombs and, in the words of a Pentagon official, "using the negotiations to pull the wool over our eyes."[3] That intensified pressures in Washington and in Seoul not to deal with Pyongyang, but to punish it for past misdeeds. "The estimate had nothing to do with policy," says a senior administration official, "except that we had to protect our policy from the flak the estimate generated."[4]

Inside the government the estimate underscored uncertainty about the past and drew some officials' attention to what was known with greater certainty, that North Korea at any moment could discharge spent fuel from the nuclear reactor at Yongbyon, containing five or six bombs' worth of plutonium, and that it was constructing two new reactors and a reprocessing plant with the capacity to separate up to thirty bombs' worth of plutonium a year. It also highlighted the risks of coercing a possibly nuclear-armed antagonist, a less certain source of North Korean negotiating leverage.

The process of producing estimates is not an analytical one in which alternative hypotheses are put forward and evidence for and against them is carefully weighed. It is a political one in which representatives of the various intelligence agencies defend their agency's point of view and negotiate the wording until they reach agreement. If they cannot, the disagreements are laid out in the text, or else agencies record their dissents in footnotes.

The November estimate began leaking to the press almost immediately. A December 3 story in the *Washington Post* dwelled on the assessment of North Korean willingness to allow inspections. The C.I.A.'s conclusion, said to be "the majority view" in the intelligence community, was that Pyongyang would open its reactor and its reprocessing plant to inspectors but would bar special inspections of its nuclear waste sites. The Defense Intelligence Agency had the most pessimistic assessment, that the North would not allow any inspections, ad hoc, routine, or special.[5] "Based on North Korea's actions to date," it read, "D.I.A. assesses that Pyongyang will continue its nuclear weapons program despite any agreement it signs to the contrary."[6] The dominant view was hedged with caveats like "based on North Korea's actions to date," which diffused the force of its conclusions.

The State Department's Bureau of Intelligence and Research (INR) dissented, saying there was no basis for concluding whether the North Koreans would relent on special inspections or not. "By November 1993," says an INR analyst, "they were moving more clearly in the direction of a compromise, but so slowly and carefully that no policy-maker could stake his position, much less his reputation, on it. More-over, it was an emotionally charged issue, one that either side could eas-ily fumble."[7] INR, says a Pentagon official who agreed with its conclu-sion, argued that "the North Koreans, by their behavior, were giving every indication that they wanted to deal." Two such indications were particularly persuasive to him: they had not reprocessed any plutonium since 1991 and they had postponed discharging spent nuclear fuel from the reactor in May 1993, when the I.A.E.A. had expected the refueling to occur. "If they weren't willing to deal, they wouldn't have restrained their technical program."[8] To build bombs North Korea had to remove the spent fuel from the reactor and extract the plutonium by reprocess-ing. Satellite imagery continued to show that the reactor remained in operation, making the discharge of spent fuel impossible without on-line refueling capabilities. I.A.E.A. inspectors had found no on-line re-fueling capabilities at Yongbyon. Inspections also showed that no re-processing had taken place at Yongbyon since 1991.

Those who disclosed the estimate believed it called diplomacy into question. Yet inspections of the reactor and reprocessing plant, while perhaps inadequate for ascertaining whether North Korea had produced one or two bombs' worth of plutonium in the past, could keep it from generating more in the future. The dominant view invited a rejoinder. As an editorial in the *New York Times* put it, perhaps the North is just stalling and would never allow inspections, but "the only way to find out is to probe diplomatically—by offering an enticing deal."[9]

The *Post* story misstated and downplayed the more explosive conclu-sion of the National Intelligence Estimate, "The document assigns what several officials said was a low probability . . . that North Korea already may have assembled one or two crude nuclear weapons or will complete one soon." Such a conclusion undercut President Clinton's commit-ment to deny North Korea a bomb. It seeped out gradually. Director of Central Intelligence James Woolsey told CNN's *Larry King Live* on No-vember 30, " 'Could have' is, I think, the right way to state it."[10] On the *McNeil-Lehrer NewsHour* December 7, Defense Secretary Les Aspin spoke of "maybe a bomb and a half at the outside, perhaps." Then he got to the point: "It is speculation because without inspections we're not going to know how many of those rods were reprocessed."[11] The estimate's exact wording was finally revealed the day after Christmas, this time in the *New York Times*. There was a "better than even" chance, it said, that North Korea already had one or two nuclear devices. It also estimated that 12 to 13 kilograms of plutonium had been extracted from the spent fuel of the Yongbyon reactor. Again, INR dissented. Again, the basis of the assessment left substantial room for doubt. Some in the State and Defense Departments called it a "worst-case" assessment. "In the face of a very high level of ignorance, nobody wants to repeat the experience of Iraq," an administration official told the *Times*.[12]

The 1993 estimate of one or two devices was an extrapolation of how many bombs' worth of plutonium could have been extracted from spent fuel in the Yongbyon reactor. The estimate was based on guesswork about the reactor's history—how long and at what power it had been operating. In its 1992 declaration to the I.A.E.A. the North had claimed it separated about 100 grams of plutonium in the spring of 1990. I.A.E.A. analysis indicated it had reprocessed spent fuel on at least three occasions—in 1989, 1990, and 1991—but could not determine how much.

Evidence of North Korea's interest in making a bomb did exist. Craters detected near Yongbyon were caused by testing conventional munitions used to trigger a nuclear device. How long it would take the North to fabricate a nuclear device was sheer guesswork, however, and not based on any firm facts. The conclusion that it had already done so was driven by the 1991 estimate that it could take North Korea "six to eighteen months" to turn extracted plutonium into a bomb.[13] Time had expired on that earlier estimate. As former director of Central Intelligence Gates put it in June 1994, "We are now well beyond the time frame of our estimate and it is highly probable that the North Koreans already have one or two nuclear devices."[14]

A February 1994 study by well-informed ex-officials for the U.S. Institute of Peace reached a different conclusion, "The C.I.A. estimate that the North has accumulated enough plutonium to make one or two bombs may be correct, but this is a worst-case extrapolation that is not based on direct evidence. There is no hard evidence—only the presumption—that the North has successfully weaponized the plutonium it has accumulated."[15] Leonard Spector, a nonproliferation specialist at the Carnegie Endowment reached a similar conclusion: "If you assume the worst about each bit of information—and that's not unreasonable—then you could conclude they have made a bomb or two." But he cautioned, "All of the assumptions in the worst-case scenario have to be true for North Korea to have a bomb."[16]

The dominant view was "very speculative," in the judgment of another INR analyst. It was "a melding of the essentialist and the technological view"—shared images of political analysts that North Korea, a Stalinist rogue state, by its very nature had to be surreptitiously bomb-making, and calculations of the reactor's potential by technical experts.[17] Again, INR was in the minority. D.I.A. had a decidedly different view. Yet Director James Clapper also had his doubts. "Personally, as opposed to institutionally, I was skeptical that they ever had a bomb," says General Clapper. "We didn't have smoking-gun evidence either way." Still, he defends the D.I.A.'s dark view of North Korea. "This is a classic debate in intelligence. Are you going to provide an assessment if you don't have the empirical evidence, or by inference, suggestion, circumstantial evidence do you build a case for a range of possibilities? In my opinion the intelligence community is irresponsible if it doesn't do the latter. In a case like North Korea you have to apply the most conservative approach, the worst-case alternative."[18]

Again, the estimate did not point to a particular policy. A December 28 *Times* editorial argued against attacking the North's bomb-making sites or imposing an economic blockade: "If the new intelligence assessment is correct, and North Korea actually has a bomb or two, Pyongyang's response could be disastrous." The only way to find out whether the worst-case assessment was warranted, the editorial added, was for inspectors to gain access to the reactor, reprocessing plant, and waste sites. "A further and compelling reason to resume regular inspections" was that the North "will soon be forced to shut down the reactor at Yongbyon and replace its nuclear fuel rods," which would allow the plutonium in them to be extracted for bomb-making. Securing those inspections would take "the right package of incentives" and "only a determined president can put that package together."[19]

The hawks were buying none of that. To them the assessment proved that the president had already failed to achieve his stated aim of not allowing "North Korea to develop a nuclear bomb" and was sure to fail in the just restated aim of getting inspections that would inhibit further North Korean bomb-making.

The conclusion of a "better than even" chance of one to two bombs could not withstand serious scrutiny. The odds had the same effect as they do for oddsmakers: they shifted the betting to a less likely outcome. They were derived in a way that even Jimmy the Greek, never mind a statistician, would have had trouble accepting—by polling the analysts. "They asked the question two ways," says a Defense Department official. "They asked, 'How many of you think they have a bomb?' More than half raised their hands. They asked the question, 'What is the probability that they have a bomb?' They averaged the answers. They got more than fifty-fifty."[20] The odds, like a weather forecaster's, revealed more about the confidence of those making the assessment than about the statistical likelihood of its being correct.

The estimate on plutonium eventually imploded as well. When experts at Livermore and Hanford redid the analysis for the Defense Department, the estimate was reduced to seven or eight kilograms from twelve or thirteen.[21] By 1996 it was lower: less than a bomb's worth.[22] It takes ten kilograms of weapons-grade plutonium to fabricate a first bomb, eight or nine for subsequent ones.[23]

Yet the facts never caught up with the estimate. Director of Central Intelligence James Woolsey, who had irked National Security Adviser Lake and others by repeatedly using intelligence in internal deliberations to make the case against deal-making, went public on February 8. In a speech in Topeka he detailed some of the C.I.A.'s conclusions. He saw "no immediate prospect" of restoring full access to North Korea's nuclear sites and he warned that the North Koreans "may decide to shut down their Yongbyon reactor soon, enabling them to extract fuel, reprocess, recover the plutonium, and use it to produce nuclear weapons."[24] His public comments stirred James Laney, the American ambassador in Seoul, to complain to the White House. "Woolsey was speaking out of turn," Laney recalls telling the President's senior political advisers, Thomas ("Mack") McLarty and David Gergen. "Most people think the D.C.I. knows more than he says. This guy was saying more than he knows."[25]

The Collapse of "Super Tuesday"

North Korea seemed determined to make an offer the United States could not refuse. Yet the November estimate poisoned the political atmosphere in Washington and Seoul. Instead of sowing caution about coercion, it renewed skepticism about negotiations. "The effect of the public arguments," says a Pentagon official, "was to reinforce the belief that many people held at the higher political levels that you couldn't back down. You had set certain conditions for dialogue and had publicized them and you had to stick to them."[26]

The Pentagon began to take precautions in case sanctions were imposed. The U.S. commander in Korea, General Luck had recommended various measures, depending on the severity of the sanctions: dispatching Patriot antimissile batteries, expediting delivery of Apache helicopters and Bradley armored vehicles, stationing an aircraft carrier off Korea, and sending air and ground reinforcements. "General Luck feels that sanctions are a dangerous option," said an administration official. "As the commander of 37,000 men there he will want to try to increase deterrence if we go that route."[27] Yet these precautions risked provoking Pyongyang into mobilizing its army, raising fears of unintended war.

President Clinton scheduled a well-publicized briefing by Defense Secretary Aspin, Joint Chiefs of Staff Chairman Shalikashvili, and General Luck on Pentagon plans. "That was very serious," says a top official who attended. "We don't do that very often." He found the discussion of reinforcement options sobering: "The intelligence people were saying this could be very provocative."[28] General Luck's assessment was just as sobering: "You could win and you could punish the North, but in the process you would punish everyone else who's a participant. The North has and will continue to have a tremendous capacity to do great damage to the South even in its weakened state."[29]

The president moved to cool things down in public. Trying to sound reassuring in an interview with *U.S. News & World Report*, he said he saw "no cause for any great alarm on the part of the American people or the North Koreans for that matter."[30]

The I.A.E.A., meanwhile, was doing its best to raise alarm. Director-General Blix told the I.A.E.A. Board of Governors on December 2 that the safeguards "cannot be said at present to provide any meaningful assurance of peaceful uses of D.P.R.K.'s declared nuclear installations and materials." That was his oblique way of saying that the film and batteries in the I.A.E.A.'s monitoring cameras at Yongbyon had been exhausted. In a slap at both Washington and Pyongyang, Blix told the Board the next day, safeguards obligations "are not subject to the course of discussions with other parties."[31] That prompted Deputy Assistant Secretary of State Robert Einhorn to fly to Vienna to ask Blix for "clarification." A senior I.A.E.A. official later recalled that "the concern on the administration's part was we should not make any statement that would be interpreted by the hawks in Washington" as reason to call off negotiations. Asked if he was pressured by Washington, Blix said, "They were not mute. But pressure, no."[32] Robert Gallucci recalls having numerous telephone conversations with the I.A.E.A. director-general: "Blix understands everything. What he decides to say is another matter. Continuity of safeguards . . . is not the way the I.A.E.A. normally does business. Part of the way the I.A.E.A. protects its international standing is to pee on us."[33]

On December 3 D.P.R.K. Ambassador Ho Jong met with Deputy Assistant Secretary of State Thomas Hubbard in New York and agreed to allow inspectors into all seven declared nuclear sites, but to limit their access inside the reactor and reprocessing plant to assuring that no spent fuel was being diverted, or in I.A.E.A. parlance, maintaining the continuity of safeguards. Ad hoc and routine inspections would have to await progress in high-level talks.[34] Ho had a formal rejoinder to the new American proposal: "The D.P.R.K. would only resume working-level contacts with the R.O.K. after the South showed its sincere attitude with respect to nuclear exercises and international pressure efforts against North Korea." Two could play the preconditions game: if North-South talks came first for Seoul, suspending Team Spirit came first for Pyongyang.

A Principals' Committee meeting convened on December 6 to consider North Korea's proposal. In the course of the meeting, Defense Secretary Aspin again advocated approaching Kim Il Sung directly with a package deal, but his rambling intervention made it sound like "a one-time take-it-or-leave-it" offer that would also "spell out to him the defense preparations we would make if it failed."[35] It led to heated exchange with National Security Adviser Lake. "Aspin came in at the last minute with a proposal that I had never heard of and no one had really thought through before," says a top official. "It wasn't coherently presented at all. It didn't sound like it would work." Just then the president joined the meeting. Lake, the official says, began "trying to review the options in a way that didn't piss all over it," but making clear that Aspin's option was "a non-starter."[36]

President Clinton decided, instead, to try to use the North Korean opening to get back to high-level talks. His comment afterward was cryptic: "Obviously we're not entirely satisfied." Yet the offer of inspections met the administration's recently revised aim of inhibiting further plutonium production and, if the new intelligence estimate was to be believed, further bomb-making as well. As Defense Secretary Aspin put it on NBC's *Meet the Press* at week's end, "Whatever happened in 1989, the situation is not deteriorating now. They are not developing more plutonium in order to be able to make more nuclear bombs."[37] Pyongyang was prepared to permit access to help assure that remained so.

The I.A.E.A. was still openly dissatisfied. "There must be unrestricted access to all declared sites," insisted the agency's spokesman, David Kyd. "Restrictions on the two facilities are not negotiable."[38] The I.A.E.A. was holding out for nothing less than full compliance with the safeguards agreement and did not want to resort to deal-making to achieve it. The I.A.E.A. preferred to have North Korea abandon the Nonproliferation Treaty altogether than remain partially in and partially out. As Bruno Pellaud, the I.A.E.A.'s deputy director-general, would say in July 1994, the D.P.R.K.'s departure from the treaty would at least clarify its noncompliance status.[39] The I.A.E.A. seemed more preoccupied with preserving the sanctity of its own standard operating procedures than with preventing proliferation in North Korea.

South Korea was also unhappy. It wanted suspension of Team Spirit linked, not to inspections, but to an exchange of North-South special envoys, and it wanted serious North-South talks to take place before U.S.-D.P.R.K. high-level talks got underway.

After consulting with Seoul, Washington nevertheless kept negotiating with the D.P.R.K. on a set of steps to be taken simultaneously: suspension of Team Spirit, resumption of North-South talks, and inspections with enough latitude for the I.A.E.A. to assure itself that no diversion had taken place at the Yongbyon reactor and reprocessing plant since its monitoring cameras had gone dark. "The problem," says Deputy Assistant Secretary of State Hubbard, who was conducting the negotiations, was that the North Koreans, "were trying to force me to speak for another party."⁴⁰ In a meeting with D.P.R.K. representatives in New York on December 10, Hubbard acknowledged North Korea's "unique status" and said the United States wanted it "to accept the technical requirements for maintaining the continuity of safeguards, not the agency's legal requirements."⁴¹

Talk about resumption of talks left the hawks infuriated, moderates doubtful, and nonproliferation specialists scornful. "Talk Means Nothing to Gangsters," read the headline atop Lally Weymouth's column in the *Post*. With unintended irony, she wrote that "the time for impassioned policy debate has passed." The administration "has already afforded diplomacy ample opportunity, and it has utterly failed." In conclusion she quoted former Secretary of State Lawrence Eagleburger, "If you're not prepared to use force, then you're nowhere."⁴² Former Secretary of Defense Caspar Weinberger was equally contemptuous. He told a Heritage Foundation symposium that an offer to cancel Team Spirit was "totally misplaced" and a deal was out of the question: "There is nothing you could really offer that is going to please them."⁴³ A RAND Issue Paper was almost as categorical, "North Korea seems determined to acquire nuclear weapons." Because "nothing that the United States can realistically offer" will increase the life expectancy of the regime in Pyongyang, "it is unlikely that a strategy of positive incentives will work." Washington instead "will have to rely increasingly on sticks."⁴⁴

Doubt about diplomacy was infectious. "We seem to be getting some motion, but perhaps no movement at all," commented centrist Senator William Cohen (R-ME). "I think we have to look at their response with some skepticism."⁴⁵ Randy Rydell, a staff member of the Senate Government Operations Subcommittee chaired by John Glenn (D-OH), dismissed administration policy as "nothing but a series of unilateral U.S. concessions" and laughed off the idea of Senate approval for a transfer of reactor technology to the D.P.R.K.⁴⁶ "Clinton Administration officials bristle, of course, at any suggestion that their proposed concessions prove that nuclear blackmail works," wrote David Sanger in the *Times*. "But that is the subtext of the whole drama."⁴⁷ Perhaps a more judicious reading of the subtext was that the administration was still having trouble making promises and keeping them, in part because of a widely shared misreading of North Korean intentions.

American and North Korean negotiators reached agreement by telephone December 29, 1993. The D.P.R.K. was "prepared to take the steps necessary to assure the continuity of inspections," but the details were left for it and the I.A.E.A. to work out.⁴⁸

North Korea had already told the I.A.E.A. on December 20 what it would and would not permit: "If the D.P.R.K. accepts the agency technical inspection for maintaining the continuity of safeguards" and if

Team Spirit 1994 is stopped, the third round of high-level talks could be held. If there is agreement on a package solution in those talks, the D.P.R.K. "will accept the agency's full inspection" and consult on arrangements. It is also "ready to discuss and permit, within a reasonable scope, more inspection activities required" in order to "recover the period in which the surveillance equipment was out of operation."[49]

In his annual New Year's Day message, Kim Il Sung went out of his way to give his support to the agreement, declaring that it paves the way for the nuclear issue to be "settled fairly," but he cautioned, pressure "may invite catastrophe."[50]

Putting the telephone agreement on paper proved difficult, however. "We never could get a consistent definition of continuity of safeguards out of Washington," says an American negotiator, "and we could never get from the 'ROKs' a consistent definition of who would do what first."[51]

Without a written text to make public, the administration invited confused speculation about the details. "It was the battle of the leaks," says a Pentagon official. "Someone would leak their version, which then compelled the other side to leak their version."[52] Both the *Washington Post* and the *New York Times* misleadingly reported that the administration had accepted a single inspection of all seven declared nuclear sites.[53] A *Times* editorial just as misleadingly overstated the results: "The North has agreed to allow the resumption of regular international inspections of all seven of its declared nuclear sites."[54] An arms control official told a *Times* reporter, "It's one of these cases where the administration was huffing and puffing and backed down. There's nothing wrong with trying to come out of this without starting a war." A U.S. official added, "We need to coax the North Koreans back to the Nonproliferation Treaty regime without falling on our own sword over phony principle."[55]

Undersecretary of State Lynn Davis was sent out at the State Department daily briefing January 5 to dispel the notion of a onetime inspection.[56] She did not clarify much else. Senior officials were now ruefully acknowledging they had done a "lousy job" of defending their policy in public.[57] Yet they remained reluctant to define the policy, let alone defend it. Instead, they tried to stem the flow of unauthorized disclosures. "In December," says a Pentagon official," everything on North Korea was put into a special channel with the goal of cutting out most people."[58] That inhibited contact between officials and informed outsiders without sealing the leaks. It also assured that most leakers were uninformed and the press and public, misinformed.

The skeptics and the hawks were not reassured. "Yesterday's promise by North Korea to allow inspections of its seven nuclear sites, even if it pans out, will not help much," wrote Richard Betts, director of security studies at Columbia University's School of International and Public Affairs, in a *Times* op-ed. "Pyongyang can bow to American demands and still proceed with its nuclear program."[59] Brent Scowcroft and Richard Haass weighed in with an op-ed of their own: "Any arrangements for inspections must provide for not one-time but regular and full access to all sites—not merely the seven apparently agreed upon—that are known or suspected of having nuclear-weapons activities." The United States, they insisted, "should continue joint military exercises and strengthen the defenses of the South against attack from the North, whether nuclear or conventional."[60] Columnist Charles Krauthammer was more strident. "I half expected this wobbly president to surrender," he wrote. "But even I was stunned by the extent of the capitulation." The results? "The N.P.T. is dead," the "I.A.E.A., if it goes along with this sham, is corrupted beyond redemption," and "American credibility—not very high after Clinton's about-faces in Bosnia, Somalia and Haiti—sinks to a new low."[61] To Senator John McCain (R-AZ), canceling Team Spirit "for the sake of a single concession which is entirely inadequate as a means of determining the extent of North Korea's nuclear program is without a doubt the worst signal the United States could send." Arnold Kanter could "see the case for having made this deal," but complained, "We've made a series of concessions, and we are not even back to the problem."[62]

News reports exaggerated what Washington was offering Pyongyang and devalued what it was getting in return. The *Times'* David Sanger reported that "limitations on the first round of inspections virtually assure that nothing new will be learned about how close Pyongyang has come to making a nuclear weapon," but "will probably prevent the Communist Government of Kim Il Sung from diverting more nuclear material from its reactors to its weapons program." The *Times* headline rendered its judgment: "U.S.-North Korean Atom Accord Expected to Yield Dubious Results."[63] That said a lot about the misplaced priorities of most observers.

While the administration was being castigated for making concessions it had yet to make, Representative Gary Ackerman (D-NY) was urging it to offer some: "We should not try to induce the North Koreans with the whiff of a carrot. Rather, we should show them the entire carrot patch."[64] Ackerman's criticism struck closer to home. As Robert Gallucci acknowledged at the time, "We have demonstrated our willingness to be forthcoming, but we haven't really had the opportunity to make these concessions that some of the critics think we have."[65]

The United States, having settled for inspections "to certify that continuity of safeguards has been maintained," was now insisting that "the number and scope of inspections required is a matter for the I.A.E.A, not the United States, to decide."[66] By saying so, says a State Department official, "we became a prisoner of the I.A.E.A."[67]

Maybe Washington was not about to fall on its sword over phony principle, but the I.A.E.A. was determined to uphold its right to conduct ad hoc and routine inspections. On January 7, 1994, the D.P.R.K. invited I.A.E.A. inspectors to come to Yongbyon and work things out "on the spot." Nothing doing, replied the I.A.E.A., inspections had to be agreed in advance and could not be limited to "containment and surveillance." On January 10 it handed D.P.R.K. representatives a detailed list of what it wanted to do. On January 17 Pyongyang refused to go along with the full list. It would allow inspectors "to verify non-diversion of nuclear material from the nuclear facilities since the last inspection" and allow them to do what they required "to remedy the gaps" in the continuity of safeguards because the cameras had stopped taping, but it insisted that inspections "not exceed the scope which was permitted in the past."[68] On January 20 the I.A.E.A. went public, saying that North Korea had balked at "a significant number of measures on the list" and adding that Blix had made it clear to the North that "this is not a negotiation" and that "we will not send an inspection team unless there is full agreement." A State Department spokesman backed the agency: "If the I.A.E.A. is unhappy, we are unhappy."[69]

Pyongyang was unmoved. On January 24 it told the I.A.E.A. that the agency's proposal "goes beyond the scope of the present consultation and is the same as the scope of routine and ad hoc inspections under the safeguards agreement."[70]

On January 25 officials disclosed that the Pentagon was "looking favorably" on shipping about three dozen Patriot antimissile batteries to South Korea.[71] President Clinton had not yet made a decision, but was expected to approve the deployment if the North had not agreed to inspections by February 21, the date that the I.A.E.A. Board of Governors was scheduled to reconvene. The Pentagon characterized the Patriots as defensive, but Pyongyang could well view the deployment as provocative. The U.S. bases they would fortify against air and missile attack could be used to launch air strikes on Yongbyon and other targets in North Korea.

The story said nothing about South Korean approval. Seoul had not yet been asked. The Patriot deployment had been initiated by the commander-in-chief of Pacific Command, Admiral Charles Larson. "You have this oriental potentate out there," says a State Department official, who "had gone a long way before the civilian side knew it. I discovered they hadn't been sold to the South. He'd run it by the Ministry of Defense."[72]

The day before the Patriot disclosure, Aspin's deputy, William J. Perry, had been nominated to succeed him. The Pentagon had been in some disarray since Aspin's ouster in December; Bobby Ray Inman had been named to succeed him only to self-destruct in public. Aspin's departure had been rumored ever since American troops stumbled into a deadly firefight in Somalia shortly after he had turned down a request by the American commander for tanks. The Somalia experience was not lost on senior civilians in the Pentagon. With Republicans in Congress demanding reinforcements, the Patriot deployment would protect the administration, if not the 37,000 troops in Korea, against hostile fire. The Patriot disclosure burnished Perry's hawkish credentials in Seoul. It also led Pyongyang to call the deployment an "unpardonable, grave military challenge" and warned that trying to "subdue the D.P.R.K. with pressure and threat" was "a big mistake."[73]

On January 31 a Defense Ministry spokesman in Seoul stepped up the pressure, saying it would resume Team Spirit exercises "unless the North agrees to *full* nuclear inspections."[74] Pyongyang reacted immediately. A statement issued that day by the D.P.R.K. Foreign Ministry accused the United States of reneging on the December 29 agreement and accused the I.A.E.A. of ignoring Pyongyang's unique status, partly in and partly out of the N.P.T.: "The demanded full-scope inspections clearly goes against the spirit of the D.P.R.K.-U.S.A. agreement and it is absolutely beyond discussion at this point in time when the U.S. nuclear threat remains yet to be removed [and] I.A.E.A. partiality and injustice remain yet to be redressed." It accused the agency of delaying consultations until its monitoring cameras had run out of film. North Korean representatives in Vienna later asked I.A.E.A. officials to circulate the statement to all members.[75] American news reports ignored the North's charges.

On February 2 Gallucci sent a message to Kang reassuring him, "We understand that inspections sought by the I.A.E.A. for the continuity of safeguards are designed to ensure non-diversion of nuclear material since the previous full inspection."[76] The I.A.E.A. was seeking that, and more. On February 7 a senior I.A.E.A. official said it had repeatedly told North Korea that "neither you, nor the United States, nor the two of you together, should decide what safeguards are requisite."[77] That led the *New York Times* to wonder, "Who Is Running Our Korea Policy?" The editorial began, "The Clinton Administration insists it will never subcontract its foreign policy to any international institution. Yet it is doing just that in its nuclear diplomacy with North Korea. It is letting the International Atomic Energy Agency decide how to carry out a deal Washington reached with Pyongyang. By changing the terms of that deal, the I.A.E.A. could embroil the United States in a dangerous confrontation on the Korean peninsula."[78]

Confrontation was just what some hawks had in mind. Senator Chuck Robb (D-VA), in a close re-election contest with Oliver North of Iran-Contra fame, introduced a resolution February 1 calling on the administration to "prepare to reintroduce" nuclear warheads to Korea. The Senate passed a milder resolution instead, urging the President to "ensure that sufficient U.S. forces are deployed in the Pacific region." In a long February 6 article in the *New York Times* detailing American military preparations in Korea, former National Security Adviser Brent Scowcroft argued in favor of additional carrier and fighter deployments: "I would be ostentatiously strengthening my position."[79] Two days later the House Republican Policy Committee accused the administration of "insufficient attention to the security of threatened American forces in the region"—fighting words on Capitol Hill—and called for the immediate dispatch of the Patriots.[80] On February 13 Senator John McCain (R-AZ) renewed the call for the "return of nuclear weapons to South Korea."[81]

All but lost in the barrage of threats was any thought that reassurance might be a better way to coax a country like North Korea into giving up nuclear-arming. A report by a U.S. Institute of Peace study group, including a number of prominent officials from the Bush Administration, tried to make that point. After calling the late November 1993 intelligence estimate into question, the group concluded, "It would be inappropriate to view Pyongyang's program to construct nuclear weapons in its current state of development as constituting an immediate military crisis." The alarmist view "plays into Pyongyang's game of threat and intimidation while slighting our many strengths for dealing with the situation." It cautioned against muscle-flexing, calling a credible military deterrent "the underpinning of diplomacy, not a strategy for problem-solving." Instead, the group contended, "The options for negotiations are potentially more productive." Arguing that a "negotiating approach which focused only on the nuclear issue" did not address either American and South Korean security interests or North Korea's concerns, the study group recommended that the administration clearly spell out a package proposal: "it can remove any ambiguity in Pyongyang's thinking about the benefits to be achieved by abandoning its nuclear program, it can reinforce those within the North Korean leadership inclined toward a course of engagement . . . and it can provide the policy context for sustaining the international coalition that opposes Pyongyang's proliferation efforts." Observing that "the complexity of the issues and the diversity of perspectives within the U.S. government and the broader policy community over priorities, strategy, and tactics have made it difficult for the United States to develop and articulate a clear policy position," the group recommended that a senior coordinator be appointed to negotiate with North Korea, oversee the bureaucracy, act as public spokesperson on this issue, and coordinate policy with key allies.[82] That one recommendation, not the reasoning behind it, received most of the news coverage.

The danger of threat-mongering was not lost on the American ambassador in Seoul, James Laney. "I was concerned that the rhetoric in
the United States was beginning to get out of hand." He sent a cable to
alert Washington about the need to evacuate American dependents in
Korea in the event of sanctions. "It hadn't crossed their minds," he says.
"We're not going to tell people you've got to go, but, by God, you're
going to have a big exodus and you're going to have a lot of hysteria and
the Korean economy is going to go kaput." Laney intended to do more
than encourage preparations. He was reminding Washington of the risks
of coercive diplomacy: "I sent that in, in part to give them a cold dose
of reality."[83] He did succeed in one respect. State Department officials
became concerned that if the cable leaked, it "might trigger some sort of
panic."[84]

As threats reverberated in Washington, Seoul tried to sound conciliatory. President Kim Young Sam held a well-publicized meeting of his
national security advisers on February 8, which put off the Patriot deployment, criticized "erroneous" American news reporting for raising
tensions, and pledged that "dialogue will be maintained as long as possible." Foreign Minister Han Sung Joo told the *Times*, "There needs to
be a calming down on both sides."[85] Seoul sent a secret message to
Washington doubting that sanctions would "have much bite" because
"primarily the provincial authorities" in Northeast China rather than the
central government in Beijing were making the decisions on trade and
investment with North Korea.[86] Meanwhile, China was rebuffing de-
marches by the United States, Britain, France, and Russia to threaten
Security Council sanctions.[87]

With the pressure off North Korea, the I.A.E.A. relented and agreed
on February 15 to an inspection for the purpose of verifying that, in its
words, "nuclear material in these facilities has not been diverted since
earlier inspections."[88] The D.P.R.K. and the I.A.E.A. both declared victory. According to the North Korean Foreign Ministry, "The U.S. and
the I.A.E.A. secretariat voluntarily withdrew their demand for routine
and ad hoc inspections and said they would seek an inspection exclusively for the continuity of safeguards, and this made it possible to decide upon the inspection scope."[89] According to I.A.E.A. spokesman
David Kyd, "They simply agreed to all of the measures."[90] A State Department official was not quite so categorical, saying that I.A.E.A. officials "got like 98 percent of what they wanted."[91] It would have taken
ingenious diplomatic draftsmanship for both the I.A.E.A. and the
D.P.R.K. to have been correct. More likely both read too much into the
agreement, with the I.A.E.A. determined to follow its inspection proto-
col to the letter and the D.P.R.K. insistent that the aim of continuity of
safeguards govern inspections. That set the stage for trouble.

On February 24, 1994, U.S. negotiators Thomas Hubbard and Gary Samore finally nailed down a written agreement with D.P.R.K. negotiators Ho Jong and Han Sung Ryol. "Actually Samore and I went up to New York without real authority to do that," recalls Hubbard. "Then we had a terrible task of selling Washington and Seoul on it." He later rued it as "my most miserable moment" in three years of negotiating with North Korea: "I had been too persuasive. It was my language. I battered Ho into accepting it." The agreement "had too many moving parts, too many things that had to happen at the same time, and given the parties we were dealing with, getting all that to happen was unlikely."[92]

On March 1, or "Super Tuesday" as some officials called it, the simultaneous steps agreed to December 29 finally took effect. Two days later, with I.A.E.A. inspectors in Yongbyon, the United States at last released the text of the "agreed conclusions":

> Pursuant to the consultations, both sides have agreed to take four simultaneous steps on March 1, 1994 as follows: 1. The U.S.A. announces its decision to agree with the Republic of Korea's suspension of Team Spirit '94 joint military exercise. 2. The *inspections necessary for the continuity of safeguards* as agreed between the I.A.E.A. and the D.P.R.K. on February 15, 1994, *begin* and will be completed within the period agreed by the I.A.E.A. and the D.P.R.K. 3. The *working level contacts resume* in Panmunjom for the exchange of North-South special envoys. 4. The U.S.A. and the D.P.R.K. announce that the third round of U.S.-D.P.R.K. talks will begin on March 21, 1994, in Geneva. Each of these simultaneous steps is required for the implementation of these agreed conclusions.[93]

Besides these "agreed conclusions," the State Department also made public a U.S. unilateral statement: "The undertaking of the United States regarding Team Spirit '94 and a third round of U.S.-D.P.R.K. talks are based on the premise that the I.A.E.A. inspections *will be fully implemented* and the North-South nuclear dialogue will continue *through the exchange of special envoys*."[94] Needless to say, a unilateral statement by Washington was not the same as an agreement with Pyongyang.

It was also a blank check to South Korea, which immediately cashed it. Seoul insisted it would not call off Team Spirit until a North-South exchange of special envoys took place, says Deputy Assistant Secretary of State Hubbard, and it "tightened the conditions for the exchange of envoys very stiffly."[95] D.P.R.K. negotiator Kang Sok Ju complained of "ill-boding moves." The agreement, he said, only mentioned renewed talks about an exchange of envoys between the two Koreas and "did not touch on fulfillment of the exchange."[96] Pyongyang insisted that Team Spirit be suspended unconditionally before it agreed to an exchange of envoys. That was consistent with the agreed text, but Seoul said otherwise and Washington backed it up. Worse yet, Seoul made the suspension contingent on *completion of the I.A.E.A. inspections*, again stretching the terms of the U.S.-D.P.R.K. agreement to the breaking point. Once again, Washington publicly backed Seoul. Assistant Secretary of State Winston Lord told a March 3 State Department press briefing, "These inspections have to be successfully carried out. . . . And if that happens *and if the North-South envoy exchange happens*, then we will go to a third round, and then the Team Spirit decision will kick in."[97] His interpretation was based on the unilateral statement by the United States, not on the U.S.-D.P.R.K. agreed statement. Lord's backing for Seoul, says Charles Kartman, deputy chief of mission in Seoul, was "a public acknowledgement of the reality. The South Koreans had come to a hard and fast decision about what their requirements were and couldn't be budged off them, and Winston acceded to that reality."[98] A less charitable interpretation was that the Bureau of East Asian and Pacific Affairs was deferring to a client.

Pyongyang, in turn, barred inspectors from taking sample smears at a hot cell for handling spent nuclear fuel, citing "external factors," a reference to Seoul's refusal to suspend Team Spirit and its insistence that exchange of North-South special envoys precede the reconvening of U.S.-D.P.R.K. high-level talks. First Deputy Foreign Minister Kang wrote Gallucci offering to resume inspections if South Korea retracted its demand for a North-South exchange of special envoys.

Most American officials believe that the North deliberately picked a fight with the I.A.E.A. The I.A.E.A. insisted it needed the sample smears to determine whether any recent reprocessing had taken place. Pyongyang correctly concluded they would also enable the agency to clear up discrepancies in the D.P.R.K.'s initial declaration. North Korea assailed the I.A.E.A. for giving its inspectors "instructions inconsistent" with the February 15 agreement, which it interpreted as permitting inspections solely for the purpose of continuity of safeguards. Sampling at the hot cell, it insisted, "contradicts the I.A.E.A. document which says that 'this inspection does not include verification of the completeness of the initial inventory of nuclear material.'"[99] The sample smears were on the list of I.A.E.A. activities that the North had agreed to, however. "The North Koreans probably made a bad deal," says Robert Gallucci. "How did they get themselves in this position? They are not the best nuclear engineers in the world and they were constantly trying to figure out what techniques the I.A.E.A. was using."[100]

Yet one experienced Korea watcher in the State Department thinks the North Koreans were just retaliating for South Korean efforts to change the terms of the February 24 agreement and never intended to start a confrontation. They were surprised by the I.A.E.A.'s overreaction.[101] Agency spokesman Hans Meyer had initially dismissed the dispute as commonplace in dealing with other host countries, "There is never an inspection where you don't have an argument."[102] On March 15, however, the I.A.E.A. abruptly withdrew its inspectors, saying it was unable to verify that no diversion had taken place. The next day the United States canceled high-level talks with the North. The I.A.E.A. was once again forcing the issue.

With South Korea still insistent on its preconditions for an exchange of envoys, North-South talks collapsed on March 19. After South Korea's representative threatened to seek sanctions, the North's responded with a threat of his own, "We are ready to respond with an eye for an eye and a war for a war. Seoul is not very far from here. If a war breaks out, Seoul will turn into a sea of fire."[103] A D.P.R.K. Foreign Ministry spokesman on March 21 accused the United States of committing "a perfidious act" that "may bring the Korean nation back to the phase of confrontation and war." The R.O.K. reacted by alerting its armed forces.

On March 19, 1994, the day that North-South talks broke off, the Principals' Committee met and opted for another round of coercive diplomacy. It decided to resume Team Spirit exercises, to consult with Seoul on dispatching Patriot antimissile batteries to Korea, and to mobilize support for sanctions in the U.N. Security Council.[104] Two days later the Patriot deployment was announced.

Washington now moved to ratchet up the crisis by seeking sanctions. In visits to Seoul, Tokyo, and Beijing, Secretary of State Christopher was finding little enthusiasm for swift action. He tried to put the best face on his conversations in Beijing, "I would say that if we work at it carefully and patiently in the United Nations and bring the Chinese along, that they will not block the imposition of sanctions." Enforcing them was another matter. Appearing on "Face the Nation" on March 20, Christopher acknowledged he had no assurances of a Chinese abstention in the Security Council: "What we do have is their encouragement to pursue patient diplomacy."[105] Two days later Prime Minister Li Peng left no doubt about China's opposition to coercing North Korea, "If pressure is applied on this issue, it can only complicate the situation on the Korean Peninsula and it will add to tension there."[106]

On March 21 the I.A.E.A. Board of Governors passed a resolution urging North Korea "immediately to allow the I.A.E.A. to complete all requested inspection activities *and* to comply fully with its safeguards agreement."[107] It then voted 25 to 1 to refer the dispute to the U.N. Security Council. Libya was the sole nay, but China and eight others abstained.

China was not about to press North Korea or back sanctions. President Jiang Zemin made that clear to President Kim Young Sam in talks in Beijing on March 28. China succeeded in replacing a U.S. draft resolution with a March 31 statement by the Security Council president urging the North "to complete the inspection activities agreed between the I.A.E.A. and the D.P.R.K. on 15 February 1994, *as the first step* in fulfilling its safeguards agreement," a weaker formulation than the I.A.E.A.'s. At China's behest, the U.S. language was watered down further. It urged the continuation of dialogue, omitting the qualifying phrase "after the I.A.E.A. completes all inspections," dropped the reference to a deadline, and replaced the phrase "further Security Council action," implying sanctions, with "further Security Council consideration" if the Council's importuning went unheeded.[108]

The Clinton Administration was trying to abandon the crime-and-punishment approach, but was having trouble doing so because of the actions of its allies. Having set its aim of constraining future plutonium production by Pyongyang, it went along with I.A.E.A. and South Korean attempts to get at North Korea's past plutonium production, thus reneging on its agreement with the North. Having started down the road to a third round of high-level talks, it allowed itself to be sidetracked into treating the resumption of talks, once again, as a reward to be withheld until Pyongyang did what it wanted. As a result, the United States would not hold a third round of high-level talks with North Korea until July 1994, a year after the second round.

Let Bygones Be Bygones, for Now

The March inspection did record one accomplishment. The I.A.E.A. confirmed what American intelligence had detected in 1991, that a second reprocessing line was under construction at the Yongbyon plant. When completed, it would double North Korea's capacity for extracting plutonium from spent reactor fuel.[109] That underscored the need for the Clinton Administration to get its priorities straight—curbing future bomb-making in North Korea before worrying about its nuclear past. It also lent new urgency to resuming inspections before the North began to shut down the Yongbyon reactor for refueling, an event the I.A.E.A. had anticipated for nearly a year. The inspectors' presence could keep the spent fuel in the reactor, with its five or six bombs' worth of plutonium, from being spirited away for bomb-making.

The administration finally put a process in place to help it set priorities. On April 4 the president approved formation of a Senior Policy Steering Group on Korea, chaired by Gallucci, with Daniel Poneman, N.S.C. senior director for nonproliferation, as vice-chair. The group was authorized to report directly to the Principals' Committee of the National Security Council, elevating its bureaucratic status. Gallucci was given the rank of ambassador-at-large and freed from his duties as assistant secretary of state for politico-military affairs.[110]

Until then no official at the level of office director or above could devote undivided attention to nuclear diplomacy with North Korea. It was just one issue among many for officials in a position to do something about it. Gallucci now had the time to review the negotiating history and consult with experts in and out of the government. "Most of the key people working on this did not know anything about Korea. I knew the capitals. That was about it," says a Pentagon official. "It was actually surprising how long it took for Gallucci to have a whole set of briefings on everything—a lot more than just the technical stuff. There was a lot on Korea. He asked for every bit of data that we had."[111]

Up to now, much of the administration's time had been spent getting to high-level talks, not negotiating. Most of the give-and-take had taken place within the U.S. government deciding what to put on the table. "We didn't really acquire much of a feel for what the North Koreans were saying to us," says Charles Kartman of the State Department. "We would thrash out internally what we wanted. All sorts of theology from the nonproliferation community got thrown into that. Then we would have to negotiate with the R.O.K. and thrash that out. By the time we were done with those two processes, not only were there no carrots left. There were no negotiations. We would throw this thing on the table at the North Koreans and tune out. Until Bob Gallucci really got engaged, nobody was really willing to listen to the North Koreans and adjust our positions to what they were saying."[112]

Gallucci at last had the bureaucratic authority to fill the package proposal with specific contents, but he still needed backing from his bureaucratic superiors to commit the United States to a deal. He took advantage of a mid-April trip to Seoul with Defense Secretary Perry to discuss the negotiations at some length. "That was a terrific opportunity," says Gallucci. "As secretary of defense, he was able to do what I couldn't do, force people to focus on North Korea's future production. The intelligence was being used as a club to say that the North was going ahead with its nuclear program and was not serious about negotiating. He used the intelligence about the facilities under construction to establish our priorities."[113]

Perry became a pivotal ally of Gallucci's. The secretary of defense concentrated his energies on policy in places where the use of force was a possibility. North Korea was at the top of the list. He alone among top officials in the Clinton Administration was prepared to take responsibility for the issue. Alone among them he was also an apostate: he no longer believed the shared images of nuclear diplomacy. In the coming days he and Gallucci would make Korea policy by articulating it in public, giving it a modicum of coherence for the first time.[114]

The Pentagon began a public campaign to defend the logic of letting bygones be bygones, trying to keep North Korea from removing spent fuel and reprocessing it for more bombs, before returning to the past. If the November intelligence estimate was to be believed, North Korea had already reprocessed the plutonium extracted when the Yongbyon reactor was shut down in 1989, had fabricated it into one or two bombs, and had stopped reprocessing plutonium. If North Korea had not in fact extracted enough plutonium for a bomb, it might not want to let the I.A.E.A. call its bluff. If it had extracted enough, it might resist turning over the material to the I.A.E.A. for safeguarding. Either way, if the United States insisted on ascertaining how much plutonium the North may have extracted in the past, North Korea might deny access to the inspectors and resume reprocessing. At a background briefing for reporters, Assistant Secretary of Defense Ashton Carter referred to "Bush's plutonium." A State Department official told *Time* magazine columnist Michael Kramer, "As soon as the bombs' existence is confirmed unambiguously, you have to do something about it. Better to let what is be and move on to cap it at the present low-level threat."[115] Unnamed administration officials steered *Post* columnist Jim Hoagland down the same path: "The Clinton Administration is prepared to live with the strong probability that North Korea has built, or can quickly build, a single nuclear bomb. The plutonium North Korea has already diverted from its reactors is so much spilt milk. The administration will not publicly admit that it is resigned to Pyongyang's keeping a proto-bomb for the foreseeable future, but that is the basis of existing policy. Washington has drawn the line against an extension of Pyongyang's nuclear capability on Clinton's watch."[116] It was not until April 3 that Perry said as much on the record. He told panelists on *Meet the Press* that North Korea had to freeze its nuclear program and then roll it back, but he said as much about the administration's ultimate priority as he did about its immediate one: "To the extent that they actually have one or two nuclear bombs now, we want those to be removed. That's a very clear objective."[117] Perry was more explicit in an April 11 interview with *Time*: "Our policy right along has been oriented to try to keep North Korea from getting a significant nuclear-weapon capability." Asked about the one or two bombs it supposedly had already, he replied, "We don't know anything we can do about that. What we can do something about, though, is stopping them from building anything beyond that."[118]

Perry and Gallucci held consultations in Seoul on April 16–20. While they were there, a Patriot antimissile battery arrived. North Korea's leader Kim Il Sung also gave two conciliatory interviews. In a rare public appearance, at a reception for journalists and diplomats, Kim renounced any nuclear ambitions and implied his willingness to freeze the North's nuclear program: "Never in the future will we have nuclear weapons, I promise you."[119] He disowned the "sea of fire" remark by the D.P.R.K. representative to the North-South talks, calling it "a mistake." The negotiator who made it was later sacked. In a written reply to questions from Japanese public broadcasting, Kim alluded to the recent reneging without rancor, "The way to resolve the problem is for the United States to abide by its pledges." He reaffirmed that the nuclear issue was negotiable: "If the United States would simply agree to top-level talks with no preconditions, we could solve the problem."[120]

Kim Il Sung was not the only Korean to sound conciliatory. Seoul was not about to be blamed if war should break out. It dropped its insistence on an exchange of North-South envoys before U.S.-D.P.R.K. high-level talks could be held. After consultations with Perry and Gallucci, it also deferred a decision to reschedule Team Spirit.[121] That cleared the way for Pyongyang to permit the I.A.E.A. to complete its March inspection.

Perry also used the occasion of his visit to Seoul to draw attention to the need to resume inspections before the pending shutdown of the Yongbyon reactor for refueling and to sound reassuring in public: "There is no imminent danger of a military conflict on the Korean peninsula."[122] In private with Perry, General Luck and Ambassador Laney argued just the opposite. They were "of one mind to make sure he knew how serious this was," says a senior military officer who took part. Laney was determined that "people felt the wool on the hair shirt, and Dr. Perry did." Luck's view was that "we were ready to do all the military things, no question about it, and we were willing to exercise them. But his contention was that a good, strong, ready force was a diplomatic tool," the officer says. Luck "didn't want us to bungle our way into war when we could handle it another way—with astute diplomatic manipulation." To him, the situation was "too important to screw up with politics and bravado."[123] Laney pressed Perry to send a high-level emissary for urgent talks with Kim Il Sung. Laney, an Atlanta resident, recommended Senator Sam Nunn (D-GA) for the job. Nunn and Senator Richard Lugar (R-IN) contacted Perry on his return to Washington and volunteered to undertake the mission, but Pyongyang rebuffed the approach.[124]

By the end of April the interagency process had also begun to sort out the U.S. negotiating position for the third round of high-level talks. American demands were divided into those that would be sought up front and those that would be deferred to a later date. In phase one, "what we wanted from them was a return to the N.P.T., full cooperation with the I.A.E.A. including ad hoc and routine inspections, measures to resolve plutonium declaration discrepancies and agreement in principle on special inspections," says a key participant in the interagency process. If that was not enough, the phase-one list included progress on implementing the North-South denuclearization declaration and bans on reprocessing, removal of spent fuel from the reactor, and missile exports. "There was a lot of back and forth about whether to put conventional forces in phase one."[125] Though predictably long and front-loaded, it was no wish list.

The list of potential concessions was a lot shorter, but it was partially responsive to the North's package proposal of October 1993: "agreement on nuclear non-use and non-deployment, opening some sort of diplomatic relations at the lowest level, lifting some sanctions, forming a multilateral energy group and facilitating cooperation with the United Nations Development Program and trial inspections at U.S. bases."[126] An attempt to work out wording for security assurances had foundered, however. Gallucci had fought hard with the nuclear theologians in the Pentagon to get language that would renounce any threat of first use of nuclear arms by the United States once the North complied fully with the Nonproliferation Treaty. That would extend to Pyongyang the same pledge that the United States makes to all treaty members in good standing. When Gallucci broached the subject during a visit to Tokyo in March, Shunji Yanai, director of politico-military affairs in the Foreign Office, objected strenuously on the grounds that it punched a hole in the American nuclear umbrella.[127] Despite the lack of security assurances, for the first time since high-level talks had begun in January 1992, there was interagency agreement on some give as well as take.

On May 3 Defense Secretary Perry publicly promulgated what had been the administration's aim since October 1993: first freezing, then rolling back the North's nuclear program. He welcomed the North's invitation to have inspectors present when the spent fuel was unloaded: "Observation of the refueling is a most important first step in containing the North Korean nuclear program because it assures us that the fuel is not reprocessed and that it stays under international observation." It was an oblique way of urging the I.A.E.A. to accept the North's invitation. He restated the administration's objectives: "But we need to go further than simply containing this nuclear program. We want to achieve a nuclear-free Korean peninsula through implementation of the North-South Denuclearization Accord which was reached last year and through a determination of what happened to fuel that was removed when the reactor was shut down previously, in the absence of outside monitoring." Perry ruled out military pressure for now because of "the risk of large-scale war," but he warned that "if North Korea were to break the continuity of safeguards, for example, by refusing to allow adequate I.A.E.A. monitoring of the spent fuel rods it will remove from the 5-megawatt reactor, the issue would return to the United Nations, where the United States and others would consider appropriate steps, including sanctions." Perry tried to strike a posture of nonprovocative preparedness. After warning that the allies "would decisively and rapidly defeat any attack from the North," he noted, "Certainly we will not initiate a war with North Korea. Moreover, we will not provoke a war with North Korea by rash actions, now or later. But we will not invite a war by neglecting appropriate defense preparations."[128] The trouble was that North Korea might see those preparations as provocative.

Stumbling to the Brink

Just as the administration had finally abandoned the crime-and-punishment approach and was concentrating on first things first, Pyongyang abruptly shut down the Yongbyon reactor and began removing the spent fuel rods. It was a provocative way to draw world attention to its nuclear potential and away from its nuclear past. Once the rods cooled, they could be reprocessed, extracting five or six bombs' worth of plutonium. The reactor could be refueled and restarted, generating more spent fuel.

North Korea had told the I.A.E.A. it was ready to let the agency resume the interrupted March inspection, even to permit smear samples "as a special exception" in return for dropping the precondition on exchanging North-South special envoys.* It was also willing to have inspectors witness the refueling of the Yongbyon reactor to verify that spent fuel was placed in nearby cooling ponds and not diverted to bomb-making. But it balked at ad hoc and routine inspections and it refused to let the inspectors remove 300 fuel rods,** a cross-section of

---

* Besides the nuclear dispute, it had also been trying to replace the 1953 armistice agreement with a formal peace treaty. On April 28, 1994, it declared the agreement invalid and announced its intent to withdraw from the Military Armistice Commission.

** The fuel rods are clustered in channels. Knowing precisely what channel a rod came from was important to the I.A.E.A. for two reasons. First, it was looking for "discontinuities in burnup history, such as would occur if some rods were . . . replaced with others during the life of the core. If the inspectors don't know where the rods were, however, they cannot predict the burnup they would see and cannot, therefore, confirm that the rod is original." Second, the North Koreans had identified one channel where they had replaced the rods early in the reactor's operating history. "The rods removed from this channel could, therefore, be a most useful tool for confirming the early operating records of the reactor."

the 7,500 rods in the reactor, for analysis. That could help determine the reactor's operating history—how many bombs' worth, if any, of spent fuel may have been removed in the past.[129] The North was also unwilling to set aside a sample for subsequent analysis. "We can never permit these activities," the Ministry of Atomic Energy told the I.A.E.A., because they go "beyond the D.P.R.K.-I.A.E.A. agreed scope of the inspection activities for the continuity of safeguards" in disregard of "the D.P.R.K.'s unique status based on its temporary suspension of the effectuation of its declared withdrawal from the N.P.T." It added that "these activities would be permitted after a package solution to the nuclear issue is achieved at the next round of D.P.R.K.-U.S. talks."[130] Only "after the nuclear issue is settled in a package deal," the Foreign Ministry reiterated in a public statement, would it allow the sample to be drawn. "If the United States and the I.A.E.A. secretariat, ignoring our good will, rudely demand sampling," the statement cautioned, "we will have to regard it as a sinister political invention."[131]

A senior official made the Clinton Administration's priorities clear: "We are obviously interested in a historical inquiry," but "if the risk is losing track of a large quantity of plutonium, then the agency should accept the North Korean plan. Any approach that would squander the opportunity to sample at a later time, we would oppose."[132]

The I.A.E.A. did not share those priorities. It was determined to apply its preferred sampling procedures and to conduct ad hoc and routine inspections as well. It did not want to go to Yongbyon just to observe the defueling—or as it told Washington, "to be at the scene of a crime."[133] In response, "we begged them to go," says a Defense Department official, "and, as the cable said, 'be the eyes of the world.'"[134]

In the I.A.E.A.'s estimation, forcing North Korea out of the Nonproliferation Treaty was preferable to bribing it to comply. As Director-General Blix told Secretary of State Christopher in Washington in late March, the I.A.E.A. would be better off having North Korea out of the Nonproliferation Treaty.[135] The I.A.E.A. was run by lawyers like Blix who were preoccupied with the precedents it would set by treating North Korea differently. Moreover, a new director had just taken over the agency's safeguards department and he "decided he was going to be as virtuous as one could be," says an American who dealt directly with the I.A.E.A. in Vienna in this period. "He started reciting what under normal circumstances a routine inspection would require. He wanted to be clear that the North Koreans rejected it, not that the I.A.E.A. hadn't asked for it. From the I.A.E.A, in its own bubble, that's a workable strategy. With a world crisis hanging on whether this moves forward or not, this became less than viable."[136]

Some top policy-makers in Washington had become aware of the problem when Blix visited Washington in late March. "The impression," recalls a senior Defense Department official who met with him, "was that the I.A.E.A. was a group of scientists who were taking an overly formalistic view of things."[137] Another Pentagon official recalls, "We said to Blix, 'do you want to take responsibility for starting the second Korean War?'"[138]

The I.A.E.A.'s approach encountered resistance in Pyongyang, which warned the United States on May 2, 1994, that it was about to begin refueling. It may have had good technical reasons for shutting down the reactor, but not for removing spent fuel. Once the reactor was shut down, the spent fuel could remain in it indefinitely. That same day Gallucci sent a reply to Vice Foreign Minister Kang urging the North to defer discharging the fuel rods to a later date and to contact the I.A.E.A. about any safety problems arising from the delay. Gallucci proposed that the disposition of spent fuel be dealt with in the third round of high-level talks "in the context of converting to light-water-reactor technology." He warned that the United States would break off high-level talks: "If the reactor is unloaded without I.A.E.A. presence, we will be forced to conclude that the D.P.R.K. no longer wishes to resolve the nuclear issue through dialogue. Thus it will be impossible for the United States and the D.P.R.K. to continue our efforts to pursue negotiated resolution of the nuclear issue."[139] Once again, the North was in no mood to deny itself more nuclear leverage. In the words of State Department official, its reply was "Up yours."[140]

On May 4 the I.A.E.A. rejected North Korea's proposal to allow monitoring of the refueling in order to forestall diversion of spent fuel, but not to set aside a sample of fuel rods for future assay. On May 5 Gallucci sent another note to Kang warning, "If the D.P.R.K. begins to discharge fuel without allowing the I.A.E.A. to simultaneously select and store some fuel rods for future measurements it will forever destroy the ability of the I.A.E.A. to take such measurements. We will have to conclude that the D.P.R.K. has no intention of leaving open the possibility of resolving the nuclear issue through our broad and thorough discussions." That redrew a red line it had drawn a year earlier. "When you looked back at the original formulation, it looked sloppy and inadequate to the needs of the moment," says a senior official.[141] Understandably unwilling to repudiate the I.A.E.A., the United States now had to back the agency's preferred method for getting at North Korea's nuclear past.

Kang's reply insisted the issue had to be negotiated with the United States: "We can never permit the storage of some fuel rods because of the D.P.R.K.'s unique status." On May 12 the North notified the agency that it had begun removing the fuel rods from the reactor. The I.A.E.A.'s hand was forced. It decided to send inspectors to consult on sampling the fuel rods, complete the March inspections and, above all, observe the defueling.

To most outsiders, unaware of North Korea's year-long delay in refueling, the discharge of the fuel rods seemed confirmation of their worst suspicions, that North Korea had been stalling until it could make more bombs. The hawks went ballistic. So did prominent moderates. Senate Majority Leader George Mitchell (D-ME) and Minority Leader Robert Dole (R-KS) backed sanctions in a joint appearance on *Meet the Press*.[142] William Taylor, a dove just back from Pyongyang, where he met with Kim Il Sung, turned hawkish in a *Washington Post* op-ed. President Clinton has just offered "a hand of friendship," he wrote, but "Pyongyang has disregarded or misread the message" and is now in danger of crystallizing a "bipartisan consensus" for sanctions. "Pyongyang's leaders," he warned, "need to understand now that the decision is really up to them whether to bite the hand of friendship and suffer the consequences."[143] Jim Hoagland was already thinking about taking the next step up the escalation ladder: "President Clinton's advisers believe North Korea will probably deal at the brink rather than defy the world over nuclear weapons. But that belief is dwindling, and serious consideration must now be given to how America would prepare for and fight a second Korean war."[144]

On May 20, with about 5 percent of the fuel rods in the cooling ponds, the I.A.E.A. reported to the U.N. Security Council that North Korea's discharge of spent fuel without an agreement on sampling "constitutes a serious safeguards violation."

That same day the Principals' Committee convened on North Korea. "The most difficult day I remember," says a Pentagon official, "was in May in Perry's office, trying to decide what position he should take going into the Principals' meeting." Perry was told it would still be possible to determine how much spent fuel had been removed in the past, but that would mean publicly breaking with the I.A.E.A. "He still wanted to send a high-level emissary directly to Kim Il Sung and lay all the cards out." The issue was, the official recalls, "Do we let the dialogue fail and go to sanctions or do we let it fail and send someone to Pyongyang?" He felt, "We could let the process die and start a new process. State's backup plan was that the U.N. debate over sanctions would take a while and generate pressure on the North Koreans to bring them back to the table."[145]

With Perry in the lead, the administration decided to offer a resumption of high-level talks on condition that the North allow the March inspections to be completed, admit inspectors to observe the removal and storage of spent fuel in order to impede its diversion to bomb-making, and preserve the possibility of eventually clearing up the anomaly in its initial declaration to the I.A.E.A. about past reprocessing.[146] It took courage to hold open the possibility of diplomatic give-and-take in the face of the domestic political reaction to North Korea's about-face.

After the Principals' Committee meeting, Defense Secretary Perry tried, once again, to direct attention to the North's nuclear future, and away from its nuclear past: "The I.A.E.A., in fact, has told us that it is confident that there has been no diversion of the fuel that has just been discharged."[147] Senior officials depicted the North's action as a "technical violation" of I.A.E.A. protocols. With North Korea scheduled to resume consultations with the I.A.E.A. on May 25, even Director-General Blix held out hope: "It still seems possible to implement the required safeguards measures" because the key fuel rods had yet to be removed from the reactor.[148]

Perry and Blix were both acting on the premise that it would take the North Koreans three to six months to unload all the fuel rods, time for diplomacy to take its course. Three months was the C.I.A.'s estimate; six months, the I.A.E.A.'s. The estimates were based on how many damaged fuel rods were in the reactor and inspectors' observation of how long it had taken to unload two damaged rods in the past. Both estimates were wrong.

On May 27, as the North continued defueling "at a very fast pace," the I.A.E.A. alarmed Washington by telling U.N. Secretary-General Boutros Boutros-Ghali that its ability to "verify the amount" of plutonium accumulated in the past would be "lost within days." At a meeting with mid-level U.S. representatives in New York that day, the D.P.R.K. rejected a proposal to resume high-level talks on the grounds that it was unwilling to satisfy the I.A.E.A. by segregating selected fuel rods for future analysis. U.S. negotiator Gallucci in an interview warned that continued defueling would "force us to go back to the Security Council where sanctions would be one of the options."[149]

The Security Council president issued a statement on May 30 urging the North to discharge the reactor "in a manner which preserves the technical possibility of fuel measurements, in accordance with the I.A.E.A's requirements."[150] Nothing doing, replied the North. "The refueling is going on," declared Yun Ho Jin, its chief representative. "It cannot be stopped."[151]

With the fuel out of the reactor, everyone knew North Korea was a critical step closer to making bombs. In the administration apprehension and anger were beginning to show. One official who had been optimistic about a deal told the *Washington Post*: "There is nobody who believes this is some clever gimmick." He angrily denounced the North Korean action as "provocative, gratuitous . . . a direct and contemptuous challenge to us."[152] Joint Chiefs of Staff representatives on the negotiating team were particularly incensed, asking in effect, "How long are we going to let them walk all over us?"[153] Senator Bill Bradley (D-NJ) and House Minority Whip Newt Gingrich (R-GA) joined the ranks of those calling for sanctions and Senate Armed Services Committee Chairman Sam Nunn (D-GA) urged that defenses in Korea be strengthened in preparation for sanctions.[154]

On May 31 President Clinton met with the Principals' Committee to set U.S. sanctions strategy. Tokyo and Beijing were still cool to sanctions and the Pentagon, concerned about appearing too provocative, preferred to "go low and slow."[155] The administration adopted a phased approach to coercive diplomacy: first a warning by the Security Council, then a thirty-day grace period to be followed by a gradual tightening. The initial measures were modest: a halt to all cooperation that could contribute to North Korea's nuclear know-how, an end to U.N. economic assistance, a cutback in diplomatic activities with the North, a curtailing of cultural, technical, scientific, commercial, and educational exchanges, and a U.N. ban on arms trade with the North.[156] On June 3 Washington withdrew its offer to resume high-level talks.

The administration quietly sounded out South Korea, Japan, and China on the possibility of attacking Yongbyon, should North Korea begin removing spent fuel from the cooling ponds and reprocessing it. The reaction was negative. Japan does not regard North Korea as its adversary, Tokyo responded. "Every action has an equal and opposite reaction," replied the Chinese official who was contacted. Asked how he thought North Korea would react, he replied, "Not North Korea, China."[157]

The hawks were implacable. "We must now decide," wrote *Times* columnist William Safire on June 2, "whether to continue the protracted runaround, hoping vainly that Kim Il Sung wants to be bought off, or to enforce international law—which would require the credible threat of war." Laying down the law meant coercing the allies, not just the North Koreans: "First, get absolute, public assurances from Japan . . . that it will wage economic war. . . . Second, tell South Korea that its days of appeasement and complacency are over—no more only 4 percent of G.N.P. for defense—and full scale mobilization is in order." If they did not go along, Washington should go it alone: "If you are not with us in stopping nuclear spread here and now—we're out of the Far East. . . . If our leadership of proliferation police is rejected, we should await better leaders there and here; we can use the savings from troops drawn down to build a space shield, thereby protecting America from the next decade's nuclear bandits."[158] That "self-delusion" on North Korea has reached "pathological" levels was Charles Krauthammer's analysis: "Cannot these senior officials finally understand that Kim is determined to acquire nuclear weapons?" He ended on a portentous note, "We now enter the time that always follows appeasement: the time of acute danger." The headline said it all: "Get Ready for War."[159] Even the usually restrained *New York Times* lost it momentarily: "Enough is enough.

North Korea has responded to the United States' patient and hopeful diplomacy with recalcitrance and provocative nuclear maneuvering." It warned that "the Clinton Administration and its South Korean allies will be under enormous pressure to impose sanctions, even if that leads the North to bar inspectors and make more bombs."[160]

Obscured in the ensuing uproar was the fact that I.A.E.A. inspectors could still witness the defueling, impeding diversion of the fuel rods to bomb-making, and that Washington was again letting the preoccupation with North Korea's nuclear past take precedence over concern about its nuclear future. President Clinton told a June 2 press conference in Rome, "If the I.A.E.A. certifies that the chain of proof is broken, that they cannot establish what has happened, then the question of sanctions will have to be moved to the U.N. Security Council."[161] In a statement released a few hours later in New York, where it was sure to get attention, the I.A.E.A. asserted that Pyongyang "has now made it impossible to select fuel rods for later measurements which would show whether there has been any diversion of fuel in past years."[162]

The North's nuclear history was not in fact irretrievable. An American technical team went to Vienna to show the I.A.E.A. ways to retrieve it. One way was to assay the twenty-one damaged fuel rods that the North had previously removed from the reactor. "We were fairly sure of the discharge dates because inspectors had come before and after and because two of them were discharged while inspectors were present," says a technically informed Pentagon official. Another way was to analyze a larger sample of fuel rods than the structured sample the I.A.E.A. had hoped to draw. "If you have all of the rods, it is much more time-consuming, much more expensive and less accurate. But can you tell the difference between scenario A and scenario B? Yes." There are still other ways but the I.A.E.A. did not want to try them. "It's like trying to get a conviction in a court of law under a new legal theory. You don't like to resort to that."[163] In a June 2 report to the U.N. Secretary-General, Blix acknowledged as much. "The agency has concluded that the limited opportunity which had remained for it to select, segregate, and secure fuel rods for later measurements *in accordance with agency standards* has been lost," he wrote. "Accordingly, the agency's ability to ascertain, *with sufficient confidence*, whether nuclear material from the reactor has been diverted in the past has also been lost."[164] But he hinted at other ways to get at the past: "For the agency to be able to verify non-diversion, it is essential for the agency to have access to all safeguards relevant information and locations. To achieve that, a paramount requirement is the full cooperation of the D.P.R.K."[165]

North Korea was trying to appear cooperative, but, as usual, on its own terms. A D.P.R.K. diplomat in Vienna said that the fuel rods were being put in the cooling ponds "after writing the location and serial numbers on the rods, with monitoring cameras operating."[166] A Foreign Ministry spokesman claimed that "the refueling is taking place in such a manner as to fully preserve the technical possibility of measuring the fuel rods at a later date as requested by the I.A.E.A. when our unique status comes to an end." The spokesman added that "it will be possible to reconstruct the channels and positions of any fuel rods and measure them correctly in the future."[167]

On June 3 Ambassador Gallucci outlined three ways to get at what had happened in 1989, 1990, and 1991: "One way is by additional information that could be provided by the D.P.R.K. A second way is by special inspection at the radioactive waste sites and by sampling. And a third way was to reconstruct the reactor operating history through nondestructive analysis of fuel when it was discharged from the reactor." It was the I.A.E.A's preferred technique for doing nondestructive analysis that was now precluded. "The overall ability to get at what happened in the past has been," in Gallucci's carefully chosen words, "seriously eroded. That does not mean destroyed."[168] By then, however, says a Pentagon official, the issue "had become so political because we had told North Korea that a condition of continuing the dialogue was that the I.A.E.A. had to be satisfied."[169] In an effort to avoid undercutting the I.A.E.A., the United States was allowing itself to become hostage to it.

Once again, the I.A.E.A. had tried to get its way with North Korea. Once again, its way was not the only way. Once again, its way, the crime-and-punishment approach, had reached a dead end.

On June 9 Gallucci testified that the administration had yet to obtain agreement on sanctions. China was still openly opposed: "At this time we do not favor the resort to means that might sharpen the confrontation," said a Foreign Ministry spokesman.[170] Privately Beijing had been trying to encourage Pyongyang to resume dialogue by displaying the benefits of defense conversion and by offering reassurances, including a reaffirmation of their mutual security pact.[171] That week President Jiang Zemin played host to a high-level North Korean military delegation headed by Army Chief of Staff Choe Kwang. Jiang used the occasion to reaffirm China's alliance with North Korea: "China and Korea are friendly neighbors, as closely related as lips and teeth."[172]

To get around a possible Chinese veto, the United States in consultations with Japan and South Korea broached the idea of imposing economic sanctions without Security Council endorsement. Both were ready to go along with the first phase of sanctions, but they were unenthusiastic about going ahead without Security Council approval.[173]

Japan had taken steps to impede remittances to North Korea, despite opposition to sanctions by the Social Democratic Party, a partner in the ruling coalition.[174] Japan's representative, Shunji Yanai, told a reporter, "The United States wants to apply sanctions faster than we do."[175] After the three issued a joint statement that the United Nations should "urgently consider an appropriate response, including sanctions," President Clinton did not sound too eager to impose them, either: "There's still time for North Korea to avoid sanctions actually taking effect if we can work out something on the nuclear inspectors."[176] The sanctions strategy did gain some ground in Moscow, which dropped its opposition— but only after Washington dropped its opposition to a Russian proposal for an international conference on North Korea prior to the imposition of sanctions.[177] Officials used talk of economic sanctions to put pressure on Pyongyang, but with insufficient backing, the administration decided to opt for political pressure, while postponing economic sanctions.[178]

On June 10 the I.A.E.A. suspended technical assistance to North Korea. China's Foreign Minister Qian Qichen expressed regret, saying sanctions will be "ineffective," and appealed for the resumption of dialogue. Pyongyang reacted by notifying Washington of its intent to withdraw from the I.A.E.A. That was not the same as withdrawing from the Nonproliferation Treaty, which would have crossed one of the red lines drawn by the United States. On June 13 a Foreign Ministry spokesman declared that "the inspections for the continuity of safeguards, which we have allowed in our unique status, will no longer be allowed. Any unreasonable inspections can never be allowed until it has been decided whether we should return to the nuclear Nonproliferation Treaty or completely withdraw from it." The spokesman "strongly reaffirmed our position that the U.N. sanctions will be regarded immediately as a declaration of war." A declaration of war was not the same as the start of hostilities, but it did portend an end to talks: "Sanctions and dialogue are incompatible. It is our inevitable option to counter expanded sanctions by hostile forces with expanded self-defense measures."[179]

The risks of the crime-and-punishment approach were becoming apparent. At a meeting in Hawaii with U.S. ambassadors in the Asian and Pacific region convened by Assistant Secretary of State Lord, Ambassador Laney issued a stern warning. "I told them we were on the road to war," he recalls. "It stunned a lot of people and got Lord's attention."[180] President Clinton was also having his doubts. One senior administration official is emphatic: "I can tell you with 1,000 percent confidence, the president was not eager for sanctions."[181] On June 4 Clinton sought to calm things down, "I don't want a lot of saber rattling over this, or war talk. This is peace talk."[182]

Ignoring his injunction, the news media exploded with war talk and demands from the hawks that Clinton himself engage in it.[183] "War—conventional sooner or nuclear later—is topic A," wrote columnist William Safire on June 9. "Let's hear from him now, in prime time and sober detail from the Oval Office, about our risk and his resolve." He dismissed peace talk out of hand, "Anyone who still thinks Kim Il Sung is not trying to become a nuclear power is a fool."[184]

The administration itself was doing its share of war talk. In an unusually explicit reference, Assistant Secretary of Defense Carter said in a speech on June 10 that the United States was "significantly increasing our intelligence assets" in Korea and studying "scenarios" in which North Korea might use nuclear and other forces if confrontation led to war.[185] President Clinton scheduled a meeting with his principal foreign policy advisers to set sanctions strategy and take military precautions in the event of hostilities.

Loose talk of war and calls for substantial reinforcements in Washington aroused the concern of General Luck and Ambassador Laney in Seoul. They met over breakfast once a week and came to trust one another. "It was probably the closest relationship between a military commander and an ambassador that ever happened," says a high-ranking officer who was privy to the conversations. "We were all worried. We were talking about evacuating all civilians, ratcheting it up, going on a wartime footing."[186] American precautions could trigger North Korean preemption. A large-scale American buildup in Korea, given Pyongyang's paranoia, could be misread as a signal that war was imminent, prompting an attack by the North before the American troops could arrive. "We both agreed," recalls Laney, "that if we started to bring in several divisions, the North Koreans would think they were about to be attacked." Deterring North Korea was not the problem in Laney's view. "If one side is weaker and thinks the other side is building up, they would be tempted to preempt." He and Luck both favored a diplomatic deal with North Korea to avert a war. "Why are we going to risk killing a million people? A bomb or two can't even do that."[187]

Laney and Luck were not alone in their concern that precautions might prove provocative. Charles Kartman, the deputy chief of mission, met every week over lunch with Luck's chief of staff. The reinforcement decision, he recalls, was "Washington-generated." To Washington it may have looked like a response to threats by the North Koreans: "Their intent was to make you believe that the decision for sanctions was a decision for war." Yet American officials in Seoul feared that reinforcements could set off an action-reaction cycle. "There is no question," recalls Kartman, "that in the summer of 1994 we were headed toward a substantially increased possibility of war."[188]

With Washington on the verge of dispatching reinforcements, there were signs of panic in Seoul. The South Korean stock market plummeted and shoppers emptied store shelves of provisions. As one State Department official remarked shortly thereafter, "This is what it looks like when two countries blunder into war."[189]

5

DEADLOCK

One good turn deserves another.
(*Petronius*, Satyricon)

AT ANY TIME from 1992 on, North Korea could have shut down its nuclear reactor at Yongbyon, removed spent fuel rods, and reprocessed them, extracting plutonium to make five or six nuclear weapons. It did not. For a country supposedly hell-bent on bomb-making, its self-restraint seems difficult to explain. North Korea's actions, instead, could be seen as signs that it was trying to trade in its nuclear weapons program for what it may have thought it needed more—security assurances and political economic ties to the United States.

Yet for three years, the United States could not bring itself to engage in sustained diplomatic give-and-take with North Korea. It first insisted that North Korea comply with the I.A.E.A. as a precondition for talks, then entered into talks with extreme reluctance. Even when it engaged in negotiations, it was unwilling to specify what it would give North Korea in return for abandoning nuclear-arming. When it did make commitments, they were not always kept, often because the United States was dependent on others to fulfill them.

South Korea was one cause of the unkept promises. Unable to manage its domestic politics, the government vacillated between cooperation and hostility. Whenever U.S.-D.P.R.K. talks were on the verge of breaking down, Seoul tried to supply the lubricant to keep them going. Whenever they lurched ahead, Seoul applied the brakes, leading Washington to renege on pledges to Pyongyang.

The I.A.E.A. was another cause of the reneging. It acted like a prosecutor carrying out the law. It was dissatisfied with anything less than full and prompt compliance with the safeguards agreement, even when Washington was prepared to settle for less in order to prevent Pyongyang from nuclear-arming.

There was a discernible pattern to North Korea's responses, had anyone cared to look closely:

When Washington unilaterally offered nuclear assurances, Pyongyang reciprocated in December 1991 by signing a denuclearization accord with

Seoul and a safeguards agreement with the I.A.E.A. It halted reprocessing and delayed removing spent nuclear fuel from its reactor.

When Washington refused to engage in high-level talks after January 1992, Pyongyang was slow to let its safeguards agreement come into force.

After Washington ignored Pyongyang's proposal for replacement reactors in June 1992 and instead resumed Team Spirit in March 1993, and the I.A.E.A. demanded special inspections, Pyongyang announced its intent to renounce the Nonproliferation Treaty and reneged on inspections.

When Washington agreed to resume high-level talks and pledged in principle to refrain from nuclear threats and respect North Korean sovereignty in June 1993, Pyongyang agreed to suspend its withdrawal from the Nonproliferation Treaty and resume nuclear inspections.

When the I.A.E.A. insisted on full access for its inspectors and Washington refused to offer anything in return from mid-1993 on, Pyongyang confined the inspectors to monitoring that no diversion of spent fuel or further reprocessing was taking place.

In December 1993 Washington accepted a package deal in principle but not in practice. When Seoul did not suspend Team Spirit and put preconditions on North-South talks in March 1994, Pyongyang again impeded the inspectors' access.

When Washington tried to threaten sanctions in order to widen access for the I.A.E.A. in May 1994, Pyongyang began refueling its reactor without allowing the I.A.E.A. to set aside a sample of spent fuel rods.

Pyongyang, in short, appears to have been playing **tit-for-tat** in nuclear diplomacy. Washington did not seem to notice.

Just in case its behavior was misunderstood, Pyongyang repeatedly made its tit-for-tat strategy clear in its statements. "It is the disposition and will of our people and army," it declared in a typical example, "to answer dialogue with dialogue and strength with strength."[1] In October 1993 a senior North Korean official warned that in the event of sanctions, the D.P.R.K. would follow the practice of a "slap for a slap."[2] When the South Korean representative to the North-South talks threatened to seek sanctions against North Korea in March 1994, his Northern counterpart responded angrily, "We are ready to respond with an eye for an eye and a war for a war."[3] On June 3, 1994, a senior North Korean representative in New York privately warned that it would respond in kind to sanctions. For example, a ban on noncommercial flights or technical assistance might lead to a denunciation in North Korea media, controls on remittances from Japan could prompt North

Korean withdrawal from the N.P.T., and a full-scale embargo on North Korean trade "would provoke war."[4] A senior North Korean officially put it more positively in May 1993 when he urged the resumption of high-level talks: "Koreans have a saying, 'Sword to sword, ricecake to ricecake.' It is time to throw away the sword and hold up the ricecake."[5]

The tit-for-tat pattern is significant. In his path-breaking work, *The Evolution of Cooperation*, Robert Axelrod demonstrates experimentally how cooperation can emerge from conflict between distrustful adversaries by following a tit-for-tat strategy. If one side begins by cooperating and then responds tit-for-tat—reciprocates if the other side cooperates and retaliates if the other side reneges—a relationship of cooperation can evolve.[6]

Cooperation is more likely, Axelrod noted, if the two sides recognize that their decisions are interdependent, if they can each observe the other and react in a timely way and if they focus on long-run interests, not momentary advantage.

Domestic politics in the United States, as well as in South Korea and Japan, made all those conditions less likely to be satisfied. Preoccupation with the home front distracted their attention from dealings abroad. It overwhelmed officials with noise from nearby, blurring signals from overseas. It interfered with prompt and sensitive responsiveness. It fostered a short-run perspective—the next news cycle, the weekend talk shows, the latest poll results.

Outside the government, members of the American foreign policy establishment paid little attention to North Korea's moves to accommodate. Those who relied on the American press were misled because, as chapter 8 will show, conciliatory North Korean statements and actions went virtually unreported.

Shared images of nuclear diplomacy also interfered with careful observation of North Korea. Pyongyang's bizarre bargaining behavior only seemed to confirm believers' worst fears. The dominant interpretation in the U.S. intelligence community was that North Korea was engaged in delay and deception, or else that its actions were ad hoc with little discernible pattern. A handful of U.S. officials, however, did begin to see a method in North Korea's madness. They interpreted its halt in reprocessing and its delay in removing spent fuel as signs of seriousness about negotiating.

Whatever its internal divisions, North Korea played the game with greater internal coherence than did the United States, according to one U.S. official. "They had the advantage of focusing their best talent on *the* central foreign policy issue for them," he says. "We were divided all over the place."[7] While there is a temptation to overestimate the coherence and consistency of other states, in this case there are grounds for accepting his conclusion.

Domestic political pressures kept pushing the Bush and Clinton Administrations toward coercing North Korea instead of cooperating with it. The pressures were generated by hawkish members of Congress and the foreign policy establishment who believed that the only way to assure a nuclear-free North Korea was to topple the communist regime there, even at the risk of war.

Yet the most striking feature of the political landscape was the coolness toward cooperation among non-hawks. Diplomacy had few defenders. One reason was the pervasive skepticism about the prospects for a deal, grounded in widely shared images within the foreign policy establishment that North Korea was a rogue state determined to nuclear arm, that it could not be induced to stop, and that coercion, not cooperation, was the only way to prevent proliferation. These shared images of nuclear diplomacy shaped the mind-set of American officials, blinding them to the tit-for-tat pattern in North Korea's bargaining behavior.

Perhaps the most telling comments came from *Washington Post* columnist Jim Hoagland, a centrist. He saw "little to admire or like" in the administration's effort to buy off North Korea. His reason?

> Real presidents don't coax. Real presidents lead, squeeze, intimidate or persuade. If none of those tactics works, real presidents zap their enemies with the C.I.A. or the 82nd Airborne. That constantly implied threat made American diplomacy far more brilliant and productive throughout the Cold War than would have otherwise been the case. But that is not credible under this president, who has made clear his deep aversion to using force abroad. . . . To blame the president alone, as some of his critics do, is to compound the problem. Americans need to reflect on the costs of the retreat from global leadership that many now advocate, and not take themselves off the hook by blaming everything on Bill Clinton's character.[8]

The idea that an American president could also demonstrate leadership, as presidents did throughout the Cold War, by making and keeping promises and avoiding needless wars, seems never to have occurred to many in the foreign policy establishment.

The result was deadlock, and a growing danger that confrontation could spin out of control. As domestic politics continued to paralyze diplomacy, a handful of nongovernmental actors stepped in to try to save the Clinton Administration from itself.

PART II

COOPERATION SUCCEEDS

6

OPEN COVENANTS, PRIVATELY ARRIVED AT

> As a permanent structure with a system of rational rules,
> bureaucracy is fashioned to meet calculated and recurrent
> needs by means of a normal routine. . . . Charisma knows
> only inner determination and inner restraint. The holder of
> charisma seizes the task that is adequate for him and demands
> obedience and a following by virtue of his mission. His
> success determines whether he finds them.
> *(Max Weber)*[1]

JIMMY CARTER and Tony Namkung make the most unlikely of partners. Carter, nuclear engineer and Navy submariner, peanut farmer and born-again Christian from Plains, Georgia, catapulted from the governorship to the presidency. Since leaving the White House, he has become an earnest missionary for nonviolence, election monitor, and emissary at large—talking peace and preaching reconciliation from Ethiopia to Nicaragua and staking his personal prestige on getting results. Namkung, born in Shanghai and schooled in Tokyo with the children of U.S. occupation troops, is an American citizen and a Korean patriot. Like many Koreans of his generation, he has kin on both sides of the 38th Parallel. Also like many prominent Koreans of his generation, he attended university in the United States. Unlike them, he stayed on. By emigrating, he avoided swearing allegiance to one side or the other of Korea's ideological divide. He remains, like his forebears, an independent Korean nationalist.

Carter and Namkung, with the help of a handful of foundation officers, ex-officials, and nongovernmental organizations, kept nuclear diplomacy with North Korea from derailing and stopped the United States from plunging into war on the Korean Peninsula.

When Jimmy Carter left for Pyongyang on June 12, 1994, talks with North Korea had broken off. The International Atomic Energy Agency, unable to get North Korea to comply fully with the Nonproliferation Treaty, had referred the matter to the U.N. Security Council, where the United States was trying, without success, to get China's support for sanctions against North Korea. Pyongyang had repeatedly denounced sanctions as "a declaration of war." It had just announced the expulsion of the I.A.E.A. inspectors who were monitoring the Yongbyon reactor to prevent the diversion of spent fuel for the production of bombs. As a precaution in the event that sanctions were imposed, the Clinton Administration was on the verge of dispatching reinforcements to Korea, a fateful step that the American commander there believed could provoke a war.

Carter returned to the United States with Kim Il Sung's personal pledge to freeze North Korea's nuclear program, allowing the inspectors to remain in place and monitor compliance, and to discuss dismantlement of its reactors and reprocessing plant in high-level talks with the United States.

Some government officials minimize the significance of the Carter mission, insisting it yielded nothing new. The real breakthrough came, they say, only after Carter's return when U.S. negotiator Robert Gallucci spelled out the terms of the freeze in a letter to Vice Minister Kang and Kang confirmed them. There is something to this argument, but not much. It depends on whether sanctions and the military precautions that accompanied them would have provoked war and whether Carter, by spurning the sanctions strategy and committing Kim Il Sung himself to freeze North Korea's nuclear program, kept the crisis from spiraling out of control. "If Jimmy Carter had not gone to North Korea," says a State Department official, "we would have been damned close to war."[2] Stopping sanctions was essential to delaying the dispatch of reinforcements. "The Joint Chiefs of Staff were operating on the assumption that the North Koreans would take sanctions as an act of war and therefore if we were going to sanctions we had to be prepared for immediate war," says Thomas Hubbard. "It was very dangerous and Carter headed it off." Yet he, like others, does not credit Carter personally. "If Carter hadn't gone, someone else would have."[3] Another diplomat who dealt directly with Carter disagrees. In his view, no one else could have done what Carter did: "A perfectly free man, a perfectly determined man is a fearsome thing, and that is what I saw in Carter. His way of operating was very different from what anyone else's could have been. You needed a bold outsider, an ex-President who lacked fear, was beholden to nobody, and had nothing to worry about except history."[4]

The difference in judgment hinges on whether anyone else would have had the will and ability to repudiate the sanctions strategy publicly. Once Carter did that, Security Council support evaporated. Although the Clinton Administration pressed on with its campaign for sanctions, countries that had previously been unenthusiastic about coercive diplomacy were now firmly committed to temporizing. That allowed diplomatic give-and-take to resume.

Of course, Carter could not have succeeded without the tacit encouragement of some American officials and the grudging tolerance of others. Yet the Carter initiative was the turning point in nuclear diplomacy with North Korea. That is testament to just how paralyzed by domestic divisions, just how prone to coercion, and just how incapable of cooperating with other nations the United States had become.

That private citizens could make national security policy on their own is rare enough. That they could overturn existing policy and accomplish what the government could not is virtually unprecedented in recent years. The Carter mission was a triumph of Track II diplomacy.

Others had a much less charitable view. Indeed, it is remarkable how little support Carter received at the time. The initial reaction of some senior Clinton Administration officials was outrage that Carter had renounced the sanctions effort and had relegated them to the sidelines while he undid American policy in talks with North Korea's Great Leader. "We look forward to his reentry to this planet," said one State Department official, "so he can sit down and tell what actually did happen." Other officials cast Carter as a dupe of Kim Il Sung. "We are dealing with a guy who is capable of the big lie," said one, "and it's possible he just took in a former president of the United States as his stooge."[5]

That was temperate compared to what critics of the administration had to say. The hawks' anger was understandable. Their strategy for stopping proliferation in North Korea, the crime-and-punishment approach, after repeated failure, was publicly undercut by Carter. Worse yet, their central contention, North Korea had to be compelled to comply by imposing stringent economic sanctions, or else be disarmed by air strikes and war, was refuted. After sanctions were repudiated by Carter and the Clinton Administration publicly backed away from air strikes, Carter still won Kim Il Sung's commitment to freeze his nuclear arms program. The freezing and eventual dismantling of that program was formalized in the Agreed Framework of October 1994, which, if fully implemented, will lead to a non-nuclear North Korea. Cooperation succeeded where coercion had failed.

How that came about is, in critical respects, a story of private covenants privately arrived at—and then formally acknowledged in diplomatic channels.

Private Contacts with Pyongyang

With the easing of the ban on travel in 1988, Americans began visiting North Korea in larger numbers and a few North Koreans attended conferences in the United States. They served as extra-governmental channels of communication between Washington and Pyongyang, and between Seoul and Pyongyang. While these exchanges were examples of Track II diplomacy, broadly construed, they had little direct effect on

the policies of any of those governments. Insofar as they had any discernible influence, it was to inform a wider group of experts in the
United States and in North and South Korea who interacted with policy-makers. By funding these early efforts, the foundations made it politically easier for program officers in other foundations to pick up where
they had left off.

While Pyongyang was being very selective about whom it talked to, it
was careful to choose people from across the American political spectrum, a sign of its sophistication. In 1989 Robert Scalapino and Gaston
Sigur were each invited to Pyongyang. John Lewis of Stanford University hosted meetings of North Korean, American, and South Korean
officials in July 1990 and in December 1991. In November 1991 a delegation put together by the Social Science Research Council and the
American Council of Learned Societies went to Pyongyang. The following year North Korea hosted a delegation from the American Freedom
Coalition that included Douglas MacArthur II.

By 1992 contacts were multiplying. In March the Reverend Billy Graham visited Pyongyang. In May the Institute for Global Conflict and
Cooperation at the University of California at San Diego hosted a conference addressed by Ambassador Ho Jong, a D.P.R.K. delegate at the
United Nations. Staff members of the Carter Center went to Pyongyang
in July.

Perhaps the most frequent visitor to North Korea from the United
States was Stephen Linton, a research associate at the Center for Korean
Research of Columbia University and a descendant of three generations
of American missionaries in Korea. He accompanied Reverend Billy
Graham on his visits. The most noteworthy of these came on January
26, 1994, the day after the Pentagon disclosed its willingness to send
Patriot antimissile batteries to Korea. Reverend Graham arrived in
Pyongyang with a letter from President Clinton to President Kim, the
first ever from an American chief executive to his North Korean counterpart. All it said was "the President sends his personal regards."[6] It was an
attempt to reach out to the North Koreans and "offer them a sense that
we were taking them seriously," says a top official. "The medium was the
message."[7] Yet the message was not well received despite Graham's best
efforts. The letter did little to establish personal rapport—sincerity, in
Korean terms—between the two top leaders, which can be decisive in
dealing with North Koreans.[8] Graham had also been fully briefed on administration policies and tried to cast them in a favorable light, but he
had nothing specific to offer. "I stressed that he was speaking with the
president's knowledge and approval," says the top official, "but that this
was not a negotiating medium." American officials were disinclined to
try Track II channels while diplomatic channels remained open.[9]

Another frequent visitor was Selig Harrison of the Carnegie Endowment for International Peace, who first went to Pyongyang as a journalist in 1972 when North Korea was seeking engagement with the United States. He was granted an interview by Kim Il Sung, to promote a new North Korean conventional arms control initiative. Harrison went to the North again in 1987 and 1992. In late May 1989 he hosted a five-man North Korean delegation at a conference at the Carnegie Endowment in Washington. Harrison was one of the earliest public proponents of what would later become the essence of the package deal, that the nuclear issue was "inseparable from the broader problem of normalizing its relations with the Kim Il Sung regime" and could not be settled on its own. He also made the critical link between the North's willingness to give up nuclear-arming and its survival: "The South should recognize that the nuclear issue is not likely to be settled in the absence of meaningful and continuing steps to reassure Pyongyang that it is not seeking a German-style unification-by-absorption." He urged the United States to spell out what economic and political rewards North Korea could expect for abandoning nuclear-arming. Yet he thought the North would demand more than the United States was prepared to give for renouncing its nuclear option: he repeatedly said that it would not "accept an airtight inspection regime" without "the removal of the nuclear umbrella."[10]

Harrison went to Pyongyang April 28–May 4, 1992, with a Carnegie Endowment Study Group that also included General Edward C. Meyer, James Leonard, and Leonard Spector. In a stop in Seoul en route, they met with Kim Yoon Ho, who had served as chairman of the South Korean Joint Chiefs of Staff in 1983. Over lunch Kim suggested that the United States "sell" light-water reactors to the North. In Pyongyang, Harrison asked Choe Jong Sun, Director of the Foreign Affairs Bureau of the Ministry of Atomic Energy, "whether they would be interested in buying light-water reactors." Harrison recalls Choe's response, "'Yes, very interested.'"[11] Less than two weeks later, Choe broached the idea of obtaining light-water reactors with I.A.E.A. Director-General Hans Blix. Buying them was not quite what Choe had in mind.

In talks with North Korean representatives at the United Nations starting in October 1993, Harrison tried to persuade them to freeze their nuclear program in order to open the way for a comprehensive settlement of the issue. The North Koreans insisted that the freeze would have to come after the replacement reactors were in operation. Harrison also tried to get an invitation to see Kim Il Sung. He made little headway on either front until May 1994, when he was suddenly invited to Pyongyang June 4–11. When he met with Kim Il Sung, he proposed a package deal: a ban on reprocessing, a halt in construction of two new reactors, and no refueling of the reactor at Yongbyon. Kim looked "somewhat interested" but "not prepared," recalls Harrison, and turned to negotiator Kang Sok Ju for a six- or seven-minute conversation. He then replied, "Such a freeze is possible and would be the best way to allay your concerns and proceed to friendly relations."[12] He stressed the need to make any commitment to supply replacement reactors "completely binding on you." He then suggested that Russia might supply the reactors, noting that Gorbachev had reneged on their previous reactor deal. Harrison held a news conference when he reached Beijing to relate Kim's comments. He got some press attention, but the news was lost in the noise of intensifying confrontation and became a footnote to Carter's intervention.

To government Korea-watchers and policy-makers, the information gathered through Track II diplomacy was "one more data point," according to a sympathetic INR analyst. "Much of it didn't prove out. A lot of it was garbled. It was nice to have, but it was rarely very different from what we received elsewhere or had gleaned ourselves." Officials had some grounds for skepticism, he adds. "The history of Track II information is at best spotty. Don't forget, we've been dealing with a lot of people over the years and many of them, unfortunately, don't build confidence in this sort of channel."[13] Charles Kartman, director of Korean affairs in the State Department from 1991 until the summer of 1993, says, "We were trying to figure out what the North Koreans were about. There were some people available who had insights into North Korea of unproven value." From the insights of Tony Namkung, Alan Romberg, and Selig Harrison, "we came up with the idea of high-level talks."[14]

Some government officials resent the intrusion of outsiders into foreign policy-making. More than professional jealousy or the prerogative of office is at issue. Officials often look upon outsiders as sources of political pressure rather than as helpful informants and intermediaries. Knowledge, after all, is power. Outsiders often have a desire to demonstrate influence, intense policy preferences, and a tendency to hear what they want to hear from foreigners. Officials, who typically have access to a wide range of information sources on other countries, worry that outsiders may all too willingly let themselves be used by foreign governments, who can disown an unofficial contact more readily than they can an official one. For these reasons, officials may be all too ready to discount or discredit nongovernmental sources of information, especially when it is discrepant with their own.

Still, there is much to be gained from nongovernmental approaches. Outsiders may feel freer to speak their minds to foreigners and probe more deeply than officials can. Officials act under instruction, which keeps them on a short leash. They are also wary, knowing that a probe may reveal as much as it gathers. In cases where U.S. intelligence is limited, Track II diplomacy can open a window onto a closed society. Yet the enormous uncertainty about North Korea and controlled nature of the nongovernmental contact with North Koreans, as well as the strength of shared images held by American officials, minimized the impact of nongovernmental informants.

The increasing contact with North Korean officials informed a small but widening circle of Americans about the North's views on the nuclear question and related issues. It also informed the North Koreans. Yet none of these interactions had much of a demonstrable effect on the policies of the governments involved. That more significant form of Track II diplomacy was yet to come.

Pyongyang Reaches Out

No American spent more time talking to North Koreans than K. A. ("Tony") Namkung. He was born Namkung Kun in Shanghai, the scion of a prominent Korean family whose history mirrors that nation's troubled last century. In the 1910s his great-grandfather edited Seoul's first pro-independence newspaper, whose attacks on Japan's annexation of Korea still resonate today in Korean demands for Japanese reparations. His grandfather, Namkung Hyuk, was educated at Princeton and Union Theological Seminary in the early 1920s and became a leading theologian, translating the Bible into Korean and founding a missionary school that educated, among others, Kim Il Sung's father. Growing up in a compound with Christian missionaries from abroad and exposed to the swirling intellectual currents of the times, three of his children, Tony's uncles, embraced communism in the 1920s, three became staunch anti-communists, and three, including Tony's father, remained independent, democratic-minded nationalists. During the late 1930s, Tony's grandfather joined Korea's government-in-exile in Shanghai. He returned home in 1949 to become secretary-general of the South Korean Council of Churches and an opponent of the Syngman Rhee dictatorship. When the Korean War broke out, he was seized by invading North Korean troops along with other South Korean religious leaders and taken north, where he may have been tortured and killed. When Tony asked North Korean officials for an account of his grandfather's death, they said he was killed by an allied air attack.

Instead of returning to Korea when the communists seized power in China in 1949, Tony's father took his family to Hong Kong. When Hong Kong seemed on the verge of being overrun, they fled to Tokyo, where, thanks to the intervention of John Foster Dulles, a roommate of Namkung's grandfather at Princeton, they were housed in the American compound on Pershing Heights. Tony—his older sister thought he needed to sound American and named him after movie star Anthony Quinn—attended American schools in Tokyo. Later, along with South Korea's Deputy Prime Minister Lee Hong Koo and former Foreign Minister Han Sung Joo, Namkung went to the United States for his higher education. Fluent in English, Chinese, Japanese, and Korean, he got a doctorate in history at Berkeley, where he caught the eye of Robert Scalapino who appointed him his deputy at the Institute of East Asian Studies there. Namkung subsequently spent three years as a visiting scholar in Seoul. After running a consulting firm on U.S.–South Korean trade, he served for three years at the Asia Society as executive director for education and contemporary affairs. As an adviser to a Wall Street law firm, Shearman and Sterling, he helped draft North Korea's regulations on joint ventures. He now heads the Project on the United States and East Asia at the Atlantic Council.

Namkung was first approached by Ambassador Ho Jong, then permanent observer to the United Nations, shortly after the North Korean arrived in New York in fall 1989. Ho was determined to cultivate American contacts. That is what any sophisticated diplomat does, but it was especially important in North Korea's case, given its long isolation and limited understanding of the United States. Ho got in touch with Namkung at the Asia Society after watching him interviewed on CNN. They met over a hundred times, usually at Ho's initiative, often on weekends in casual dress, almost always with a junior North Korean diplomat present. Namkung initially deflected questions about nuclear and other relations with North Korea and mostly discussed personal matters.

Their conversations led to an invitation to visit Pyongyang in December 1990. North Korea was beginning to reach out to Americans and Namkung was one of the first. The ostensible purpose was to prepare for an Asia Society study mission to Pyongyang that May and for North Korean participation in a conference in Washington that September. His conversations suggest that the North Koreans had something more in mind. His principal interlocutors were Li Hyong Chol and Kim Byong Hong, respectively director and deputy director of the Institute of Disarmament and Peace, an arm of the Foreign Ministry. He also met informally with the director-general of the Ministry's newly established Bureau of American and Japanese Affairs, Song Rak Un.

Namkung was told that North Korea had just made three major policy decisions, which, if true, would have marked a fundamental turnabout for the autarkic communist regime. One was to normalize relations with longtime foes, the United States and Japan. A second was to seek peaceful coexistence, as distinct from unification, with South Korea. The third was to introduce market reforms. A leadership fearful of imminent collapse might have been more defensive and less willing to open up North Korea's nuclear facilities or its economic and political system to outsiders. What struck Namkung was the confidence of the North Koreans that these changes would "demonstrate the superiority of their *juche*-based system of self-reliance," not undermine it.[15]

Three policy implications flowed from the North Korean decisions, Namkung was told. First, Pyongyang expected Washington to establish ties, to encourage Japan to engage in dialogue with North Korea, and to play "a coordinating role" in improving North-South relations. To allay American concern that North Korea was trying to "drive a wedge" between the United States and South Korea, his interlocutors took the line that "you are free to nurture South Korea if you wish, but you should understand that South Korea is not the whole Korea." Second, they blamed Washington's so-called "five-point policy" for impeding direct dialogue by imposing five preconditions for talks, but said they were encouraged that October when Assistant Secretary of State Richard Solomon had dropped all but one, acceptance of I.A.E.A. safeguards on its nuclear facilities. They urged that diplomats from the United States and the D.P.R.K. sit down face to face and try to understand each other. Otherwise, it would be impossible to move ahead on nuclear safeguards. Third, they felt disarmament and relaxation of tensions should proceed in tandem with economic cooperation. They promised concrete proposals by the Asia Society's visit in May. The optimism in Pyongyang was palpable, says Namkung. The North Koreans were convinced that people-to-people diplomacy would persuade the United States to deal.[16]

A year later, in late May 1992, Namkung visited Pyongyang again, this time alone, to prepare for a second Asia Society mission to North Korea. It was four months after the first round of high-level talks and just after the I.A.E.A.'s first visit to Yongbyon. The North Koreans wanted the United States to upgrade talks. Why, they complained, did it just rely on the Beijing channel? He also learned of North Korea's interest in developing non-nuclear energy resources as a quid pro quo for stopping its bomb program. He was told of possible joint ventures with Bechtel, General Electric, and Westinghouse. En route home, he reported this interest to a commercial attache in the U.S. embassy in Beijing, who was not impressed.[17]

When Namkung accompanied the Asia Society study group to Pyongyang in October 1992, his fourth visit there, the optimism of a year ago had evaporated. The North Koreans, says Namkung, were shocked that some American visitors, like Robert Scalapino, left Pyongyang open to the possibility of dealing with the North but skeptical, while others, like Karen Elliott House of the *Wall Street Journal*, returned home and attacked the idea. That led Pyongyang to a sober reassessment of people-to-people diplomacy and the political prospects of a deal with Washington. High-level talks were moribund, North-South dialogue was falling apart, and Team Spirit was scheduled to resume, turning Pyongyang's pessimism into paranoia.

During the October visit, the North Koreans repeatedly complained to Namkung that the United States was "moving the goalposts" by adding democracy, human rights, and missile sales to its original conditions for upgrading the dialogue with North Korea.[18] One night Namkung watched a three-hour television program featuring officers in the high command who denounced diplomacy as a fraud and warned that Team Spirit was about to resume. Later that evening two of his North Korean interlocutors visited him in his hotel room to underscore the message.

By now Namkung was persuaded that his contacts with the North Koreans were serious because, with one exception, they had made no effort to convert or recruit him. It was quite another matter to persuade distrustful American policy-makers of their seriousness. Indeed, it would take until 1994 for Namkung to gain a personal hearing from any senior U.S. official.

On April 26, 1993, three days after the United States agreed to resume high-level talks, North Korea's senior representative at the United Nations, Kim Jong Su, asked to see Namkung in New York. Namkung passed along four impressions of the meeting to American officials: that nuclear inspections could not be the only issue on the agenda of the talks; that the meeting could not be another one-time affair, like the high-level talks in January 1992, but the first in a series of meetings to improve relations; that the atmospherics would be critical and the dialogue had to be a two-way exchange of views, not simply another occasion for the United States to lecture the D.P.R.K.; and that it was desirable to work out the results of the meeting in advance, either directly or through a third party. The third party the North Koreans had in mind was Namkung.

The Hidden Hand in the First Joint Statement

In late May 1993, just before high-level talks were to resume in New York, Namkung made his fifth visit to Pyongyang. He met with First Vice Foreign Minister Kang Sok Ju and other members of the D.P.R.K. negotiating team as they were about to board a plane for New York. It was then that Namkung had his first detailed discussions with North Korean officials on issues to be addressed in the negotiations. From these

conversations he concluded that Pyongyang intended to redirect attention to the 1991 North-South denuclearization accord and away from
I.A.E.A. inspections. While postponing its withdrawal from the Nonproliferation Treaty and hinting that agreement could be reached with
the I.A.E.A., it would try to delay inspections and hold out for protracted talks with the United States.

Namkung encouraged his North Korean interlocutors to remain partially in the treaty. He also surprised them by urging them to try for a
joint statement with the United States in the coming round of high-level
talks. It was an idea he had gotten from a State Department official.[19]
The North Koreans asked him to suggest communique language that
the United States might find acceptable, and Namkung, drawing on the
wording of the U.N. Charter, jotted down a few broad principles on a
sheet of paper and handed it to the North Koreans. His handwritten
notes read:

> Seek to reach early agreement on broad principles: nuclear-free peninsula,
> coexistence and co-prosperity and reunification, and contribution to peace
> and prosperity of Asia/Pacific region.
> Extract commitment *in principle* to: cancellation of T[eam] S[pirit], nega-
> tive security assurance, inspection of military bases in South, ban on nu-
> clear testing, transfer of technology for peaceful purposes.
> Work towards joint statement embracing broad principles and looking for-
> ward to regular talks at Assistant Secretary level.[20]

In Beijing en route home on June 1, Namkung telexed Charles Kartman, director of Korean affairs at the State Department, that "the
D.P.R.K. has braced itself for imposition of sanctions" and "the mood
in Pyongyang remains defiant and self-righteous." Yet he saw a way out:
"I sensed that if the U.S. were to show them that it regarded the
D.P.R.K. as an equal partner in the talks and that it sought a political
solution to the nuclear issue, they would give in" and remain in the
Nonproliferation Treaty, and agree to special inspections and implementation of the North-South denuclearization accord of December
1991. Based on his conversations in Pyongyang, Namkung sketched out
a comprehensive deal "clearing up suspicions about its nuclear program
in exchange for such concessions as have already appeared in the press—
cancellation of T[eam] S[pirit], inspection of U.S. bases, some kind of
security guarantee, and some kind of statement recognizing the legitimacy of their regime, or their right to exist as a sovereign state."
Namkung now put into U.S. diplomatic channels what he had planted
in Pyongyang: "It is my personal view that the D.P.R.K. may seek to
negotiate a very general joint statement that talks about what both parties agree to, as a way to create the right atmosphere for a deal"—the

principles he had proposed to the North's negotiators. "No one took this [telex] seriously," says Namkung.[21]

Namkung returned to the United States on June 12, 1993, the day after the first U.S.-D.P.R.K. Joint Statement was announced. He picked up a newspaper and found to his amazement that the text repeated verbatim the principles he had suggested to the North Koreans.[22] A member of the U.S. delegation picks up the story:

> There must have been 24 hours of discussion with those guys. They said we don't trust you and you don't trust us. We've got to get something to send back home. What's your bottom line? I said you cannot leave the N.P.T. What do you want? They said, can you give us security assurances and can you give a statement that you will respect our sovereignty and treat us with respect. . . . My response was how in the world can we say we respect each other's sovereignty when you are threatening the world's nonproliferation regime. Ho Jong said we're not asking for anything more than you committed to in the U.N. Charter.[23]

Two years later this official was unaware, as were nearly all his colleagues, that the North Korean draft had come from a private citizen of the United States.

During his May visit Namkung had also transmitted a proposal to the North from an acquaintance of his, South Korea's Deputy Prime Minister for Unification Affairs Han Wan Sang. It suggested a meeting of presidential envoys at the deputy prime minister level, leading to a summit meeting between the two presidents, as a way to circumvent the stalemated prime ministerial talks.[24] The proposal seems to have been Han's own initiative. North Korea announced its acceptance the next day, May 23, 1993, only to have South Korea turn it down.

In the course of the visit the American desk officer at the D.P.R.K. Foreign Ministry, Song Rak Un, took Namkung aside and asked him to serve as a back-channel to the State Department. Namkung parried the request, calling it premature. Yet from that time on, he became a one-way back-channel, passing on reports of his meetings with North Koreans to the Korea desk and the Bureau of Intelligence and Research in the State Department and to the Central Intelligence Agency.

In September 1993, anticipating a breakdown in the high-level talks, North Korean representatives in New York asked Namkung to meet with them every few days. In the course of these conversations he became aware that they were trying to stretch the July 19, 1993, agreed statement to mean that the United States had committed itself to replacement reactors before the third round of talks. They were construing the word *chunje*, translated as "premise" in English, to mean "precondition."[25] He tried to disabuse the North Koreans.

In November 1993 Namkung was handed a proposal by a North Korean representative in New York and instructed to convey it to the State Department as his own idea. To break the deadlock in high-level talks, the North Korean said, the United States should send a special high-level envoy to Pyongyang.[26]

An analyst in INR whom Namkung was informing of his contacts with the North says that while his reports had little effect on their own judgments, they "reinforced our confidence that we were, broadly, on the proper track." It also eased their sense of isolation among Korea-watchers. Namkung's reports might have been news to top policy-makers, had they seen and believed them. "We do have a tendency to deny ourselves potential benefits from Track II," the INR analyst says, "but it is a mistake to say we ignore it."[27] Namkung's reports had no known effect on C.I.A. assessments.

Namkung's Track II diplomacy did have some influence in Pyongyang, where he helped broker the June 1993 Joint Statement by getting the North Koreans to adopt a diplomatic formula that the United States would find acceptable. Track II diplomacy's influence on the American government would have to await Jimmy Carter's involvement.

Two Foundations Try to Jump-Start Diplomacy

The Rockefeller Brothers Fund had provided much of the financial support for Namkung's initial visits to North Korea. With diplomacy deadlocked and the U.S. government unable to agree on a set of inducements to North Korea, program officers George Perkovich at the W. Alton Jones Foundation and Thomas W. Graham at the Rockefeller Foundation picked up where the Rockefeller Brothers Fund left off. Both had worked on nonproliferation, Perkovich on the staff of Senator Joseph Biden (D-DL) and Graham at the Arms Control and Disarmament Agency, and both took a strong personal interest in the issue. In 1993 they began funding small projects designed to lay the intellectual groundwork and improve the political climate for a diplomatic deal with North Korea. From 1991 to 1994, W. Alton Jones spent $998,000 and Rockefeller $700,000 on grants relating to North Korea. That was a sizeable share of their security programs, but a small sum by foundation standards: in 1990 the Rockefeller Foundation made grants of $74.4 million in all. Total foundations grants for international affairs that year totaled $140.4 million, about 28 percent of that for programs on peace, security, and arms control.[28] Substantial sums, including funding from Rockefeller and W. Alton Jones, went to experts who opposed dealing with North Korea.

Most foundations do not act like venture capitalists. They play it safe, avoiding impolitic subjects like North Korea and funding well-established institutions and well-respected experts who did not get their reputations by taking great risks. "Who can quarrel with a $2 million grant to Harvard or Stanford," says one program officer, "even if it plows the same old ground."[29] Graham and Perkovich were exceptions.

They could not have done so without the support of their bosses and boards of directors. Involvement in North Korea was not controversial with the board at W. Alton Jones, says Perkovich. "It was clear that there was potential for proliferation in the region and that it was important to fund people who understood the dynamics and had strategies for dealing with them."[30]

Graham had the firm backing of Peter Goldmark, president of the Rockefeller Foundation. In March 1993, nine months after joining the foundation, Graham proposed a $1 million project on North Korea. Goldmark turned down the proposal on the grounds that not enough was yet known about North Korea to justify such an expenditure, but he endorsed the project in principle. Within three weeks he approved Graham's request for a small grant. Even more important, on April 6, 1993, he approved a letter to Jimmy Carter committing the foundation to pay his expenses for a mission to Pyongyang, should he ever decide to go.

Graham's motives and methods are clear from his private correspondence. He saw a resemblance between the failure of government and academic experts to anticipate or track the collapse of the Soviet Union and what was happening now with North Korea. "The system for collecting and screening information on North Korea (both in government and [the] NGO/press community) was the same that had 'failed' in the past," he wrote on October 27, 1994. "As a result, I was not confident that the U.S. government either had all the right information or was interpreting the information correctly." Graham, who had graduated from Stanford University and gotten his doctorate from M.I.T., felt those who had been more prescient about the Soviet Union "tended to be outside of the Cambridge–Washington–Palo Alto mainstream," where "their ideas were not taken seriously." Graham started looking for the same sort of outsiders and risk-takers "who had traveled to North Korea and who had sustained contact with the D.P.R.K. over several years." He found that "what they were saying was at odds not only with the public debate in the United States but also with the private thinking of many officials in the Executive Branch."[31] Tony Namkung was one such person. Another was Peter Hayes, an Australian-born, American-trained physicist who was studying alternative energy sources in Asia and had written a book on American nuclear forces in Korea.

Hayes, whose work had been supported by the W. Alton Jones Foundation, was Graham's first grantee on North Korea. He gave Graham the idea of trying to involve Jimmy Carter in Track II diplomacy with North Korea. Hayes had first visited Pyongyang in late September 1991, arriving the day President Bush announced the withdrawal of U.S. nuclear arms from South Korea. He met with a number of North Korean officials including Kim Yong Sun, Undersecretary of State Kanter's interlocutor at the January 1992 high-level talks. The North "welcomed" the Bush announcement, according to Kim, the first time it had ever welcomed an American initiative. If the arms were withdrawn, he added, the signing of the safeguards accord would follow "automatically."[32] Hayes was able to provide the North Koreans with details of the withdrawal, including the fact that all the warheads would be withdrawn and that a leak to the press to the contrary was false. He also tried to disabuse them of their inflated estimate of American nuclear warheads in the South. On his return to Seoul Hayes briefed American embassy and South Korean officials on his discussions.

Hayes returned to Pyongyang in November 1992, a month after the resumption of Team Spirit exercises had been announced. He was told that some North Koreans would use the issue to stir up an air of crisis for domestic political purposes, putting all pragmatic moves on hold. He had a long conversation with Choe U Jin, the D.P.R.K. representative to the North-South Joint Nuclear Control Commission, who warned him that North Korea might disrupt I.A.E.A. inspections if Team Spirit went ahead: "What is the use of discussing inspections when we are exposed to nuclear threats and nuclear war maneuvers by the United States and South Korea?"[33] Hayes passed the warning on to U.S. intelligence.

Graham funded Hayes's third trip to Pyongyang on May 8–11, 1993, which culminated in another long conversation with Kim Yong Sun. Kim stressed the need for high-level talks to ease mutual suspicions and resolve the nuclear issue. He hinted at revival of the light-water reactor proposal: "If we seek broad scientific exchanges, why not nuclear cooperation?"[34] He appealed to American interests: "The United States has nothing to lose politically or economically by improving relations." In relations among nations, Kim noted, there are no permanent enemies and no permanent friends.[35] It was a preview of themes that North Korean negotiators would soon replay at the talks.

Hayes's contacts showed the value and limitations of informal channels of communication for sharing information and perspectives from the United States and South Korea with North Korean officials, and vice versa. "It is amazing," Hayes says, "that these two political cultures were able to communicate about anything, given how personalistic and centralized the system is in Pyongyang and how bureaucratic, legalistic and rationalist the system is in Washington."[36] While Hayes had both the technical and cultural know-how to bridge the two, his infrequent visits did not allow him to nurture the sustained personal relationships that are essential for establishing trust in North Korean society. He also had difficulty reaching senior U.S. officials. "The major effect I had was not on the inside," he says, "except to confirm the views of those who already agreed with me," a handful of intelligence specialists. He tried to influence the climate of opinion, especially in Seoul, where his articles in *Sisa Journal*, widely circulated among political elites, posed an early challenge to the conventional wisdom there.

W. Alton Jones and Rockefeller also financed Hayes's brainchild, the Nautilus Pacific Research institute. To overcome inadequate reporting in the American press, Nautilus established an e-mail network that disseminated an on-line daily compilation of news reports from around the world on the North Korean nuclear issue, as well as papers by experts. That kept a small but influential circle up to date on the subject and reduced the impact of the blatant propaganda in wide circulation on North Korea. It was a way to use the new information technology to gather and disseminate information in real time at least as well as the intelligence agencies could.

Nautilus also did several ground-breaking studies designed to improve the knowledge base about North Korea. The first of these studies, on North Korean decision-making, was undertaken by Alexandre Mansourov, a young Soviet expatriate who had worked in Pyongyang. Hayes himself directed studies of North Korea's energy needs. The most influential of those studies showed how replacing North Korea's gas-graphite reactors with light-water ones would reduce, though not eliminate, the risks of proliferation. It also analyzed the inadequacy of North Korea's power grid for transmitting the electricity that the replacement reactors would generate, and the inefficiencies in its distribution and use of coal and other energy resources.[37] He recommended a comprehensive survey of North Korea's energy needs, a suggestion that American officials later took up with the D.P.R.K. in an effort to open up alternatives to the replacement reactors.[38] He also recommended that nongovernmental organizations help meet North Korea's energy and environmental needs, a proposal later funded by the W. Alton Jones Foundation.[39]

Besides supporting Hayes's work, the Rockefeller Foundation commissioned a study by Scott Snyder at the Asia Society on the feasibility of cooperating with North Korea. Though initially hesitant about accepting the grant out of fear that it would alienate backers in South Korea, the Asia Society went ahead and canvassed 150 policy-makers, nongovernmental experts, and others in the United States, South Korea, and Japan between October 19 and November 10, 1993. It generated a range of inducements much broader than the government was then considering. It also produced a snapshot of expert opinion at the time.

A majority of the eighty-one respondents recommended considering inducements, but only if they were coupled with disincentives for North Korean noncooperation. In short, they favored a version of stated U.S. policy. Yet "a substantial minority," the report found, "stressed that no inducement is likely to convince the D.P.R.K. to cooperate sufficiently to allow the United States to achieve its policy objectives on the Korean peninsula." Some thought only sticks would work; others thought nothing would convince the North to give up its nuclear program. Almost all of those who favored inducements thought that political cooperation was more essential than economic or technical cooperation.

A small minority felt the nuclear threat was overblown and that the United States should wait until North Korea realized it could not afford nuclear-arming before expanding cooperation. Another small set of respondents thought that talks would not succeed unless they occurred at a much higher level and recommended appointing a personal representative of the president, a former official empowered to deal directly with leaders in Pyongyang.[40] Marshall Boutin of the Asia Society briefed the findings to State Department officials, citing a number of cooperative projects with North Korea that the government could support.

Tony Namkung, who became a consultant to the Rockefeller Foundation in 1994, began encouraging Graham to explore other avenues of potential cooperation. He had two purposes in mind. One was to provide suitable inducements for an eventual nuclear deal, and meanwhile give North Korean diplomats something to show for their efforts. Another was to weave a web of nongovernmental contact and cooperation, a safety net for U.S.-D.P.R.K. relations in the event that high-level talks stalemated. Namkung himself was pessimistic about the chances of American acceptance of a deal anytime soon. "No one who has followed North Korea closely," he wrote Graham on March 3, 1994, the day the agreement on four simultaneous steps was announced, "can possibly believe that their 'package solution' will bring about an end to the crisis."[41] He came up with three potential areas of cooperation: rice-breeding, energy conservation and use, and educational exchanges by medical practitioners.

Namkung added to the list in June. He suggested cultural exchanges, including an exhibition of ceramics at the Asia Society; a tour of the United States by a North Korean operetta; interviews with North Korean officials, including Kim Il Sung, on the *McNeil-Lehrer NewsHour*; a visit to Wall Street by a leading D.P.R.K. reformer, Vice Minister of

Economic Affairs Kim Jong U, to explain his country's new foreign investment laws; and the establishment of a private task force with government endorsement to hold high-level discussions in Pyongyang. He also broached the idea of a scientific exchange that he got from a senior North Korean diplomat in New York. A team of North Korean nuclear scientists would be invited to the United States to discuss issues relating to the replacement reactors. In turn, a team of American scientists would visit Yongbyon, take samples at the nuclear waste sites, and determine how different methods of computation could account for the differences between the North Korean initial declaration and the I.A.E.A. analysis. Upon conclusion of a peace treaty, the two sides could discuss removal from North Korea of any nuclear material it had accumulated.[42] That, of course, was a way around special inspections by the I.A.E.A., which made it unacceptable to American officials.

Namkung did succeed in expanding the list of inducements available to the American government, say U.S. officials. Yet he failed to provide much of a safety net for U.S.-D.P.R.K. relations because the administration was discouraging nongovernmental contact and cooperation and insisting that any arrangements be subject to cancellation in the event Pyongyang reneged on agreements with Washington.[43]

Graham wanted to thicken the web of nongovernmental ties with North Korea in just that event. The Rockefeller Foundation aide was also eager to jump-start nuclear talks through Track II diplomacy. In May 1994 he arranged for Gallucci to meet with a group of Korea experts, including, for the first time, Tony Namkung. The thrust of most experts' remarks was that the United States needed to address more than nuclear issues with North Korea in order to get anywhere in the talks.[44]

When Jimmy Carter showed an interest in going to North Korea, Graham was ready with both money and information. He had become convinced that Carter's understanding of the issues, his acceptability to North Korea, his access to CNN, and his religious background made him the ideal person to approach Kim Il Sung. Graham made good on Rockefeller's April 1993 commitment to fund Carter's travel expenses. In December 1993 he briefed a key Carter aide, Marion Creekmore, about Namkung's contacts with the D.P.R.K. On the eve of the Carter mission, Graham also arranged for Namkung to prepare background papers for him to take to Pyongyang. Graham's own memorandum to Carter summarized what he had learned about dealing with North Korea: "Officials in the government often discount D.P.R.K. statements, underestimate the willingness of the D.P.R.K. senior leaders to take risks, find it difficult to interpret the meaning of *juche*, place too low a value on indirect communications that the North has with N.G.O. actors, and virtually ignore the cultural side of the equation." He recommended that Carter "talk directly with the most informed 'dove' in the administration after you have received your group briefing" and "with the most informed Asian specialist *who speaks Korean* as your last briefing." He also suggested reading "the written work of the most informed skeptic who knows North Korea, speaks Korean, but thinks the D.P.R.K. will never bargain away the bomb."[45]

Namkung's memorandum listed the cultural obstacles that had to be overcome in dealing with North Koreans. One was that they have trouble "talking to 'secular,' 'modern' Westerners. They do not know how to deal with the deep cynicism that pertains to matters of the 'spirit' or the metaphysical. This is probably why people like the Rev. Billy Graham have been such a big hit in Pyongyang while others like Stephen Solarz have been such miserable failures." A second is that "when Koreans, both North and South, fight (verbally, within their families and within their own culture) they engage in *righteous indignation*. They start from an assumption that they are totally right, the other side is totally wrong, and that extreme language should be used to communicate that one is both 'serious' and 'moral.'" The North Koreans also interpret diversity and disunity as "national weakness." In contrast to the factional politics of democratic societies, Kim Il Sung and his cadre of senior leaders took pride in having imposed discipline on their society in order to achieve unity. "The sooner they are exposed to the notion that diversity is strength, the less room there will be for mistakes that have profound consequences for all parties concerned." Finally, they favor mediation as a face-saving way of negotiating.[46]

Namkung recounted how he had been told of three fundamental policy changes during his first trip to North Korea. "What made their proposed reforms even more interesting to me was that they seemed to stem not from some apprehension or fear about their ability to compete in the world or about the future of their system but from some kind of internal resilience about which the outside world had *very little knowledge*." The choice, as Namkung saw it, was "*not* between sanctions and the prospects of eventual military action, on the one hand, and North Korean compliance with its obligations under the I.A.E.A., on the other." The choice was, instead, "Will the United States exercise its moral and legal authority to steer and even guide North Korean moves to make peace with its neighbors and promote economic growth, or will it take steps which are intended to send a clear and strong message but have the effect of further isolating and destabilizing an already paranoid, dangerous and extremely suspicious military power?"[47]

Peter Hayes, Han Park, a professor at the University of Georgia, and others also sent briefing papers to Carter. These papers framed the issue very differently from those who thought that North Korea only understood the language of force, which struck a chord in Carter. As he told a CNN interviewer on his return: "The North Koreans are not on their knees begging for economic aid from the United States and they're not begging that the United States have diplomatic relations. They look upon themselves as a proud and respected sovereign nation who would like to have this relationship on a mutually respectful basis."[48] It was a disarming way to talk to strangers.

Jimmy Carter Refuses to Take "No" for an Answer

Jimmy Carter had first shown an interest in Korea when, within a month of becoming president, he had raised human rights concerns with South Korean President Park Chung Hee. He tried intermittently, and unsuccessfully, to secure the release of political prisoners held by the Park regime, most notably opposition leader Kim Dae Jung. Yet Carter remained suspect on the left as well as the right in South Korea. Rightists resented his raising the issue. Leftists blamed him because, after Park's assassination and the 1979 coup, U.S. officials worked openly with the new military rulers in Seoul, and after demonstrations took place in Kwangju, the U.S. commander in Korea, who commanded South Korean as well as American forces there, did not prevent a redeployment of R.O.K. troops who participated in the infamous Kwangju massacre, killing hundreds of civilians.[49]

Carter also had a technical grasp of nuclear issues and a healthy distaste for nuclear arms. In his 1977 inaugural address he endorsed as "our ultimate goal—the elimination all nuclear weapons from this Earth." His commitment was not just rhetorical. He was personally more engaged than any other president in curbing the spread of nuclear arms, in South Korea among other places. He also tried to remove American nuclear arms from the Korean peninsula, along with U.S. troops. The move elicited a favorable response from Kim Il Sung, who called Carter "a man of justice," but Carter's decision was eventually reversed by bureaucratic resistance in Washington and opposition in Seoul, which threatened a revival of the South Korean nuclear arms program.[50]

During the Bush and Clinton Administrations, Carter had watched with rising concern as the nuclear crisis heated up. He encouraged his staff to track events closely and received briefing memos from them every two or three weeks. Besides extensive talks with Graham and others at the Rockefeller Foundation, he spoke to Reverend Billy Graham and others who had visited North Korea. He also talked with the Chinese on several occasions and "found them to be the most knowledgeable. It was their opinion that convinced me they could not accept inter-national condemnation of their country and their Great Leader," says Carter.[51] "His firm belief," says an aide, "was that the sanctions ap-proach was just the wrong way to deal with the North Koreans and that they would react very adversely to a move toward sanctions. To him the key issue was whether or not sanctions were voted, not whether they would be implemented or how they would be carried out."[52]

The American ambassador in Seoul, James Laney, who until his ap-pointment had been president of Emory University, site of the Carter Center, also tried to stir the former president's concern. In mid-May, Laney recalls, "I told him this is getting real bad." He vented his frustra-tion about administration efforts to head off the intensifying crisis and urged Carter to get involved.[53] Laney had earlier suggested sending Sen-ator Sam Nunn (D-GA) to Pyongyang as a special emissary, a proposal picked up by Defense Secretary Perry but turned down by the North. Carter's name had been on Perry's list of possible emissaries in Decem-ber, says a Pentagon official, but he was ruled out because "he did not have high marks with the South Koreans or with domestic audiences."[54]

The idea of such a mission appealed to Carter. In early 1991 and again in 1992 he had received invitations to Pyongyang from North Ko-rean visitors to the Carter Center. Laney had discouraged him from ac-cepting the second invitation because it was "inappropriate": 1992 was an election year in both the United States and South Korea. Members of the Carter Center staff went instead. This time Carter was determined to go himself.

He called President Clinton on June 1 to express his unease and the White House arranged for Robert Gallucci to come to Plains on June 5 to brief him. Gallucci had been trying without success to put more American give into the diplomatic give-and-take and recited the history of the diplomatic effort in some detail, including internal differences of views. Far from mollifying Carter, the meeting convinced him of "the seriousness of the problem" and the need to communicate directly with Kim Il Sung, "the only person in North Korea who could change the course of events." Gallucci's recollection is more nuanced: "I wanted to give him a good technical briefing because I knew that he, as a former nuclear engineer in the Navy, would appreciate that. I hoped to build credibility that I understood this stuff. I also wanted him to understand why we had prioritized our objectives the way we had. I didn't have to be told that the risk was Carter would decide we had it wrong and that he would go off to achieve other objectives."[55]

After the briefing Carter sent a letter to President Clinton saying he intended to go to North Korea. Vice President Al Gore telephoned Car-ter the next day, who told him "I was strongly inclined to go." Gore said he would call Clinton in Europe, where the president was commemorating the fiftieth anniversary of D-Day. Gore called back June 7 and said that "President Clinton had approved my going."[56]

To North Korea, which had just been denied a meeting with an assistant secretary of state, the presence in Pyongyang of a former president, especially one who had tried to ease tensions on the Korean peninsula when he was in office, was a token of American respect. Carter was someone Kim Il Sung could do business with.

To the Clinton Administration, the Carter mission was a gamble. If he freelanced, he could always be disowned, but not without political repercussions. Even if he succeeded, the administration would be open to criticism by Republicans and South Koreans who disparaged Carter's willingness to take risks for peace. Yet turning down the former President was also risky, especially if it came to be portrayed publicly as a missed opportunity to avoid war. In the end Carter won Clinton's assent. "The president," says a top aide, "had been interested all along, and I agreed, though carefully, in finding ways to allow the North Koreans to move, and in ways that saved their face and established a high-level dialogue with them."[57]

Carter flew to Washington June 10. He was met at the airport by National Security Adviser Lake and N.S.C. staff member Daniel Poneman. Lake tried to make clear, says a top official, "Carter's role was to offer them a way out. It was not to offer them a new American policy that turned everything around."[58] Lake told Carter that he had no authority to speak for the United States, that he was going, in Carter's words, "without any clear instructions or official endorsement."[59]

He then received another lengthy briefing from Gallucci and others. It covered the technical issues, what was permitted under the Nonproliferation Treaty and what was not, where the North Korean program stood, and differing views on the relative importance of getting at the future and the past. It also dealt with whether Kim Il Sung or Kim Jong Il was running things in Pyongyang. "Carter particularly had trouble with some of the statements about how the North Koreans would likely react to sanctions," says an aide. "Carter made it very clear that to believe that you could vote the sanctions as a warning [and get a reaction only when you] implement them was a misreading of the psyche of the North Koreans."[60] Carter also took issue with one intelligence briefer's contentions that Kim Il Sung was getting old, that he had his good days and bad days and that most of the day-to-day policy-making, including the nuclear issue, was in the hands of his son, Kim Jong Il.[61] "The session did not go well," says an official who attended. "Carter kept asking the briefers, 'Have you ever been to North Korea? How do you know?'"[62]

Later Carter wrote out his talking points and read them to Gallucci. A determined ex-President was not someone who could be tied down by negotiating instructions from a mere ambassador. Gallucci proposed no changes.

The political context was no more auspicious than the sendoff. North and South Korea had begun mobilizing their armed forces. On Carter's arrival in Seoul June 13, Secretary of State Christopher called to tell him that North Korea was about to eject the I.A.E.A. "The outcome of the whole crisis," Carter recalls Christopher saying, "could depend on what happened to the inspectors."[63]

Carter arrived in Pyongyang on June 15. That very day the United States began circulating a draft resolution in the Security Council on a strategy of graduated sanctions: first a warning statement by the Security Council president, then a thirty-day grace period, followed by the phasing in of political and economic sanctions. Sanctions were to be imposed only if North Korea ejected the remaining I.A.E.A. inspectors, withdrew from the Nonproliferation Treaty, or reprocessed more plutonium.[64] During the first phase, the U.S. draft included a mandatory ban on the sale of arms and their components; suspension of all development aid; a ban on air traffic other than passenger flights; a ban on technical and scientific cooperation; a ban on cultural, commercial, and educational exchanges; a ban on participation in athletic events; and a request, though not a requirement, to curtail the size and scope of diplomatic activities. A second phase would freeze most remittances. The third phase was not spelled out, but could involve a total trade embargo including oil.[65] Because of fear of a violent reaction in North Korea, the gradual imposition of sanctions was the most that South Korea and Japan—or the Pentagon—would accept. Even so, Chinese acquiescence was unlikely. If the Security Council was unable to act, the United States was prepared to form a coalition to impose sanctions without U.N. authorization.[66]

On June 15, as Carter was meeting with North Korean officials, pressures were mounting in the United States to apply coercion. "Negotiations, pleas and promises of cooperation for good behavior haven't had the slightest effect," argued Karen Elliott House in the *Wall Street Journal*. "Nevertheless we now have the spectacle of global arbitrator Jimmy Carter, who sought to pull U.S. troops out of South Korea during his presidency, traipsing off to Pyongyang when President Clinton ought to be sending Norman Schwarzkopf—perhaps with a few sample photos of high-tech warfare in the Gulf. The emissary's message: Here's what we will do *for* you [diplomatic relations, aid] if you abandon nuclear ambitions; here's what we will do *to* you if you don't." She left no doubt about what had to be done: "The administration has to be willing not only to go to war on the Korean peninsula but also to put the U.S.-China relationship on the line. . . . [I]t must tell Beijing privately that the U.S. is prepared to sink any Chinese ship that approaches North Korea and bomb any Chinese transport as soon as it crosses the border into North Korea."[67] To stop North Korea from bomb-making, House was ready to risk war with China.

That same day the *Washington Post* ran an op-ed by two former Bush Administration officials, National Security Adviser Brent Scowcroft and Under Secretary of State Arnold Kanter, blasting Clinton's strategy and demanding "more decisive action." Pyongyang is "on the brink of pulling out of the N.P.T." in preparation for resuming the reprocessing of spent fuel to extract plutonium, they asserted. "It is also hard to imagine that the 'phased' economic sanctions being proposed by the United States—if and when they are imposed—could possibly be effective in time to slow or halt possible North Korea reprocessing plans." They favored an ultimatum to Pyongyang: "It either must permit continuous, unfettered I.A.E.A. monitoring to confirm that no further reprocessing is taking place, or we will remove its capacity to reprocess." Acknowledging that bombing the reprocessing plant and spent fuel in the cooling ponds could launch a second Korean war, they urged a military buildup in South Korea.[68] Though the op-ed was intended to toughen the administration's stance, the timing of its publication was a coincidence; it had been submitted just after the North Koreans had begun removing plutonium-laden fuel rods from their reactor.

The Carter visit also intensified partisan rivalry in South Korea. Opposition leader Kim Dae Jung had proposed a package solution in a speech to the Korea Society on May 18 and had endorsed a high-level American mission to Pyongyang at a Washington press conference.[69] He was in a position to claim credit if Carter succeeded. On the other end of the political spectrum, any talks between Americans and North Koreans that left out the South Koreans was disconcerting to Seoul's hard-liners, who suspected North Korea would use the visit to drive a wedge between Washington and Seoul or to boost its own prestige. President Kim Young Sam raised these concerns in a meeting at Blue House with Undersecretary of State Peter Tarnoff on the eve of Carter's arrival in Seoul, en route to Beijing, "Kim Il Sung might attempt to convey a message of peace to the West through Carter, while telling his people that the former U.S. president is in Pyongyang to pay respects to him."[70] His remarks were promptly disclosed to reporters. When Carter paid calls on Kim and his top advisers, by Carter's own account, "They seemed somewhat troubled about our planned visit."[71]

Carter also called on the commander-in-chief in Korea, General Luck, who "was deeply concerned about the consequences of a Korean war."[72] Luck "tried to give him a feel for what might occur if we fought." He shared his assessment, "If you fight, you win. But you spend a billion dollars, you lose a million lives, and you bring great trauma and hardship on the psyche of both countries, so I'm not sure winning is a win." Luck often admonished others, "Every day we don't fight, we win."[73] An aide says Carter "came away from that conversation reinforced in his view that the situation could very quickly deteriorate."[74]

That same concern prompted President Clinton to convene a council of war on June 16, Washington time, to authorize reinforcements for Korea in anticipation of sanctions. The Pentagon proposed three options, depending on the severity of the sanctions. Its preferred option was to deploy 23,000 troops, mostly to handle logistics, in preparation for the 400,000 additional troops General Luck had said he would need in the event of war. A second option would also dispatch 30–40 aircraft, including fighter planes, to South Korea and F-117 stealth fighter-bombers and other bombers to Guam. An even more robust option would also station a second aircraft carrier in the region and send more Army and Marine combat troops.

The National Intelligence Officer for Warning, Charles Allen, briefed President Clinton on the sobering possibility that reinforcements could trigger North Korean mobilization, raising the risk of preemptive war. Such war warnings are customarily given to the president only when war seems imminent. "I don't recall a big alarm bell going off," says a top official who was there. One reason was that C.I.A. and D.I.A. disagreed: "C.I.A. was more worried about the danger of war."[75] Also, the risks of not sending reinforcements were clear after Somalia. Defense Secretary Perry and Joint Chiefs of Staff Chairman Shalikashvili emphasized those risks and the President approved the Pentagon plans. The reinforcement decision was page-one news in the *New York Times* the next day. A report of the Carter breakthrough in Pyongyang was buried on an inside page.[76]

The Carter-Kim Deal

Carter's first meeting in Pyongyang took place that same day, or June 15, Korea time, with Foreign Minister Kim Yong Nam, who informed him that the I.A.E.A. inspectors would be ousted and would not be allowed back in until a deal could be worked out in a third round of talks. A diplomat saw it as a "ritual flexing of biceps."[77] Carter did not. "The responses to my proposal on how to end the impasse were quite hard line," Carter reports, "with an apparent fixation on beginning the third round of talks as a prerequisite to any affirmative actions." He was especially worried that any gap in monitoring would lead to charges that North Korea was diverting nuclear fuel to bomb-making, adding impetus to the sanctions drive. Carter was so "distressed" that he awoke at

3 A.M. the next morning to dispatch his aide, Marion Creekmore, back to Panmunjom, where he could send a message to Washington over a secure phone line.[78] He instructed Creekmore, a former ambassador, to seek authorization from the White House for a third round of high-level talks to satisfy the North Korean demand, but not to transmit the message until after he could meet with Kim Il Sung later that morning. Upon arriving at Panmunjom, Creekmore took the opportunity to speak with Ambassador Laney.

Carter began the meeting with Kim Il Sung by describing his unofficial role. He then outlined American concerns about North Korea's nuclear program, in particular, the need for total transparency "from its inception."[79] Carter found Kim "remarkably familiar with the issues," but not fully briefed on one critical point, the expulsion of the inspectors.[80] Carter later learned from his interpreter, Dick Christenson of the State Department, that Kim had asked his advisers for clarification on that point.

Reading the detailed talking points he had shown to Gallucci prior to leaving Washington, Carter proposed a freeze monitored by the I.A.E.A. Kim Il Sung accepted. "He was willing to freeze their nuclear program during the talks," says Carter, "and to consider a permanent freeze if their aged reactors could be replaced with modern and safer ones." He made one other request, for a "U.S. guarantee that there will be no nuclear attack against his country." Carter was content to accept an agreement in principle, leaving the details of the freeze for others to pin down. He had Christensen call Creekmore and tell him to return to Pyongyang without sending the message to Washington because "I now felt that I had gotten everything we needed."[81]

Others were not as sanguine. When Creekmore told Ambassador Laney what Carter was proposing, Laney recalls, "I said that won't fly politically and it won't do the job." In Laney's view, "It was just in the heat of the negotiations that he thought he had something." Carter "hung in there," he adds, and got a better deal.[82] Kim Il Sung had spoken "in generalities" and the initial reporting cable was unclear whether he had "agreed to a full freeze or not," especially whether the spent fuel in the cooling ponds could be reprocessed. "I remember worrying that this is the stuff of big misunderstandings," says a diplomat. "We were so damned close to a real confrontation. There was zero good will to paper over a misunderstanding like that."[83]

In the afternoon Carter met with Gallucci's counterpart, First Vice Foreign Minister Kang Sok Ju, to confirm the freeze. Again, Carter found one of Kim Il Sung's subordinates "not as forthcoming" as he himself had been. "On occasion," says Carter, Kang "tended to deviate in his position from what Kim Il Sung had committed to do, but when I asked him each time if he had a different policy from his 'Great Leader,' he would back down."[84]

A Pentagon official familiar with the translator's notes of the meeting says, "Carter made some mistakes." The most important of them concerned disposition of the spent fuel in the cooling ponds. "The right answer was, we'll take that off your hands," but "he indicated to the North Koreans it was all right to reprocess."[85] Carter has a different recollection. Nothing was said in the briefing he was given before leaving for Pyongyang "about moving the fuel rods out of North Korea." Reprocessing was permitted under the Nonproliferation Treaty. That was the basis of one of the talking points Carter had drafted and shown to Gallucci: "Reprocessing is not prohibited but must be subject to inspections."[86] When Carter read that to Kim Il Sung, Christenson whispered to Carter not to settle for that. "He told him he can't do that," says a diplomat who was directly involved. "We had been working for twenty years to keep reprocessing off the Korean peninsula. We couldn't say yes to the North after saying no to the South for so long. That was a bone of contention."[87]

After dinner Carter telephoned the White House. The call, about 10:30 A.M., Washington time, interrupted the council of war. Gallucci was sent out of the Cabinet Room to answer it. The conversation was guarded; it took place over an open line, enabling the North Koreans to eavesdrop. "Basically Carter said this is what I'm going to say. Bob said, I really wish you'd say that, and his position was modified."[88] Fifteen minutes later Gallucci returned and stunned the gathering with news that Kim Il Sung had agreed to freeze his nuclear arms program under I.A.E.A. monitoring, and to resume high-level talks on a comprehensive settlement of the nuclear issue. Carter, Gallucci concluded, was about to go on CNN live to announce the deal. "It blindsided us," says a top official, who was unaware that Carter had taken CNN with him.[89] "You told him not to," said National Security Adviser Lake. No, said Gallucci ruefully. The room erupted in exasperation.[90]

Moments later they tuned into CNN and some officials' exasperation turned to fury. Carter gave the back of his hand to the crime-and-punishment approach. Discussing the resumption of high-level talks, he said, "The commitment that I have received is that all aspects of North Korea's nuclear program would be resolved through good-faith talks," but not "just unilaterally letting" the I.A.E.A. conduct a special inspection of the waste sites. He also raised doubts about I.A.E.A. insistence on sampling the spent fuel rods, which had set off the crisis:

> The North Koreans are convinced that they have a feasible plan by which this could be done. The I.A.E.A. has disagreed. Today the North Koreans told me they had additional compromise proposals, which I didn't try to study, that they were prepared to pursue. I know that some scientists who are highly qualified have said that there is a good probability, with more

work, to go back and get the history of the nuclear reactor. . . . [T]he North Koreans claimed today that they have every rod that came out of the reactor identified and that they can place it in the reactor core from which it was withdrawn.[91]

Carter added that in approaches other than the I.A.E.A.'s preferred one, "the degree of confidence would be problematic."

Most important of all, Carter publicly repudiated the sanctions strategy. "Nothing should be done to exacerbate the situation now," he declared. "The reason I came over here was to try to prevent an irreconcilable mistake."[92] Carter went public deliberately. "It was obvious," Carter himself wrote at the time, "that the threat of sanctions had no effect on them whatsoever, except as a pending insult, branding North Korea as an outlaw nation and their revered leader as a liar and criminal."[93]

"Carter made clear to me he did it on purpose," says a diplomat who was directly involved. "His intent was to kill the sanctions movement." The diplomat elaborates, "The North Koreans had reiterated that a sanctions resolution in the U.N. would be the breaking point. . . . Carter didn't know where it stood but he wanted to make sure he killed it. He knew some countries were wavering and I think he figured that if he went on CNN and said we have the makings of a deal . . . it would cause any nation that was wavering to stand back and say, wait a minute, let's not rush to sanctions."[94]

The next day, June 16, Foreign Ministry spokesman Shen Guofang hardened China's opposition to sanctions: "China in principle does not subscribe to the involvement of the Security Council in the nuclear issue on the Korean Peninsula or the resort to sanctions to solve it."[95] Russian Foreign Minister Andrei Kozyrev also bridled at the U.S. draft on grounds that Russia had not been consulted in advance.[96]

Carter had gone out of his way to reassure North Korea and to distance himself, in private and in public, from prior American positions. It paid off.

The CNN interview stunned the gathering in the Cabinet Room. Some senior officials seemed more concerned about being upstaged in public than being rescued from a doomed policy. "It looked as if we were contracting out our foreign policy, like we were bystanders," said one, "and had totally lost control of it."[97] Yet the freeze could spare the administration from its own folly—a sanctions strategy that had put it on a possible collision course with disaster. The countries that had to enforce the sanctions were unwilling to, and the prospect of Security Council debate on sanctions had prompted military precautions that were threatening to explode into war. In the heat of the moment, participants let personal pique get in the way of prudent policy.

After several testy outbursts, Vice President Gore intervened with a pertinent question, "Can we make lemonade out of this lemon?"[98] He proposed taking the Carter-Kim deal and interpreting it to Washington's advantage. "The crux of his pitch was to hear what we want to hear," says a participant.[99] President Clinton recalled that during the Cuban missile crisis of October 1962, the Kennedy Administration had ignored a Soviet demand in diplomatic channels for the removal of U.S. nuclear weapons in Turkey in return for withdrawing its own missiles from Cuba and responded instead to Soviet back-channel messages asking only that the United States pledge not to invade Cuba. The so-called "Trollope ploy" in the Cuban case, of course, differed in one critical respect: the initiative for the back-channel messages had come from officials in the Soviet government.[100] The initiative for the Carter mission came from outside government.

Gore's timely intervention helped redirect the group from fulminating against Carter to trying to make the most of the opening he had given them. The president and his senior advisers reached for pads to begin drafting a reply. "Here we were doing policy in real time, no option papers, no lengthy period to staff this out," said a participant.[101]

Stanley Roth, N.S.C. senior director for East Asia, said it was important "to raise the bar" before resuming talks. He proposed a new precondition—that the North not restart the Yongbyon reactor. He had been pushing that proposal for months, with support from Assistant Secretary of Defense Carter. Gallucci and Poneman had opposed the idea on the grounds that it went beyond North's obligations under the Nonproliferation Treaty and was therefore likely to be turned down. Now that Pyongyang had removed more spent fuel from the reactor, administration officials felt they needed something more for resuming talks, something that could be portrayed as a significant new concession to help fend off attacks at home.

Relocating the spent fuel at Yongbyon to a third country also came up in the ensuing discussion. "There was a lot of blue-skying," says a participant. Someone suggested the principals' time could be better spent by leaving the drafting to Gallucci, Poneman, and Leon Fuerth, Gore's national security aide. The three went to the vice president's office down the hall and drafted a statement for the president.[102]

National Security Adviser Lake had tried to telephone Carter while he was on the air with CNN. When Carter finally got through to Lake, they spoke briefly and he was told to call back for the American response. In the meantime Secretary of State Christopher awakened the South Korean and Japanese foreign ministers to consult on what to tell the D.P.R.K. It was not until 5:30 A.M., Pyongyang time, that Lake read the reply to Carter over the telephone, again on an open line. "They had a difference over reprocessing," says an aide. Carter disagreed on another key point as well. "He didn't accept that we needed the bar raised a bit before we went back to the table. He didn't accept that they could not reload the reactor," says Gallucci.[103] Marion Creekmore, who was with Carter in Pyongyang, concurs, "Carter was disturbed by the substantial expansion of the White House demands that had been given to him and later confirmed by Gallucci. Although he assumed that they were included in Kim's commitment, he had not tried to specify no refueling as part of the agreement."[104] Carter also objected to continuing the diplomatic drive for sanctions, but Lake refused to suspend it. The blowup came over the spent fuel in the cooling ponds. "Carter knew from what we were saying that this reprocessing he had suggested they could do was wrong," says a diplomat who was directly involved. "Ultimately he and Tony Lake argued about that over the phone. That was a very unpleasant conversation. Lake was angry and Carter was angry."[105]

In the end, President Clinton seized the opportunity Carter had handed him to return to the negotiating table. He told National Security Council staffers a few days later that it would "give the North Koreans an exit. . . . If an ex-president came to them, that was something they could respond to. It would allow them a graceful climb-down."[106] At a news conference later that day, Clinton declared, "If today's developments mean that North Korea is genuinely and verifiably prepared to freeze its nuclear program while talks go on—and we hope that is the case—then we would be willing to resume high-level talks." But he added, "In the meantime, we will pursue our consultations on sanctions at the United Nations."[107] By casting the freeze in the most favorable terms, with both North Korean and American audiences in mind, the statement reminded one of its drafters of a politician who was asked during the temperance debates whether he was a wet or a dry: "If by whiskey you mean the wonderful elixir that puts a smile on a man's face, then I'm for it, but if you mean hellfire and damnation, then I'm against it."[108]

In a briefing moments later, Gallucci told reporters "we see possibly some new elements in the message. We will be exploring the meaning of the message in diplomatic channels, and only after we're able to do that, will we be able to characterize it." He interpreted the freeze expansively: "not refueling the reactor or reprocessing the spent fuel it has just removed, and permitting the I.A.E.A. to maintain the continuity of safeguards."[109]

That morning on the spur of the moment Kim Il Sung invited Carter to join him aboard his yacht. Carter took advantage of the leisurely cruise to renew discussion on reprocessing with Kim. He insisted that the freeze had to cover a ban on reprocessing for the duration of the third round of high-level talks. "I explained that a permanent commitment could be predicated on approval of light-water reactor technology." Kim gave his assent. Kang reopened the issue with Carter later on, however, insisting that the North would need to reprocess the spent fuel in the cooling ponds within three months. "He is not a nuclear expert," notes Carter, "and did not seem to understand that, once rods are removed, there are alternatives to reprocessing."[110] Carter urged Kang to take up the issue with Gallucci. A diplomat recalls, "There was a great deal of to-ing and fro-ing between Carter and Kang on specific elements, what is and what isn't okay," but in the end Carter never wrung a firm commitment from Kang to refrain from reprocessing the spent fuel in the cooling ponds.[111] The refueling issue also remained unresolved.

Carter took up two other politically significant questions with Kim Il Sung himself. One was North-South relations. Kim acknowledged that "the fault for lack of progress lay on both sides." Carter elicited an invitation from Kim to South Korean President Kim Young Sam for a summit meeting, which "should be done without preconditions or extended preparatory talks." Kim, says a Carter aide, thought it important to meet at the summit first and then let lower-level officials work out the details. "If you let lower-level officials plan a meeting, you never get to have one."[112] A summit meeting could help sell the deal to Seoul. "Carter faced a Seoul that was pretty skeptical," says a diplomat who was there with him. "When he was able to present to the South Korean government a summit possibility, that turned it from skeptical to positive because the South was no longer just an onlooker or a passive bystander. It was now in the center."

Carter also raised the issue of the remains of American soldiers killed in the Korean War. Dealing with the remains, he told Kim, would be "a significant goodwill gesture to the American people." After Kim's wife commented favorably on the idea, Kim agreed to permit joint U.S.–North Korean teams to search for the remains.[113]

In the course of the conversation Kim also expressed willingness to implement the North-South denuclearization accord, to draw back forces from the DMZ, and to reduce North and South troops by one hundred thousand. He was willing to have U.S. troops remain in Korea, but reduced in proportion to North-South cuts.

Another disagreement between Carter and the Clinton Administration was not long in coming, however, this time in public. During the cruise Carter told Kim, in words picked up by a CNN microphone, "I would like to inform you that they have stopped the sanctions activity in the United Nations."[114] He did it, knowing "that it would be traumatic and create complications in Washington and Seoul," says a diplomat. "I think he understood that and he didn't like that, but his larger purpose was to prevent the one thing from happening that the North had warned would be the point of no return. He's a brave man. That took courage."[115] President Clinton tried to downplay the differences, suggesting Carter may have been misunderstood: "There was no question and answer. There was no clarification." But others were quick to disown Carter's statement. "Carter is hearing what he wants to hear, both from Kim Il Sung and from the administration. He is creating his own reality," said one senior official.[116]

The Clinton Administration was having trouble taking yes for an answer. "The shocking thing about the Carter visit wasn't that people were disappointed that someone was going," says a State Department official. "It was that when he got the freeze people here were crestfallen."[117] The reaction to Carter in the upper reaches of the State Department did not extend to the National Security Council staff, says a top official. Lake was "glad he went because he offered them a stool on which they could dismount," but Lake objects to the conclusion that Carter, by kicking away sanctions, opened the way to a deal and averted a war.[118]

The administration was reluctant to abandon its sanctions strategy. It did not want to be seen giving any inducements to North Korea for doing what any signatory was obliged to do under the Nonproliferation Treaty. It clung to sanctions as a shield against accusations of appeasement. It wanted the appearance of having coerced North Korean compliance. Yet the uncomfortable fact was that coercion had failed to secure full inspections or an end to North Korea's nuclear program and showed little sign of succeeding anytime soon. Worst of all, it might have been on the verge of provoking a disastrous and unnecessary war.

To his credit, President Clinton used the Carter opening to begin negotiating in earnest. "North Korea's latest offer to resolve the crisis over its nuclear program appears to include little that is new," wrote the *New York Times*'s Michael Gordon in a careful appraisal, "but President Clinton's willingness to seize it as an opportunity to avoid a confrontation reflects an abrupt shift of policy."[119] It also showed his political courage in the face of fierce opposition.

The Bushmen Go on the Warpath

The Clinton Administration's political misgivings were not misplaced: Carter's detractors were vitriolic in their denunciations. The hawks went on the warpath. Fearful that North Korea was about to reprocess the spent fuel in the cooling ponds and make five or six bombs, they called for air strikes on Yongbyon while the fuel rods were still too hot to handle.

A concerted campaign was spearheaded by former Bush Administration officials. The day after the deal, June 17, the *Los Angeles Times* ran an op-ed by Robert Gates, C.I.A. director in the Bush Administration, "Bluntly put, it is too late to stop the North Korean bomb. . . . We dithered too long pursuing a course of diplomacy that was not complemented by a buildup of forces that would give clout to our political strategy and put us in a position to take military action if it failed." Echoing the call of two other Bush Administration officials, Brent Scowcroft and Arnold Kanter, two days earlier, Gates proposed "a warning to the North not to begin reprocessing the recently extracted nuclear material," and "then destroying the reprocessing plant if the North ignores us."[120] Richard Haass, an N.S.C. staff member in the Bush Administration, raised doubts about the Carter deal in an op-ed in the *New York Times*: "To say the least, Kim Il Sung's record does not warrant optimism." Haass joined in the G.O.P. air campaign, but he had a different target: "Launch a preventive military attack against North Korea's nuclear facilities at Yongbyon that is comparable to Israel's attack that destroyed Iraq's reactor in 1981." Never mind that Iraq had yet to start up its reactor, let alone possibly produce enough plutonium for a bomb. Haass did add a caveat: "But if South Korea, which would bear the brunt of any retaliation or release of radiation, did not acquiesce in U.S. military action, we should pause."[121] Former Secretary of State Lawrence Eagleburger was the next Bush Administration official to weigh in. He was "horrified" to hear Carter "taking the word of this murderer who runs North Korea."[122] Philip Zelikow, who had served on the National Security Council staff in the Bush years and had spent the first six months of the Clinton Administration working on North Korea policy in the Pentagon, called the abandonment of sanctions "an American-led retreat. Sanctions have been dropped. And what has Mr. Kim given up in exchange for this retreat? Absolutely nothing." Citing Clinton's characterization of the freeze as "a very positive development," Zelikow concluded, "It sure is, for Kim Il Sung."[123]

One former Bush Administration official did not parrot the party line, Donald Gregg, American ambassador to South Korea from 1989 to 1993 and now president of the Korea Society. The Clinton Administration, he wrote in the *Washington Post*, is "still focused entirely on the I.A.E.A.'s nuclear agenda, refusing to address broader economic concerns until these technical matters are addressed." Carter's visit "may be helpful in broadening the dialogue between Washington and Pyongyang." Gregg quoted an old friend from Seoul who was experienced in dealing with Pyongyang, "'The North Koreans think you are trying to strangle them; they want better relations with you.'" The United States has ample forces in place and the North Koreans "know this and respect it." He hoped Clinton would "figure out that he must talk to the North Koreans as well as confronting them."[124]

Carter came home to a frosty White House reception. President Clinton did not return from his weekend retreat at Camp David to greet Carter but spoke to him by telephone. Carter met instead with National Security Adviser Lake. They decided that Carter would send a note to Kim Il Sung asking him to confirm Carter's understanding of what they had agreed to, along the lines of the President's statement of June 16, and that Gallucci would send a similar note to his counterpart, Kang Sok Ju.

Afterward Carter had a caustic comment about the "so-called experts" in the government who claim North Korea will yield to the threat of sanctions, "The experts who briefed me before I left have never been to North Korea."[125] He gave reporters an upbeat assessment of his trip, "I personally believe that the crisis is over." Gallucci was cautious: "There may be an opening here, but. . .we really do need to follow up on what he has brought back to see just exactly how much is there."[126]

The next day, June 20, Gallucci wrote Kang Sok Ju, asking him to confirm what Kim Il Sung told Carter and accept the additional preconditions for talks: "We understand that your willingness to freeze the nuclear program means that the D.P.R.K. will not refuel the 5-MWe reactor nor reprocess spent fuel while U.S.-D.P.R.K. talks continue."[127] Carter sent a note to Kim Il Sung, making the identical points.

The official North Korean reply was thankfully not long in coming. Kang responded June 22, "For the immediate future, we would like to assure you that, for the sake of the third round, we are prepared neither to reload the 5-MWe reactor with new fuel nor to reprocess the spent fuel, and to permit inspections for practical safeguards, including the maintenance of presence of I.A.E.A. inspectors and agency surveillance equipment in place at Yongbyon. Issues at that stage will be subject to the discussion in the third round."[128] "They didn't like where they were," says a diplomat. "Brinkmanship is their game, but they wanted out. They were so damned grateful to get out that when it came to what a freeze was, they said freeze it all, dammit."[129] North Korea was willing to accommodate the United States by accepting an expansive definition of the freeze even though it was no longer under the threat of sanctions or war.

North Korea's reply was greeted with relief and exhilaration in the White House. President Clinton himself announced the agreement, calling it "an important step forward" and "the beginning of a new stage in our effort to pursue a non-nuclear Korean peninsula." He committed himself to the comprehensive approach: "In addition to addressing the nuclear issue, we are prepared to discuss the full range of security, political and economic issues that affects North Korea's relationship with the international community."[130] Yet the White House showed its eagerness to shove Carter offstage. The President, said National Security Adviser Lake, "used the past tense to say he did a good job rather than is doing a good job because now that's through."[131]

The critics were not done with Carter, however. Charles Krauthammer evoked the specter of Chamberlain at Munich. In a column headlined, " 'Peace in Our Time,' " he disparaged "people convinced that all that stands between war and peace is their dining with a dictator." He called Carter "the most gullible political pilgrim since George Bernard Shaw" visited the Soviet Union in 1931. Attacking Carter's contention, Krauthammer wrote, "The crisis is not over. Nothing has been done to stop the North Korean drive for nuclear weapons. But much was done by Carter to derail U.S. efforts to stop that drive." What about the freeze? "It is a sham. To safely reprocess the Yongbyon fuel rods into bomb material, the North Koreans have to wait a month or two anyway before extracting their plutonium . . . because the rods are now still relatively hot (radioactive). With time, they cool."[132] *Newsweek* headlined its June 27 report on the Carter mission, "A Stooge or a Savior."

Henry Kissinger joined the chorus of critics: "Kim Il Sung used the Carter visit to induce yet another retreat. The sanctions effort was suspended when barely started." Dismissing "the much-touted Pyongyang concessions" as "an attempt to gain time," he went to raise the bar higher: "A freeze of the North's activities, leaving it in possession of the existing weapons and the growing plutonium-producing capability would pose a mounting threat. A rollback is needed." He rejected diplomatic give-and-take for the crime-and-punishment approach that had failed repeatedly since early 1991: "The precondition for improved relations must be full compliance with I.A.E.A. inspections of all sites, an accounting for past production and a return to the Nonproliferation Treaty." He then proposed what sounded a lot like an ultimatum: "Before any military action is implemented, another serious diplomatic effort is necessary. But it must have a definite time limit."[133]

There was scattered applause for diplomacy. It was time to negotiate a package deal with North Korea, Richard Allen, President Reagan's national security adviser, told conservative columnist Robert Novak. "Advice from such odd bedfellows as Jimmy Carter and Dick Allen should be considered," concluded Novak.[134] From Carter's end of the political spectrum, *Washington Post* columnist Jessica Mathews commented, "North Korea's recent actions . . . should alter U.S. negotiating strategy, not from fear or weakness but out of an interest in what will work." She endorsed what the Pentagon had been proposing: "put North Korea's past activities on the back burner for the time being, and link the incentives we are prepared to offer only to the control of Pyongyang's present program." She tried to slow the rush for rash action: "While the fuel rods remain too radioactive to handle, further negotiations pose no security risk."[135]

Yet the defenders of deal-making in the foreign policy establishment were few in number. When the White House invited a group of outsiders to a private discussion with top officials on June 20, only two spoke out firmly in favor of returning to the negotiating table, Gregg and Selig Harrison of the Carnegie Endowment. Carter "was very effectively used by Kim Il Sung to dissipate the pressure for sanctions and split the coalition," said a former high-ranking diplomat who served in both Democratic and Republican administrations. "If Carter is right," said another ex-official, "everything we have been told about North Korea for 40 years is wrong."[136] It was a telling remark.

In contrast to the foreign policy establishment, the public was overwhelmingly supportive of negotiating. A *Newsweek* poll found 68 percent in favor of resuming talks and 25 percent opposed until inspections took place. The administration's disarray was apparent to the public, however. Asked about the president's handling of North Korea, 42 percent disapproved, 31 percent approved, and 27 percent had no reply.[137]

In South Korea, the Carter trip was under assault. Seoul, said a *Chosun Ilbo* editorial, "could not hide the bewilderment at such a turn of events."[138] South Korean President Kim Young Sam quickly took up Kim Il Sung's offer of a summit meeting and said he would meet "anytime anyplace, with no conditions."[139] That hardly assuaged his domestic opponents.

The lesson that former President Carter took away from his mission, he told CNN on June 22, is that "we should never avoid direct talks . . . with the main person in a despised or misunderstood or condemned society who can actually resolve the issue." He compared his efforts to the diplomatic breakthrough in the Middle East: "We went through this for ten years when nobody in our government would meet or talk to Yasir Arafat. The Norwegians did, and they were the ones that brought the peace agreement last summer."[140]

Unlike the Norwegians, Carter did not bring back "the makings of a deal," says a member of the American delegation to the high-level talks. "We already had that, at least in outline form, by late 1993. Carter's intervention was crucial, not because of what it added to the deal, but because it let both sides step back long enough to get back to the deal they were already working on."[141] Perhaps so, but it only happened after Carter had repudiated sanctions.

Track II diplomacy was decisive in averting a confrontation and collapse of the talks. It showed how outsiders can sometimes be better informed than American intelligence agencies, for instance, about North

Korea's energy and agriculture needs. It showed how nongovernmental actors can conduct diplomatic probes of other nations in a timely and flexible way that advances American interests. It showed how a private citizen of the United States, Tony Namkung, could influence government policy in a closed and centralized political system like North Korea. It showed how relatively small amounts of money from foundations could have a disproportionately large impact on policy.

Yet the special conditions of this case may help account for the success of Track II diplomacy. It took an insular state like North Korea that wanted a deal with the United States but did not know how to get one to listen to a Tony Namkung. It took an administration amenable to outside influence, including well-placed allies like Ambassador-at-Large Gallucci, Ambassador Laney, General Luck, and Defense Secretary Perry who were prepared to support a Track II initiative. It also took experts willing to talk and listen to strangers, and a person of the stature of Jimmy Carter who was willing to stake his place in history on keeping the peace.

7

GETTING TO YES

*"You've failed, haven't you, Mr. North Wind?
Now it's my turn," declared the sun and shone
his warm rays toward the traveler.
"Whew! It's unbearably hot! I'd better take all
this clothing off," exclaimed the traveler.
Struck with great admiration at the sun's success
the north wind admitted, "Merely using force as I did
will not enable me to succeed in moving others."
(Aesop, "The North Wind and the Sun")[1]*

JIMMY CARTER managed to move the United States and North Korea away from the brink and back to the negotiating table. Once he did, it would take negotiators just four months to conclude an Agreed Framework mapping out reciprocal steps to resolve the nuclear issue. Within a year a more detailed accord on the replacement reactors was signed at Kuala Lumpur, putting the antagonists on the path to settlement of the nuclear dispute. As of mid-1997 the D.P.R.K. had lived up to these agreements.

Washington's newfound willingness to deal led to a rapid resolution of the crisis. Its turnaround was prompted by an awareness, brought home by the June 16 warning briefing, of how imminent war seemed in mid-June. The close call chastened the few officials who were aware of it—in parts of the Pentagon, on the negotiating team, and at the very top of the administration. Going to "the brink of disaster," says Deputy Assistant Secretary of State Thomas Hubbard, "was probably the cathartic moment that we needed."[2] A top official who disputes this contention says, "I don't think we'll ever know how close we came to a huge crisis militarily on the peninsula." Yet he acknowledges in his very next breath, "It was enough to worry us very seriously."[3]

Seizing the moment, a determined Robert Gallucci led the administration to abandon the crime-and-punishment approach once and for all and engage in concerted give-and-take. "We learned some lessons after that. Earlier we had deprived ourselves of a dialogue," says a State Department Korea hand. "That deprived us of a tool to solve the problem. Now that we were back at the table we did it a little differently. We weren't just involved in conversations."[4]

The Clinton Administration tried hard to convince casual observers that the turnabout was forced on Pyongyang by threat of sanctions and military action. There is little evidence to support that claim. The sanctions strategy was moribund even before Washington abandoned it, killed off by Jimmy Carter. Air strikes had been set aside, to be used only in desperation. Nor did North Korea undergo a sudden change of heart. For over two years it had refrained from unloading spent fuel and producing plutonium in an effort to coax the United States into concluding a nuclear deal. Consistent with a tit-for-tat strategy, it became more accommodating as the threats evaporated.

Once a deal with Pyongyang became an irresistible force, however, Seoul became an immovable object. In May, when war seemed imminent, South Korea had abruptly turned conciliatory, but once the danger receded, Seoul's enduring fear of abandonment revived. Although detente between Washington and Pyongyang called into question the original rationale for South Korea's existence, antagonism to the North, its economic success and transition to democracy now provided a more sustained source of legitimation. Detente did threaten the influence of the South Korean armed forces and hard-liners who resisted it with a vengeance. That caused skittishness in Blue House, where President Kim did not want to alienate those who helped put him in power. Its domestic politics made South Korea a difficult partner from June 1994 on, strewing impediments in the way of nuclear diplomacy.

There was skittishness in the United States as well. After almost stumbling into war, a handful of officials may have undergone a deathbed conversion of sorts, but most of Washington remained oblivious to the near-miss. Many in the foreign policy establishment, not just the hawks, were convinced that the Carter freeze was a cave-in. As a result, the June 1994 events did not relax the grip that shared images of nuclear diplomacy exerted on the Congress, the foreign policy establishment, and the press. Domestic opposition to deal-making remained strong, instilling caution in the administration.

Outside the government proponents of deal-making had doubts whether American policy-makers would ever negotiate in earnest. Their pessimism was evident in a July 10 op-ed in the *Washington Post* by John Steinbruner, director of foreign policy studies at the Brookings Institution. "Within the U.S. government it is believed that Jimmy Carter's improvised intervention has actually reinforced North Korea's habits of highly adversarial bargaining," he wrote, "and that reaction will be an obstacle to the development of a comprehensive initiative." Such an initiative, he elaborated, "would involve the international financing and technical assistance necessary for a benign transformation of the Yongbyon nuclear reactor complex. It would also involve the full normalization of political relations, an economic development program to bring the country out of isolation at a pace it might be able to manage, and regional security arrangements to provide reassurance against military intimidation." That would take "more effort, more imagination, more political accommodation than anyone currently finds convenient." Steinbruner argued, "Coercive bargaining is the natural inclination of the U.S. government. A stern negotiating record suppresses the domestic dispute that would be associated with any explicit political accommodation with North Korea."[5]

Clinton's hard-line critics, meanwhile, were unrelenting. Writing in the *Wall Street Journal*, Mark Helprin warned, "Someday the West may lose a city in the nuclear detonation of a weapon now under construction in North Korea. Those already assembled (my sources never fail me) are deliverable only by truck today, but as Washington temporizes, Pyongyang is working hard to shrink its payloads and extend the range of its missiles." To Helprin it was self-evident that North Korea would keep on making such weapons of mass destruction: "That no nation will voluntarily forgo what it perceives as the means of ensuring its existence is confirmed by nuclear weapons programs from China to Brazil." Brazil had, of course, verifiably renounced bomb-making in part because of American inducements. "President Clinton deals with this threat as he does with all foreign policy questions . . . by capitulation," wrote Helprin. "North Korea's boldness is directly attributable to the fact that the short-term military balance is now more in its favor than at any time since the Korean War." While he was willing to consider using nuclear arms against the North, his preferred response was an American conventional buildup to "sober and deter the North. Only then might negotiations be appropriate."[6] Helprin is a well-known writer of fiction.

Despite lingering hostility to the Carter-Kim freeze in Washington and Seoul, diplomacy resumed auspiciously enough. The United States and North Korea quickly agreed to begin the long-delayed third round of high-level talks in Geneva on July 8. Just as quickly, North and South Korea scheduled the start of a three-day summit meeting in Pyongyang on July 25, their first ever.

The American negotiating position was set at a Deputies' Committee meeting in early July. The aim was to extend the freeze to a ban on reprocessing and a halt in construction of the 200-MWe reactor, and to assure international monitoring during the time it took to conclude an agreement. There were competing priorities, like an end to North Korean missile exports. The Pentagon had previously been preoccupied with missile as well as nuclear proliferation, but officials there who wanted the missile issue deferred in order to focus the talks on stopping the North's nuclear program got their way.

The most immediate concern was the fate of the five or six bombs' worth of plutonium in the spent fuel now in the cooling ponds at Yongbyon. One option was, of course, to reprocess the fuel rods once they were no longer too hot to handle, but reprocessing by North Korea was out of the question. Officials in the Pentagon and elsewhere who wanted the fuel rods shipped to China, Britain, France, or Russia for reprocessing, carried the day in interagency deliberations. Yet Pyongyang was unlikely to reduce its nuclear leverage by agreeing to ship out the spent fuel anytime soon.[7] That made it essential for I.A.E.A. monitoring cameras and inspectors to assure that the fuel rods stayed where they were. Eventually, the water in the ponds would corrode the metal cladding of the rods, creating all sorts of hazards like flash fires and exposure to radiation. Technical discussions would soon be needed on measures to retard the corrosion, such as replenishing the cooling ponds with denatured water and maintaining them at the proper temperature and acidity levels, before putting the rods in dry storage—special containers or casks—while a deal was consummated.[8]

Gallucci sought negotiating flexibility to offer the North firm commitments on the start of diplomatic relations, an eventual peace treaty, and the provision of replacement reactors. The Bureau of East Asian and Pacific Affairs, concerned about the reaction in Seoul, was opposed to the first two, other agencies to the third.[9] Who would supply and pay for the replacement reactors was a major problem. While the list of American demands was pared down, the package deal remained empty.

Nevertheless, on the American delegation, says Thomas Hubbard, "There was a new mood as we went off to Geneva to try to pin things down."[10] The July 8 negotiating session was declared "useful and productive" by the two sides. They discussed how to phase out North Korea's existing nuclear program and phase in the replacement reactors. In compensation for freezing work on their existing reactors, the North Koreans wanted help meeting their electricity needs until the replacement reactors were on line. They also expressed some interest in obtaining reactors from Russia. There was extensive discussion on arrangements for the spent fuel in the cooling ponds. The United States offered to help store the fuel rods safely, in preparation for shipping them out of the country. In an obvious pressure tactic, negotiator Kang Sok Ju repeated what he had said to Carter, that because of the corrosion problem some fuel rods would have to be removed from the cooling ponds for reprocessing within a month. Any more reprocessing, the Americans warned, would be a "deal-breaker." The North Koreans also wanted a peace treaty with the United States and withdrawal of U.S. forces, marking a formal end to the Korean War.[11] For the D.P.R.K. a peace treaty was also one path to diplomatic normalization of relations with the United States.

Kim Il Sung's Legacy

The importance of having had Jimmy Carter secure Kim Il Sung's personal commitment to the freeze soon became apparent. On July 8, 1994, the day that the third round of high-level talks got underway, Kim suffered a sudden stroke and died. The death of the man who had ruled North Korea throughout its half century of existence momentarily unnerved negotiators and revived doubts about the prospects for nuclear diplomacy.

As if that were not bad enough, South Korea began a public campaign to destabilize the communist dynasty rather than deal with it. It vilified the late Great Leader and sowed doubts about the chances of succession and fitness to rule of Kim Jong Il, his son and heir apparent. It rounded up pro-North dissidents for eulogizing Kim Il Sung and barred them from travelling North to attend his funeral. Seoul also alerted its armed forces and canceled all military leaves.

Government hard-liners began putting out the word that the transition in Pyongyang was in trouble. "Some South Korean officials," reported the *Korea Herald*, "have not ruled out the possibilities that the death of the North Korean leader might have been the result of a power struggle."[12] The press picked up the theme. "Kim Il Sung was able to put his son in place. However, once the father is buried, he will no longer be able to control history," wrote a *Chosun Ilbo* columnist. "History will record that Kim Il Sung was the last communist dictator."[13]

Every passing day brought some new reason for Seoul to question the orderly transfer of power in Pyongyang. A two-day postponement of the state funeral to allow more mourners to pay their respects renewed speculation. "This could be some significant sign implying a power struggle," said one senior South Korean official involved in North Korean matters. "I think there is no one in the world who would delay his father's funeral date because of the condolence ceremony."[14]

South Korean intelligence sources also started rumors disparaging Kim Jong Il, and the American press spread them. "There is some speculation," reported the *New York Times*, "that Mr. Kim became involved in terrorist attacks to try to establish his credentials as an active, heroic leader, since he lacked the esteem his father earned leading the fight against the Japanese and the Americans. Mr. Kim has also been painted as a spoiled child and playboy, with a fondness for liquor, cars and wild parties with women from Sweden and Japan. Some reports say he has recently cut back on his frolics because his health has declined a bit."[15] The *Wall Street Journal* reported, "U.S. officials believe Pyongyang's communist regime might fall within months of the death of its creator."

It went on, "The U.S. intelligence assessment of Kim Jong Il" is "that he is at best a 'flake' and at worst a psychopath. He is seen as erratic and cruel." The *Journal* repeated a story from South Korea's state-run news agency that ten North Korean army officers suspected of conspiracy were burned alive on his orders. "The report was unconfirmed, but analysts say such behavior would fit a man who is widely regarded as the brains behind a 1983 assassination attempt in Rangoon, Burma, on then-South Korean President Chun Doo Hwan. That bombing missed the president but killed several of his cabinet members." The story also revived a rumor making the rounds of Pyongyang's diplomatic community in the late 1980s: "While driving his imported convertible at high speeds through the North Korean countryside, the story goes, he ran down and killed a group of pedestrians."[16] South Korean disinformation and journalistic credulity seemed equally unbounded. Any doubt that Kim Il Sung, after devoting a half century of his life to building up North Korea, would have groomed an incompetent madman to take over the enterprise apparently did not cross the minds of intelligence sources in Seoul or reporters who passed along their speculation.

Kim Il Sung's death seemed to confirm the experts' doubts about nuclear diplomacy. "With his father gone from the scene," argued Jonathan Pollack, an East Asia specialist at RAND, in a typical assessment, "there is little to suggest that the younger Kim will be prepared to barter away the one instrument of North Korean power that could keep the outside world and his internal rivals at bay."[17] Other analysts went further and predicted the imminent collapse of the regime. "The C.I.A. had said that when the old man dies, everything would go to hell," recalls a State Department Korea hand. "It was wrong. They're navigating on the course he set."[18]

A few longtime government analysts dissented. While acknowledging how little they knew about North Korea's inner workings, they downplayed the likelihood of any dramatic discontinuity. "These nuclear talks have been Kim Jong Il's talks. He is the leading figure in organizing and settling nuclear policy," said a member of the American delegation at the high-level talks. "We have never seen clear or even unclear signs of a debate on nuclear issues."[19]

Many Korea watchers feared that Kim Jong Il would take a confrontational stance on the nuclear issue in order to consolidate his support among military and party hard-liners. Yet, if he had been in charge of Pyongyang's nuclear strategy during his father's reign, he had taken care all along to leave a way out of the apparent impasses he put himself in. In a July 26 paper written for the Nautilus Institute, Alexandre Mansourov, a Soviet expatriate who had worked in Pyongyang and was now at the Center for Korean Research at Columbia University, dissented from the dominant view. He predicted that "turf battles are likely to intensify, especially between the Ministry of Foreign Affairs and the Korean People's Army over the military applications of the North Korean nuclear program." Yet he, too, expected previously established patterns to persist in nuclear decision-making: "Whenever a perception of threat to the regime's survival increased, the fears of entrapment grew, and a coalition tilted in favor of the positions advocated by the military and hard-liners was formed, . . . and negotiations stalled."[20]

There were no early signs of discontinuity. Two I.A.E.A. inspectors remained at their post in Yongbyon. When Gallucci and Hubbard paid a condolence call on the North Korean mission in Geneva, they had a long conversation with Vice Foreign Minister Kang Sok Ju, who assured them of "continuity" in his country's nuclear policies.[21] President Clinton noted, "While they did ask that we suspend our talks with them, they asked that our representative stay in Geneva and we agreed to do that."[22]

An incident during the condolence call showed how desperate the North Korean negotiators were to get something to show for their efforts. Gallucci consulted members of the U.S. delegation about how to pay his respects and was told to sign the condolence book with an appropriate message like, "Words cannot express the sympathy I feel for the Korean people," and otherwise be guided by his hosts. Upon his arrival he was escorted past a row of North Koreans to a photograph of the departed Great Leader and told to bow. Spotting cameras poised to capture the moment, he froze, then backed away after the barest nod. Pictures of a deferential American negotiator would have jeopardized his political standing back home. His hosts looked crestfallen, but they made as much of his condolence call as they could: his words of sympathy were headline news in Pyongyang.[23]

President Clinton, on a visit to Naples, was quick to reassure Pyongyang. Just hours after word reached Washington, Daniel Poneman of the N.S.C. staff drafted and secured quick clearance of a message extending "sincere condolences to the people of North Korea on the death of President Kim Il Sung. We appreciate his leadership in resuming the talks between our governments. We hope they [the talks] will continue as appropriate."[24] Clinton added that he wanted a "personal" dialogue with Kim's successor. Senate Minority Leader Robert Dole (R-KS) was just as quick to criticize the gesture, "Perhaps President Clinton has forgotten that Kim Il Sung was responsible for the war that caused the loss of more than 54,000 American lives and 100,000 Americans wounded."[25] The reaction in Washington was short-lived. After all, when Josef Stalin died, President Eisenhower sent a condolence message to the Soviet Union.

Seoul could not bring itself to do so and was angered that Clinton had. When one opposition legislator, Lee Bu Young, broke the taboo and expressed condolences at a National Assembly hearing and three of his Democratic Party colleagues suggested that it was the proper thing for the government to do, they were pilloried in the press. "They should go to North Korea and offer sympathy," read a *Chosun Ilbo* cartoon, "and never come back."[26] Their own party disowned their remarks and they had to apologize. The reaction in Seoul was "hell no," recalls a State Department Korea hand. "The backlash was so strong that the government drew the conclusion it had to be a little tougher."[27] Kim Young Sam decided to side with the hard-liners who wanted collapse, not cooperation, in North Korea.

Foreign Minister Han Sung Joo tried to sound accommodating: "We sincerely hope that the new leadership in Pyongyang will keep alive the recently created momentum for dialogue, resolve the nuclear issue, and pursue peaceful coexistence and co-prosperity between North and South Korea."[28] Han, says Charles Kartman, now the deputy chief of mission in the U.S. embassy in Seoul, "was waging a lonely fight" for the nuclear deal.[29] His voice was swamped in a sea of vituperation. At a cabinet meeting called July 18 to review policy toward the North, Prime Minister Lee Yung Dug set the tone, "There has been a historic assessment that Kim Il Sung is responsible for a number of national tragedies, such as the consolidation of national division and the fratricidal war."[30] Who divided the nation was a matter of dispute among historians, but Seoul soon distributed documents culled from Soviet archives showing Kim's responsibility for starting the Korean War.

On July 11 the North postponed the summit meeting with the South. Within days it castigated President Kim Young Sam for not taking the occasion to promote reconciliation: "Our nation will surely settle accounts with him for his towering crime, which will be cursed down through the generations."[31] Its reaction strongly implied a prolonged postponement of summitry.

That suited President Kim Young Sam just fine. He might have been willing to go to Pyongyang to meet with someone of Kim Il Sung's stature, but he would not condescend to travel there to meet his son.[32] His standoffishness would keep North-South relations out of synch with those between Washington and Pyongyang, a source of continuing friction with Seoul.

Washington had always held Pyongyang solely to blame for impeding North-South dialogue, but in a departure from past practice, Assistant Secretary of State Lord sounded more even-handed. "We will encourage North Korea to resume its dialogue with South Korea," he told reporters on July 22. "It's up to South Korea, together with North Korea, to figure out how to do that."[33] Three days later a D.P.R.K. Foreign Ministry spokesman warned that "if the improvement of North-South relations is set as 'a precondition' for the improvement of D.P.R.K.-U.S. relations at the [high-level] talks, a fatal roadblock would be erected in the way of the solution to the nuclear issue."[34]

Seoul continued to erect roadblocks. One was to dwell on Pyongyang's nuclear past. On July 27 the National Security Planning Agency, South Korea's C.I.A., trotted out another North Korean defector, an official of a trading company said to be the son-in-law of the country's prime minister. He alleged that Pyongyang already had five bombs and might make more. "Some say North Korea is only using the nuclear issue as a card," he told reporters. "I don't think so. There is a firm belief that the only way to sustain the Kim Jong Il system is to have nuclear capabilities."[35] How he was in a position to know any of that was open to question. Two days later, after consultations with Washington, Seoul formally dismissed the defector's claims, but the damage was already done.[36]

Seoul's campaign of vilification did not amuse Washington. "It does not seem to me," Gallucci icily told an August 2 State Department press briefing, "that it added clarity and warmth to the dialogue."[37]

Putting Some Chips on the Table

Negotiations had made little headway in the past because the United States never offered any substantial incentives for North Korea to end its bomb-making. With Congress unwilling to approve replacement reactors for North Korea, or even a significant share of the $4.7 billion cost of the project, representatives of the richest country in the world were reduced to travelling from capital to capital, hat in hand, begging foreigners to solve what Washington considered its most significant security concern.

The administration's initial impulse had been to find other sponsors for North Korea's light-water reactors and have Russia's nuclear agency, Minatom, build them. That would have satisfied two American nonproliferation aims at once: buy off Minatom, which had been resisting entreaties to put its nuclear material under international control, and persuade Pyongyang to become nuclear-free. Minatom, desperate to stay in the nuclear business, wanted to build a new, as yet untested design, not its older, accident-prone models. Yet South Korea was not about to foot the bill for Russia to build the reactors. "Everybody's first conclusion was that the only thing that made sense in carrying out the L.W.R. project was Russian reactors," recalls Thomas Hubbard, who did not think the R.O.K. and Japanese would find them acceptable. Hubbard came up with the idea of a multilateral consortium, instead.[38]

A July visit to the region convinced Gallucci that a consortium could be patched together. With the high-level talks in recess until August 5, Gallucci started in Seoul, where he secured an unwritten pledge from Foreign Minister Han on July 21 that the South would "actively assist" the North in replacing its reactors with South Korean ones if it gave up nuclear-arming.[39] South Korea, which depends on nuclear reactors to generate over one-third of its electricity, had already built two light-water reactors of its own, both modifications of an American model. According to Hubbard, who accompanied Gallucci, "What surprised us was that the R.O.K. came in and said, if you do the R.O.K. reactors . . . we'll pick up the lion's share of the cost."[40]

Some South Korean legislators bridled at paying for Pyongyang's reactors at Washington's behest and others wanted special inspections to precede any pledge to provide them. In an effort to sell the reactor deal in Seoul, proponents recast it as a foundation for unification, featuring South Korea in a "central role." Deputy Prime Minister Lee Hong Koo put it this way, "The project should promote the construction of a national community in Korea and the promotion of the national welfare."[41] Other South Korean officials were less diplomatic, taunting Pyongyang for needing Seoul's help to meet its energy needs. Seoul "could always be counted on to rub their noses in it," says Hubbard.[42]

Gallucci then traveled to Tokyo, where he embraced Japan's willingness to pay for some heavy fuel oil to satisfy North Korea's interim energy needs. A few experts held out the hope that the oil would meet North Korea's needs without having to build new nuclear reactors at all.

Hostility to a reactor deal was on the rise in Washington as well. Opposition in Congress and the expert community was fueled by disclosures from intelligence sources that American satellites had observed preparations to install turbines at Yongbyon to make it appear as if the reactor were used to generate electricity. "Based on all the information I have, the current nuclear capacity of North Korea exists solely for the purpose of [making plutonium] and not now and never has been attached to the national power grid," said Senator Phil Gramm (R-TX). "The argument that they will be hampered in electricity production by shutting down the reactor complex is ridiculous." Leonard Spector, a proliferation specialist at the Carnegie Endowment, said the deal risked "teaching North Korea about modern nuclear engineering and construction techniques" and urged "the utmost caution."[43] On July 15 the Senate, by 95 to 0, passed an amendment to the Foreign Assistance Act of 1995 barring aid to North Korea unless the President certified that it did not possess nuclear arms, had halted its nuclear program, had come into full compliance with both the Nonproliferation Treaty and its safe-guards agreement, and did not export weapons-grade plutonium or missiles.[44] In an August 2 *Washington Post* op-ed, Victor Gilinsky, a former Nuclear Regulatory Commission member, argued that overriding "our strict statutory standards for nuclear exports" to provide North Korea with nuclear technology "would make us accomplices to its violations of Nonproliferation Treaty inspection rules. By thus buying off an international trouble-maker, we would be giving the wrong idea to others similarly inclined." Coal-fired plants "would make much more sense," he argued. So would improving the efficiency of the way the North Koreans "transmit and use electricity."[45]

The Gilinsky op-ed drew an August 5 rejoinder from Robert Manning, a State Department adviser on Asia policy in the Bush Administration, and James Przystup, director of Asia studies at the Heritage Foundation, warning that "an odd coalition of technical purists, anti-nukers, and political partisans threatens to scuttle the already slim hope of a deal." In return for the replacement reactors, the United States "would effectively cap North Korea's weapons program and open the door to rolling it back."[46] Deal-making also gained support from another unexpected source, former Congressman Stephen Solarz, who had opposed negotiations by the Bush Administration. "We should offer North Korea full diplomatic relations, a no-first-use pledge about the use of nuclear weapons, and whatever economic assistance it needs for its legitimate energy requirements, including, if necessary, a light-water nuclear reactor." Anticipating that North Korea might agree to forgo future production of fissile material but insist "that its past program is off-limits," Solarz felt that "the future of the North Korean program should concern us more than its past."[47]

High-level talks resumed August 5 in Geneva. Disposition of the eight thousand fuel rods and an end to construction at two reactor sites took up most of the eight hours of negotiating that day. D.P.R.K. negotiator Kang denied pledging not to reprocess the fuel rods in the cooling ponds in talks with Jimmy Carter, and a search of the American notetaker's records backed him up.[48] Kang now rejected shipping the fuel rods abroad for reprocessing. He insisted the North would halt construction of two new reactors when a replacement reactor was "actually" provided, which could mean either when a firm commitment was made to supply the reactor or a construction contract was signed.[49] The North was also unwilling to extend its freeze on reloading the Yongbyon reactor beyond September. Kang indicated that it intended to refuel, then freeze. "They made a big deal of it," says Thomas Hubbard.[50] So did the Americans, who were not about to give North Korea more nuclear leverage than it already had.

North Korea also expressed its displeasure with South Korean reactors. After Gallucci repeatedly made it clear that neither the United States nor anyone else besides South Korea would put up the money for replacement reactors and that South Korea was not about to pay for anyone else to build them, "Kang made a statement that clearly implied they would accept the South Korean reactors and we took it as that," says Hubbard, "and he nodded when we said we were going to take it as that."[51]

The two sides made significant progress on another key issue: the North agreed that as part of a settlement it would implement full-scope safeguards. That required it to clear up anomalies in its nuclear history—by special inspections, if necessary. The timing remained unsettled, as did the timing of dismantling the North's existing reactors. In a significant concession, the North also took the peace treaty off the table for now.[52] That was not the only indication of North Korean interest in accommodation.

To some on the American delegation a deal now seemed in sight. An INR analyst who had been poring over North Korea's public statements detected "clear signs" that "a final decision had been made" on special inspections and the North was "laying the groundwork in public." Nevertheless, he adds, "Even the best I could say was that they were no longer rejecting the idea of special inspections publicly; there was no way of knowing the outlines of their final position."[53]

A week later, on August 12, the talks yielded another agreed statement, listing four pairs of reciprocal acts that "should be part of a final resolution of the nuclear issue." The United States committed itself to "make arrangements" for the provision of light-water reactors and interim energy supplies; in return the D.P.R.K. said it would remain in the Nonproliferation Treaty and implement its safeguards agreement. "Upon receipt of U.S. assurances" on the reactors and the interim energy supplies, the D.P.R.K. would freeze construction of its two new reactors and seal its reprocessing plant. The sides agreed to establish liaison offices in Washington and Pyongyang and "to reduce barriers to trade and investment, as a move toward full normalization of political and economic relations." In return for "assurances against the threat or use of nuclear weapons" from the United States, the D.P.R.K. would implement the North-South denuclearization accord. Expert-level talks would be held to work out storage and disposal of the spent nuclear fuel in the cooling ponds at Yongbyon, the supply of alternative energy, and arrangements for the liaison offices. The two sides recessed the high-level talks until September 23. The North pledged to maintain the freeze and inspections for continuity of safeguards in the meantime, but it refused to extend its commitment not to refuel the Yongbyon reactor beyond the next round of talks.[54] (Text in appendix II.)

There was a last-minute hitch. When the agreed text was sent to capitals on August 11 for concurrence, Pyongyang balked at committing itself to "full-scope safeguards."[55] The sides instead settled on the language, "The D.P.R.K. is prepared to remain a party to the Treaty on the Nonproliferation of Nuclear Weapons and to allow implementation of its safeguards agreement under the Treaty." The safeguards agreement explicitly provided for special inspections. After a late-night session haggling over the revision, Gallucci told a 2 A.M. August 13 news conference what he had been telling the North Koreans all along: "There is no chance that there will be a light-water reactor constructed in a country that does not accept full-scope safeguards. In this case the requirement . . . includes the acceptance of special inspections."[56] Gallucci's North Korean counterpart, Kang Sok Ju, was upbeat, hailing the accord as an expression of "our clear intentions to resolve our nuclear issue." He repeated the North Korean view, "We on our part do not recognize the special inspections," but "the future of that issue," he added, "depends on whether the D.P.R.K. and the United States build up trust and the D.P.R.K. and the I.A.E.A. build up trust."[57]

The South Korean Foreign Ministry called the agreement "a step in the right direction to insure past, present and future nuclear transparency." Yet others in Seoul were privately critical that the agreement made no mention of the source of the reactors or South Korea's "central role" in supplying them. The issue would dog the negotiations for many months to come. "The South," says Thomas Hubbard, "wanted to keep pinning it down in such a way that would be embarrassing to the North Koreans. So they would decline to write it in a public way, but they never backed down on their willingness to accept it."[58]

Others in Seoul criticized the absence of any specific commitment to special inspections, which they believed to be a foolproof way to ascertain whether or not North Korea had a bomb. "It's a positive step forward," said Kim Kyung-Won, former ambassador to Washington and president of the Seoul Forum for International Affairs, "but it doesn't really take care of the one fundamental concern that we have."[59]

Seoul had another fundamental concern as well: it was opposed to the exchange of liaison offices or any moves toward diplomatic normalization between the D.P.R.K. and the United States. "There is a sense of feeling left out," said Yang Sung Chul, a professor of political science at Kyunghee University.[60] The Americans had consulted with the South Koreans during the round. "We flagged that all the way through," says Hubbard. "Yet when it hit the papers in Seoul they went berserk." Privately South Korean officials began insisting that the United States not exchange liaison offices until North-South talks made progress. "Between August and September the South tried to get us to accept that linkage. We tried not to make a public issue of it, but we made it clear to them that we hadn't accepted it," says Hubbard. "They threw the blame on us, saying we didn't consult. Rarely has that been the case. It's almost always been something they've accepted." To Hubbard the lesson was "there's no way you can consult enough with them because they can't manage their own domestic politics."[61] It would take a lot longer for the rest of Washington to absorb that lesson of alliance management.

President Kim Young Sam did not mute his misgivings. In an August 15 speech, he formally offered to supply North Korea with two nuclear reactors but on tough conditions that the North was unlikely to accept anytime soon. One was ad hoc, routine, and special inspections: "If and when the North guarantees the transparency of its nuclear activities, we are ready to support their development of the peaceful use of nuclear energy, including light-water nuclear reactor construction, by providing them with the necessary capital and technology." Unnamed presidential aides also told reporters Seoul would insist on playing "a central role" in building the reactors. Kim went on to declare victory in the Korean Cold War: "The competition between the South and the North over which can create a better society has been decided." He cast his offer as a step toward unification on the South's terms: "This could well become the very first joint project for national development, leading to the establishment of a single community of the Korean people." He alluded to the North's dependence in a way that was sure to be seen as patronizing: "The problems of the North are our own problems."[62] Kim called for the rivals to "stop slandering each other." He also called on North Korea "to undertake bold reforms including improvement of the human rights situation." Substantial improvement was surely needed, but Seoul, whose own human rights record was hardly unblemished, often treated the issue as a way simply to slander the communist regime and threaten its survival. Kim said nothing about setting a new date for the postponed North-South summit meeting.

Privately President Kim still insisted that the nuclear past took precedence over the nuclear future. In a forty-minute telephone call the next day, he urged President Clinton to condition any pledge to provide reactors on completion of special inspections. That was a potential deal-breaker. Clinton was prepared to be patient about the past. He reaffirmed the American position, that construction of the reactor, not the commitment to provide them, would have to await full North Korean compliance with its safeguards agreement. An American official fudged the distinction in public: "We're making it very clear that the North Koreans will have to solve this problem with the inspections before anyone will deliver a reactor to them." A White House official said, "As we get into this very difficult stage with the North Koreans, there is a great deal of emphasis to make sure South Korea and the U.S. are in lock-step coordination."[63] The South Koreans were not making it easy.

The North Korean Foreign Ministry objected to "setting the special inspection" as a "precondition to the solution of the issue" and rebuffed the South Korean demand, "We will never allow the inspection of the military sites at the expense of our sovereignty to receive light-water reactors." Yet the Foreign Ministry added that "we are willing to involve ourselves in clearing up 'nuclear suspicion' in the future."[64] Press reports interpreted the statement as a repudiation of North Korea's August 12 commitment, without mentioning South Korea's demand. An August 28 broadcast on Pyongyang radio restated the point for anyone who bothered to listen: "It is foolish of the South Korean authorities to blare that they would offer the light-water reactor only when the North accepted special inspections."[65] For North Korea to acknowledge its dependence on its sibling rival to power its economy was humiliating enough without also having to satisfy South Korean preconditions.

Seoul also kept sowing doubts about the succession in the North, producing another spate of stories in the American press, some of them skeptical of Seoul's claims. South Korea's state news agency Yonhap, citing an unidentified Western diplomat in Seoul, reported that leaflets were dropped at embassies in Pyongyang August 19 bearing the slogan, "Down with Kim Jong Il." Two foreign diplomats in Pyongyang contacted by the Associated Press dismissed the report as groundless, but the story was carried by the *New York Times* and other newspapers.[66] Noting Kim Jong Il's reclusiveness and the delay in his formal installation as party general secretary and head of state, stories speculated whether, as a *Los Angeles Times* report phrased it, "something is rotten in Pyongyang." It cited James Lilley, a former U.S. ambassador to Korea, "You get these gnawing signs that something is wrong."[67] The article neglected to mention that Lilley had been saying all along it would take a collapse of the communist regime to resolve the nuclear issue. On August 25, after a meeting of top-level officials, South Korea issued a statement, "The government is keeping a close watch on North Korea, as there seems to be uncertainty regarding the change of power." In reporting it, the *Washington Post* added that "much of the evidence of a conspiracy against the younger Kim either has proved false or, upon examination, looks rather flimsy."[68] A page-one news story in the *New York Times* wondered, "Who is in charge in North Korea?" It went on, "In recent days there has been a string of reports, some from North Korea, some amplified by the South Korean Government for its own purposes, hinting at strife over choosing a successor to Kim Il Sung."[69] Just what those purposes were, the story left unsaid. The news reports were inadvertently promoting a campaign by some South Koreans to try to destabilize North Korea rather than deal with it.

On September 1 the United States and the D.P.R.K. announced that working-level talks would begin on September 10. Talks on the disposition of the fuel rods and the provision of replacement reactors and interim energy supplies were slated for Berlin with Gary Samore, a State Department proliferation specialist, to represent the United States. Talks on the liaison offices would be held in Pyongyang with Lynn Turk of the State Department's Korea desk to head the U.S. delegation. Although diplomats had unofficially accompanied Americans to Pyongyang, this was the first time an American diplomat would hold official talks there.

The announcement set off another round of intense criticism in Seoul. Citing an "erosion in cooperation and collaboration with the U.S.," *Chosun Ilbo* said, "South Korea faces a total crisis in foreign affairs, especially in dealing with North Korea." The newspaper with the largest circulation in Korea, *Chosun Ilbo* had waged a long crusade against cooperation with North Korea. That sent Foreign Minister Han Sung Joo flying to Washington for a hastily scheduled visit. Han expressed concern that improvement in U.S.-D.P.R.K. relations was leaping too far ahead of North-South relations instead of proceeding "in parallel," and sought a delay in the exchange of liaison offices. An aide to President Kim Young Sam said, "We hope the U.S. government can persuade the North to come to terms with the South in return for, if not a precondition of, Washington's recognition of Pyongyang."[70] Han also sought assurances that the United States would not sign a peace treaty with North Korea. Concern about the peace treaty was kindled by China's abrupt announcement on September 2 of its withdrawal from the Military Armistice Commission, which supervised the truce in the demilitarized zone.

Secretary of State Christopher sounded vaguely reassuring, "We cannot finally resolve the nuclear issue until and unless the North resumes its dialogue with the South." A final resolution could, of course, take years. "We are saying that the North-South issue is part of the solution," said an administration official, "but we are not trying to establish any mechanical linkage."[71] A U.S. official blamed Seoul's campaign of vilification for the lack of parallelism: "It is South Korea that poured the gasoline and lit the match."[72]

The brouhaha would cost Han his job at year's end. He had long been under attack by the hawks in Kim Young Sam's entourage for being too willing to negotiate with the North, but President Kim thought of the U.S.-educated Han as someone who could handle the Americans. Now that critics were assailing Kim himself, accusing him of letting Washington race ahead of Seoul in dealing with Pyongyang, Kim shifted the blame to Han.

Having tried to appease the hawks, Kim now tried to placate the business community by easing a ban on South Korean firms from doing business directly with North Korea. The ban had been maintained at American behest in order to pressure North Korea to resolve the nuclear issue. Although the volume of indirect trade was on the rise, the *chaebol*, Korea's conglomerates, fearful of losing market share to the Japanese and other competitors, argued that the restraints still chafed. "There is a feeling that something has to be done to reach a breakthrough in inter-Korean relations as the U.S. and Pyongyang move [toward rapprochement] faster than before," said a presidential spokesman.[73] It was a better way to keep "in parallel."

The Clinton Administration was also getting heat at home. North Korea, said Douglas Paal, director of the Asia Pacific Policy Center and an Asia specialist on the National Security Council staff in the Bush Administration, "senses that the United States will seek an agreement at any price."[74] Paul Wolfowitz, undersecretary of defense in the Bush Administration, took the same tack, "It seems to me that we are in a situation where we are paying more and more for less and less."[75] When an op-ed by George Perkovich of the W. Alton Jones Foundation ran in the *Washington Post* arguing that a deal would not set a bad precedent for other potential proliferators, George Stephanopoulos, the president's senior adviser, took the time to call to thank him.[76]

So beleaguered was the administration that some officials began offering a new rationale for a nuclear deal: killing North Korea with kindness. They characterized the construction of replacement reactors as a "crowbar" to pry open the country to outside influences that would cause its collapse and a "poison pill" for its assisted suicide. The argument that the problem was about to disappear was eagerly picked up by Democrats on Capital Hill. "Time is on our side," a Congressional source told the *Los Angeles Times*. "As long as we can maintain the current freeze and continue talking, it is to our advantage. I think we're never going to see a light-water reactor up and running in North Korea, because there's a good chance there won't be a North Korea at the time it is ready."[77] Yet it was difficult to be sure how much staying power the regime had and whether North Korea's collapse was something to be desired or feared.

The October Agreed Framework

With high-level talks due to resume on September 23, the talks in Berlin bogged down. The issue was compensation for the electricity that in theory might have been generated by the reactor to be shut down under the freeze and for the sunk costs of the two new reactors whose construction was to be halted. The United States had offered interim energy supplies, either in the form of fuel or non-nuclear generating capacity. "In Berlin we got some different ideas that were a little grander," Gallucci said.[78] He was referring to a statement by D.P.R.K. negotiator Kim Jong U at a September 12 negotiating session that economic planners in Pyongyang were opposed to replacing the reactors unless the United States fully offset all related costs, which Americans reckoned could add $2 billion to the price of the deal.

In Berlin the North Korean negotiator did react positively to the idea of a consortium, while insisting that an American firm act as prime contractor. He objected to the South Korean reactors as "unsafe, uneconomical, and politically unsuitable."[79] There was some truth to the third objection, but publicly the North Koreans spoke mostly about the first, expressing interest in a reactor being developed by Siemens on the grounds that it was "much safer and more secure."[80] It was the North's way of disparaging the South. From the beginning the United States had told North Korea that the only country willing to supply replacement reactors was South Korea and Seoul was not about to pay anyone else to build them. As Gallucci put it at a September 14 press conference, "The only viable—technically viable, financially viable, politically viable—construct for a light-water reactor project is one where South Korea plays a central role."[81] North Korean naysaying did not trouble most members of the American delegation. "For a lot of us," says one, "the feeling was, we said that enough times, they heard us and they never said, forget it."[82] With Gallucci in Seoul to secure South Korea's commitment in writing to providing the reactors, Kim Jong U told reporters in Berlin, "The right of selection of light-water reactors is in the hands of the D.P.R.K. Whether South Korea is to finance the project or not, we are not concerned."[83]

Gallucci later said, "I couldn't quite explain why we were confronting positions in Berlin which were quite inconsistent with understandings we just so recently reached in Geneva."[84] One reason was amour propre: the North wanted to play down the centrality of the South's role in replacing the reactors. A more immediate reason was that South Korea was insisting that special inspections be held before it would promise to supply the reactors. A *New York Times* editorial warned, "Don't Feed Seoul's Hawks." It argued that the South Korean government was under pressure from hawks not to postpone the special inspections, "but those special inspections are among the few bargaining chips the North has, and it is not likely to concede them until it is assured of getting the light-water reactors."[85]

Within the week Seoul dropped its insistence on completing a special inspection before committing itself in writing to provide the reactors. Shortly after Gallucci's departure, President Kim Young Sam sent President Clinton a letter on September 20 saying that Seoul "will play a central role in providing North Korea with light-water reactors if the North guarantees the transparency of its nuclear activities."[86]

The next day Gallucci appeared at the State Department noon briefing to preview the upcoming round of high-level talks. He told reporters of his consultations with South Korea, Japan, China, Russia, and other countries in Europe and Asia about joining a consortium, the Korean Energy Development Organization (K.E.D.O.), to supply replacement reactors and meet North Korea's interim energy needs. As yet he had no commitments, he said, but he stressed, "The best way to characterize the South Korean role is that it will be central." Asked by a South Korean reporter whether South Korea would be "dominant," he replied, "I believe the word I tried to use was 'central.' I like 'central,' and I hope you'd come to develop some affection for it too."[87] Reporters laughed.

High-level talks resumed two days later in Geneva. The issue of compensation was resolved without much trouble. The North Koreans asked for "cash or alternative fuel," recalls Thomas Hubbard. "We said coal. They said heavy fuel oil." The United States calculated that 500,000 metric tons of oil a year would make up for the electricity theoretically foregone by freezing the North's nuclear program. The dispute came over how soon the oil would flow. The United States agreed to a first shipment once the freeze was verifiably in place. As it had with the replacement reactor, the North resisted referring to K.E.D.O. as the supplier of the oil, says Thomas Hubbard. "They wanted the United States on the hook."[88]

Getting Pyongyang to commit itself not to refuel the reactor as part of the freeze was a problem. "The North Koreans said that their nuclear scientists were hot to trot" about refueling, but the real issue was nuclear leverage, says Hubbard. "It was a power play." Two other issues were even more contentious: when the North would have to ship out the spent fuel and when it would have to clear up the discrepancies in its account to the I.A.E.A. of its nuclear past—by special inspections if necessary. "The two elements of leverage they insisted on holding onto were the fuel rods and the special inspections," says Hubbard. The North wanted a commitment from the United States to a finished light-water reactor by the year 2000. The United States accepted 2003. "Then the question became when in the LWR process did various things happen," says Hubbard. "They wanted to lock us in as deeply as possible to the LWR before they had to ship the fuel rods out and do special inspections."[89]

The American delegation was in agreement on which mattered most: "We had all come around to the view that the fuel rods were more important than the special inspections." That priority was not shared in

Seoul, or in much of Washington. After the Bush and Clinton Administrations had made so much of the importance of special inspections to ascertain whether the North may have already reprocessed one or two bombs' worth of plutonium, they had convinced others that "if you don't get them, then you haven't gotten anything." Clearing up the past became the principal point of contention with the North. The United States initially wanted that done before construction began on the first replacement reactor. Its fallback position was within six months of the signing of a contract to deliver light-water reactors. The D.P.R.K. said it would "completely eliminate the so-called suspicions" only after the reactors were completed.[90] "The thing we argued the most about was when and how," recalls Hubbard. "Kang would say, you're taking my pants off." Again and again the word "pants" recurs in Hubbard's notes.[91]

At this delicate moment an unauthorized American threat made Pyongyang bristle. The day of Gallucci's briefing, *Pacific Stars & Stripes* published an interview with the U.S. commander-in-chief in the Pacific, Admiral Ronald J. Zlapoter, disclosing that the United States had dispatched the aircraft carrier *Kitty Hawk* to the Sea of Japan, off Korea. He cited Haiti as an example of how "some very strong military force can influence diplomacy. And that's why we're putting the carrier battle group up there off the Korean peninsula. I think it sends a very strong message."[92]

The history of American gunboat diplomacy is familiar to North Koreans. An American man-o-war, the *General Sherman*, tried to open Korea to commercial penetration in 1866. After it ran aground near Pyongyang, Koreans killed the crew and burned the ship. To avenge the killing and force Korea open, the United States dispatched an armada in 1871, but it too was forced to withdraw.[93] A century later, carriers armed with nuclear-capable aircraft were used to threaten North Korea.

The D.P.R.K. Foreign Ministry reacted a day after Zlapoter's comments, warning that "undisguised military provocations" could wreck the talks and end the freeze on its nuclear activities. In a pointed rejoinder to Seoul, it added, "If the dishonest forces created difficulties in the provision of LWRs, insisting on 'special inspections,' the D.P.R.K. would not feel the need to freeze its independent graphite-moderated reactor program." The spokesman added, "It is unthinkable that the D.P.R.K., which regards independence as its life and soul, would open even its military sites to get LWRs."[94] The D.P.R.K. Defense Ministry reacted more sharply three days later, "Now that the United States is seeking a military showdown, we cannot stick to talks indefinitely." It added, "Our people's army . . . will never allow any attempt to have our military sites opened through special inspections."[95] The *Kitty Hawk* was withdrawn on October 3. An official complained, "The feeling among the [negotiating] team is how can I negotiate when they [North Koreans] say, 'Send the carrier away' and we send it away?"[96]

Now it was the South Korean Defense Ministry's turn to toy with coercive diplomacy. It staged an Armed Forces Day parade, its first in four years, to display its latest weapons.[97] With Defense Secretary Perry due in Seoul on October 6–7 for an annual Security Consultative Meeting, it began suggesting that Team Spirit might be resumed.[98] Even after Defense Secretary Perry deferred a decision, a senior South Korean official told Reuters following a meeting of senior national security advisers with President Kim on October 11, "It is the government's position to go ahead with Team Spirit military exercises next month unless the North shows sincerity to resolve the nuclear problem."[99]

The hawks' efforts to dynamite deal-making finally drew return fire from the highest-ranking dove in the government. Foreign Minister Han Sung Joo did his best to close the gap between perceptions and reality in Seoul. "Because of its desperate situation," he told journalists on September 24, "North Korea has been forced to take a passive and defensive posture. In my opinion, the North has been clinging to its nuclear card with the aim of improving its diplomatic ties with the United States so as to break out of this plight."[100] A week later Han was berated when he testified before a committee of the National Assembly. Backbenchers from the ruling Democratic Liberal Party complained that engagement between Pyongyang and Washington was outpacing North-South ties and that the reactor deal was unfortunate. One warned the government to be wary of K.E.D.O. "because other foreign countries, if they are allowed to participate in the consortium, will surely have a larger voice on the issues of the Korean Peninsula."[101]

Domestic opposition to direct dialogue between Washington and Pyongyang was unnerving the government in Seoul. In an October 7 interview with the *New York Times*, President Kim Young Sam revealed his unease in an outburst of naked hostility: "The problem is we think we know North Korea better than anyone. We have spoken with North Korea more than 400 times. It didn't get us anywhere. They are not sincere." He lashed out at American compromises that could extend the life of the communist regime: "We should not make more concessions in the future. Time is on our side." Responding to a question from *Times* publisher Arthur Sulzberger, Jr., he took direct aim at the *Times*'s editorials as well as at Washington: "If the United States wants to settle with a half-baked compromise and the media wants to describe it as a good agreement, they can. But I think it would bring more danger and peril."[102]

Press reports of deadlock fueled pessimism about the talks. Foreign Minister Han warned, "If the current situation continues, the talks will collapse."[103] In fact, negotiators had reached the final stage of hard bargaining where a deal seems possible but some of the most difficult issues remain to be resolved. "There's a distance between the two sides, and on our side at least it's worth taking some time to figure out where we go from here," a delegation member told a reporter.[104] To bridge the distance, negotiator Gallucci asked for a brief recess on September 29 to return to Washington for new instructions.

Three key issues remained. One was how firm a stand to take on barring the refueling of the reactor, to prevent the North from generating more spent fuel. In a meeting with Secretary of State Christopher and White House adviser David Gergen, Hubbard recalls arguing, "Look, Mr. Secretary, the important point is that they don't reprocess." They were persuaded: "They gave us some room to maneuver on the reloading." It proved unnecessary; the North relented and agreed not to reload. The other key issues were how long to postpone the I.A.E.A.'s scrutiny of the past and when to phase in the dismantling of the reprocessing plant and the shipping out of the spent fuel. As Gallucci had said at a State Department briefing, the nuclear waste sites "are not going anywhere," so "there is no urgency" for a special inspection.[105] Construction could begin, but none of the nuclear components of the reactor could be lawfully transferred to North Korea until it came into full compliance with the Nonproliferation Treaty.

The Principals' Committee of the National Security Council convened over lunch on October 3. With strong backing from Defense Secretary Perry, Gallucci won approval to defer special inspections until key nuclear components of the reactor were about to be delivered. Depending on the pace of construction, that could be five years away. The principals also approved postponing the requirement to dismantle the reprocessing plant until then on condition that it remained sealed under I.A.E.A. supervision. Deputy Secretary of Defense John Deutch objected to the delay in putting the spent fuel into casks and the failure to require removal of the spent fuel generated by the replacement reactors. Gallucci was instructed to insist on canning the spent fuel once the reactor contract was signed, deferring the need to reprocess it. Handling of future spent fuel would be covered by the contract for replacement reactors.[106]

Deutch renewed his objections in a letter to President Clinton. He also questioned whether the interim fuel supplies could be misused by the North Korean military. Heavy fuel oil could be used for heating and generating electricity, but not to power an airplane or a tank. Resentment on the delegation had not yet dissipated a year later. Three members dismissed Deutch's letter as "ludicrous," "pretty stupid," and "a real nuisance." Another took it as a ploy to look technically sophisticated and politically tough-minded. The delegation cabled Washington, urging that the issue be deferred until contract talks and warning that trying to commit the North Koreans to ship out the spent fuel could lead them to insist that the United States guarantee their supply of nuclear fuel.[107]

The Deutch letter occasioned a lengthy airing of these issues in an October 18 National Security Council meeting.[108] That prompted Hubbard, who was negotiating the text of the accord, to take a chance. "I was on a roll with Kim Gye Gwan," Hubbard recalls, "and without authorization I said, do you mean you're not going to reprocess the rods that come out of the LWR? He said, of course, we're shutting down, we're sealing, we're not going to reprocess."[109] The Deutch letter had another, less salutary effect. It led negotiators to pin down the precise uses for the heavy fuel oil, a source of needless trouble later on. Detailed arrangements for storing and disposing of the spent fuel would await expert-level talks.

On October 12 the United States agreed to defer a full accounting of the D.P.R.K.'s nuclear past and dismantling of its existing nuclear facilities. Two days later the Agreed Framework was concluded.

South Korea objected that the accord made no mention of North-South talks. North Korea was not alone in resisting a commitment to North-South talks in the text. Some Americans were also wary of an overly tight linkage, for fear that it could impede conclusion of a deal and its implementation. Settling the issue in a way that mollified the South Koreans took a week. The North promised to "engage in North-South dialogue" and "consistently take steps to implement" the 1991 North-South denuclearization accord.

Clinton, citing the "unanimous recommendations" of his advisers, gave his assent. On October 21 the United States and the Democratic People's Republic of Korea signed the accord.

The Agreed Framework was just that—an agreed framework, not a treaty, sidestepping the need for Senate action. (Text in appendix II.) The accord carefully avoided obligating the United States to supply two replacement reactors and set just one fixed date, that the first reactor would be ready by the end of 2003. Instead, it laid out a detailed road map of reciprocal steps, leaving both sides some leverage against reneging. The D.P.R.K. pledged to remain a party to the Nonproliferation Treaty and to freeze its nuclear program by not refueling its reactor, cooperate in arranging temporary safe storage of the spent fuel rods pending their eventual removal, and seal its reprocessing plant to prevent it from extracting plutonium from those fuel rods. Implementation of the freeze under I.A.E.A. monitoring was an immediate test of the North's good faith. In return, the United States promised to move toward political and economic normalization, an exchange of liaison offices, and the lowering of barriers to trade and investment. A U.S.-organized consortium would construct two new nuclear reactors and provide the North a supply of heavy fuel oil in the interim.

In elaborately choreographed steps, nuclear dismantling would proceed along with the construction of replacement reactors. With construction of the plant and turbines for the first reactor complete, but before any nuclear components were supplied, the North would have to come into full compliance with its safeguards agreement, "taking all steps that may be deemed necessary by the I.A.E.A., following consultations with the agency, with regard to verifying the accuracy and completeness of the D.P.R.K.'s initial report on all nuclear material in the D.P.R.K." Unspecified but clearly implied were two steps that the agency could well deem necessary, special inspections and the safeguarding of any previously undeclared nuclear material. Then, as the reactor's nuclear components were installed, the North would ship out its fuel rods. As the second replacement reactor neared completion, the North would complete the dismantlement of its gas-graphite reactors and reprocessing plant.[110]

The United States committed itself to very little: it would supply a portion of the heavy fuel oil, at a cost of $20 to $30 million a year, and help arrange and pay for the storage of the spent nuclear fuel, at a total cost of $10 million. An American firm would supply some key nuclear components for the replacement reactors, requiring a bilateral nuclear cooperation agreement that would have to be submitted to Congress. The bulk of the estimated $4.7 billion cost of constructing the reactors and supplying the spent fuel would be borne by others, especially South Korea and Japan. If they failed to meet the North's energy needs, President Clinton in a letter to Kim Jong Il promised to "use the full powers of my office to provide, to the extent necessary, such interim energy alternatives from the United States, subject to the approval of the U.S. Congress." The letter contained a similar obligation for the replacement reactors.

The agreement meant that the world would still have to live with some nuclear ambiguity about North Korea's nuclear past for at least five years, and perhaps forever. What it does not have to live with is the near-certainty that by now the North could have many more nuclear weapons.

Decrying and Defending the Deal

Critics of the Clinton Administration immediately found fault with deferring shipment of the spent nuclear fuel to a third country, special inspections of the nuclear waste sites and putting any previously undisclosed nuclear material under I.A.E.A. safeguards, dismantlement of the North's existing nuclear facilities, and resumption of North-South talks.

Lost in the barrage of criticism were the administration's achievements. It had shut down North Korea's nuclear arms program. The agreement went well beyond the Nonproliferation Treaty to prohibit the D.P.R.K. from refueling its reactor or reprocessing and to require it to dismantle its existing nuclear facilities. The replacement reactors would make North Korea completely dependent on others for the supply of nuclear fuel, which could be cut off if it did anything untoward. That limited the plutonium-laden spent fuel it could generate.

President Clinton hailed the accord as one that "will make the United States, the Korean peninsula and the world safer." An unnamed I.A.E.A. official was still missing the point: "This means that we are living with a country that flouted the nuclear Nonproliferation Treaty and will remain in noncompliance for years."[111] That set the tone for much of the commentary to follow. "The president will take on a pretty heavy burden of defending this agreement as skepticism arises about North Korea's behavior," said Douglas Paal, an Asia specialist on the National Security Council staff in the Bush Administration. Supposition about clandestine nuclear sites in the North was another point of contention. "If they only let us into places they just declare, have you really got their whole program? We won't know," worried James Lilley, ambassador to Seoul in the Reagan Administration.[112] Collapse, not cooperation, remained the goal of some opponents toward North Korea. "When the history of this week's agreement is written," intoned an editorial in the *Wall Street Journal*, "we suspect what will be remembered is that the world started pouring money into the Kim regime just as it should have been allowed to crash."[113] Jim Hoagland disparaged Clinton's " 'Let's Make a Deal' approach," and "a tendency in this administration to reward its adversaries for hanging tough." The deal "leaves the most important leverage over its terms in the hands of North Korea up to the year 2003 and perhaps beyond."[114] He neglected to mention that the deal also gave the United States leverage, arguably for the first time. John Glenn told the *Wall Street Journal*, "I think the worst thing a great power can do is bluff, get caught at the bluff, and not be willing to back it up."[115] Senate Minority Leader Robert Dole commented, "It is always possible to get an agreement when you give enough away."[116] William

Safire quoted James Schlesinger, "While it was not an unconditional surrender, it was a negotiated surrender."[117] Senator John McCain (R-AZ) was characteristically outspoken: "I am absolutely accusing the President and Mr. Gallucci of appeasement and going back on their commitment that they made to me and several other members of Congress that the first item of business in negotiations with the Koreans would be inspections of the two nuclear waste sites and the accounting for the plutonium that was diverted—that could have and, in the view of the C.I.A., did result in the construction of two nuclear weapons."[118]

Few in the foreign policy establishment defended the deal. "The agreement cuts the heart out of their ability to produce nuclear weapons and that is the most serious and the most immediate problem," said Leslie Gelb, president of the Council on Foreign Relations, who had once opposed deal-making.[119] Arnold Kanter, who had held the first high-level talk with the North in the Bush Administration, said, "Given the strategic decision to essentially buy out the North Korean nuclear program, then I think this is a good agreement. Would I have liked to have avoided setting that kind of precedent? Yes. Do I think it is a price worth paying? Yes."[120] *Washington Post* columnist Jessica Mathews called it "a solid win for world peace" and accused "Republicans who have leaped to blast it" of being "strikingly ill informed about its contents."[121]

The response in Seoul was bitter. A cartoon in one newspaper depicted South Korea's Kim Young Sam on the ground eating a lowly radish while North Korea's Kim Jong Il stood on a mountain eating ginseng, a delicacy prized by Koreans.[122] "Where has the nuclear transparency gone?" wondered *Chosun Ilbo* in a page-one headline. "Bewilderment" was the headline in *Kookmin Ilbo*. A backbencher in the ruling Democratic Liberal Party charged the government with failing to get special inspections "prior to construction of the light-water reactors." In a Blue House background briefing, national security adviser Chung Jong-uk sounded defensive: "Frankly speaking, it does not satisfy us. But I hope you will regard it as the second best policy." Washington, he went on, had ignored Seoul's opposition and "pushed ahead with the logic of a superpower."[123] To one Korea expert it was as if the North and South were about to be married and the South asked the United States to perform the marriage, only to have the minister run away with the bride.[124]

Defense Secretary Perry was dispatched to Seoul "to offer the Korean government the assurances that this agreement was compatible with their and our long-term security interests." He told reporters en route, "I have a reputation in Korea as being a hard-liner on this issue and, therefore, they will understand that if I'm in favor of it, that these security issues have been taken into account."[125]

Much of the American debate turned on the likelihood of North Korean compliance, but implementation of the accord also depended on substantial financial pledges from South Korea, Japan, and other consortium members, and on Congressional funding of the American share. Paying for replacement reactors was a problem for restive South Korean legislators. Paying $50–60 million a year for heavy fuel oil to meet North Korea's interim energy needs was a problem everywhere else. Finance Minister Masayoshi Takemura hinted that Japan's contribution was contingent on European participation. "This was not a precondition, in the strict sense," said one Foreign Ministry official, but another conceded, "Ultimately, it is a political decision. And it's not clear yet what is politically acceptable to the Japanese people."[126]

In the November election the Republican Party took control of both Houses of Congress. The shock was just reverberating around Washington when Secretary of State Christopher, in Seoul for a previously scheduled visit, walked into the office of President Kim Young Sam. He was "immediately hit with The Question, 'How should we read this election?'"[127] The South Korean hawks had an answer: with jubilation.

With Congress now more unlikely than before to appropriate money for the deal, the Clinton Administration tried to avoid a vote and instead drew on $4.7 million in discretionary funds in the Pentagon budget for the first shipment of 50,000 metric tons of heavy fuel oil while approaching other governments to beg for funding. The *Far Eastern Economic Review* headlined its story on the accord, "Hold the Champagne."[128] In a *Wall Street Journal* op-ed, Karen Elliott House called the deal "a house of cards." The only question, she contended, is "when it will collapse."[129]

Yet it was one thing for the deal to fall apart, quite another for opponents to assume political responsibility for blocking implementation. The new Republican majority in Congress was not about to risk that.

Nor was North Korea about to provide any pretext to undo the deal. With American experts in Yongbyon to study how best to store the spent fuel rods in the cooling pond, Pyongyang announced that it had begun implementing the freeze.[130] I.A.E.A. inspectors confirmed the North Korean claims.

Partisan maneuvering on the nuclear deal intensified after the election. The thrust of the Republican attack was that the administration, had it been a tougher bargainer, could have given away less and gotten a lot more, in particular, prompt special inspections to resolve doubts about North Korea's past diversion of nuclear fuel and whether it had already made two bombs. An editorial in the *New York Times* challenged

Senator John McCain, an exponent of that view. "The two-bomb theory may be nothing more than a figment of hypervigilant imaginations,"
it argued. "But Mr. McCain prefers to chase what may turn out to be a
will-o'-the-wisp instead of stopping the North from turning real plutonium into real bombs now."[131] Henry Sokolski, who worked on nonproliferation in the Reagan Administration, urged Republicans to withhold
money for interim fuel supplies until the accord was clarified. Yet Republican Congressional leaders drew back from renouncing the Agreed
Framework altogether. "I don't want to say we will tear up" the accord,
said Senator Frank Murkowski (R-AK), who was first in line to chair the
Subcommittee on East Asian and Pacific Affairs in the Senate.[132]

The subcommittee began hearings December 1. Questioners concentrated on the sequencing of steps and the possibility of North Korean
noncompliance. "We will be well down the road of providing economic
incentives," complained Subcommittee Chairman Charles Robb (D-
VA), "before we have the ability to confirm anything about North
Korea's true nuclear weapons capability." Gallucci emphasized that
North Korea would have to freeze its nuclear program and allow inspectors to verify that it had before it received anything in return. "If the
D.P.R.K. reneges on the deal it will have gained little," he noted, "and
other steps we would plan on taking would be easily reversible."[133] Were
that to occur five or ten years hence, he argued, the United States would
be no worse off, having postponed North Korean bomb-making.

A visit to North and South Korea made Senator Murkowski a reluctant convert. "I don't anticipate any" Republican efforts "to scuttle that
agreement," he told reporters in Seoul. He sounded reassured on compliance: "We saw, repeatedly, affirmative commitment on the part of
North Koreans to live up to [their] part of the deal." The trip also eased
his misgivings about aiding the North Koreans: "I think they are desperately in need of foreign exchange, desperately in need of energy and in
a transition of leadership, and as a consequence, they need assistance.
And I think if that assistance can properly be communicated and transmitted we can ease tensions in this part of the world."[134]

Support for the deal was still fragile on December 18 when an incident had the hawks up in arms again. An American Kiowa scout helicopter strayed across the Demilitarized Zone, 3–5 miles into North Korean territory, and was shot down. One of the two Americans on board
was killed and the other captured. The North Koreans turned over the
body of the dead pilot, but it took days of talks before they released their
captive. The Military Armistice Commission had been the venue for
handling such incidents, but Deputy Assistant Secretary of State
Thomas Hubbard flew to Pyongyang to seek the pilot's release. He was
"handed a bill of particulars" when he arrived: confess that the heli-

copter was engaged in espionage, apologize, have South Korea free some longtime political prisoners in return for the pilot's release, hold bilateral peace talks with the D.P.R.K., and hold bilateral talks on a "peace mechanism" to replace the Military Armistice Commission (M.A.C.) and supervise the truce. The United States denied the espionage charge, expressed "sincere regret," and agreed to "contacts in an appropriate forum designed to prevent such incidents in the future."[135] The North Koreans wanted talks with the United States. "For us the appropriate forum is the M.A.C. channel where the R.O.K. is present," says Hubbard. "We had a couple of talks in which only an American general and a North Korean general were present, but we did it under the auspices of the M.A.C., which allowed us to set up special representatives for special purposes. They wanted to institutionalize that. I did not agree to that."[136] Yet accidents do happen along the DMZ, raising the possibility of an exchange of hostile fire. Why risk the lives of American troops to avoid incurring the wrath of the South Koreans?

Incur that wrath it did. "Pyongyang has now set a significant precedent for direct political contact with Washington, even before their diplomatic normalization," complained the *Korea Times*, an English-language daily in Seoul. "If the U.S. knuckles under to North Korean blackmail, it could be dragged deeper into Pyongyang's traps."[137] Yet the episode showed that both the United States and the D.P.R.K. had a stake in preserving their tenuous relationship. It also suggested the need to go beyond the Agreed Framework and defuse the armed confrontation at the DMZ, which would require talks among all the parties with armed forces there, the United States, North Korea, and South Korea.

By delaying the release of the captured pilot until after Christmas, Pyongyang missed an opportunity to improve its political standing in Washington. Pyongyang could be as self-absorbed as Washington and American politics was not its concern. To a country that saw itself as threatened at every turn and prided itself on prickly self-reliance, an American incursion, however inadvertent, was not to be taken lightly.

Some saw darker forces at work, the rising power of the military in Pyongyang. "To me, it was clear," says Representative Bill Richardson (D-NM), who happened to be in Pyongyang at the time of the shootdown and helped secure the return of the dead pilot, "that the Korean People's Army was again putting up roadblocks, such as an espionage charge, to the agreement. That's why the Foreign Ministry, with some urgency, asked the Clinton Administration to send an envoy to continue negotiations."[138] If Richardson was correct, multiple channels of communication were all the more necessary. To others the evidence of increasing military ascendancy in the North was not that clear. Alexandre Mansourov of Columbia University's Center for Korean Research, saw no evidence of "a real power struggle" between the Ministry of Foreign Affairs and the army, just a wariness "of trespassing on each other's turf." When the North Korean leadership saw "the political mood in the United States [begin] to swing against them on December 27–28, they immediately made the decision to release Bobby Hall to preserve the option of normalizing relations with the United States. Despite lingering uncertainty about who rules the D.P.R.K., this decisive move shows the presence of strong political leadership in Pyongyang."[139] This was the prevailing view in the U.S. intelligence community as well.[140]

During the thirteen-day episode a much less publicized event took place that had greater potential for slowing implementation of the Agreed Framework, a cabinet shakeup in Seoul. On December 23 President Kim Young Sam sacked Foreign Minister Han Sung Joo, an advocate of the nuclear deal, and replaced him with Gong Ro Myung, former consul general in New York. Two others experienced in dealing with Americans were promoted. U.N. Ambassador Yoo Chong-ha, who had helped convince President Kim to take a hard line in November 1993, was named senior presidential secretary for foreign affairs and national security, and Kim Deok, director of the National Security Planning Agency, South Korea's C.I.A., became deputy prime minister for national unification. Those unenthusiastic about the nuclear deal were in the ascendancy. At a January 6 press conference, President Kim Young Sam made his priorities plain: "Intra-Korean talks were the most important provision of the North Korea–U.S. agreement reached in Geneva last year." Lest anyone mistake him for harboring newfound enthusiasm for such talks, Kim continued, "Presently, there is no leader in the North. Once the new leader emerges, I think it will follow for them to contact us to propose a summit."[141]

In North Korea, the party newspaper *Rodong Sinmun* and the Korean People's Army newspaper *Rodong Chongryon* jointly published an authoritative New Year's Day editorial extolling the high-level talks for "upholding the intentions of the fatherly leader" and leading to the adoption of a "historic" accord.[142]

Declaring that the D.P.R.K. had complied with the Agreed Framework by shutting down its nuclear reactor and sealing its reprocessing plant, the United States shipped the first installment of heavy fuel oil to the North.[143] On January 9, 1995, Pyongyang responded by announcing that it would lift its ban on commercial and financial transactions with the United States, a step that both sides were obliged to take under the Agreed Framework.[144] Washington grudgingly reciprocated. In addition to shipping the fuel oil, it unblocked some frozen assets and allowed direct telephone calls to the D.P.R.K., the use of credit cards by travelers in the North, the opening of journalists' offices there, and imports of magnesite, used to line blast furnaces in steel mills.[145] A U.S. official characterized the gesture as meeting "the letter of the agreement, while making a very modest change," leaving "about 99 percent" of the legal barriers to trade in place.[146]

Hearings on the nuclear accord resumed on January 24 in the Republican-controlled Senate. G.O.P. leaders were content to criticize it without trying to undo it. The deal is "very badly flawed and unacceptable" because it prolongs the existence of "a bizarre Orwellian regime," complained Senator John McCain (R-AZ), but he acknowledged, "The administration has put us in a box" on the accord. "If we refuse to fund it, we can be accused of breaking it."[147] During the hearings a week later, McCain stated the Republican case with characteristic bluntness: "I believe this agreement will fail. I believe North Korea will renege on this agreement just as they reneged on their freely accepted treaty obligations under the Nonproliferation Treaty and just as they did eight times during the past two years of negotiations leading to this deal. However, I do not think Congress should overturn this agreement. To be candid, I do not want to have Congress blamed for something that will really be the result of North Korean duplicity."[148]

Perhaps more telling than the Republican attack on the deal was the administration's defense of it. "The Agreed Framework," Secretary of State Christopher told the Senate Foreign Relations Committee, "is the product of months of determined diplomacy and firm negotiation." The air of unreality was palpable. He went on undeterred, "To ensure the success of our approach, the United States conducted intensive consultations with our allies South Korea and Japan, and other Security Council members. And to ensure the security of South Korea in a period of heightened tension, we also accelerated modernization of our military forces there. We negotiated from a position of strength." Christopher's testimony made no mention of the Carter mission in defusing the crisis, but emphasized how the administration had raised the bar. "After Kim Il Sung made a commitment to freeze North Korea's nuclear program if the United States would agree to resume talks, President Clinton responded immediately by defining what an acceptable freeze would mean." Christopher underscored, "The president set a new, higher standard for maintaining dialogue with the North by insisting that a freeze include a commitment not to reload and operate its 5-megawatt reactor—not to *produce* any more plutonium. This went beyond the North's previous commitment not to undertake any reprocessing or *separation* of plutonium." That North Korea had refrained from reprocessing and delayed unloading the reactor for as long as three years, while trying to negotiate a deal, had no place in the official history that North Korea had knuckled under: "The North Korean leadership made this decision because it understood that if it did not, the United States would pursue sanctions and was prepared to deal with the consequences. We had achieved a position of advantage—which we would carry into the negotiations when they resumed—because a consistent policy had been supported by successful diplomacy at the United Nations and evident military readiness on the ground."[149] To shield itself from Republican accusations of failing to hang tough and get a better deal, the administration stressed its success at coercive diplomacy. Neither side would let the facts stand in its way.

Defense Secretary Perry's testimony was more realistic. Economic sanctions were "both risky and costly" and a military strike even more so. If the North Koreans took military action, "that would involve a full-scale—full-scale—war."

The Issue at Kuala Lumpur: What's in a Name?

Further talks were needed to implement the Agreed Framework. Two sets of technical talks were stipulated in the accord, one to arrange for storing and disposing of the spent fuel in the cooling ponds and the other to work out the details of the supply of interim energy and replacement reactors. On January 24 technical talks in Pyongyang ended in an agreement to place the fuel rods in dry storage. Getting committees in Congress to reprogram funds for storing the rods was not as easy. Yet resistance on Capitol Hill was far less rigid than in Seoul. Talks on the consortium to provide replacement reactors would drag on for six months, with the South Korean allies generating even more friction than their brethren to the North.

Having decided not to oppose the Agreed Framework outright, members of the Senate now undertook to impede its implementation. Besides threatening to hold up funding, they backed a resolution, co-sponsored by Senator Murkowski and Senator Robb among others, that the administration "should take steps to ensure that implementation . . . is linked to substantive and rapid progress in dialogue between North and South Korea."[150] Once again, that was asking for trouble.

North and South Korea were in no mood to talk. When Deputy Secretary of State Strobe Talbott visited Seoul on January 28, he was asked to postpone an exchange of liaison offices until Pyongyang showed its "willingness to pursue inter-Korean dialogue."[151] He was also asked not to hold military-to-military talks to avoid incidents like the downing of the errant U.S. helicopter. North Korea could play the same game. Stepping up its challenge to the armistice agreement, it ousted Polish members of the Neutral Nations Supervisory Commission and announced, "The N.N.S.C. has nothing to do now."[152] In the Berlin talks with the United States it refused to sign a supplier agreement naming South Korea as the source of the two replacement reactors.

Gong Ro Myung made his first trip to Washington as South Korea's foreign minister to meet with Secretary of State Christopher on February 6. According to a U.S. official, he urged that South Korea's "central role" in supplying North Korea with replacement reactors "be spelled out for the world to see" for the sake of its "national prestige."[153] That was precisely what North Korea was refusing to do. Pyongyang knew that the reactors had to come from Seoul, but was looking for ways to play up Washington's role in the transaction. Its purpose was to minimize the appearance of dependence on South Korea. It also hoped to demonstrate the South's subservience to the United States, an impression Washington was trying to avoid. Regardless of what was done to disguise the fact, the North would remain the South's poor cousin, dependent on it to power its economy. Seoul could afford to be magnanimous, but it wanted Washington to face down Pyongyang, even if that jeopardized the Agreed Framework.

Deputy Secretary of Defense Deutch's insistence that the United States pin down the purposes for the heavy fuel oil now came back to haunt the administration. When American negotiators asked the North Koreans, they said the oil would be used for electricity production and heating. "If they'd said agricultural production," says Thomas Hubbard, "we'd have agreed to that. We might even have agreed to steel production."[154] The heavy oil could not fuel tanks or aircraft, but it could be used to heat furnaces or run generators in a steel plant. After word leaked from the Pentagon that this had happened, General Gary Luck told the Senate Armed Services Committee on February 16 that there was room for "suspicion" of such skimming, but "I think we called their hand on that and they stopped doing it."[155] The incident led Senator Mitch McConnell (R-KY) to charge that the Secretary of State was less than candid when he testified that North Korea was in "full compliance."[156]

Talks in Berlin on the replacement reactor were bogged down. As part of the reactor deal North Korea was also asking for $500 million in aid to upgrade its power grid, to make it capable of transmitting the electricity generated by the replacement reactors. It wanted 540 kilometers of new transmission lines, new substations, and a simulator to train reactor operators. One U.S. official dismissed the request as "outrageous."[157] Officially the United States offered a more considered response. "The opening position of the North Koreans is to request a maximum number of add-ons," said the State Department spokesperson. "We have no intention of agreeing to the add-ons which are outside of the normal scope" of a light-water reactor or "which would significantly increase the cost of the project."[158]

There was also misinformed press speculation that the North Koreans had rejected replacement reactors supplied by South Korea. They had not. "The real problem there," says Deputy Assistant Secretary of State Thomas Hubbard, "was describing the LWR project in a way that made clear that the South was going to play a central role and that it would be a Korean reactor. Finding the words to say that was excruciating on all sides." American and North Korean negotiators "found words in Berlin that would have been satisfactory to us, but they were not satisfactory to the South."[159]

The chief North Korean delegate at the United Nations, Pak Gil Yon, went public March 9, "Our position has been very clear. Selection of a South Korean–type of reactor is a violation of the Geneva Agreed Framework." Calling it by another name was acceptable: "If you say an American-type of reactor rather than a South Korean–type, everything would be resolved."[160] Compromise was possible, if and when South Korea was willing. The reactors were a South Korean modification of a reactor designed by a U.S. firm, Combustion Engineering, which would build at least one key nuclear component. Other parts were to be supplied by other countries, including the nuclear fuel. The Agreed Framework had stipulated, "The United States, representing the international consortium, will serve as the principal point of contact with the D.P.R.K. for the LWR contract." The supplier agreement could also designate an entity other than a South Korean firm as the titular prime contractor. One such entity was K.E.D.O.

The day Pak spoke, the United States, South Korea, and Japan formally announced the founding of K.E.D.O., a multinational consortium, to supply the reactors. Yet Seoul did not make it easier for Pyongyang to specify K.E.D.O. as its contracting partner. "In putting K.E.D.O. together," says Hubbard, "the South beat us down and put in references to the South Korean standard reactor, which made it hard for the North to say K.E.D.O." A March 17 broadcast by the North Korean Central News Agency made this explicit, "The term 'South Korean model' is the brake on the conclusion of an agreement regarding the provision of light-water reactors, and further, a root cause of killing the D.P.R.K.-U.S. framework agreement. As long as the K.E.D.O. consortium is aimed at the provision of South Korean model reactors, we will never deal with it."[161] One news report suggested the North was threatening to refuel its reactor.[162] There was renewed talk of sanctions in Washington and Seoul if it did.

The South, meanwhile, "kept escalating its demands," says Hubbard. A Blue House official, on background to a *Korea Times* reporter on March 30, spoke of President Kim Young Sam's "take-it-or-leave-it ultimatum to the North" and added that "the real master of brinkmanship is President Kim, not Kim Il Sung or Kim Jong Il." Asked about State Department allegations that Kim was taking a hard-line stance with a view toward upcoming local elections, he replied, "In the past tension on the Korean Peninsula somewhat helped the ruling party in elections. But the story is different in this case. President Kim is not in a position to make a concession. This means a political catastrophe for him and his party." He dismissed reports that American firms were lobbying to build the reactors, "Any efforts by Westinghouse or other U.S. companies will be futile once we, the principal financier of the North Korea project, decide not to pay."[163]

The Berlin talks broke off on April 20 without agreement. With the six-month period stipulated in the Agreed Framework for concluding a supply contract due to expire in a day, a D.P.R.K. official in Berlin told Reuters, "For us April 21 is the last day. We have no scope for extending the talks past this date." A State Department spokesman said the United States was "prepared to continue" the talks. Pentagon spokesman Kenneth Bacon said that North Korea had "moved in" a maintenance team to the reactor sites and warned that refueling "would be a very, very serious step." State Department spokesman Nicholas Burns added that "if North Korea breaks the freeze," the United States "would consult with our allies about returning this issue to the U.N. Security Council, including the possibility of seeking sanctions."[164]

On April 22 the D.P.R.K. Ministry of Foreign Affairs relaxed a bit, saying it considered April 21 "a target date, not a deadline" for a supplier agreement.[165] Behind the scenes the United States proposed that Gallucci and Kang meet in Geneva. Kang said he could not leave Pyongyang and invited Gallucci to come there for talks. Instead Thomas Hubbard was designated to hold talks with Kim Gye Gwan in Kuala Lumpur.

The Kuala Lumpur talks opened on May 16. Two weeks later, they "almost came a cropper," says Hubbard. Then he decided to drop all the "troublesome" references to South Korea and find a way to finesse identifying the source of the reactors. "Will you take the reactors provided by K.E.D.O.?" Hubbard asked. Yes, said Kim.[166] The way out was to draw up a supplier agreement between K.E.D.O. and North Korea, omitting any mention of South Korea, and then have K.E.D.O. announce that it had chosen South Korea to supply the reactors. The breakthrough came on June 7. The following day President Clinton telephoned President Kim. Instead of approval he got a harangue. On June 9 Ambassador-at-Large Gallucci and Assistant Secretary of State Lord flew to Seoul to convince the South Koreans.

On June 12, 1995, the deal was finally done. It came in the form of a joint statement, which said, "The reactor model, selected by K.E.D.O., will be the advanced version of U.S.-origin, design, and technology currently under production." It said nothing about South Korea's "central role": "K.E.D.O. will select a prime contractor to carry out the project. A U.S. firm will serve as program coordinator to assist K.E.D.O. in supervising overall implementation of the LWR project; K.E.D.O. will select the program coordinator."[167] Within minutes of the joint statement, K.E.D.O. announced that "the LWR project will consist of two reactors of the Korean standard plant model of 1,000 MWe each," that it "will select a qualified firm from the Republic of Korea as prime contractor" and that it was authorizing "discussions with Korea Electric Power Corporation in connection with the prime contract."[168]

K.E.D.O. was a potential mechanism for North-South cooperation. Once in operation, it became a forum for direct dialogue, since South Korea was represented at contract talks between K.E.D.O. and North Korea. At social gatherings the North and South delegates often went off in a corner to sip drinks and swap jokes and cigarettes. While negotiations were not always smooth, they did proceed apace. America's allies, South Korea and Japan, often proved more difficult negotiating partners than the North Koreans. Money was not the only reason. The North's amour propre was still a sore point for the South. No one wanted to pay for repatriation of spent fuel from the light-water reactors and Japan saw no need for it, fearing that it would raise regional concerns about the spent fuel from its own reactors.[169]

Once Washington decided to bargain in earnest, it did not take long to get an agreement that, if implemented, will rid the Korean peninsula of nuclear arms. What took Washington so long to try? One reason is the shared images of nuclear diplomacy that dominated the mind-set of people in and out of the government. Another reason is domestic politics. Many participants agree with Thomas Hubbard: "There's nothing less popular than any sign of cozying up to North Korea."[170]

Seoul did little to disguise its dismay about the Agreed Framework or the Kuala Lumpur accord. Nor did some pillars of the American foreign policy establishment. "I am not happy about the way the Korean nuclear agreement came about," Henry Kissinger told the Heritage Foundation. "I don't think it is good policy to have an American negotiation in Korea that excludes Seoul, and I am uneasy about our having acquiesced to the nuclear status quo in the peninsula." He recommended that "in all negotiations involving the future of the Korean Peninsula, we should not talk with the North Koreans without the participation of South Korea; and if the North Koreans are not willing to do this, then I don't think we should talk to them." Once again, talks were being treated as a reward for good behavior rather than a means for the United States to get what it wanted.

PART III

CONCLUSIONS

8

NUCLEAR DIPLOMACY IN THE NEWS—

AN UNTOLD STORY

*A news-writer . . . may confidently tell today what he intends
to contradict tomorrow.*
(*Samuel Johnson*, The Idler)

TO EVEN the most devoted news watchers, the story of nuclear
diplomacy with North Korea may seem unfamiliar. The reason is
simple: key parts of the story never appeared in the news. In particular, evidence that North Korea might be trying to trade away its nuclear arms program received very little media attention between 1992
and mid-1994. North Korean concessions were downplayed; crucial
proposals were virtually ignored.

Nuclear diplomacy with North Korea was largely covered as a case of
crime and punishment. North Korea was portrayed as an outlaw state
whose misdeeds warranted economic sanctions. Suspicions of its noncompliance with the Nonproliferation Treaty and evidence of its refusal
to play by the rules of diplomatic discourse were dominant features of
the news. When the D.P.R.K. balked at allowing the I.A.E.A. to conduct inspections, that was overwhelmingly portrayed as evidence of its
duplicity rather than as evidence of its unwillingness to give up nuclear
leverage without getting something in return. The news coverage had
repercussions both for politics and for policy.

Besides distributing news and advertising for a profit, the news media
act as the central nervous system of the body politic. In a political system
as dispersed as the United States, news stories are often the quickest way
to glean intelligence from abroad, to float trial balloons and gauge domestic and foreign reactions to impending policy changes, and to inform
the bureaucracy, Congress, and interested publics of decisions. If the
news media do not perform well, they can disorient the political system—
blind it to impending trouble overseas, muffle or distort reactions from
home and abroad, and misinform audiences about government actions.

American news coverage of the world is dominated by American news
sources, especially U.S. government officials and members of the foreign
policy establishment. The unintended result is that newsmaking can create a closed circle of Americans talking to themselves. In so doing, the

news mutes and distorts information from abroad, in this case, what China, South Korea, and especially North Korea itself were saying and doing.

Flawed news coverage can interfere with high-fidelity communication between government officials and the foreign policy establishment, especially feedback from the academic, business, and foundation communities, and outside experts who rely on the news media for current information about the world and American involvement in it.

That was a problem in news about nuclear diplomacy with North Korea because government officials who favored diplomatic give-and-take were initially reluctant to go public, while opponents were vocal and well covered.

The problem was compounded by the episodic attention that newsmakers gave to North Korea and the way they framed news about it. During the Cold War, relations with the Soviet Union dominated the attention of American officials and so dominated the news. That affected what stories mattered most, how to frame foreign news, even where to locate reporters. News was reflected and refracted through that Cold War lens, distorting it. The end of the Cold War has given freer play to journalistic routine and convention in shaping coverage, which may exert a subtler, but no less important distorting effect on the news.

Unfamiliarity Breeds Contempt

Reporters tended to ignore the diplomatic dialogue between the United States and North Korea. Even when news stories did focus on the talks, other concerns crowded out the details of the two sides' negotiating positions and pushed the news off page one. News stories that did discuss diplomacy cast doubt on the prospects of a deal or disparaged its desirability.

News coverage of the Korean nuclear issue was preoccupied with North Korea's nuclear past and nuclear intentions and the prospects for sanctions and war. Three questions dominated most stories: Did North Korea already have the Bomb? Was it about to start a war? How soon would it collapse, like the rest of the communist bloc? These preoccupations suggest that the Cold War frame shaped coverage of nuclear diplomacy. So, too, did the notion of North Korea as a rogue state.

North Korean threats grabbed a lot of attention—the more hair-raising they sounded, the more prominently they were displayed and replayed. Whenever Pyongyang threatened to resume producing plutonium, it set off a feeding frenzy in the news, leaving a lasting impression that cooperation was inconceivable. North Korea did not help by cloaking its concessions in threats. Yet, after a while, its bluster and bravado seemed predictable. Its concessions, arguably, were at least as news-worthy.

The news media also gave a lot of space and time to menacing utter-ances by Americans, especially people outside the Executive Branch. De-spite the inordinate attention paid to what should be done militarily, many U.S. and R.O.K. military moves went unnoticed. So did the po-tential for inadvertent war at the time of Jimmy Carter's trip to Pyong-yang in June 1994. Conjecture about American concessions, even when they had not actually been made or even considered, got some play. Re-neging on past American promises—by South Korea, the I.A.E.A., and the United States itself—got little or none. Indeed, reporters almost en-tirely missed how decisions in Seoul and Vienna were driving policy in Washington.

American concerns, by and large, dominated American coverage. Ko-rean concerns, North or South, received short shrift.

Finally, the news was, literally, one-sided. North Korea's own ex-pressed views about what it found acceptable and objectionable simply went unreported. Some examples will illustrate these points.

North Korea's Ignored Offer

On April 10, 1992, North Korea ratified a nuclear safeguards agreement with the I.A.E.A. It provided for international monitoring and on-site inspections to insure that the North's civilian nuclear plants and material were not misused to produce plutonium for nuclear arms. On May 4, 1992, North Korea handed over an inventory of its nuclear material and facilities to the I.A.E.A.—a more prompt and detailed declaration than was required, including a dozen sites previously unknown to outsiders. A story by Don Oberdorfer, which ran on an inside page of the *Wash-ington Post*, began, "North Korea has set the stage for early international inspection of its nuclear program by providing the first extensive infor-mation on its much-disputed facilities, including the surprise revelation that it has produced a small amount of plutonium, an element used in nuclear weapons." The story went on to depict the North Korean decla-ration as more than an inch thick, with "extensive information not previ-ously expected," including another "surprise listing"—a "radiochemical laboratory," or reprocessing plant at Yongbyon "designed for research on the separation of uranium and plutonium."[1]

One week after the declaration, I.A.E.A. Director-General Hans Blix began a six-day visit to North Korea, including the nuclear installations at Yongbyon. When Blix, en route home, spoke to reporters at a news conference in Beijing, a spate of stories focused on his tour of the "ra-diochemical laboratory." The *New York Times* Beijing correspondent wrote a typical lead, "The head of the International Atomic Energy

Agency said today that a mysterious building in North Korea could function as a plutonium reprocessing center if outfitted with additional equipment. Such an installation would be the core of a nuclear weapons program." The page-one story noted, "Mr. Blix was very careful to describe only what he saw and not to accuse North Korea of trying to develop nuclear weapons." Yet it added that the visit "seemed to raise as many questions as it answered about whether North Korea was trying to develop nuclear weapons and how far it might have progressed."[2]

Three questions the visit did not seem to raise, nor did Blix choose to address, were whether North Korea had made any negotiating proposals; why it was more forthcoming in its declaration to the I.A.E.A. than it had to be, much to the surprise of agency and American government experts; and how Pyongyang's disclosures may have been related to its negotiating strategy.

A partial answer to these questions came shortly, but it was obscured by the news coverage. On June 8 the *Washington Post* carried a two-inch squib citing state radio in South Korea that North Korea had offered to stop producing plutonium "if the I.A.E.A. provides it with alternative technology for nuclear power plants." It made the offer "in talks with U.S. officials in Beijing June 1."[3] On June 12 the *Washington Times* ran a Reuters dispatch on an inside page, citing an interview with Li Hyong Chol, North Korea's representative in Geneva, who said that Pyongyang was ready to stop working on technology to extract plutonium from spent fuel from its nuclear reactors if Japan agreed to provide it with know-how on light-water reactors and uranium enrichment. He added that North Korea had made the offer both to the I.A.E.A. and the United States. *Sankei Shimbun*, the dispatch noted, quoted Richard Solomon, assistant secretary of state for East Asia and Pacific Affairs in the Bush Administration, as saying North Korea had presented the proposal to Blix during his May visit.[4]

The *New York Times* of June 12 had a lead story, datelined Washington, which began, "Administration officials say that the first experts to conduct a detailed survey of North Korea's nuclear installations have confirmed that the country has been building a large plutonium-reprocessing plant, but that the inspectors have so far found no evidence that enough nuclear material has been produced to make an atomic bomb." The story asserted that the inspectors' preliminary findings, to be presented to the I.A.E.A. Board of Governors that day, "cast doubt" on C.I.A. worst-case estimates that North Korea could have nuclear arms within a few months to a year. "But some U.S. military and intelligence officials, deeply suspicious of North Korea's sudden willingness to allow inspectors into its most secret installations, say there is circumstantial evidence to suggest that another 'pilot plant' for extracting plutonium has been hidden underground or in the mountains." The story later alluded to a reference in Blix's trip report: "a small pilot plant should have preceded the 'radiochemical laboratory.'"

Not until the fourth paragraph did the story mention another reference in Blix's report: "*Senior North Korean officials told him they would abandon their reprocessing effort if Japan, South Korea or Western nations would assure a supply of nuclear fuel and technology that would allow North Korea to build civilian power plants.*" Further down, the story noted, "North Korea's surprise offer to halt its program is further evidence that Mr. Kim's Government, out of money and suddenly without help from its Chinese and Soviet allies, is beginning to abandon its philosophy of *juche*, or self-reliance."[5]

On June 20, nearly a week after the *Times* story, an article ran on an inside page of the *Washington Post*, headlined "N. Korea May Consider Reducing Atom Program." The lead read, "Senior North Korean officials have told the I.A.E.A. that the country is 'ready to consider' abandoning some elements of its nuclear program if foreign countries pledge to provide the required assistance." The story quoted a U.S. intelligence analyst, "They are trying to lay the groundwork for some sort of compromise." It also noted that this week, "a North Korean representative to the I.A.E.A. clouded the picture somewhat by insisting that the reprocessing facility, the most provocative feature of North Korea's nuclear program, be retained 'for the sake of his country's prosperity and economic growth,' an I.A.E.A. official said."[6]

Major American newspapers never again referred to the 1992 D.P.R.K. offer, even though it became the basis of the diplomatic deal with the United States two years later. The consequence is that readers were left unaware that North Korea had long offered to trade away its nuclear program and that the United States was unwilling to deal. North Korean behavior became incomprehensible without the knowledge that Pyongyang might have been prepared to yield on I.A.E.A. inspections and more, but only if it got what it wanted in return. Instead, the mistaken impression remained that North Korea was the intransigent party, toying with the inspectors while it built nuclear arms.

On Background: Tipping the Military Balance in Korea

In the summer of 1993 the Pentagon canvassed military options for destroying North Korea's nuclear program and found them wanting. Pentagon planners also concluded that a war in Korea could cost as many as 500,000 military casualties within the first ninety days, more lives than were lost throughout the 1950–52 war. That planning estimate was the military's way of casting doubt on the wisdom of air strikes or economic sanctions.

The risk of war was a major premise of the case for proposing a package deal, a step that the Clinton Administration was weighing in November 1993. To prepare the ground for diplomacy, administration officials wanted to disclose that major premise without raising doubts about American preparedness for war or leaving itself open to charges of appeasement.

Defense Secretary Les Aspin took on the assignment en route for an annual Security Consultative Meeting with South Korea, at which he was proposing a joint military assessment intended to encourage Seoul to buy new counterbattery radars, help pay for Patriot antimissile batteries, and take other precautions. Identified as a "senior military official traveling with Mr. Aspin," he gave a background briefing to Pentagon reporters. He said that North Korea's refusal to allow inspections posed a challenge "much tougher and more dangerous than Somalia and Bosnia" because "our interests are much greater in Asia" and because of the risk of "huge casualties if we make a misstep."[7] He then noted, "There is a very fine line between coercing North Korea to do what you want them to, and provoking a tremendous disaster."[8] The next day in public, Aspin raised questions about economic sanctions and said the U.S. still hopes for a diplomatic solution. "But the North Koreans should know that our deterrent posture and our defenses are strong," he added. "It is not our intention either to be weak or look weak in this process."[9]

On the plane en route home, Aspin gave another backgrounder in which he discussed at some length the military menace posed by North Korea, emphasizing its forward deployment of troops, heavy artillery, and multiple-launch rockets near the demilitarized zone. That made it possible for the North to attack with little warning, leaving no time to transport U.S. reinforcements to Korea. North Korea had been gradually redeploying forces near the DMZ for years, but Aspin left reporters with the misimpression that the redeployment was a recent occurrence, raising fears that war was imminent—war with a possibly nuclear-armed foe. "My recollection," says Assistant Secretary of Defense Ashton Carter, who accompanied Aspin on the plane, "is that Les was as surprised that he was making news as anyone else. The analyst in Les was making that point sharply without adequate attention to what the press is predictably going to do with it."[10]

The *Washington Post*'s lead was calmer than most: "North Korea has been steadily adding military forces near the demilitarized zone that separates it from South Korea while continuing to fend off international inspections of key nuclear-related sites, U.S. officials said yesterday." It quoted Aspin's comments at his press conference about American sightings of "a lot of changes that have been taking place recently . . . [that alter] the military capabilities on the North Korean side." It cited wire service stories quoting "a senior defense official returning with Aspin to Washington yesterday"—again Aspin himself—saying that roughly 70 percent of the North's 1.1 million ground troops has been moved "right up close to the border . . . over a period of the last three years or so"—as if over 700,000 had recently been redeployed! Again quoting "the official on Aspin's plane," it closed on an ominous note, "I think that we may be entering kind of a 'danger zone' here."[11]

David Sanger's version in the *New York Times* began more graphically with a description of the Aspin party being whisked off to the Foreign Ministry in Seoul, "where three photographs dominate the conference room wall. The first shows Seoul in 1945, a peaceful town of traditional-style Korean homes. The second was taken from the same site in the early 1950s, after the forces of Kim Il Sung had swept over the border, leaving nothing standing except smoldering ruins and a few chimneys. Next to it is a color photograph of the same site today, with its sweeping boulevards and office towers." Sanger's story did convey Aspin's intended message: "By the time Mr. Aspin left, he and his aides were talking openly about their growing worries that the wrong kind of pressure on the isolated North Korean Government could provoke it to lash out."[12]

By the time word reached the *Times* of London, war in Korea was page-one news, and fast approaching:

> The United States has prepared plans for a cruise missile strike to wipe out North Korea's secret nuclear bomb-making facility as its confrontation with the world's last Stalinist regime turns into President Bill Clinton's biggest foreign policy challenge. Washington fears that President Kim Il Sung, who has massed more than 70% of his 1m-strong armed forces close to the border with South Korea, will himself order a preemptive missile attack, or even an invasion of the South in a re-run of the Korean war he launched four decades ago.[13]

A Pentagon spokesman tried to slow down the journalistic rush to war at a news briefing two days later: "There has been a buildup of the conventional forces of North Korea near the border area along the demilitarized zone gradually over the past ten years. On our way back from our trip, a senior Defense official . . . described some of the worrying things. . . . But there was no mention—I want to make this clear—there was no mention that the department felt an attack by the North Koreans was imminent."[14]

On November 15, the day that the National Security Council met to choose diplomatic options, including a package solution that would eventually satisfy some of North Korea's demands, the *Washington Post* carried a story whose next-to-last paragraph tried to put the military assessment in the context of the administration's opting to negotiate with North Korea: "The backdrop for the debate includes what several officials said is a chilling military assessment of the results of any confrontation on the Korean peninsula."[15]

It was too little, too late. The prospect of Korean War II had taken on a life of its own. The dire assessment also allowed critics to cast a cloud of appeasement over diplomatic efforts. In a December 12 page-one story on the military balance in the *Washington Post*, the headline captured the problem: "Trepidation at Root of U.S. Korea Policy." The coverage implied what a December 12 *New York Times* headline said, "North Korea's Game Looks a Lot Like Nuclear Blackmail," and that the United States was yielding. It also sparked demands from hawks in Congress and elsewhere to reinforce American troops in Korea and attack North Korea's nuclear sites, provocative moves that were contrary to the diplomatic strategy Aspin had intended to encourage.

Drowning in a "Sea of Fire"

One recurrent feature of North Korea's bargaining style was brinkmanship. It often warned of the risk of war, but it was usually careful not to make outright threats of attack. For instance, it frequently denounced the proposed imposition of economic sanctions by the United Nations Security Council as "a declaration of war," which it technically was under Chapter VII of the U.N. Charter. Pyongyang responded to threats of sanctions and military action with bristling bravado. The North's warnings usually made headlines. The context was nearly always lost in the noise.

For instance, as the D.P.R.K. continued to rebuff I.A.E.A. efforts to gain fuller access to its nuclear sites and the United States remained reluctant to spell out its quid pro quo for full North Korean nuclear transparency, South Korea saw to it that North-South talks went nowhere by making the completion of inspections a precondition for suspending Team Spirit. Under the terms of the agreed statement of February 1994, the D.P.R.K. was not obliged to do that, but only to begin "the inspections necessary for the continuity of safeguards." South Korea and the United States, however, were obliged to suspend Team Spirit.

North-South talks turned into a slanging match. After months of hesitancy, South Korea agreed to a U.S. deployment of Patriot antimissile batteries. On March 19, with the I.A.E.A. on the verge of referring the dispute to the Security Council, the Clinton Administration decided to seek a Security Council resolution warning North Korea of economic sanctions if it did not comply with I.A.E.A. demands for inspections. The *New York Times* reported the decision on page one, noting that it had come just hours after North Korean representatives had walked out of talks with South Korea and "threatened war if Washington and Seoul mounted a pressure campaign. 'Seoul will turn into a sea of fire,' Park Young Su, the North Korean delegate said before abruptly ending the talks."[16]

The "sea of fire" remark was repeated in one news story after another. Two days later, the North Korean challenge was headline news in the *Financial Times*: "N. Korea's 'Sea of Fire' Threat Shakes Seoul—Pyongyang May Be Set on Cultivating a Nuclear Madman Image." The story quoted the threat in full, "It does not matter what sanctions are applied against us. We are ready to respond with an eye for an eye and a war for a war," said Mr. Park. "Seoul is not far away from here. If a war breaks out, Seoul will turn into a sea of fire. Mr. Song, you won't survive the war."

The story put the remark partly in context: "The outburst was triggered when Mr. Song Young-dae, the chief delegate for South Korea, mentioned the possibility of UN sanctions being applied against North Korea for its refusal to accept full international nuclear inspections." It was a case of tit-for-tat: one threat by Seoul elicited another by Pyongyang. The story went on to quote a South Korean official who saw the challenge as carefully orchestrated: "The North's whole strategy on the nuclear issue is based on intimidation, playing on international fears that they will lash out if they are pushed too far."[17]

Yet North Korea was not the only party engaging in political theatrics, something neither story mentioned. The source for the text of Park's fulminations, Don Oberdorfer reported five weeks later, was South Korea's chief delegate, and the President's office released a videotape of the incident for national newscasts.[18] Seoul, it seems, was out to shake itself. Three weeks later, in an interview with Japan's NHK television, Kim Il Sung repudiated the North Korean delegate's action as "out of place." Shortly thereafter, Park was relieved of his post, an act that received scarce mention in U.S. news coverage.[19]

Never Say Never

It became an article of faith in news coverage that North Korea would never allow special inspections. Time and again, stories made that assertion, or quoted sources making it. Some stories cited North Korean statements purportedly saying that. Others were inspired by I.A.E.A. sources to adopt this interpretation. Yet a careful reading of North Korea's words provides clues to the contrary.

For example, on June 7, 1994, after North Korea abruptly began removing spent fuel rods from its Yongbyon reactor, the *New York Times* ran a story by its Pentagon correspondent, datelined Washington, saying that the pace of the defueling was alarming Washington because the rods contained five or six bombs' worth of plutonium. The penultimate paragraph read: "The prospects for a compromise look dimmer than ever. Yun Ho Jin, North Korea's representative to the I.A.E.A., said today that the North would never allow inspectors to visit two nuclear-waste sites to try to determine how much plutonium might have been diverted in past years."[20] The next day, a *Washington Post* story led with the same assertion: "North Korea told the I.A.E.A. today that his government 'will never allow inspections' of two suspected nuclear-waste sites." It later quoted Yun as telling reporters, "Our position is clear and unchanged. [North Korea] will never allow inspections of the two sites."[21]

Perhaps so, but in the joint statement of June 11, 1993, North Korea had formally accepted the principle of "peace and security in a nuclear-free Korean peninsula, including impartial application of full-scope safeguards."[22] Full-scope safeguards, enumerated in its agreement with the I.A.E.A., included special inspections. The commitment was certainly ambiguous insofar as North Korea kept denouncing the I.A.E.A.'s request for special inspection of the nuclear waste sites as a sign of the agency's partiality. Somewhat less ambiguously, North Korea, both in talks with the United States and in consultations with the I.A.E.A., insisted on maintaining "a clear distinction between the guarantee of continuity of safeguards"—inspections to impede any diversion of spent nuclear fuel to bomb-making by checking seals and data and keeping monitoring equipment in working order, which it would permit—"and full compliance with the safeguards agreement," which would require "a package solution" in high-level talks with the United States.[23] News stories rarely, if ever, made that critical distinction.

In the agreed statement of August 12, 1994, negotiated with the United States after Jimmy Carter's breakthrough visit, the D.P.R.K. pledged that as part of a final settlement, it was "prepared to remain a party to the [Nonproliferation Treaty] and to allow implementation of its safeguards agreement under the treaty."[24] The safeguards agreement explicitly provided for special inspections, if necessary, even though the timing of those inspections remained a sticking point in the talks.

In August South Korea pledged to construct replacement reactors for North Korea as part of an eventual deal, but it conditioned its commitment on completion of special inspections. The North Korean Foreign Ministry rebuffed the South Korean demand, "We will never allow the inspection of the military sites at the expense of our sovereignty to receive light-water reactors." The American press interpreted the statement as a repudiation of North Korea's August 12 commitment. "In a potentially significant policy turn," read the *New York Times*'s lead,

"North Korea has thrown cold water on a week-old nuclear agreement with the United States by rejecting American demands that it permit international inspections of two critical nuclear sites." The story never mentioned the South Korean demand. Yet the North Korea statement objected to "setting the 'special inspection' that we have never admitted and cannot admit in the future either, as a 'precondition' to the solution of the issue." It went on, "Therefore, we declare once again that we will never allow a 'special inspection,' though we are willing to involve ourselves in clearing up 'nuclear suspicion' in the future."[25] The implication was that the I.A.E.A. would eventually be allowed to do what it wanted to try to clear up the past, so long as it was not called a special inspection.

On September 21, two days before the third round of high-level talks were to resume, Robert Gallucci revealed the U.S. negotiating position at a State Department briefing: "[S]ince special inspections are of two radioactive waste sites which are not going anywhere, there is no urgency to the conduct of the inspection in a technical sense. That said, and recognizing that this is a sensitive political issue for all, and particularly for the North, we're prepared to defer the conduct of the inspections until somewhat into the settlement process." U.S. negotiators, he went on, "have not been specific about exactly what point the inspection . . . would have to take place," but "have indicated certainly that it would have to be before any" nuclear components of light-water reactors would be delivered to the North.[26] The revelation brought harsh reactions from opponents of a deal in South Korea and the United States who, consistent with the crime-and-punishment approach, wanted special inspections to take place before any concessions were made to North Korea.

The very day of Gallucci's briefing, an interview with Admiral Zlapoter, U.S. commander-in-chief in the Pacific, appeared in *Pacific Stars & Stripes*, disclosing the dispatch of a carrier battle group to the Sea of Japan off Korea, and adding, "I think it sends a very strong message."[27] The fact of the deployment and the admiral's comments got little immediate notice in other news media, but they were not missed in Pyongyang. The Foreign Ministry reacted a day later, warning that "undisguised military provocations" could wreck the talks and threatened to end the freeze on its nuclear activities: "If the dishonest forces created difficulties in the provision of LWRs, insisting on 'special inspections,' the D.P.R.K. would not feel the need to freeze its independent graphite-moderated reactor program." The spokesman added, "It is unthinkable that the D.P.R.K. . . . would open even its military sites to get LWRs." A Reuters dispatch carried the remarks on special inspections but not the reference to "military provocations."[28] The Defense Ministry reacted more sharply three days later, "Now that the United States is seeking a military showdown, we cannot stick to talks indefinitely." It added, "Our people's army . . . will never allow any attempt to have our military sites opened through special inspections."[29]

The Defense Ministry statement made headline news. "N. Korea Threatens to Quit N-Talks," read the *Financial Times*. The story from Geneva noted, "Yesterday's statement from Pyongyang said North Korea would 'never' allow special inspections of military sites."[30] The story neglected to mention the carrier deployment, or that North Korean negotiators in Geneva had never threatened to break off talks and the North's negotiating position remained unchanged on special inspections. It also neglected to note that the two sides had in fact narrowed their differences over the timing of the special inspections.

A September 28 story in the *Washington Post* headlined, "U.S.-N. Korea Nuclear Talks at Stalemate as Pyongyang Takes Hard-Line Stance," tried to sum up the state of the talks. The North Koreans do not speak for themselves in the story. American officials speak for them:

> U.S. and North Korean officials have made no progress in five days of negotiations on North Korea's nuclear program, and in some respects are further away from an agreement than they were at the end of talks a month ago, according to U.S. officials. The officials blamed North Korea for the apparent stalemate, asserting that diplomats from the isolated state had made unacceptable demands in the talks that had undermined a preliminary understanding reached by the two nations in Geneva on Aug. 12. But the officials conceded that Washington also came to the negotiating session without any major new ideas, despite having learned of the North Korean demands earlier this month during informal discussions in Berlin. . . . U.S. officials were at a loss to explain why North Korea appeared to be pursuing a more hard-line stance.[31]

Within three weeks the two sides reached agreement.

Reporters who took their cues from I.A.E.A. officials and nongovernmental experts concluded that North Korea would never accede to the inspections necessary to clear up its nuclear past. Yet North Korean negotiators never quite said never. They seemed to be saying, not anytime soon, if ever, which left some wiggle room for diplomacy. That led the Clinton Administration to try to stop future production of plutonium by North Korea first and wait to ascertain what it may have produced in the past. It also made the October 21 Agreed Framework possible.

The clues that North Korea was preparing to reverse course were subtle, easily misread, and not always convincing to close observers. The news ignored them.

Explaining News on Nuclear Diplomacy

The conventional wisdom about news is that it tries to sensationalize events in order to attract a larger audience. The possibilities that a one-time foe could be nuclear-armed or that a second Korean war might soon erupt were certainly sensational, if true. Yet they are no less sensational than what was demonstrably truer: after years of hostility, North Korea was trying to reach an accommodation with the United States. Moreover, sensationalism offered little of the supposed benefits to the bottom line: news about North Korea was hardly the stuff that would sell more U.S. newspapers or boost network news ratings.

News is also supposed to be about the unexpected, but it is the expected, the conventional, the routine that dominates the news. If anything was unexpected, for instance, it was a nuclear accord between Washington and Pyongyang. Antagonism was expected, and that is what reporters paid attention to.

Political explanations of news are also commonplace. The contention is that news coverage reflects editorial policy. Yet it is difficult to distinguish the news stories in the *Wall Street Journal* from those in the *New York Times* although the editorial lines of the two papers differ sharply. Indeed, the line of causation was the reverse in the case of nuclear diplomacy. The news coverage influenced the slant of the editorials, although less at the *Times*, where the editorials tried on occasion to correct the news coverage.

Another like-minded explanation is that journalists as a class, or editors and publishers, share an ideological orientation—be it liberal or conservative, hawk or dove—that biases news coverage. Yet it is difficult to demonstrate such shared orientations or to show how they systematically bias the news. While journalistic biases do affect the news, they are of another sort, stemming from the ways journalists cover news.

An alternative explanation of the coverage of nuclear diplomacy with North Korea begins with the idea that news is not what happened. News is what *somebody says* has happened. That is especially so when events are invisible to all but the participants, as most events in foreign policy are.

The somebodies are **news sources**, and newsgathering consists of **organizational routines**, or standard operating procedures (SOPs), for selecting and excluding news sources. Among the most important of these SOPs are deadlines, which truncate a reporter's search for information, and legwork, interviewing sources in person or by telephone rather than analyzing statistical data or poring over documents in a library. Journalists also have their own **conventions** for selecting the stories and sources that are considered newsworthy. For example, the "news peg" embodies the value journalists place on timeliness. Stories are more likely to make the news if they are timed to coincide with discrete events, even those staged for the purpose of receiving coverage. The less recent the event, the less likely a story will be judged timely, or newsworthy.[32] That gives an episodic cast to news coverage.

Reporters are generalists, which makes it easy for editors to deploy them and to overrule their news judgments. One consequence is that they seldom know very much about the countries they cover, or speak the local language. They rely heavily on informants who speak English.

Most reporters do not roam the world randomly searching for news. They are assigned to **bureaus** and **beats**, locations where news is produced and disseminated to them routinely through press releases, news conferences, or background briefings. Covering a beat means making occasional checks with a network of contacts, or potential news sources—above all, "authoritative sources," people in formal positions of authority in the institutions reporters cover. Specializing in a bureau or on a beat allows reporters to develop some familiarity with subjects that recur repeatedly, even a bit of expertise.

Perhaps the most important factor in newsgathering on North Korea is that no Western news organization had a bureau there. Indeed, few news organizations had bureaus in South Korea; most covered Korea from bureaus in Tokyo or Hong Kong.* Moreover, no news organization seems to have assigned a reporter to cover nuclear diplomacy with North Korea full time. Between 1991 and 1994, for instance, twenty-two different reporters had byline stories on the subject in the *New York Times*. At least a dozen more contributed to the wire service stories carried by the *Times*. The story was covered by reporters in various locations—the State Department, Pentagon, C.I.A., White House, and other beats around Washington; Seoul, where the wire services had bureaus; the United Nations and Geneva, where the talks were held; Vienna, where the I.A.E.A. was headquartered; Tokyo and, on occasion, other foreign capitals. What reporters at all these locations have in common is that news about North Korea is not a major object of their attention. Reporters covered nuclear diplomacy with North Korea as a by-product of covering other beats, sources, and stories.

Even in these locations, reporters did not routinely seek out North Korean sources, nor did North Koreans routinely make themselves avail-

---

* It is expensive for news organizations to staff many bureaus. Most organizations have very few. Two primary considerations determine their location: the historical importance of a place to the news organization's home country and logistics, the ready availability of air and telecommunications links to other locations in the region and the world. Logistical considerations are especially important in deploying staff efficiently to wherever news may be breaking.

able to the press. The exceptions are noteworthy. The Foreign Ministry in Pyongyang did conduct occasional news briefings and issue official statements, or press releases. So did the Ministry of Atomic Energy. D.P.R.K. diplomats at the United Nations and D.P.R.K. representatives to the I.A.E.A. also held occasional background briefings or press conferences, as did North Korean diplomats in other capitals. These statements were sometimes carried in North Korea's official news media, where they were transcribed by the Foreign Broadcast Information Service and sometimes picked up by Reuters or the Associated Press. As a rule, however, North Korea did not routinely disseminate information to Western news organizations.

By and large, even when they did put out information, North Koreans themselves were seldom sources for news about North Korea or its negotiating positions. This may seem somewhat surprising in view of the fact that North Korea was one of two parties to the high-level talks.

Reporters did not routinely read translations of North Korean news by the Foreign Broadcast Information Service. Nor did they avail themselves of information circulating among outside experts by e-mail and fax.

American reporters, instead, relied primarily on American officials as sources, and secondarily on South Korean and I.A.E.A. officials. That accounts for the passing reference to North Korea's 1992 negotiating proposal. American and I.A.E.A. officials did not make anything of it at the time, and most forgot about it soon thereafter. So did reporters. That also suggests why North Korea's turnabout on special inspections went unnoticed in the news. Few American officials felt confident enough to talk about the possibility because they either did not think it possible or because doing so would set the talks up for failure. Finally, the reliance on South Korean rather than North Korean sources helps account for coverage of the "sea of fire" incident.

The patterns of news coverage are also explained by the conventions of American journalism. Perhaps the most important convention is that news consists of "stories." Once a story line becomes established, it is difficult to shake, and "the story" of nuclear diplomacy was that North Korea, "a rogue state" and an old-style communist one at that, was guilty of violating the Nonproliferation Treaty and nuclear-arming, a crime that deserved punishment.

Another important journalistic convention is that stories about conflict are deemed more newsworthy than stories about cooperation, and stories about war are deemed the most newsworthy of all. That may help explain why, even though cooperation between foes seems more unexpected than conflict, news coverage concentrated on the differences in the nuclear dispute, even ignoring when they were resolved.

That also helps account for the play given to the possibility of war, especially after the 1993 Aspin briefing.

Perhaps less explicable in this respect is that the news coverage largely ignored conflicts between the United States and the I.A.E.A. and between Washington and Seoul. Reliance on American sources, who were reluctant to draw attention to these conflicts, may account for this.

Journalistic conventions do more than influence what the news media deem newsworthy. They serve as crude rules of evidence or epistemological premises for journalists, affecting their judgments of what is valid and what is dubious. The convention of "objective news" is one example. It is a procedure of story composition, avoiding value-laden adjectives and the explicit intrusion of reporters' personal opinions into stories by leaving the colorful phrase-making and attributing interpretation to news sources. Needless to say, the convention of objectivity does not keep stories free of interpretive bias and selectivity. It does require reporters to quote sources.

The convention of "authoritative sources" validates some informants and not others. In public affairs, the higher-ranking the officials, the more authoritative they are presumed to be. Former officials are also presumed to be more authoritative than nonofficials. To American journalists, North Koreans were simply not reliable sources, even though they presumably knew more about North Korea's nuclear stance than outsiders.

The routines and conventions of journalism produced stories in which North Korea's views were interpreted by others—mostly U.S. officials and occasionally American experts and South Koreans, many of whom had never talked to a North Korean or seen North Korea. News of North Korea was reflected and refracted through the lenses of outsiders, many of whom had a stake in their characterizations of North Korea.

Press inattention to North Korea's 1992 proposal is mainly due to the sampling of news sources available to reporters. So are the dearth of news coverage of the diplomatic talks and the skepticism, if not downright hostility, toward a possible deal. American officials, especially senior officials, were reluctant to talk to anyone, including North Korea, about a diplomatic deal in any detail until 1994, and even then, were hesitant to defend diplomacy except in understandably uncertain tones. Most outside experts on nuclear proliferation as well as foreign policy generalists also had doubts or reservations about a deal. Opponents of diplomacy, partisan or otherwise, and those who preferred economic sanctions or military action were ready to speak out forcefully, without having to take responsibility for their advice. Defenders of the deal were relatively few in number, especially in Washington and Seoul. Unless reporters expanded their rolodexes, they were likely to talk to sources who cast doubt on the likelihood or the wisdom of a diplomatic deal.

Journalists have to cope with endemic uncertainty and resulting conflict over what is news and what it means. To the extent that they follow the same routines and embrace the same conventions, they are more likely to replicate each other's stories. That raises fewer doubts in the minds of editors and readers—or their own minds—about what "the story" really is. In this way, newsmaking is a **consensual** activity. The common social setting in which journalists moved may have had a subtle effect on their coverage of nuclear diplomacy of North Korea. Running into few people who believed a deal was both likely and desirable, they were influenced by the conventional wisdom to think that the negotiations were not especially newsworthy.

Op-Eds and Editorials

Editorials on North Korea mostly embraced the crime-and-punishment approach. So did op-ed writers and columnists. Most of the commentary was critical of administration policy for being too soft or too ambivalent about applying sanctions or using force to compel North Korea's compliance. There were important exceptions, and they helped broaden and deepen the discourse a little on what to do about North Korea's nuclear activities. The *Wall Street Journal*, both in its editorial and its op-eds, gave voice to hard-liners who contended that no reliable deal could be done with the communist regime and that the only solution was to topple it, by war if need be. The *Far Eastern Economic Review* echoed the *Journal.* Starting in 1990, the *New York Times* took issue with prevailing sentiment and editorialized in favor of reassuring the North and then offering a specific set of quid pro quos for opening up and shutting down North Korea's bomb-making.[33] The *Boston Globe* and other editorial pages occasionally chimed in. A few op-ed pages, most notably those of the *Los Angeles Times* and the *New York Times* gave some space to diverse currents of opinion. The former also paid attention to the Asian context. National Public Radio's news programs and, on occasion, the *McNeil-Lehrer NewsHour* did so, as well.

Among the columnists, Charles Krauthammer and Lally Weymouth were the most strident hawks. Only Jessica Mathews was sometimes willing to defend diplomatic deal-making. Krauthammer, in particular, had some effect on policy in 1993, says one official, prompting the administration to shrink from offering inducements to North Korea. "Early on, when people were still skittish, he caused major contortions."[34]

In theory, editorials are supposed to express opinions, unconstrained by the need to put them in the mouths of sources. Editorial writers can raise subjects that news sources do not want to talk about. They are also free to disagree with news coverage. They can introduce facts and assertions not reported in news stories, even contradict those in news stories. In this sense, editorials can reorient readers disoriented by the news. In practice, editorial writers seldom have the inclination, the time, the expertise, or the support of editors to do so. They are largely reactive, both to the flow of the news and to lobbying by interested parties in and out of the government. They take the news as fact. They accept the existing political discourse as a given and comment on the players and their proposals—"calling balls and strikes" as one *Times* editor put it. Editorials advocating a diplomatic deal with North Korea by the *New York Times* were a partial exception. Sometimes they deliberately took issue with reporters' depictions of events, and they framed alternatives to the policies under consideration in Washington.

The op-ed pages, in theory, provide another open space for political discourse on nuclear diplomacy. To most editors, op-ed means not just physically opposite the editorial page; it means opposing the editorial line and giving new meaning to the news. The op-ed pages offer space for commentary that is off the news or, occasionally, itself makes news by virtue of the originality of the argument or the authority of its author.

In practice, editorial writers and op-ed editors adhere to some routines and conventions of their own that constrain them. Perhaps the most obvious routine, and the most constraining one, is that newspapers are dailies. The small staffs—in this period the *Times* editorial page had fourteen editorial writers, four of them editors, and the op-ed page had four editors—have to fill the page daily. They do not have a lot of time to research, write, and edit pieces on a wide array of subjects. This puts a premium on easily written and edited pieces.

Editors also feel bound by conventions of timeliness to comment on recent events. That makes commentary episodic, mostly tied to events. Timeliness has two major consequences for op-ed editors. Overwhelmed by many more submissions than they have the space or time to accommodate, they use the "news peg" as a sorting device. The need for timely pieces also leads them to round up the usual suspects, soliciting pieces from a small stable of commentators they can rely on to turn well-written drafts on demand, quickly.

The convention of authoritative sources also applies to op-ed pieces, with some qualification. People in formal positions of authority are presumed to be more authoritative commentators than anyone else. Name recognition may also weigh more heavily than expertise in the choice of authors. On the assumption, however, that administration officials have access to the news pages as sources, or can voice their views in letters to the editor, the op-ed page affords space to opponents of administration policy, many of them dissenting officials, ex-officials, or would-be officials. Backing for administration policy tends to come from surrogates, often members of Congress or ex-officials whom the administration may stimulate to write op-eds or even provide drafts to, usually without the op-ed editors' knowledge.

Editors also follow a convention of balancing the page among policy areas and between policy pieces and lighter or more literary ones. The *Times*, for instance, seldom ran more than one foreign policy editorial a day and tried to mix national, local, and cultural commentary. The convention of balancing the page was compounded by the constraints on space. Editorials in the *Times* average little more than four hundred words; op-eds about six hundred. That put severe limits on how many times and at what length any subject is addressed.

In short, the space and scope for political discourse may be wider on the editorial and op-ed pages than it is on the news pages, but the opening is narrower in practice than in theory.

Possible Consequences of News Coverage

While news stories contained much talk about carrots and sticks, few reporters bothered to ask exactly what carrots the United States had actually put on the table and officials were reluctant to say. They instead dwelt mainly on the sticks the United States could use to coerce North Korean compliance. American news coverage was also preoccupied with North Korean sticks and ignored its carrots. This tendency was particularly pronounced when Pyongyang made one of its sporadic threats to resume producing plutonium. Saturation coverage of the threats drowned out North Korean hints of a way out of the crisis.

This pattern of coverage had several pernicious effects. One was to drive the policy process. "In the Clinton Administration," contends one highly placed official, "the White House operated at a very accelerated pace of reaction in foreign policy. Its idea of when to do something was driven by the news cycle."[35]

Another consequence was to make diplomacy virtually incomprehensible to most readers and to heighten the impression that war was likely. That inspired the hawks to intensify their calls for reinforcements to Korea, precisely the step that could trigger war. Their appeals fell on deaf ears among the public at large, which was sharply divided about the use of American troops in Korea, but it played better in elite audiences, especially the foreign policy establishment.[36] The almost daily reminders of the risks in the news may have made senior American and South Korean officials more cautious and more inclined to negotiate. Yet it made them skittish about saying so in public. The result was a vicious circle, in which the administration itself was the major source for the portrayal of dealings with North Korea as a matter of crime and punishment which, in turn, later made it loath to describe nuclear diplomacy as a matter for give-and-take between sovereign states. Even after Jimmy Carter repudiated sanctions and brought home the makings of a deal, administration officials tried to put the focus on its effort to impose sanctions. Even when the Agreed Framework of October 1994 was done, the president and members of his cabinet were reluctant to justify the concessions. With such reticent defenders and plenty of voluble detractors, it was understandable why news coverage dwelled on the doubts. As the *Wall Street Journal* headlined its report of the accord, "U.S. Will Sign Pact with Korea Amid Skepticism."[37] Even that was an improvement on the *Times*, whose subhead, "For Korean Vow to End Arms Program, U.S. Will Provide $4 Billion in Energy," was flat wrong.[38] It is difficult to determine how the news coverage affected the North Koreans.

Another effect was to create a vicious circle in the news media as well. The more the coverage was framed as a matter of crime and punishment, the more the "crimes" and "punishments" became "the story." Past news coverage affected editors' and reporters' perceptions of what was newsworthy about North Korea's nuclear program. It also influenced what appeared on op-ed and editorial pages.

The North Korea story seemed to fit the Cold War frame that shaped how foreign news was depicted in the American press. The Cold War was one of the longest running stories. Yet that frame has now been shattered by the implosion of the Soviet Union.

Observers have often noted the way that Cold War categories affected news coverage. Less noted has been a subtler impact of the Cold War: it made foreign news matter to editors, increasing the volume of foreign coverage. Without the Cold War story line, foreign editors are finding it more difficult to justify the space they give to foreign stories in the news, or to justify the costs of gathering news from abroad. A December 1992 memo from Bernard Gwertzman, foreign editor of the *Times*, to his staff, made this point:

> When one looks back, it is remarkable but not astonishing how much of newspaper coverage since World War II was devoted to foreign affairs, and how much hinged on the Cold War and East-West rivalries. This competition consciously and subconsciously dominated government policies, affecting newspaper coverage as well. We are not talking here just of major crises like the establishment of the Berlin Wall and the Cuban missile con-

frontation, but also of lesser developments that received heavy attention because they were related to the larger East-West themes. The Soviet Union and the United States were the nuclear superpowers, and a conflict between them could literally have destroyed the world. Thus, there was a credible, overarching relevance to covering every aspect of this competition. . . .This created a considerable market for foreign coverage, since virtually any foreign story could have some East-West, war-peace resonance, and therefore correspondents were encouraged to poke deeply into the domestic fabric of a society that might otherwise safely remain fairly obscure to our readers on the explicit or implicit understanding that an East-West competition was taking place and so it was important to know what was going on.[39]

At a time when most news organizations are reducing foreign coverage, they may inadvertently contribute to American ignorance of the world and feed isolationism. Yet lack of coverage was not the problem in the North Korea case. How the news media covered nuclear diplomacy was.

News organizations are cutting back staffing overseas and substituting stringers for full-time correspondents in order to cut costs.[40] As overseas staffing is drastically reduced, newspapers depend more on wire service dispatches; television news, on footage shot by independent camera crews. This material is integrated into stories filed by reporters based elsewhere, most often in Washington. With fewer reporters overseas to offer on-the-scene judgments, greater control over coverage rests in the hands of editors back home in the United States. The centralization of newsmaking may also leave news content much more subject to the conventional wisdom around Washington.

Journalists with an interest in foreign news sometimes yearn to replace the Cold War frame with an equally compelling one. None has emerged. The Gwertzman memo attempts to develop one:

> In many ways we are asking more, not less, of our correspondents, even though the proportion of front-page, hard news stories from overseas may have dropped in the past year. We still have as large a foreign staff as before the end of the Cold War. What is new in the current situation is not that we are covering foreign news less, but that we have to cover it differently. . . . We are interested in what makes societies different, what is on the minds of the people in various regions.[41]

Perhaps so, but even at the *Times* threat-based coverage is still the norm in judging what countries and events are most newsworthy, and a supposedly nuclear-arming North Korea was ideally suited to receive such coverage.

So long as administration officials were hesitant about justifying deal-making with North Korea, the news media were organizationally biased to transmit threatening news and commentary about the prospects and desirability of negotiating with North Korea. So it should not be surprising that, excluding administration officials, the sources quoted in news stories were preponderantly hostile to or skeptical of a deal with North Korea. So, too, were editorials, op-eds, and columnists.

9

THE POLITICS OF DISCOURAGEMENT

The mind is slow in unlearning what it
has been long in learning.
(*Seneca*, Troades)

T HE CLINTON Administration took advantage of the June
1994 mission by Carter to reverse field and begin negotiating in
earnest. Within four months it concluded the Agreed Framework. Within a year it reached agreement in Kuala Lumpur on the replacement reactors. Yet the highest officials in the Clinton Administration seemed initially hesitant to defend their success.

To fend off criticism that it was too eager for compromise, the administration talked about the threats it had brandished to compel the North.
Yet U.S. threats to embargo North Korea or destroy its nuclear sites,
whatever their value as ammunition against hawks at home or in South
Korea, were little more than bluff at best, counterproductive at worst.
North Korea bristled at every threat, becoming more intransigent instead of more pliable. The result was diplomatic deadlock. North Korea
needed little reminder of the history of American nuclear threats and the
continuing American military presence on the peninsula. It needed reassurance that the United States was intent on dealing with it, not out to
destroy it. Belated promises, not threats, brought it around.

To understand why Track II diplomacy was essential—why the administration was so reluctant to probe North Korean intentions by engaging in diplomatic give-and-take and so fearful of being accused of
appeasement when it did make a deal—it is necessary to examine the
politics of nuclear diplomacy both in and out of the government.

No Interest in a Deal

Nuclear diplomacy with North Korea was unusually demanding. It was
politically risky to conduct a probe of North Korean intentions because
of the possibility of failure. It was also potentially costly, politically if not
economically: it was difficult to get government agencies to commit resources to a package of inducements. Diplomatic probes and promises
required the involvement of top decision-makers.

Many countries and issues compete for their attention. During the Cold War the involvement of senior officials was assured if the country or issue was seen to bear, however remotely, on Soviet-American relations. With the end of the Cold War, officials no longer have a sorting mechanism for establishing priorities. That makes it very difficult to allocate their own time to issues or to sustain a coherent line of policy, any line of policy. Coherence is impeded by the sheer complexity of the American government and the competing organizational interests of the various departments and agencies.

Complexity is built into the bureaucracy by statutes that govern the Executive Branch. Congress has parceled out authority and responsibility for preventing proliferation, for instance, among the Arms Control and Disarmament Agency, the Bureau of Politico-Military Affairs in the State Department, and a newly established office for nuclear security and counterproliferation in the Department of Defense headed by an assistant secretary. Dealing with Korean matters was the job of assistant secretary of state for East Asian and Pacific affairs and a deputy assistant secretary of defense for regional affairs. There was a similar division of labor on the National Security Council staff. Military matters were the primary concern of the armed services, especially the commander-in-chief in Korea, an Army general; the commander-in-chief of the Pacific, a Navy admiral; the service chiefs of staff and the president's principal military adviser, the chairman of the Joint Chiefs of Staff.

Congress has also written conflicting responsibilities into law. For instance, the Department of Energy and its weapons laboratories had a stake in the transfer of nuclear technology as well as in the prevention of proliferation.

With complexity has come the need for coordination and policy direction. Increasingly that has been the job of the National Security Council staff, but N.S.C. officials hesitated to take the lead in proposing a package deal to North Korea, in part because they were trying to forge a consensus among agencies with different interests, stakes, and stands, in part because they, like others, saw deal-making as a lost cause and a political liability.

In the first five months of the Clinton Administration, conducting nuclear diplomacy with North Korea was particularly difficult because it was no one's job. Those who worked on the issue did not know much about Korea, North or South. They also had many other things to do, such as winning Senate confirmation, which distracted them from much sustained attention to the North Korean nuclear issue.

The reluctance of senior officials to take charge of dealing with North Korea or to promote deal-making in public was perhaps the most telling evidence of the politics of the problem. Domestic politics reinforced the bureaucratic impulse to play it safe and not to become involved in putting a deal together.

Pyongyang's adversarial bargaining behavior interacted with Washington's political aversion in perverse ways. North Korea floated compromises upon a sea of threats. Without experienced Korea hands at top policy-making levels of the American government who were more attuned to the North's tactics, Pyongyang's pledge-breaking, double-dealing, and brinkmanship gave qualms even to the handful of officials who favored a strategy of inducement and reassurance. Its personal attacks on I.A.E.A. Director-General Hans Blix helped convince many American officials that it would never live up to its treaty obligations.

Organizational interests, the main motive in bureaucratic politics explanations, also predisposed most government agencies against a deal with North Korea.[1] The armed services were a partial but critically important exception.

The State Department has an interest in maintaining good relations by cooperating with other governments. Yet cooperation with North Korea was not a concern of the State Department since the United States did not have relations with the D.P.R.K. Instead, the Bureau of East Asian and Pacific Affairs was mainly concerned about maintaining good relations with ally South Korea. That inclined officials to show sympathy for Seoul's point of view and to favor steps that did not endanger the alliance. The ambassadors to Seoul at the time, Donald Gregg and James Laney, were not career Foreign Service officers, however, and took a broader view of their responsibilities. They both gave critically needed support to nuclear diplomacy with North Korea.

The State Department also has an interest in negotiating with other governments. That interest leads it to insist on conducting negotiations on behalf of the United States. It does not necessarily incline the department to favor negotiations, especially when officials believe that talks will be fruitless, or worse, when they feel the other side will take advantage of talks to pursue its nuclear ambitions.[2]

The State Department also has an interest in preventing proliferation, but this function was never regarded as one of its essential roles and missions, or **organizational essence**. It was distinctly less important than maintaining good relations with other governments, as has been evident in past dealings with Israel, Pakistan, India, South Africa, Brazil, and Argentina. As a technical function, furthermore, nonproliferation has low status in the Foreign Service. FSOs are often content to let civil servants in the State Department, like Robert Gallucci, take on this chore, or to relegate it to the Arms Control and Disarmament Agency (A.C.D.A.).

To nonproliferation specialists in the State Department and especially in A.C.D.A., preventing proliferation was seen as synonymous with preserving and protecting the prerogatives of the I.A.E.A. Nonproliferation specialists in the Pentagon defined their interests differently. They were preoccupied with preventing North Korea from producing any more plutonium or diverting what it had to bomb-making. The difference in outlook led them to take opposing stands at interagency meetings, according to one senior participant: "Everybody kept taking a classical institutional position. O.S.D. in both administrations came in and said, we don't care so much about the I.A.E.A. and safeguards. We care about the plutonium. The State Department came in with the opposite view and A.C.D.A. even more so."[3]

A.C.D.A. has significant nonproliferation responsibilities under its legislative charter. It is also the repository for technical expertise on the subject. That inclines the agency to treat arms control as a question of engineering, a technical perspective that it shares with the I.A.E.A.

That was partly a matter of political necessity. Lacking the interagency clout to assemble incentives for deal-making, it regarded political questions like normalization of political and economic relations with North Korea as beyond its purview. By the 1990s, moreover, its political support on Capitol Hill had eroded to the point where its very existence was in jeopardy. To shore up its standing, career officials at A.C.D.A. took a much harder line against proliferators, favoring the crime-and-punishment approach and opposing rewards for compliance.

The Department of Energy has conflicting interests on proliferation issues. It has historically borne responsibility for designing and building nuclear warheads and for promoting nuclear power. Neither of these responsibilities inclined it to see the prevention of proliferation as a pressing concern. Quite the contrary, some in the weapons labs saw proliferation as a rationale for continued nuclear-arming and nuclear testing.

With the collapse of the Soviet Union, however, demand for new warhead designs in the armed services contracted and the possibility of a comprehensive ban on nuclear tests led the weapons laboratories to seek new roles and missions. One area of Congressional concern, and budgetary growth, was nonproliferation, where Livermore and Sandia had significant expertise.

While interest in nonproliferation has grown, it has yet to become a dominant interest of the labs. Their essence remains, in the latest euphemism, "stockpile stewardship," insuring that the warheads still in the nuclear arsenal are safe and reliable and retaining the expertise to replace them when they decay.

North Korea impinged on the interests of the Army, Navy, and Air Force in several ways. Acquiring the capabilities and budgets they need to carry out their responsibilities is their constant preoccupation. In a world without the Red Army, the North Korean threat was critical to the two-war strategy that the armed services used to justify retaining their substantial capabilities and budgets after the Cold War.

Yet the armed services need threats, not wars, and North Korea was no exception. Threat inflation served two purposes: justifying sizable forces and opposing the use of force to solve the nuclear problem. Once the Clinton Administration completed its bottom-up review and decided to maintain an excessively large force structure and to draw the bottom line on the defense budget at $265 billion a year, the services' interest in avoiding war in Korea came to the fore, and they stressed just how costly such a war could be.

The North Korea contingency was especially important for the capabilities and budget of a twelve-carrier Navy. The Navy used that contingency to justify stationing an aircraft carrier and its companion ships in Northeast Asia and the Pacific. The Navy had long preferred to rotate carriers instead of crews. By the Navy's rule of thumb, for every carrier permanently on station, one was in overhaul and another on home leave. In practice, the ratio was closer to four carriers in the fleet for each one on station. In addition, the Navy was expected to reinforce its position by rushing five more carrier battle groups to the region in the event of war. The Korea contingency thus drove a sizable share of the Navy's force structure and budget, at least four out of twelve carrier battle groups. That may have predisposed the Navy to display carrier battle groups off the coast of North Korea.

North Korea impinged on the Army's interest in capabilities as well. Force readiness was central to that interest. Readiness required exercises in Korea, but not exercises so provocative that they increased the likelihood of war.

The Army had two brigades deployed in Korea. Another 5⅓ active Army divisions of reinforcements would be committed there in the event of war. The North Korea threat thus helped sustain a ten-division Army. Without it, there would be less justification for the requirement to wage two major regional contingencies, nearly simultaneously. Yet the U.S. commander-in-chief in Korea had no interest in seeing that latent threat become manifest. That interest made him wary of dispatching substantial reinforcements during the June crisis.

The Air Force, since its inception, has had an interest in strategic bombing, striking targets other than those on the battlefield, especially targets like urban industrial areas that it believed would affect the enemy's ability and will to resist. While the Air Force regarded strategic nuclear roles and missions as its essence during the Cold War, it has come to view conventional bombing as increasingly essential since the collapse of the Soviet threat. That shift is evident in the promotion of aviators in the Tactical Air Command to top posts in the Air Force, including the command of its intraservice rival, the Strategic Air Command. It was also evident in the change of S.A.C.'s motto in the mid-1980s from "Peace Is Our Profession," which implied nuclear deterrence, to "We Are Warriors," which strongly implied the use of conventional weapons. This interest, aided by improvements in guidance technology, led the Air Force to stress its effectiveness at precision bombing of strategic targets, like nuclear facilities, without having to resort to nuclear arms.

The Central Intelligence Agency's interest in the Korean nuclear question was far less tangible, but perhaps no less important, because its interest influenced assessments in ways that agency analysts may not have recognized and would not acknowledge. In particular, the agency treated nonproliferation primarily as a problem of denying potential proliferators the technology and material they needed for bomb-making and directed its assets accordingly. Having defined its nonproliferation mission to be denial, the agency treated proliferators as adversaries, and tried to catch them in the act of acquiring the means to make bombs. Unless tasked to do so, it did not look for ways to induce potential proliferators to give up their quest.

The C.I.A. lacked good sources of political intelligence on North Korea. The C.I.A. did not have agents in Pyongyang with access to top political authorities or its nuclear program. Nor did it have extensive intelligence liaison with South Korea, which could have biased its assessments.[4] Nor did it place much confidence in other human intelligence sources. Defectors, especially those trotted out by South Korean intelligence, are notoriously unreliable. Less explicably, analysts were also discouraged from talking to North Korean diplomats and visitors or to academics who studied North Korea. All of this made the C.I.A. especially dependent on national technical means.

Much of the best political intelligence comes from careful culling of public sources, like reading reports in the North Korean media, but within the intelligence community this source is not considered as reliable as more esoteric technical means, like satellite photography and communications intercepts, or spies. The C.I.A., in the vernacular of the intelligence community, relies more on sigint, comint, and humint than on "askint" and "readint," giving technical analysts more influence than regional political analysts.

American intelligence was able to detect some important things from satellites. Yet the dearth of data collected on North Korea's nuclear program left unusually large room for interpretation. That interpretation was unduly influenced by the domestic political climate, in particular, by shared images widely held in the foreign policy establishment.

The domestic climate exerted even greater influence over political analysis. With the end of the Cold War, the intelligence community and especially the C.I.A. had come under intense Congressional scrutiny. The accuracy of its assessments, in particular its failure to anticipate the collapse of the Soviet threat or to detect much of Iraq's nuclear program, were open to question. So were its bloated budget and its main mission. How could a C.I.A. that had concentrated so much of its staff and other resources on the Soviet Union meet the country's intelligence needs after the Cold War? Under Robert Gates the C.I.A. moved to deflect this question by contending that political analysts were generalists who could readily apply their skills to North Korea as to the Soviet Union. Since North Korea was a growth sector in the C.I.A., it attracted some analysts who had once worked on the Soviet Union but had little or no Korea expertise and who were much more attuned to political realities at home than to those in North Korea. They were more inclined to take an "essentialist" view of North Korea, ascribing its behavior to the very nature of the beast.

The C.I.A. faced opposition both on the left and the right on Capitol Hill, but even before the Republicans took control of both houses of Congress, the right had become much more powerful than the left. The agency's interest in preserving its budget and its influence also may have led it to overestimate the nuclear threat posed by North Korea, for fear of underestimating as it had with Iraq. It also led it to discount the possibility of cooperating with an unpredictable communist regime in Pyongyang.

In contrast to the C.I.A., political analysis was closer than technical analysis to the organizational essence of the State Department's Bureau of Intelligence and Research, as career INR officials define it. In the intelligence community, "there are two cultures," says an INR analyst. "The regional types are more oriented to political analysis. They tend to be acutely aware of the security situation and are more prone to question what difference a bomb or two or three would make. For the nonproliferation types North Korea was a totally new discovery. They knew nothing about it initially, although after they had been on it for a year or two, they became as sophisticated as anyone."[5] INR had far fewer analysts. As a result they could not afford to specialize in military or economic or political affairs and were accustomed to integrating the military and technical with the political. That made it easier to bridge the culture gap, keeping technical intelligence from "being treated as facts that could be understood in isolation, or that somehow spoke for themselves," according to another INR analyst. "In turn, the technical specialists armed the regional people so that they were not overwhelmed or bamboozled by technical presentations."[6]

INR was also institutionally somewhat predisposed to give diplomacy a chance. In the words of a senior State Department analyst, "If you believed that the North Koreans were determined to build bombs and were unwilling to make a deal, that left you with no policy except to go to war."[7] These differences of interest and perspective made INR a dissenter within the intelligence community.

For the Pentagon, surprise can prove fatal. So can mobilizing against a foe that did not intend to attack. Yet intelligence estimates serve other purposes than divining a potential foe's intentions and capabilities. They help justify expensive capabilities and demanding roles and missions. To armed services confronting shrinking budgets, estimates that cast doubt on North Korea's capabilities or readiness for war are fighting words. North Korean nuclear intentions and potential were also the central justification for an expansive new mission in the Pentagon, that of counterproliferation. The bias of the Defense Intelligence Agency and armed service intelligence assessments was to overestimate North Korean capabilities.

A major contention of the bureaucratic politics approach was succinctly stated by Rufus Miles, "Where you stand depends on where you sit." The performance of the intelligence community suggests a corollary to Miles's dictum: What you see depends on where you sit and where you stand.

Organizational interests biased intelligence assessments and predisposed many bureaucrats against nuclear deal-making with North Korea. Yet the main cleavages did not always form neatly along the division of labor among departments. Organizational interests were not always compelling enough to determine bureaucratic stakes and stands.

If the government has trouble probing North Korea or engaging in diplomatic give-and-take, the role, in theory, could be filled by outsiders. Yet, far from facilitating diplomacy, the expert community was largely hostile to that endeavor. So was the rest of the foreign policy establishment. Domestic politics, even more than bureaucratic politics, predisposed officials against deal-making with North Korea.

The Foreign Policy Establishment

An expert is someone who gives policy-makers good reasons why something is a problem and why a proposed solution cannot work. An academic is someone who is not interested in the problem or the solution. A journalist is someone who can always find an expert to quote. A foundation executive funds experts. The foreign policy establishment is populated by people who read what journalists write and believe what experts say.

Success in Track II diplomacy with North Korea depended on people who did not fit these descriptions. They helped turn the American government around to negotiate an agreement that, if fully implemented, will keep North Korea from nuclear-arming.

The American foreign policy establishment, people active in or attentive to foreign affairs, was largely skeptical about, if not hostile to, negotiating with North Korea. Very few members of the establishment were prepared to be quoted in public in favor of a deal, even after it was concluded. For some the hostility was partisan in nature. For others it was ideologically motivated: to unreconstructed cold warriors North Korea was not a partner to make deals with but a foe to be destabilized or destroyed. Yet outright hostility to deal-making was a minority view. The dominant view was skepticism that North Korea wanted a deal and would keep any deal it made. The skepticism was so infectious that it kept all but a handful of those involved in the public debate from lending support to nuclear diplomacy and discouraged officials from taking risks for deal-making.

Two groups of specialists influenced what the news media reported and what the foreign policy establishment knew about nuclear diplomacy with North Korea: nonproliferation experts and Korea experts. For very different reasons both groups lent support to coercive diplomacy and opposed cooperation. Foundation funding largely went to experts who were part of the problem, not part of the solution. Some of these experts were in think tanks and other N.G.O.s, others at universities.

The rest of the academic community was largely uninvolved. The exception was a handful of generalists in international relations who were quoted in the news media or contributed to the op-ed pages, nearly all of whom expressed doubts about denying nuclear arms to North Korea. Most saw proliferation as inevitable, short of war. Some were sanguine about living with a nuclear-armed North Korea and relying on the American nuclear deterrent to check any aggressive ambitions it might have. Others favored coercive responses, even war.

The Partisan Opposition

Nuclear diplomacy came under fierce fire from hawks in South Korea and their allies in the Republican Party. South Korean hawks, wary of rapprochement between North Korea and the United States, preferred to destabilize the North rather than deal with it. That would likely preclude agreement, freeing the North to build bombs that a unified Korea would inherit. For a few hawks in Seoul, that was not far-fetched. For others, nuclear-arming by North Korea was a way to justify nuclear-arming by South Korea. For most, accommodation with North Korea was simply anathema.

Why Republicans in Congress were so eager to make common cause with South Korea's hawks is less obvious. Some on the party's right wing were opposed to foreign aid of all sorts, especially aid to a hateful communist regime, but why question a deal that obliged South Korea and Japan to pay nearly all of the $5 billion in costs? One possible reason is that if the United States could not prevent proliferation, that would strengthen the case for the right wing's pet project, ballistic missile defense of the United States. Yet other Republicans favor deep cuts in the budget and are unwilling to lavish billions on Star Wars defenses. Many Republicans also want the United States to act on its own and are hostile to all sorts of collective action. They seem inclined to rely on military rather than economic means to cope with proliferation threats. Militarily, the United States can afford to be self-reliant, if it chooses to, but economic measures require international cooperation. The irony is that resistance in Congress to paying the price of conciliation forced the administration to approach the allies, hat in hand, to obtain financing for the deal.

What drove the Republicans was disbelief that the D.P.R.K. could ever be weaned from its nuclear program. Their political strategy has been to make a sport of denouncing nuclear diplomacy with North Korea in the expectation that it would fail, which would allow them to claim credit for foresight—but to stop short of sabotaging the deal, which could leave them open to blame, alienate America's allies, Japan and South Korea, and worst of all, come 1997, possibly confront a Republican President with a war in Korea. Former Secretary of State James Baker put it succinctly in testimony to Congress, "If you cut it off up here on the Hill, then you're taking on your shoulders the responsibility for what might happen if the United States unilaterally walked away from an agreement it has negotiated with North Korea, even though I don't think the other side is going to keep it, and even though I think it's a bad agreement."[8]

The Proliferation Experts

Experts on proliferation in the academic world, think tanks, and other nongovernmental organizations seemed to spend most of their time calling attention to the problem instead of seeking a solution. The experts' attention-getting helped mobilize support for coercive measures, ranging from economic sanctions and antimissile defenses to air strikes and other forms of counterproliferation. That was not necessarily their intention.

Most proliferation experts acted as if they had an interest in drawing attention to the problem for its own sake, not because they had a policy to advocate. Simply documenting the problem of proliferation is difficult enough without trying to solve it. Would-be proliferators conduct surreptitious bomb programs disguised as peaceful power plants or research. They are careful to cloak their purchases of dual-use equipment and nuclear material. So are the sellers of such wares. Intelligence agencies and even international inspectors do unearth suspicious patterns and practices and occasionally conduct briefings for outside experts, but they are often reluctant to disclose their discoveries for fear of revealing their sources and methods.

As a result, nongovernment experts rely on unauthorized disclosures to supplement what they can glean from publicly available sources. Often the leaks are motivated, sometimes to probe proliferators' reactions, sometimes to publicize a personal assessment that was rejected by other intelligence analysts, sometimes to push a policy. Nongovernment experts may not share the leakers' motivation but they are willing to be used. They serve as intermediaries, brokers of information, gathering it from open and official sources and packaging it for dissemination to the news media and Congress. Documenting the problem attracts publicity, and foundation funding. A reputation for scrupulous attention to detail still matters to some proliferation experts, but given the news media's inattention to past performance and its preoccupation with bumper-sticker slogans, all too many find that overstatement is the way to fame and fortune in the expertise business.

Experts who do promote their own solutions tend to apply the same prescriptive template to all potential proliferators: denial and safeguards to keep technology and material from being used in bomb-making. That template did not fit the circumstances in North Korea, however. Its nuclear program was too far along for denial to work. It already had the know-how, the technology, and the nuclear reactor fuel it needed to make bombs. Safeguarding its nuclear material and facilities against misuse was a feasible policy, but how to do that was the main point of contention in nuclear diplomacy. North Korea was unwilling to comply with the I.A.E.A.'s demands without getting something in return. With few exceptions, most notably Spurgeon Keeny of the Arms Control Association, nonproliferation experts opposed giving North Korea what it wanted.

To nonproliferation hawks North Korea's defiance showed the bankruptcy of traditional nonproliferation policies. To them the I.A.E.A. was either feckless or toothless. North Korea could not be trusted, whether or not it agreed to allow inspections. It could always throw out the inspectors and resume bomb-making or build a clandestine nuclear program in addition to its known facilities. If the United States was serious about keeping North Korea from getting a bomb, it had to apply coercion.

For some hawks, nonproliferation became little more than a pretext for destroying North Korea and unifying the Korean peninsula. One who made this aim unusually explicit was a former Pentagon official, Henry Sokolski. In testimony before the House Armed Services Committee, he argued that "we need to back off our preoccupation with nuclear inspections for North Korea and get on with the serious business of containing and transmuting this threatening, tyrannical regime." He proposed interdiction of North Korean shipments of missile or nuclear equipment, but his ultimate policy was to eliminate North Korea by having the South absorb it. In his words, "the only sure way to defuse the North Korean strategic threat is to defuse the regime."[9] Other hawks openly argued for a stringent embargo to cause North Korea's collapse or an attack on its nuclear installations. The hawks defined the problem in a way that defied solution. The North's neighbors were not about to impose a total embargo and the United States itself has historically rejected preventive war as a way to deal with the problem of proliferation, against the Soviet Union in the 1950s and against China in the 1960s and 1970s.

More traditional nonproliferation experts thought that I.A.E.A. inspections could help constrain North Korea's nuclear program. The traditionalists wanted to strengthen the I.A.E.A. by upholding its right to inspect. Yet that led them to treat noncompliance as a crime that deserved punishment. In their view, a deal that rewarded North Korea for noncompliance was damaging to the nonproliferation regime. Some also found fault with the form of the reward: replacement reactors, which may have been proliferation-resistant but were not proliferation-proof, and might end up only postponing the problem.

Why were such experts so disinclined to deal? They tended to treat proliferation as a technical and functional problem. On their map of the world, there were no nations, just potential proliferation problems. Insofar as they focused on North Korea, or any other country, they studied the details of its nuclear capabilities, not its internal politics, its foreign policy, or its motives for acting the way that it did. Yet preventing proliferation required an intimate knowledge of North Korea's peculiar fears, wants, and needs, not just the plutonium-producing potential of its reactor.

The proliferation experts' judgments about the prospects for negotiating with North Korea may have been colored by their own research on its bomb-making efforts. Inferring a country's nuclear intentions from its nuclear capabilities, they were inclined to doubt the prospects for disarming.

For the outside experts to do their job, they also had to maintain close contact with I.A.E.A. and American officials working on nonproliferation, especially in the intelligence community. Dependent on them for information, outsiders tended to absorb the insiders' perspectives. To the I.A.E.A. the crime-and-punishment approach was the appropriate response to North Korean noncompliance. Until late 1993 it was also the policy of the United States. Most of the intelligence community, which regarded its main nonproliferation mission as denial, had concluded that diplomacy would not work. Nongovernment experts came to share these views. To challenge them was to risk being dismissed as naive or out of touch, and worse, having contact and cooperation curtailed. For much of the expert community, open dissent from government policy was a risk, especially without influential support from opponents in Congress.

To judge from the contents of news articles and op-eds, dissent in the community of nonproliferation experts with few exceptions took the form of more dire assessments of the problem rather than a more imaginative view of the solution.

The Korea Experts

To most Korea experts the problem was North Korea, not proliferation, and the solution was to do whatever South Korea thought best. A few dissenters from the dominant view were critical to resolving the crisis.

Some Korea experts were Americans raised in Korea, mostly the children of missionaries. Others had served in Korea in an official capacity. Many had personal ties and privileged access to officials in Seoul. Some spoke the language and followed the Korean press and could interpret current South Korean thinking to American officials. The problem was that most South Korean officials and nearly all the South Korean press were opposed to direct negotiations between the United States and North Korea. The South Korean government was also assiduous in cultivating American Korea-watchers and using a cadre of "American-handlers," many of them educated in the United States, to keep in contact and lobby on its behalf. In contrast, remarkably few Korea experts had any contact at all with North Korean officials posted at the United Nations and elsewhere.

As a consequence, the Korea experts were usually good at anticipating trouble from Seoul, but seldom helpful in understanding Pyongyang. They were experts on South Korea. With few exceptions they embraced South Korean views of North Korea. Most saw preservation of good relations with South Korea as the dominant American interest, one far more important than keeping North Korea non-nuclear. They also deplored the lack of Korea expertise in the senior ranks of Washington officialdom. They had a point, but they made too much of it. At the height of the nuclear crisis the Korea country desk had two of the Department's most fluent Korea-speakers, but it was manned mostly by Foreign Service officers who spoke Japanese, not Korean. The Korea experts' solution was questionable. They recommended appointment of someone who specialized in Korea, or at least Northeast Asia, to replace Robert Gallucci, a nonproliferation specialist, as the American negotiator.

The dissenting Korea experts fell into roughly two camps, those who thought that American policy should aim primarily at improving relations between the two Koreas rather than preventing proliferation and those who favored cooperative engagement with North Korea. Among the most prominent dissenting Korea experts who backed engagement were Selig Harrison, James Laney, Donald Gregg, and Bruce Cumings. Many of the dissenters, however, were Americans of Korean extraction, often first-generation immigrants, who tended to be marginalized in the policy debate, both by the other experts and by U.S. officials.

A survey by the Asia Society in October 1993 on inducements for North Korea provides some evidence for these contentions. Of the 150 contacted, 40 were identified as East Asia experts. Another 41 were identified as Korea specialists and 13 of them were of Korean extraction. The majority of the Korea experts favored the carrot-and-stick approach then being pursued by the Washington and Seoul. A substantial minority thought that no inducements would ever convince the North to abandon bomb-making. A small minority saw South Korea as a source of inducements or insisted that any inducements be coordinated with Seoul. By contrast, at least 8 of the 13 experts of Korean extraction unequivocally favored offering American inducements to North Korea.

This case suggests that as a polyglot society, the United States has much to learn about the world from the immigrants who are drawn to its shores, but only if it listens, and not just to a chosen few.

Other Scholars

A handful of other scholars ventured public comment on nuclear diplomacy with North Korea, most of them generalists in international politics and nearly all of them adherents of the realist school of thought.

Yet the reach of realism extended well beyond the walls of academe. Most officials embraced it. So did many politicians and experts. It informed the shared images of nuclear diplomacy.

Those shared images exerted greater influence on bureaucratic politics than did organizational interests. They also affected the play of partisan politics. They were the unstated premises of most experts' analyses. In short, they influenced much of the American foreign policy establishment about the chances of cooperating with North Korea. The establishment's belief in these shared images allowed the hawks to dominate the public discourse on North Korea. To officials desperately trying to make a deal with North Korea, that was a persistent source of discouragement.

10

WHY WON'T AMERICA COOPERATE?

*The test of a first-rate intelligence is the ability to
hold two opposed ideas in the mind at the same time
and still retain the ability to function.*
(F. Scott Fitzgerald)

FOUR SHARED images shaped the politics of nuclear diplomacy
in the United States: first, that "rogue states" with an aggressive
intent in acquiring nuclear arms are the main proliferation menace; second, that as an archetypal rogue state, and an old-fashioned
communist one at that, North Korea was hostile to the United States
and hell-bent on nuclear-arming; third, that once a state decides to
build the Bomb, it cannot be induced to stop; and fourth, that the only
way to get states to abandon their nuclear ambitions is to demonize
them as outlaws and force them to disarm—the crime-and-punishment
approach to nonproliferation.

Given the endemic uncertainty about North Korean nuclear capabilities and intentions and the history of hostility, these certitudes filled the
vacuum of knowledge of North Korea for policy-makers. Even when
their grip on policy-makers' minds began to loosen by the fall of 1993,
the four shared images still retained their hold over many vocal members
of the foreign policy establishment who influenced the domestic politics
of nuclear diplomacy in the United States. Establishment opposition to
a deal with North Korea predisposed policy-makers to favor the crime-
and-punishment approach over diplomatic give-and-take.

The shared images of nuclear diplomacy are rooted in two rival intellectual traditions which dominate the American orientation to international politics: liberalism and realism.

The liberal tradition, as espoused by Woodrow Wilson and his many
followers, emphasizes the common interests of states and the potential
for cooperation in international society. It is a central tenet of liberalism
that international conflict and war are caused by states with flawed domestic structures. Democratic states with market-oriented economies,
liberals believe, are likely to cooperate with one another, and conversely,
exceedingly unlikely to go to war with one another. The same cannot be
said of a corporatist state with a command economy, authoritarian rule,
and a cult of personality. Nor does it apply to a garrison state with obses-
sive secrecy and repressive internal surveillance that allots a substantial

portion of its budget to military purposes. For liberals, North Korea was a decidedly bad state, a rogue that could not be trusted to cooperate but, instead, was prone to wage war on its neighbors.

For liberals who embraced a live-and-let-live policy toward the rest of the world, North Korea was an unattractive nuisance, not much to worry about. Other liberals of a more crusading bent wanted to pry open this last outpost of communism and transform it, or else compel it to collapse. The crime-and-punishment approach to proliferation had some appeal to liberals of both persuasions, who share a legalistic view of international relations.

American foreign policy, like the United States itself, was "born liberal," in Louis Hartz's phrase, so it is not surprising that American officials would try to justify their policies with liberal arguments. Liberalism infuses National Security Adviser Anthony Lake's depiction of rogue states such as North Korea:

> Ruled by cliques that control power through coercion, they suppress basic human rights and promote radical ideologies. While their political systems vary, their leaders share a common antipathy toward popular participation that might undermine the existing regimes. These nations exhibit a chronic inability to engage constructively with the outside world, and they do not function effectively in alliances—even with those like-minded. . . . Finally, they share a siege mentality. Accordingly, they are embarked on ambitious and costly military programs—especially in weapons of mass destruction and delivery systems—in a misguided quest for a great equalizer to protect their regimes or advance their purposes abroad.[1]

There is also a distant echo of Woodrow Wilson's call to "make the world safe for democracy" in President Clinton's 1993 appeal to the United Nations, "If we do not stem the proliferation of the world's deadliest weapons, no democracy can feel secure."[2] The attempt to associate the threat of proliferation with undemocratic states ignores the fact that most nuclear-armed nations are democracies. So are many other states that have maintained their option to make nuclear arms.

Along with liberalism, the other principal source of the shared images of nuclear diplomacy is realism. Realism's central contention is that the structure of relations among states, not the domestic structure within states, best explains international relations. Starting from the premise of international anarchy, realists account for war and peace by the operation of the balance of power. Realism treats states as if they were unitary actors, calculating the most efficient way to achieve their national interests, above all, military security.

Realism took a primitive form in the public discourse on North Korea. Realists view the world as a war of all against all. They were quick to dismiss cooperation as, in a word, unrealistic and to favor coercive diplomacy. To most realists it was self-evident that nuclear arms make their possessors secure by so strengthening deterrence to make war unthinkable. They favored deterring a nuclear-arming North Korea by a conventional buildup and nuclear threats. Other realists feared that North Korea was too irrational to deter. They wanted North Korea disarmed but despaired of disarming it short of all-out war. Few realists were willing to entertain an alternative hypothesis, that countries might also suffer from economic and political insecurities and might be moved by economic and political inducements to abandon their nuclear ambitions.

In more sophisticated forms, realism and liberalism dominate the American academic discourse on international relations as well. The scholarly literature is worth exploring because the North Korean case poses as much of an intellectual challenge to the reigning schools of thought about international relations in the United States as it does a political challenge to the dominant beliefs of the American foreign policy establishment. The case raises doubts about some contentions at the core of both realist and liberal thinking. The question is not merely academic. The scholarly discourse helped inform the public discourse, both because American foreign policy-makers were schooled in realism and liberalism and because some of the leading scholarly proponents of these ideas took part in the public debate that affected official and popular attitudes toward nuclear diplomacy with North Korea.

Realism

Academic realists hold that states value national security above all other goods and that military preponderance makes them secure. Most see nuclear arming as inevitable and nuclear disarming, especially by means of cooperative strategies, as very unlikely. As Kenneth Waltz of the University of California at Berkeley has written, "The United States opposes North Korea's presumed quest for nuclear military capability, yet in the past half-century, no country has been able to prevent other countries from going nuclear if they were determined to do it."[3] The word "presumed" seems to qualify whether Waltz's tautology applies to Pyongyang, but almost all realists share his assumption that states as insecure as North Korea are determined to go nuclear.

Some leading theoreticians like Waltz follow the logic of realism to its ultimate conclusion: that the further spread of nuclear arms is not only inevitable, but also desirable. Coexisting in a condition of anarchy, with war an ever-present possibility, states have to rely on themselves for security. They may form alliances but cannot depend on them. They make prudential calculations about the costs and benefits of war, calculations that err on the side of caution. War is risky and nuclear war, prohibitively so. As Waltz puts it, "*Uncertainty* about the course that a nuclear war might follow, along with the *certainty* that destruction can be immense, strongly inhibits the first use of nuclear weapons."[4]

More questionable propositions follow from this premise. The prospect of nuclear war deters states from waging *any* premeditated war, conventional as well as nuclear. By the same token, nuclear deterrence makes coercive threats against nuclear states less credible. Even if conventional war breaks out, the risk of nuclear war will keep it from escalating out of control. Nuclear war is so fearful that states take precautions to avoid any chance of preemptive or accidental war. States will also not risk waging preventive war against a North Korea out of fear that it may have built a bomb or two. In short, by strengthening deterrence, nuclear proliferation promotes peace and stability.[5]

Nuclear arsenals like those amassed by the United States and the Soviet Union are absurdly excessive for deterrence, in Waltz's view. A few survivable warheads will suffice, a lesson that the United States and the Soviet Union never did absorb. Their possessors will also take the necessary precautions to insure that they are safe from attack or accidental use, something the United States and Soviet Union did not always do. Small arsenals will be easier to disperse and protect while assuring tight control over their potential use. "Nuclear forces are seldom delicate," he concludes optimistically, "because no state wants delicate forces, and nuclear forces can easily be made sturdy."[6]

The logic of deterrence, asserts Waltz, applies with equal force to the North Koreas of the world. He rightly rejects the ethnocentric view of Third World countries as inherently less prudent. Yet he does so on the questionable grounds that states will behave like states, regardless of their cultures, political systems, political instability, and leadership. "With nuclear weapons any state will be deterred by another state's second-strike forces," he writes. "One need not be preoccupied with the characteristics of the state that is to be deterred or scrutinize its leaders."[7] Domestic structures do not matter; the balance of power governs behavior.

Other realists are not as sanguine about proliferation as Waltz. They believe that nuclear arms in the hands of others, especially potential foes, would not be beneficial to American security. Yet they agree with Waltz that states will not willingly relinquish nuclear arms or forgo nuclear-arming.

In theory, realists do not rule out cooperation among rival nations, but they do consider it improbable and precarious. In practice, noncooperation is a premise, not a hypothesis, for many realists. They contend that anarchy in the international system leads states to seek autonomy and control rather than interdependence and cooperation. In Waltz's words, cooperation will occur "only in ways strongly conditioned" by the anarchy of the international system.[8] Dispute settlement is unlikely without a credible threat of force.[9]

In giving priority to deterrence, realists also discount the value of norms like the one enshrined in the Nonproliferation Treaty, that the spread of nuclear arms is wrong. Were it not for that norm, however, the near-unanimous opposition in the United Nations to North Korea's stance would be difficult to explain.

Realism captures aspects of the North Korean nuclear problem. From North Korea's vantage point, it was at a serious military disadvantage with arch-rival South Korea. Even worse, the North's allies, the Soviet Union and China, had become increasingly unreliable, while the South was firmly allied with the United States, which could bring its formidable forces to bear in the event of war.

For realists like Waltz, North Korea's increasing insecurity should have led it to accelerate its nuclear-arming, even to undertake a crash program. It did not. Contrary to realist expectations, the communist regime's economic insecurity may have motivated it to sacrifice its nuclear program in return for aid, investment, and trade from the West. Yet it was willing to make that sacrifice only if political relations with the United States improved, alleviating its military insecurity. Given the threatening context, reassurance and reciprocity were essential if the D.P.R.K. were to abandon its nuclear ambitions.

Realists were pessimistic about cooperating with North Korea. Most favored strengthening deterrence by sending reinforcements to Korea and making nuclear threats. Insofar as realists could conceive of ending North Korean bomb-making, they believed it would require coercion. Yet North Korea took steps to abandon nuclear-arming only when coercion was no longer credible—after the Clinton Administration had rejected air strikes and Jimmy Carter had publicly repudiated sanctions, undermining Security Council support for them.

To realists war is the *ultima ratio* and the threat of war makes states more amenable to compromise. Yet the close call in June 1994 had no discernible effect on North Korea, which had been trying for more than three years to strike a nuclear bargain with the United States. It did have an effect on some Clinton Administration officials, convincing them to abandon the crime-and-punishment approach for good and to engage in sustained diplomatic give-and-take instead.

Realist theory is at least well-reasoned. In their public comments on North Korea, however, theorists of international relations all too often espoused a simplistic form of realism without the scholarly caveats and qualifications. So did most U.S. officials and the Americans who influenced them. Indeed, realism seems to be the secular religion of the foreign policy establishment. Those who want to play a part in policy-making believe in it, or at least pay lip service to it by acting as if they believe in it, even if they do not.

Realist theoreticians concentrate on conflict to the virtual exclusion of cooperation. Yet conflict and cooperation coexist in international politics. The conditions under which one or the other is more prevalent is not simply a matter of theory; it is a subject for empirical research. To regard one as the norm and the other as the exception is not a sound basis for understanding how states interact. Scholars can afford to simplify reality in order to deepen their understanding of aspects of it. Statesmen cannot.

The North Korea case also bears on other issues raised in the scholarly literature about the calculus of cooperation. One is whether states are motivated to cooperate by the expectation of absolute or relative gain, or whether cooperation is more likely when the relative gain is shared equitably. The North Korea case calls into question whether the theory can be made operational by suggesting how difficult it is to measure relative gain and how subjective any evaluation must be. The two sides' values were incommensurate and their expectations of payoff uncertain. The United States and North and South Korea, this study contends, benefited in absolute terms from the Agreed Framework. Yet which side stood to gain absolutely or relatively was hotly contested in the United States. Indications are that it was in the D.P.R.K. as well. Uncertainty about another Korean war or economic collapse in the North dominates the calculations.

A second proposition also rests on beliefs about the future. Willingness to cooperate is enhanced by the expectation on both sides that they will continue to interact from now on. The Agreed Framework was structured to foster that expectation, which begs the question of whether the anticipation of prolonged interaction preceded the accord. That was certainly the hope if not the expectation in Pyongyang. Indeed, some North Korean officials expressed the wish that the relationship would evolve into a security partnership of sorts in which American antagonism would diminish over time. They want to see the United States become a guarantor of the North's security, a peace broker and economic go-between, restraining the South, mediating between North and South and opening the way to expanded trade, investment, and aid with the outside world. To what extent that expectation is widely shared in Pyongyang is not known. It still has almost no resonance in Washington.

The Liberal Challenge to Realism

Other schools of thought have long warred with the realists over the potential for cooperation in international society, and offer very different policy prescriptions. One such school is liberal institutionalism. Starting from many of the same premises as the realists, liberal institutionalists try to account for cooperation amid anarchy. Their main contention is that cooperation is facilitated by international regimes, defined as norms, rules, and procedures that structure actors' expectations.[10]

Regimes, the liberal institutionalists assert, foster cooperation by monitoring compliance and by increasing the political costs of noncompliance. That was so in this case. Despite North Korean accusations that the I.A.E.A. was biased, it was politically more palatable for Pyongyang to grant access to I.A.E.A. inspectors than to allow South Korea or the United States to monitor its nuclear facilities. Contrary to the conventional wisdom in Washington, I.A.E.A. inspections were also more effective than American satellite imagery in narrowing the range of uncertainty about North Korea's nuclear past and present. Without substantial sanctions or armed force at their disposal, neither the I.A.E.A. nor the United Nations Security Council were effective enforcement mechanisms. Yet the norm of nonproliferation and the existence of the I.A.E.A. and the Security Council made it easier for the United States to mobilize international political support in order to persuade North Korea to abandon bomb-making and implement the Agreed Framework, once it was reached.

The nuclear nonproliferation regime encouraged cooperation in other, more subtle ways. It helped redefine interests, raising the value of compliance on a particular issue through linkages with other issues. Acceptance of I.A.E.A. inspections was an internationally approved way for the D.P.R.K. to demonstrate its willingness to get along with the outside world. Signing an accord with the I.A.E.A. was a way to satisfy the American interest in a nuclear-free Korea in the expectation that the United States would reciprocate. When that expectation was not fulfilled, limiting the access of inspectors was North Korea's way of compelling American reciprocity.

Yet the behavior of the I.A.E.A., the institutional embodiment of the nuclear nonproliferation regime, poses a fundamental challenge to liberal institutionalist theory. The agency's internal rules, procedures, and organizational interests became impediments to reciprocity. Having been judged a failure in Iraq, the I.A.E.A. was determined to uphold its safeguards accord with North Korea to the letter and to insist on full-scope safeguards. At times the agency seemed more preoccupied with getting at North Korea's nuclear past than with preventing future bomb-making. At other times, most notably in fall 1993 and May 1994, when it nearly abandoned monitoring altogether rather than accept limits on its inspections, it seemed more concerned about upholding the sanctity of its own procedures than about preventing proliferation. Because the I.A.E.A. was determined to lay down the law in North Korea, it became part of the problem. Contrary to liberal institutionalists' expectations that the I.A.E.A. would facilitate cooperation, relying on the agency as a instrument of nonproliferation led to adoption of the crime-and-punishment approach, impeding diplomatic give-and-take.

Yet another approach to understanding cooperation across borders emphasizes what have been called "epistemic communities," whose members are united by a shared profession and a common understanding of a problem and its solution.[11] In the North Korea case, a tiny informal network of nongovernmental organizations and a handful of allies in governments recognized the pernicious cause-and-effect relationship between the American approach to nuclear diplomacy and North Korean responses and agreed that any solution to the proliferation problem could not be isolated from other political, economic, and security issues on the Korean peninsula. Using the internet, e-mail, and other new tools of communication, the extra-governmental network gathered and disseminated intelligence, sometimes more rapidly than government agencies did. The role of this epistemic community went beyond providing alternative information and interpretation. In June 1994 it changed American policy. By means of Track II diplomacy it defused the nuclear crisis and opened the way to cooperation.

Yet cooperation was slow to emerge principally because of American unwillingness to deal. Neither realist nor liberal institutionalist theories can adequately account for that unwillingness, which was not rooted in the structure or institutions of international politics but in the shared images of American bureaucratic and domestic politics—images shared, above all, by realists and liberals.

Cooperating with Strangers

The American foreign policy establishment proved remarkably resistant to trying cooperative threat reduction. Instead, it reflexively favored coercion—economic sanctions and air strikes—that brought the United States to the brink of war.

This suggests a dangerous lack of perspective. It is unrealistic to expect the American people to be eager to go to war to stop the spread of nuclear arms, never mind to uphold the right of the I.A.E.A. to collect radioactive samples from a glove box or to determine how soon inspectors could visit nuclear waste sites to try to ascertain whether North Korea had diverted a few grams or a few kilograms of spent fuel from a nuclear reactor.

For supposed pragmatists, most members of the American foreign policy establishment, officials included, behaved in a remarkably doctrinaire way. Were it not for Track II diplomacy by Jimmy Carter, the North Korea crisis might have ended in war.

A generation of American students and practitioners of foreign policy have been schooled in the lessons of the 1962 missile crisis. What the Cuban missile crisis was to the Cold War, the nuclear crisis with North Korea may well be to the current era. The United States will need to absorb the implications of this case if it is to attain its aims abroad, and in particular, to stop the spread of nuclear arms. Yet even now the foreign policy establishment resists drawing appropriate lessons from the success of diplomatic give-and-take: that it is possible to reverse a state's decision to "go nuclear," that inducements work, that cooperation is far less costly than coercion, and that the international norm against nuclear-arming facilitates cooperation, not only among those trying to prevent proliferation but also by the would-be proliferator.

Much of the establishment is eager to assert American global leadership and seems fearful of American disengagement. It also tends to identify engagement with a willingness to intervene militarily and it deplores the consequences for American credibility of an inability to make and carry out threats.

Yet the foreign policy establishment seems unconcerned about America's inability to make and keep promises. That inability could prove far more deleterious to its influence in the world.

If the United States is to cooperate with other countries, these establishment beliefs cannot go unchallenged. It is a mistake to define American interests in the world mainly in terms of military security or to think of American engagement primarily in terms of coercive diplomacy and the use of force. The American people do not oppose involvement abroad per se, but they are distinctly unenthusiastic about sending American troops to die abroad in doubtful causes. A foreign policy establishment that emphasizes military might to the detriment of other ends and means of American engagement in the world may feed isolationism.

The establishment must be more willing to try cooperation. Cooperation means talking with strangers and listening to what they have to say. It means making promises, not just threats.

Cooperation is often thought of as the norm with allies, not foes. Yet cooperation occurs even in war, setting limits on both means and ends.

Conversely, even allies sometimes find it difficult to cooperate because of conflicting interests. That was certainly the case in nuclear diplomacy with North Korea. The South Korean government could not make up its mind whether to seek collapse or cooperation in North Korea. Indeed, at times it was easier for Washington to cooperate with Pyongyang than to cooperate with Seoul. Japan was also reluctant to bear much of the cost of cooperating with North Korea. That made a cooperative strategy more difficult for the United States, whose own unwillingness to supply replacement reactors and heavy fuel oil to North Korea made it dependent on South Korea and Japan.

Events since the conclusion of the October 1994 Agreed Framework seemed to confirm South Korean unwillingness to cooperate with North Korea. South Korea continues to impede American efforts to deal with the D.P.R.K. In the fall of 1996, a North Korean submarine ran aground while apparently dropping off spies on a reconnaissance mission. Such spying is routine among states, as shown by the arrest of a South Korean spy in Washington within days of the submarine's discovery. Yet South Korea charged the North with launching a "commando raid" as a prelude to all-out war. It exploited the incident to delay ground-breaking for construction of the replacement reactors, thereby delaying removal of six bombs' worth of plutonium in the spent nuclear fuel now in North Korea, as well as delaying I.A.E.A. efforts to clear up the anomalies in North Korea's nuclear past. Seoul also prevailed on Washington to postpone talks with Pyongyang on curbing its exports of ballistic missile technology.

South Korean ambivalence about dealing with North Korea could also prove an impediment in the four-party talks aimed at a peace treaty, writing a formal end to the Korean War. Seoul has to choose cooperation rather than collapse as its goal in dealing with Pyongyang, if the military confrontation on the peninsula is to be defused.

It is also misleading to identify international cooperation with international institutions. That was implicit in the policy of "assertive multilateralism," the Clinton Administration's ill-chosen phrase. It meant using international institutions to get others to do what it wanted, as the Bush Administration had done in the Persian Gulf War. Cooperation should not be seen as necessarily synonymous with working through inter-national institutions. The United States can try cooperation on its own.

The American approach to the I.A.E.A. and the United Nations Security Council in the North Korea case suggests why. The I.A.E.A. was regarded as a witness for the prosecution, if not an instrument to impose America's will on North Korea. Since the I.A.E.A. is powerless to go where a sovereign state will not allow it, this approach reduced the nonproliferation regime to a means for provoking confrontation, if not war, with North Korea. The Security Council was an effective forum for rallying support to the nonproliferation cause. Yet taking the issue to the United Nations was diversionary. The Security Council has no independent power to impose sanctions or deploy military force. That power depends on U.N. members, many of whom were unwilling to do either against North Korea. Yet administration officials kept deploying sanctions as a shield against accusations from opponents at home that they were unwilling to stand up to North Korea and force it to disarm. In blaming the United Nations for inaction, American officials were using it as a convenient whipping-boy for their own unwillingness to choose cooperation instead of coercion to prevent North Korean bombmaking.

The United States will undoubtedly face that choice again, in Iran and elsewhere. So long as the United States persists in criminalizing proliferation and demonizing so-called rogue states in order to confront them, it will leave itself with politically unpalatable alternatives, to live with more nuclear-armed states or to disarm them, temporarily, by force.

The American aversion to cooperating in order to prevent proliferation is perverse. It is much less costly than coercion, and it works. Thanks to cooperation, to date at least eight countries have been persuaded to abandon nuclear-arming: South Korea, Taiwan, Brazil, Argentina, South Africa, Ukraine, Belarus, and Kazakhstan. Thanks to cooperation, thousands of nuclear warheads are being dismantled in Russia and many more could be. Thanks to cooperation, North Korea, which by now could have made at least five or six bombs, has none. That may be anathema to Americans who believe in going it alone, but such a one-sided approach poses a clear and present danger to American security.

It is possible to prevent proliferation, but only if Washington learns to stop fighting the problem and tries to solve it. At a minimum, that requires cooperative engagement with potential proliferators. In the North Korean case this was facilitated by the withdrawal of American nuclear arms from the Korean peninsula. Ultimately it may require a nuclear quarantine, marginalizing the role of nuclear arms. It is not enough to promote nonproliferation as a norm. If the United States continues to emphasize the importance of nuclear arms to its own defense, it can hardly expect all other nations to forgo them forever.

APPENDIXES

APPENDIX I

NORTH KOREA'S TIT-FOR-TAT NEGOTIATING BEHAVIOR

	UNITED STATES (ROK, IAEA)	*NORTH KOREA*
	COOPERATES	**RECIPROCATES**
9/27/91	Bush withdraws nuclear arms	
11/11/91	Security Consultative Meeting: Team Spirit canceled for 1992	
12/13/91		Agreement on Reconciliation Non-Aggression, Exchanges, and Cooperation with ROK
12/31/91		Joint Declaration with ROK on Denuclearization of the Korean Peninsula
		Halts reprocessing
		Delays refueling reactor
1/30/92		Signs IAEA Safeguards Agreement
	RENEGES	**RENEGES**
1/22/92	High-level talks: US refuses more talks or detailed discussion of quid pro quos until North allows IAEA, ROK inspections	Delays implementing Safeguards Agreement
	INCREMENTAL MOVEMENT	
5/4/92		Initial declaration to IAEA admitting past reprocessing, asks for help in building replacement reactors, during Blix visit to Yongbyon nuclear sites
6/1/92	US ignores DPRK reactor proposal made in Beijing channel	
7/8–18/92		Allows IAEA ad hoc inspection that discovers inconsistencies with its initial declaration
9/11–14/92		Allows IAEA radiological measurement at Building 500, revealed as below-ground waste site by US satellites

	RENEGES	RENEGES
10/8/92	Security Consultative Meeting sets resumption of Team Spirit in 1993	
2/9/93		Rejects IAEA request for special inspection at waste sites, confines IAEA to "continuity of safeguards"
2/25/93	IAEA one-month deadline for access	
3/8/93	Team Spirit begins	
3/12/93		Gives 90-day notice of intent to renounce Nonproliferation Treaty

	COOPERATES	RECIPROCATES
4/22/93	Accepts high-level talks	Accepts IAEA monitoring to impede diversion, reprocessing of spent fuel ("continuity of safeguards"), but not ad hoc and routine inspections
		Does not refuel reactor
6/11/93	High-level talks first joint statement, agrees to more talks	Suspends withdrawal from NPT
7/9/93	In high-level talks agrees to "explore" replacing reactors	Agrees to consult with IAEA on safeguards and "begin" ROK talks

	RENEGES	RENEGES
8/3–10		IAEA inspectors discover tampering with seals, try to do ad hoc and routine inspection but are harshly rebuffed
11/1/93	IAEA allows monitoring cameras to run out of film to force ad hoc and routine inspections. UNGA by 140–1 vote demands DPRK cooperate, but China abstains	
11/16/93	Working-level US-DPRK talks: US agrees to comprehensive approach in principle, to resume high-level talks and suspend Team Spirit once DPRK agrees with IAEA on inspections, engages in talks with ROK	
11/23/93	ROK President Kim Young Sam in meeting with Clinton balks at package deal and bars suspension of Team Spirit until exchange of special envoys with DPRK. US backtracks in talks with DPRK	

INCREMENTAL MOVEMENT

12/29/93	Agrees to third round of high-level talks, suspension of Team Spirit	Accepts "inspections necessary for continuity of safeguards," resumption of working-level talks with ROK
3/1/94	"Super Tuesday," simultaneous steps agreed December 29, 1993, to be implemented	

RENEGES	**RENEGES**

3/3/94	ROK makes suspension of Team Spirit contingent on exchange of special envoys, "full" IAEA inspections.	
	US unilateral statement: suspension of Team Spirit, high-level talks on premise that inspections "fully implemented," North-South dialogue continues through "exchange of special envoys"	
3/5/94		Lets IAEA see second reprocessing line under construction but bars some agreed procedures, citing "external factors." IAEA breaks off inspection
3/19/94	ROK-DPRK talks break off. US consults ROK on Team Spirit, deploys Patriots	

RENEGES	**RENEGES**

4/29/94		Invites IAEA to complete March inspection, monitor refueling, but not ad hoc and routine inspections, sampling of fuel rods
5/4/94	IAEA rejects offer. US redraws red line: if no sampling, no high-level talks	
5/12/94		Notifies IAEA, US that refueling begun
5/13/94	IAEA agrees to complete March inspection, monitor refueling	
6/10/94	IAEA suspends DPRK technical assistance	
6/13/94		Notifies US of intent to leave IAEA and oust inspectors

COOPERATES	**RECIPROCATES**

6/15/94	Carter disavows sanctions	Kim Il Sung accepts freeze monitored by IAEA, summit with ROK, confirmed in subsequent exchange of letters

APPENDIX II

KEY DOCUMENTS

JOINT STATEMENT OF THE D.P.R.K. AND THE U.S.A.
NEW YORK, JUNE 11, 1993

The D.P.R.K. and the U.S.A. held government-level talks in New York from the 2nd through the 11th of June, 1993. . . . At the talks, both sides discussed policy matters with a view to a fundamental solution of the nuclear issue on the Korean peninsula. Both sides expressed support for the North-South Joint Declaration of the Denuclearization of the Korean Peninsula in the interest of nuclear nonproliferation goals.

The D.P.R.K. and the United States have agreed to principles of:

—assurance against threat and use of force, including nuclear weapons;
—peace and security in a nuclear-free Korean peninsula, including impartial application of full-scope safeguards, mutual respect for each other's sovereignty, and noninterference in each other's internal affairs; and
—support for the peaceful reunification of Korea.

In this context, the two Governments have agreed to continue dialogue on an equal and unprejudiced basis. In this respect, the Government of the D.P.R.K. has decided unilaterally to suspend as long as it considers necessary the effectuation of its withdrawal from the Treaty on the Nonproliferation of Nuclear Weapons.

AGREED STATEMENT BETWEEN THE U.S.A. AND THE D.P.R.K.
GENEVA, JULY 19, 1993

The delegations of the U.S.A. and the D.P.R.K. met from July 14–19, 1993, in Geneva for a second round of talks on resolving the nuclear issue.

Both sides reaffirmed the principles of the June 11, 1993, joint U.S.A.-D.P.R.K. statement.

For its part, the U.S.A. specifically reaffirmed its commitment to the principles on assurances against the threat and use of force, including nuclear weapons.

Both sides recognize the desirability of the D.P.R.K.'s intention to replace its graphite-moderated reactors and associated nuclear facilities with light-water moderated reactors (LWRs). As part of the final resolution of the nuclear issue, and on the premise that a solution related to the provision of LWRs is achievable, the U.S.A. is prepared to support the introduction of LWRs and to explore with the D.P.R.K. ways in which the LWRs could be obtained.

Both sides agreed that full and impartial application of I.A.E.A. safeguards is essential to accomplish a strong international nuclear nonproliferation regime.

On this basis, the D.P.R.K. is prepared to begin consultations with the I.A.E.A. on outstanding safeguards and other issues as soon as possible.

The U.S.A. and the D.P.R.K. also reaffirmed the importance of the implementation of the North-South Joint Declaration on the Denuclearization of the Korean Peninsula. The D.P.R.K. reaffirms that it remains prepared to begin the North-South talks, as soon as possible, on bilateral issues, including the nuclear issue.

The U.S.A. and the D.P.R.K. have agreed to meet again in the next two months to discuss outstanding matters related to resolving the nuclear issue, including technical questions related to the introduction of LWRs, and to lay the basis for improving overall relations between the D.P.R.K. and the U.S.A.

AGREED STATEMENT BETWEEN THE U.S.A. AND THE D.P.R.K. GENEVA, AUGUST 12, 1994

The delegations of the U.S.A. and the D.P.R.K. met in Geneva from August 5–12, 1994, to resume the third round of talks.

Both sides reaffirmed the principles of the June 11, 1993, U.S.-D.P.R.K. joint statement and reached agreement that the following elements should be part of a final resolution of the nuclear issue:

(1) The D.P.R.K. is prepared to replace its graphite-moderated reactors and related facilities with light-water reactor (LWR) power plants, and the U.S. is prepared to make arrangements for the provision of LWRs of approximately 2,000 MW(e) to the D.P.R.K. as early as possible and to make arrangements for interim energy alternatives to the D.P.R.K.'s graphite-moderated reactors. Upon receipt of U.S. assurances for the provision of LWRs and for arrangements for interim energy alternatives, the D.P.R.K. will freeze construction of the 50 MW(e) and 200 MW(e) reactors, forego reprocessing, and seal the Radiochemical Laboratory, to be monitored by the I.A.E.A.
(2) The U.S. and the D.P.R.K. are prepared to establish diplomatic representation in each other's capitals and to reduce barriers to trade and investment, as a move toward full normalization of political and economic relations.
(3) To help achieve peace and security on a nuclear-free Korean peninsula, the U.S. is prepared to provide the D.P.R.K. with assurances against the threat or use of nuclear weapons by the U.S., and the D.P.R.K. remains prepared to implement the North-South Joint Declaration on the Denuclearization of the Korean Peninsula.
(4) The D.P.R.K. is prepared to remain a party to the Treaty on the Non-Proliferation of Nuclear Weapons and to allow implementation of its safeguards agreement under the Treaty.

Important issues raised during the talks remain to be resolved. Both sides agree that expert-level discussions are necessary to advance the replacement of the D.P.R.K.'s graphite-moderated program with LWR technology, the safe storage and disposition of the spent fuel, provision of alternative energy, and the establishment of liaison offices. Accordingly, expert-level talks will be held in the U.S. and D.P.R.K. or elsewhere as agreed. The D.P.R.K. and U.S. agreed to recess their talks and resume in Geneva on September 23, 1994.

In the meantime, the U.S. will pursue arrangements necessary to provide assurances for the LWR project to the D.P.R.K. as part of a final resolution of the nuclear issue, and the D.P.R.K. will maintain the continuity of safeguards, as agreed in the June 20–22, 1994, exchange of messages between Assistant Secretary of State Robert L. Gallucci and First Vice Minister of Foreign Affairs Kang Sok Ju.

THE AGREED FRAMEWORK OF OCTOBER 21, 1994

Delegations of the Governments of the United States of America and the Democratic People's Republic of Korea held talks in Geneva from September 23 to October 17, 1994, to negotiate an overall resolution of the nuclear issue on the Korean peninsula.

Both sides reaffirmed the importance of attaining the objectives contained in the August 12, 1994, Agreed Statement between the U.S. and the D.P.R.K. and upholding the principles of the June 11, 1993, Joint Statement of the U.S. and the D.P.R.K. to achieve peace and security on a nuclear-free Korean peninsula. The U.S. and the D.P.R.K. decided to take the following actions for the resolution of the nuclear issue:

I. Both sides will cooperate to replace the D.P.R.K.'s graphite-moderated reactors and related facilities with light-water reactor (LWR) power plants.

1. In accordance with the October 20, 1994, letter of assurance from the U.S. President, the U.S. will undertake to make arrangements for the provision to the D.P.R.K. of a LWR project with a total generating capacity of approximately 2,000 MW(e) by a target date of 2003.
—The U.S. will organize under its leadership an international consortium to finance and supply the LWR project to be provided to the D.P.R.K. The U.S., representing the international consortium, will serve as the principal point of contact with the D.P.R.K. for the LWR project.
—The U.S., representing the consortium, will make best efforts to secure the conclusion of a supply contract with the D.P.R.K. within six months of the date of this document for the provision of the LWR project. Contract talks will begin as soon as possible after the date of this document.
—As necessary, the U.S. and the D.P.R.K. will conclude a bilateral agreement for cooperation in the field of peaceful uses of nuclear energy.

2. In accordance with the October 20, 1994, U.S. letter of assurance concerning interim energy alternatives, the U.S., representing the consortium, will make arrangements to offset the energy foregone due to the freeze of the D.P.R.K.'s graphite-moderated reactors and related facilities, pending completion of the first LWR unit.
—Alternative energy will be provided in the form of heavy oil for heating and electricity production.

—Deliveries of heavy oil will begin within three months of the date of this document and will reach a rate of 500,000 tons annually, in accordance with an agreed schedule of deliveries.

3. Upon receipt of U.S. assurances for the provision of LWRs and for arrangements for interim energy alternatives, the D.P.R.K. will freeze its graphite-moderated reactors and related facilities and will eventually dismantle these reactors and related facilities.

—The freeze on the D.P.R.K.'s graphite-moderated reactors and related facilities will be fully implemented within one month of the date of this document. During the one-month period, and throughout the freeze, the I.A.E.A. will be allowed to monitor this freeze and the D.P.R.K. will provide full access to the I.A.E.A. for this purpose.

—Dismantlement of the D.P.R.K.'s graphite-moderated reactors and related facilities will be completed when the LWR project is completed.

—The U.S. and D.P.R.K. will cooperate fully in finding a method to store safely the spent fuel from the 5 MW(e) experimental reactor during the construction of the LWR project, and to dispose of the fuel in a safe manner that does not involve reprocessing in the D.P.R.K.

4. As soon as possible after the date of this document U.S. and D.P.R.K. experts will hold two sets of experts talks.

—At one set of talks, experts will discuss issues related to alternative energy and the replacement of the graphite-moderated reactor program with the LWR project.

—At the other set of talks, experts will discuss specific arrangements for the spent fuel storage and ultimate disposition.

II. The two sides will move toward full normalization of political and economic relations.

1. Within three months of the date of this document, both sides will reduce barriers to trade and investment, including restrictions on telecom services and financial transactions.

2. Each side will open a liaison office in the other's capital following resolution of consular and other technical issues through expert-level discussions.

3. As progress is made on issues of concern to each side, the U.S. and D.P.R.K. will upgrade bilateral relations to the Ambassadorial level.

III. Both sides will work together for peace and security on a nuclear-free Korean peninsula.

1. The U.S. will provide formal assurances to the D.P.R.K. against the threat or use of nuclear weapons by the U.S.

2. The D.P.R.K. will consistently take steps to implement the North-South Joint Declaration on the Denuclearization of the Korean Peninsula.

3. The D.P.R.K. will engage in North-South dialogue, as this Agreed Framework will help create an atmosphere that promotes such dialogue.

IV. Both sides will work together to strengthen the international nuclear non-proliferation regime.

1. The D.P.R.K. will remain a party to the Treaty on the Nonproliferation of Nuclear Weapons (NPT) and will allow implementation of its safeguards agreement under the Treaty.

2. Upon conclusion of the supply contract for the provision of the LWR project, ad hoc and routine inspections will resume under the D.P.R.K.'s safeguards agreement with the I.A.E.A. with respect to the facilities not subject to the freeze. Pending conclusion of the supply contract, inspections required by the I.A.E.A. for the continuity of safeguards will continue at facilities not subject to the freeze.

3. When a sufficient portion of the LWR project is completed, but before delivery of key nuclear components, the D.P.R.K. will come into full compliance with its safeguards agreement with the I.A.E.A. (INFCIRC/403), including taking all steps that may be deemed necessary by the I.A.E.A., following consultations with the Agency, with regard to verifying the accuracy and completeness of the D.P.R.K.'s initial report on all nuclear material in the D.P.R.K.

Kang Sok Ju   Robert L. Gallucci

TEXT OF PRESIDENT CLINTON'S LETTER TO KIM JONG IL

I wish to confirm to you that I will use the full powers of my office to facilitate arrangements for the financing and construction of a light-water nuclear power reactor project within the D.P.R.K., and the funding and implementation of interim energy alternatives for the D.P.R.K. pending completion of the first reactor unit of the light-water reactor project. In addition, in the event that this reactor project is not completed for reasons beyond the control of the D.P.R.K., I will use the full powers of my office to provide, to the extent necessary, such a project from the United States, subject to approval of the U.S. Congress. Similarly, in the event that the interim energy alternatives are not provided for reasons beyond the control of the D.P.R.K., I will use the full powers of my office to provide, to the extent necessary, such interim energy alternatives from the United States, subject to the approval of the U.S. Congress.

I will follow this course of action so long as the D.P.R.K. continues to implement the policies described in the Agreed Framework Between the United States of America and the Democratic People's Republic of Korea.

NOTES

CHAPTER 1
UNCOOPERATIVE AMERICA

1. "Threats and Opportunities on the Korean Peninsula," Speech at the Korean Information Center, Washington, July 20, 1994.

2. A 1993 poll found 54 percent of the establishment believed the United States had lost influence; 30 percent of the public did. Seventy-five percent of the establishment wanted the United States to play the most active role in the world, compared to 37 percent of the public. Andrew Kohut, "Societal Change in the United States and Its Transatlantic Consequences from an Empirical Perspective," *Estranged Friends*, eds. Max Kaase and Andrew Kohut (New York: Council on Foreign Relations Press, 1996), pp. 81, 88.

3. For instance, while 86 percent of the foreign policy establishment favored going to war if North Korea invaded South Korea, just 31 percent of the general public did. Kohut, "Societal Change," p. 78. Cf., Stephen Kull, "What the Public Knows that Washington Doesn't," *Foreign Policy* 101 (Winter 1995–96), pp. 102–15.

4. It is a maxim of bureaucratic politics succinctly stated by Graham Allison and Morton Halperin: "Ask who in another government wants to do what you want for his own reasons. If you locate him, strengthen him. If you do not, despair." Graham T. Allison and Morton H. Halperin, "Bureaucratic Politics: A Paradigm and Some Policy Implications," in Raymond Tanter and Richard H. Ullman, eds., *Theory and Policy in International Relations* (Princeton: Princeton University Press, 1972), p. 75.

5. Mitchell Reiss, *Bridled Ambition: Why Countries Constrain Their Nuclear Capabilities* (Washington: Woodrow Wilson Center Press, 1995), ably details all but the first two cases. Inducements also played a part in earlier efforts to keep Sweden and Australia non-nuclear. In all these cases, domestic political considerations were important influences on decisions to disarm or refrain from nuclear-arming.

6. Secretary of State Warren Christopher, testimony before the Senate Foreign Relations Committee, January 24, 1995.

7. Elaine Sciolino, "Clinton Ups Atom Stakes," *New York Times*, October 20, 1994, p. A-7.

8. Among those who make the case for appeasement are Winston Churchill, *The Gathering Storm* (Boston: Houghton Mifflin, 1948), chap. 18; Hans Morgenthau, *Politics Among Nations*, 3rd ed. (New York: Knopf, 1962), pp. 64–67; Evan Luard, "Conciliation and Deterrence: A Comparison of Political Strategies in the Interwar and Postwar Periods," *World Politics* XIX, 2 (January 1967), pp. 167–89; and Alexander L. George, *Bridging the Gap: Theory and Practice in Foreign Policy* (Washington: U.S. Institute of Peace, 1993), chap. 5.

9. Senator John McCain, Conference on the U.S. Nuclear Agreement: Current Status and Prospects for the Future, The Heritage Foundation, Washington, June 15, 1995.

10. Memorandum by K. A. Namkung, June 7, 1994. Namkung was a key intermediary with North Korea.

11. Korean Central News Agency (KCNA), September 25, 1994, in Foreign Broadcast Information Service, *East Asia* (henceforth *FBIS*), September 26, 1994, pp. 41–42.

12. John Merrill and William J. Taylor, Jr., "R.O.K.-U.S. Security Relations in 1991," *Korea Briefing, 1992*, ed. Donald N. Clark (Boulder: Westview, 1992), p. 63.

13. Cost was Defense Secretary Dick Cheney's main reason for cancelling Team Spirit in 1992. Interview with senior Bush Administration official, June 28, 1996.

14. Government Accounting Office, *Navy Carrier Battle Groups: The Structure and Affordability of the Future Force* (Washington: Government Printing Office, February 1993), p. 19. The annual cost could approach $3.7 billion if indirect acquisition and other costs are taken into account. Cf., Andrew Krepinevich, Jr., *A New Navy for a New Era* (Washington: Center for Strategic and Budgetary Assessment, 1996), p. 20.

15. Defense Secretary William Perry and General Edward Luck, U.S., Congress, Senate, Armed Services Committee, *Security Implications of the Nuclear Non-Proliferation Agreement with North Korea*, 104th Cong., 1st Sess., January 26, 1995, pp. 22, 32. If the impact on regional economies is taken into account, the cost was estimated at $1 trillion.

16. Interview with senior Defense Department official, February 5, 1996.

17. The term, "shared images," is used in Morton H. Halperin, *Bureaucratic Politics and Foreign Policy* (Washington: Brookings, 1977), p. 11. On the relationship between images and perception, see John Steinbruner, *The Cybernetic Theory of Decision* (Princeton: Princeton University Press, 1974), chap. 4; Robert Jervis, "Hypotheses on Misperception," *World Politics* XX, 3 (April 1968), pp. 454–79; and *Perception and Misperception in International Politics* (Princeton: Princeton University Press, 1976), chaps. 4, 7; and Alexander L. George, *Presidential Decisionmaking in Foreign Policy: The Effective Use of Information and Advice* (Boulder: Westview, 1980), chaps. 2–3.

18. By early in the next century, according to C.I.A. Director James Woolsey, U.S. Congress, Senate Select Committee on Intelligence, Hearing: Global Threat Assessment, January 10, 1995. Estimates in previous years were 8–10 years. In 7–15 years, according to Defense Secretary William Perry, in Clyde Haberman, "U.S. and Israel See Iranians 'Many Years' from A-Bomb," *New York Times*, January 10, 1995, p. A-3. Perry was contradicting Israeli and American officials who contended it would take Iran just five years, who were quoted in Chris Hedges, "Iran May Be Able to Build an Atomic Bomb in 5 Years, U.S. and Israeli Officials Fear," *New York Times*, January 5, 1995, p. A-10.

CHAPTER 2
THE BUSH DEADLOCK MACHINE

1. Robert Carlin, "North Korea," *Nuclear Proliferation after the Cold War*, ed. Mitchell Reiss and Robert S. Litwak (Washington: The Woodrow Wilson Center Press, 1994), p. 129. Carlin, as chief of the Northeast Asia Division,

Bureau of Intelligence and Research, was the senior North Korea–watcher in the State Department.

2. Leonard S. Spector, with Jacqueline R. Smith, *Nuclear Ambitions: The Spread of Nuclear Weapons, 1989–1990* (Boulder: Westview, 1990), p. 129; and Michael J. Mazarr, *North Korea and the Bomb* (New York: St. Martin's, 1995), p. 41.

3. Thomas W. Graham, "The International Atomic Energy Agency: Can It Effectively Halt the Proliferation of Nuclear Weapons?" *U.S. Policy and the Future of the United Nations*, ed. Roger A. Coate (New York: Twentieth Century Fund Press, 1994), pp. 89–112.

4. Barry M. Blechman et al., *Force without War: U.S. Armed Forces as a Political Instrument* (Washington: Brookings, 1978), pp. 2, 48, 51, 128; Richard K. Betts, *Nuclear Blackmail and Nuclear Balance* (Washington: Brookings, 1987), pp. 31–47; Alexander L. George and Richard Smoke, *Deterrence in American Foreign Policy: Theory and Practice* (New York: Columbia University Press, 1974), pp. 238–41; Roger Dingman, "Atomic Diplomacy during the Korean War," *International Security* XIII, 3 (Winter 1988–89), pp. 60–66, 72, 75, 79–86; Rosemary Foot, "Nuclear Coercion and the Ending of the Korean Conflict," *International Security* XIII, 3 (Winter 1988–89), pp. 98–101; Peter Hayes, *Pacific Powderkeg: American Nuclear Dilemmas in Korea* (Lexington, MA: Lexington Books, 1991), pp. 60–62, 127–28, 131–33; and Leonard S. Spector and Jacqueline R. Smith, "North Korea: The Next Nuclear Nightmare," *Arms Control Today* XXI, 2 (March 1991), p. 10. Admiral Arthur Radford, chairman of the Joint Chiefs of Staff, made the first explicit nuclear pledge to South Korea in January 1955, declaring that the United States "would be ready to use atomic weapons, if needed" in the event of North Korean aggression.

5. Hayes, *Pacific Powderkeg*, has a detailed history of American nuclear deployments and strategy in Korea.

6. Kim Tae-woo, Korean Institute of Defense Analyses, "The United States and North Korea: A South Korean Perspective," Paper presented at the Carnegie Endowment for International Peace, Symposium on "The United States and North Korea: What Next?" Washington, November 16, 1993 (unpublished), p. 4. Cf. Spector, *Nuclear Ambitions*, chap. 8.

7. Joseph Yager, "South Korea," in Jozef Goldblat, ed., *Non-Proliferation: The Why and Wherefore* (London: Taylor and Francis, 1985), p. 199.

8. South Korea began nuclear-arming in 1971 after the Nixon Doctrine was promulgated and one American division was withdrawn from the peninsula. It resumed its program in 1977 when President Carter proposed withdrawing another division. North Korea may have learned from South Korea's experience. In September 1990 as Moscow moved toward establishing diplomatic relations with Seoul, Pyongyang warned that it would have to seek "some weapons for which we have so far relied on the alliance." KCNA dispatch, in *FBIS*, September 19, 1990, p. 15.

9. Reflecting those assessments, Senators Sam Nunn and Richard Lugar carefully noted in a statement on the Korean Peninsula on February 23, 1994, "Both U.S. and South Korean forces maintain a qualitative edge over their North Korean counterparts in most force categories, especially in the air and at sea." These assessments make worst-case assumptions about the other side's ca-

pabilities to wage war against the United States. American analysts then engage in mirror-imaging and assume that the other side shares their conclusion, but what if the other side does a worst-case assessment of its own? Its military disadvantage may have seemed even greater in Pyongyang, given this fundamental asymmetry in net assessments.

10. The numbers are from International Institute for Strategic Studies, *The Military Balance, 1996–97* (London: Oxford University Press, 1996), pp. 186–89.

11. Interview with General James Clapper, October 31, 1996.

12. Albert Wohlstetter and Gregory S. Jones, "'Breakthrough' in North Korea?" *Wall Street Journal*, November 4, 1994, p. A-12.

13. Robert A. Manning, "Economic Sanctions or Economic Incentives?" Paper presented at the Carnegie Endowment Symposium on "The United States and North Korea: What Next?" Washington, November 16, 1993 (unpublished), pp. 3–4, and Report of the Symposium on North Korea and Prospects for Korean Unification, La Jolla, May 25–27, 1995 (unpublished), pp. 8–10. The data are drawn from South Korean sources. They may overstate the decline in GDP by underestimating private economic activity in the North, which goes unreported, as well as "off-the-books" trade across the Chinese and Russian borders and with South Korea and Japan.

14. Robert L. Carlin and John Merrill, "North Korea's Relations with the United States and Japan," *Korea 1991: The Road to Peace*, ed. Michael J. Mazarr, John Q. Blodgett, Cha Young-koo, and William J. Taylor, Jr. (Boulder: Westview, 1991), pp. 118–21.

15. John Merrill, "The Regional Political Context of Inter-Korean Economic Cooperation," in Korea Economic Institute, *Korea's Economy, 1994*, vol. X (Washington: K.E.I., 1994), p. 2.

16. For a history of earlier efforts, see Carlin and Merrill, "North Korea's Relations with the United States and Japan," pp. 125–27; and Ralph N. Clough, *Embattled Korea: The Rivalry for International Support* (Boulder: Westview, 1987), pp. 111–21, 184–203.

17. Interview with State Department official, March 25, 1996.

18. Deputy Assistant Secretary of State Desaix Anderson, U.S., House, Subcommittee on Asian and Pacific Affairs, *Hearing on Korea: North-South Nuclear Issues*, 101st Cong., 2nd Sess., July 25, 1990 (Washington: Government Printing Office, 1991), p. 19.

19. Don Oberdorfer, "Bush, Roh Act to Reassure North Korea," *Washington Post*, June 7, 1990, p. A-29.

20. Ibid.

21. Ruth Sinai, "Bush Administration Approved Major Trade Deals with North Korea," Associated Press, March 17, 1993.

22. Interviews with U.S. officials, January 11, 1991, December 27, 1991, January 11, 1996.

23. Interview with Richard Solomon, February 27, 1996.

24. Colin Powell, *My American Journey* (New York: Random House, 1995), p. 540. Powell's skepticism about nuclear arms is abundantly apparent on pp. 45, 47, 112–13, 323–24, 452, 485–86.

25. Philip Zelikow and Condoleezza Rice, *Germany Unified and Europe Transformed* (Cambridge: Harvard University Press, 1995), pp. 304–5, 312–13. R. Jeffrey Smith, "U.S. to Seek to Eliminate Most A-Arms in Europe," *Washington Post*, May 3, 1990, p. A-1.

26. Interview with senior Bush Administration officials, February 27, 1996, and June 28, 1996.

27. Interview with Donald Gregg, August 21, 1996.

28. Powell, *My American Journey*, p. 540.

29. "Issues and Opportunities in U.S.-Korean Relations," A Report of the Committee on U.S.-R.O.K. Relations, cosponsored by the East-West Center and the Seoul Forum for International Affairs, February 11, 1991 (unpublished). Another ex-chairman of the Joint Chiefs of Staff, Admiral William Crowe, favored removal of U.S. arms but only after North Korea guaranteed it would not develop nuclear arms of its own. William Crowe and Alan Romberg, "Rethinking Security in the Pacific," *Foreign Affairs* LXX, 2 (Spring 1991), p. 134.

30. For instance, Joseph Churba and Sol Sanders, letter to the editor, *Washington Post*, July 13, 1991, p. A-18.

31. Leslie H. Gelb, "The Next Renegade State," *New York Times*, April 10, 1991, p. A-25.

32. Interview with Roh Tae Woo, September 23, 1991.

33. *Korea Times*, July 4, 1991, p. 2, in *FBIS*, July 5, 1991, pp. 21–22, and *Korea Herald*, August 9, 1991, p. 2, in *FBIS*, August 9, 1991, pp. 25–26

34. Don Oberdorfer, "U.S. Refuses to Shift Nuclear Arms in South Korea," July 3, 1991, p. A-23.

35. *Korea Herald*, August 9, 1991, p. 2, in *FBIS*, August 9, 1991, pp. 25–26, reflecting a July 3 South Korean backgrounder.

36. Mazarr, *North Korea and the Bomb*, p. 65.

37. Interview with senior U.S. official, March 30, 1997.

38. "Nuclear Developments," *Nonproliferation Review* I, 3 (Spring/Summer 1994), pp. 132, 134, and II, 2 (Winter 1995), p. 97.

39. Interview with senior Bush Administration official, June 28, 1996.

40. Powell, *My American Journey*, p. 541. Cf., Andrew Rosenthal, "Arms Plan Germinated in Back-Porch Sessions," *New York Times*, September 29, 1991, p. 14.

41. Interview with senior Bush Administration official, June 28, 1996.

42. Interviews with U.S. officials, December 27, 1991, February 16, 1996. Cf., Don Oberdorfer, "U.S. Decides to Withdraw A-Weapons from S. Korea," *Washington Post*, October 19, 1991, p. A-1.

43. His "diplomatic sources" seemed familiar with President Bush's meeting with President Roh Tae Woo on September 23, where the subject did not come up, but not with the earlier Wolfowitz-Kim consultation. Don Oberdorfer, "Airborne U.S. A-Arms to Stay in South Korea," *Washington Post*, October 12, 1991, p. A-20.

44. Shim Jae Hoon, "Early signs," *Far Eastern Economic Review*, November 7, 1991, p. 11.

45. James Sterngold, "Seoul Says It Now Has No Nuclear Arms," *New York Times*, December 19, 1991, p. A-3.

46. Reiss, *Bridled Ambition*, pp. 238, 292 n. 24.

47. Interview with State Department official, March 25, 1996.

48. Interview with Donald Gregg, August 21, 1996.

49. Interview with senior military officer, May 2, 1997.

50. David Easter, "Korea Talks Gain Amid Nuke Scare Campaign," *Guardian*, November 20, 1991, p. 17.

51. Interview with senior Bush Administration official, February 27, 1996.

52. Interview with senior Bush Administration official, June 28, 1996.

53. Joint Communique of the 23rd R.O.K.-U.S. Security Consultative Meeting, Seoul, November 20–22, 1991.

54. David Sanger, "Cheney, in Korea, Orders Halt to U.S. Pullout," *New York Times*, November 22, 1991, p. A-7.

55. Mazarr, *North Korea and the Bomb*, p. 67.

56. R.O.K. Ministry of Defense press release, January 7, 1991.

57. Interview with Richard Solomon, February 27, 1996.

58. Statement of the D.P.R.K. Foreign Ministry, in *FBIS*, November 25, 1991, pp. 6–7.

59. Mazarr, *North Korea and the Bomb*, p. 72.

60. Mike McCurry carefully noted at the State Department daily briefing April 4, 1994, "It's important that we have not seen any evidence, at this point, that North Korea has separated any plutonium over the last three years." Cf., Reuters, "UN Body Sees No More N. Korean Plutonium Extraction," September 12, 1994.

61. John Merrill, "The Korean War: Questions of Leadership," The Sanwa Lecture Series, Fletcher School of Law and Diplomacy, Medford, MA, Spring 1994.

62. Jim Hoagland, "Stopping North Korea's Bomb," *Washington Post*, October 24, 1991, p. A-23.

63. Reiss, *Bridled Ambitions*, pp. 245–46.

64. For example, Stephen Chapman, "A Nuclear North Korea: The Danger We Can't Ignore," *Chicago Tribune*, November 14, 1991.

65. Yonhap, September 27, 1991. It was the second such suggestion he had made publicly. On April 12 he told a group of Korean editors that South Korea might be forced to mount an Entebbe-style raid against North Korea's nuclear facilities. He later retracted his remark, causing three South Korean newspapers to delay publication. David E. Sanger, "Furor in Seoul over North's Atom Plant," *New York Times*, April 16, 1991, p. A-3.

66. Thomas Friedman, "China Undercuts U.S. Anti-Atom Effort on Korea," *New York Times*, November 15, 1991, p. A-12.

67. Interviews with senior officials, December 27, 1991, February 27, 1992, June 12, 1992. Cf., Mazarr, *North Korea and the Bomb*, p. 58. Douglas Paal, the National Security Council's Asia specialist, also favored negotiations, but was unable to convince his boss.

68. Interview with senior Bush Administration official, June 28, 1996.

69. Interview with a senior State Department official, February 27, 1996.

70. Notes of meeting with Kim Il Sung, December 1991. Interview with Stephen Solarz, January 16, 1992. Solarz was accompanied by Stanley Roth and Ralph Clough.

71. Reuters dispatch, December 23, 1991.

72. David E. Sanger, "Bush Warns Seoul of Pace of Pacts with North Korea," *New York Times*, January 6, 1992, p. A-1. The differences between what should be negotiated were not as profound as the differences over who should do the negotiating.

73. Interview with Charles Kartman, December 3, 1996.

74. Ibid.

75. Interview with senior Bush Administration official, February 27, 1996.

76. Interview with a U.S. official, March 25, 1996.

77. Interview with participant, March 26, 1996.

78. Interview with senior Bush Administration official, February 27, 1996.

79. Interview with senior Bush Administration official, February 27, 1996, and with senior U.S. official, February 27, 1992, and D.P.R.K. official, November 23, 1993. Cf., Robert S. Greenberger and Steve Glain, "How U.S., North Korea Went from Promise to Peril in Two Years," *Wall Street Journal*, June 8, 1994, p. A-1; Mazarr *North Korea and the Bomb*, pp. 70–71.

80. Interview with Charles Kartman, December 3, 1996.

81. Interview with administration official, March 30, 1997.

82. Mazarr, *North Korea and the Bomb*, p. 51.

83. Arnold Kanter, "Carrots and Sticks," Paper for the Carnegie Endowment Symposium on "The United States and North Korea: What Next?" November 16, 1993 (unpublished), p. 1.

84. Reiss, *Bridled Ambition*, p. 296 n. 51.

85. Interview with Defense Department official, February 16, 1996.

86. Don Oberdorfer, "North Korea Describes Nuclear Reactor Program," *Washington Post*, April 15, 1992, p. A-32.

87. David E. Sanger, "North Korea Plan on Fueling A-Bomb May Be Confirmed," *New York Times*, June 15, 1992, p. A-1.

88. "N. Korean Proposal," *Washington Post*, June 8, 1992, p. A-13.

89. Interview with senior Administration official, March 25, 1996.

90. Interview with State Department official, March 25, 1996.

91. Interview with State Department official, March 25, 1996.

92. Interviews with five participants, February 27, 1996, March 22, 1996, March 25, 1996, April 9, 1996, and April 9, 1996.

93. Interview with Charles Kartman, December 3, 1996.

94. "Fearing North Korea Too Fast," *New York Times*, March 2, 1992, p. A-14 (emphasis in original). Elaine Sciolino, "C.I.A. Chief Says North Koreans Are Hiding Nuclear Arms Projects," *New York Times*, February 26, 1992, p. A-1. His testimony was previewed for Don Oberdorfer, "N. Korea Seen Closer to A-Bomb," *Washington Post*, February 23, 1992, p. A-1.

95. Elaine Sciolino, "U.S. Agencies Split over North Korea," *New York Times*, March 10, 1992, p. A-1.

96. Interview with INR analyst, February 27, 1995.

97. R. Jeffrey Smith, "N. Koreans Accused of Arms Ploy," *Washington Post*, February 28, 1992, p. A-29.

98. Bruce Van Voorst, Interview with Robert M. Gates, Jr., *Time* CXXXIX, 16 (April 20, 1992), p. 62.

99. Interview with State Department and intelligence officials, April 9, 1996.

100. Warren Strobel, "N. Korea Hiding Nuclear Plants?" *Washington Times*, June 21, 1992, p. 1.

101. T. R. Reid, "North Korea Reveals Existence of Nuclear Reactor Unknown in West," *Washington Post*, April 17, 1992, p. A-7. Its existence was in fact known to U.S. intelligence.

102. Gary Milhollin, "North Korea's Bomb," *New York Times*, June 4, 1992, p. A-23. Blix himself began making the case for the prototype. In his June 15 report to the Board of Governors, which was leaked to the press even before he formally presented it, he noted, "The timetable of the operations and the industrial logic seemed to suggest that a small pilot plant should have preceded the 'radiochemical laboratory.'" But he added, "the existence of any such pilot plant was categorically denied" by the D.P.R.K. Sanger, "North Korea Plan on Fueling A-Bomb May Be Confirmed."

103. Speech at the Heritage Foundation, Washington, May 20, 1992. Cf., interview on SBS-TV, Seoul, May 18, 1992, *Korea Update*, p. 4.

104. Interview with senior administration official, February 27, 1992. The talks were conducted by A.C.D.A. Director Ronald Lehman and Assistant Secretary of State for Politico-Military Affairs William Rope.

105. Interview with State Department official, April 6, 1996.

106. Interview with State Department official, April 9, 1996.

107. Interview with State Department official, February 27, 1996.

108. Yonhap dispatch, November 30, 1991, in *FBIS*, December 3, 1991, p. 16. Cf. Reiss, *Bridled Ambition*, p. 240.

109. Interview with Defense Department official, May 20, 1996.

110. Interview with U.S. official, February 16, 1996.

111. Interview with State Department official, June 27, 1996.

112. Interview with Donald Gregg, August 21, 1996.

113. Interviews with U.S. officials, February 22, 1993, February 16, 1996.

114. Interview with State Department official, June 27, 1996.

115. Interview with State Department official, April 9, 1996.

116. Interview with senior military officer, May 2, 1997.

117. Interview with senior Bush Administration official, June 28, 1996.

118. Interview with State Department official, April 9, 1996.

119. Interview with INR official, March 25, 1996.

120. Interview with State Department official, April 9, 1996.

121. Interview with INR official, March 25, 1996.

122. Interview with State Department official, April 9, 1996.

123. Ibid.

124. Interview with Charles Kartman, December 3, 1996.

125. Interview with Donald Gregg, August 21, 1996.

126. *FBIS*, October 13, 1992, p. 17.

127. *FBIS*, October 22, 1992, p. 21.

128. KCNA, press statement by Kim Jong-u, chairman of the North-South Joint Economic Cooperation and Exchange Commission, *FBIS*, October 23, 1992, p. 21.

129. Peter Hayes, "Nuclear Inspections in Korea: Rough Waters Ahead?" *Sisa Journal* (Seoul), November 20, 1992.

130. Reiss, *Bridled Ambition*, p. 244.

131. Interview with State Department official, April 9, 1996.

132. John J. Fialka, "U.S., Allies Seem Set to Give North Korea Time to Consider Treaty Withdrawal," *Wall Street Journal*, March 18, 1993, p. A-9.

133. Interview with Defense Department official, April 25, 1996.

134. Interview with Assistant Secretary of Defense Ashton Carter, March 3, 1997.

135. Interviews with participants, February 22, 1993, December 14, 1995, and February 5, 1996.

136. Interview with U.S. official, February 16, 1996.

137. Interview with State Department official, June 27, 1996.

138. Interview with Defense Department official, May 20, 1996.

139. R. Jeffrey Smith, "N. Korea and the Bomb: High-Tech Hide-and-Seek," *Washington Post*, April 27, 1993, p. A-1.

140. T. R. Reid, "Shake-Up in North Korea Leaves Experts Guessing," *Washington Post*, December 10, 1993, p. A-47.

141. David E. Sanger, "The Nonproliferation Treaty Bares Its Toothlessness," March 14, 1993, p. IV-18.

142. Statement of the D.P.R.K. Government Declaring Withdrawal from the Nonproliferation Treaty, March 12, 1993.

143. Ruth Sinai, "Bush Administration Approved Major Trade Deals with North Korea," Associated Press, March 17, 1993.

144. David Sanger, "South Korea, Wary of the North, Debates Building a Nuclear Bomb," *New York Times*, March 19, 1993, p. A-8.

145. "The Korean Peninsula Heats Up," *New York Times*, March 12, 1993, late edition, p. A-28.

146. Robert A. Manning and Leonard S. Spector, "North Korea's Nuclear Gambit," *Washington Post*, March 21, 1993, p. C-3.

147. T. R. Reid, "Overtures Made to N. Korea," *Washington Post*, March 17, 1993, p. A-25.

148. "North Korea's Bomb Threat," *Wall Street Journal*, March 17, 1993, p. A-14.

149. David Kay, "Don't Wait for a Change of Heart in North Korea," *Wall Street Journal*, March 18, 1993, p. A-12.

CHAPTER 3
THE CLINTON ADMINISTRATION TIES ITSELF IN KNOTS

1. Quoted in Roger Hilsman, *To Move a Nation* (Garden City, NY: Doubleday, 1967), p. 15.

2. Interview with State Department official, April 9, 1996.

3. Interview with senior Clinton Administration official, February 5, 1996.

4. Interview with senior administration official, May 1, 1997.

5. Douglas Jehl, "Seoul Eases Stand on Nuclear Inspections of North," *New York Times*, March 30, 1993, A-13. Cf., Don Oberdorfer, "South Korean: U.S. Agrees to Plan to Pressure North," *Washington Post*, March 30, 1993, p. A-14.

6. Interview with Daniel Poneman, March 30, 1997.

7. Interview with a senior D.P.R.K. diplomat, March 9, 1993.

8. I.A.E.A., "Safeguards in the D.P.R.K.: Chronological Background," 94-2-15, February 15, 1994 [henceforth cited as I.A.E.A. Chronology], p. 12.

9. Jim Hoagland, "China Policy: Back to Bush?" *Washington Post*, April 1, 1993, p. A-23.

10. Thomas L. Friedman, "China Undercuts U.S. Anti-Atom Effort on Korea," November 15, 1991, p. A-12.

11. The sole exception had occurred in the case of Iraq, after vigorous diplomacy by U.N. Ambassador Thomas Pickering.

12. Interviews with Chinese official, March 10, 1993, and March 2, 1994.

13. Interview with senior administration official, May 2, 1994.

14. Interview with senior administration official, April 23, 1996.

15. Interviews with Chinese officials, February 10, June 23, and August 11, 1993.

16. Lena H. Sun and Jackson Diehl, "Arms Issue Reported Causing Rift Between China, N. Korea," *Washington Post*, April 28, 1993, p. A-13.

17. Interview with U.S. official, February 15, 1996.

18. D.P.R.K. Foreign Ministry Statement, April 6, 1993.

19. Interview with State Department official, April 9, 1996.

20. Interview with senior administration official, March 30, 1997.

21. Interview with Ashton Carter, March 3, 1997.

22. Interview with Defense Department official, April 24, 1996.

23. Interview with Defense Department official, May 20, 1996. For the hawks' account, see Kenneth R. Timmerman, "Going Ballistic," *New Republic*, January 24, 1994, pp. 12–15.

24. Interview with Ashton Carter, March 3, 1997.

25. Interview with Defense Department official, April 24, 1996.

26. Interview with Thomas Hubbard, June 27, 1996.

27. Interview with Ashton Carter, March 3, 1997.

28. "Washington Whispers," *U.S. News & World Report*, March 29, 1993, p. 18.

29. Jim Mann, "N. Korea Intent on Becoming a Nuclear Power, Experts Say," *Los Angeles Times*, March 31, 1993, p. A-1.

30. Aidan Foster-Carter, "North Korea and the Bomb," *Financial Times*, April 4, 1993, p. 8.

31. Arms Control Association briefing, Washington, April 6, 1993.

32. Mann, "N. Korea Intent on Becoming a Nuclear Power, Experts Say." Harrison was one of several Americans, myself included, who were hearing this argument from the North Koreans.

33. Ahn Byung Joon, "The Options for North Korea," *Far Eastern Economic Review*, May 6, 1993, p. 23.

34. Warren Strobel, "U.S.-North Korea talks a possibility," *Washington Times*, April 14, 1993, p. 1.

35. I.A.E.A. Chronology, p. 16.

36. Interview with Defense Department official, May 20, 1996.

37. David E. Sanger, "North Korea Stirs New A-Arms Fears," *New York Times*, May 6, 1993, p. A-7.

38. Interview with Ashton Carter, March 3, 1997.

39. Interviews with State Department officials, April 9, 1996.

40. Douglas Jehl, "U.S. Agrees to Discuss Arms Directly with North Korea," *New York Times*, April 23, 1993, p. A-10.

41. Douglas Jehl, "U.S. Sees Conciliatory Atom Steps by North Korea," *New York Times*, May 13, 1993, p. A-11.

42. R. Jeffrey Smith, "U.S. North Korea Set High-Level Meeting on Nuclear Program," *Washington Post*, May 25, 1993, p. A-14.

43. R. Jeffrey Smith, "U.S. Outlines Compromise in Korea Talks," *Washington Post*, May 27, 1993, p. A-42.

44. U.S., Senate, Foreign Relations Committee, Asia and Pacific Subcommittee, Hearing, May 26, 1993.

45. Interview with Deputy Secretary of State Thomas Hubbard, June 27, 1996.

46. Interview with a delegation member, March 30, 1997.

47. Interview with State Department official, April 9, 1996.

48. Interview with Robert Gallucci, February 27, 1996.

49. Interviews with Thomas Hubbard, July 27, 1996, and with a delegation member, March 25, 1996.

50. Robert Gallucci, press conference, New York, June 11, 1993.

51. U.S.-D.P.R.K. Joint Statement of June 11, 1993.

52. Interview with a U.S. delegate, March 25, 1996.

53. Interview with State Department official, April 9, 1996.

54. Correspondence with INR analyst, October 22, 1996.

55. Douglas Jehl, "North Korea Says It Won't Pull Out of Arms Pact Now," *New York Times*, June 12, 1993, p. 1.

56. Interview with U.S. official, February 15, 1996.

57. Interview with State Department official, March 25, 1996.

58. Lally Weymouth, "Bearing Down on North Korea," *Washington Post*, June 18, 1993, p. A-25. The editorial referred to was "To Assure a Nuclear-Free Korea," *New York Times*, June 12, 1993, p. 20.

59. Frank Gaffney, Jr., "Delusions over North Korea," *Washington Times*, June 16, 1993, p. G-3.

60. "We know that they are not building bombs right now," Defense Secretary Les Aspin told reporters on background November 2. T. R. Reid, "Aspin Reassures Japanese," November 3, 1993, p. A-10.

61. Interview with Defense Department official, May 20, 1996. A third training session took place in the United States.

62. General Uri Sagui, chief of military intelligence, disclosed this assessment in an interview with *Yediot Ahranot*, April 17, 1992.

63. Jim Mann, "U.S. Tactics in Curbing Arms Spread Debated," *Los Angeles Times*, March 13, 1992, p. A-2. Cf., Elaine Sciolino, "U.S. Tracks a Korean Ship Taking Missile to Syria," *New York Times*, February 21, 1992, p. A-9; Barton Gellman and Ann Devroy, "U.S. to Board N. Korean Ship Carrying Scuds if It Nears Gulf, Officials Say," *Washington Post*, March 8, 1992, p. A-32; John Lancaster, "Suspected Scud Shipment Reaches Iran," *Washington Post*, March 11, 1992, p. A-11; Barton Gellman, "U.S. Failed to Detect Ship," *Washington Post*, March 12, 1992, p. A-1.

64. Michael Parks, "Fearing Its Foes May Buy N. Korean Missiles, Israel Gets Down to Business," *Los Angeles Times*, June 29, 1993, p. A-3. Cf., Clyde Haberman, "Israel Seeks to Keep North Korea from Aiding Iran," *New York Times*, June 20, 1993, p. 6.

65. Reuters, "S. Korea Asks Peres Not to Visit N. Korea," June 21, 1993; "Israelis Say U.S. Opposes North Korean Deal," *New York Times*, August 15, 1993, p. 3; David Hoffman, "Israel Agrees to Suspend Contacts with North Korea," *Washington Post*, August 17, 1993, p. A-15; Robert S. Greenburger, "North Korea's Missile Sales in Mideast, Along with Nuclear Issue, Raise Concern," *Wall Street Journal*, July 19, 1993, p. A-6.

66. Interview with senior administration official, March 30, 1997.

67. Frank J. Murray, "Japan Sees N. Korean Nuclear Threat," *Washington Times*, July 7, 1993, p. 1.

68. Jim Mann and Leslie Helm, "Japan Shifts Its Stand on Ruling Out A-Bomb," *Los Angeles Times*, July 9, 1993, p. 1.

69. Gwen Ifill, "In Korea, Chilling Reminders of Cold War," *New York Times*, July 18, 1993, p. IV-1.

70. "Clinton's Warning Irks North Korea," *New York Times*, July 13, 1993, p. A-6. Japan's Foreign Minister could not resist going further at a late July news conference. Asked whether Japan might go nuclear, Muto replied, "There is a clause in the N.P.T. allowing withdrawal from the treaty. If North Korea develops nuclear weapons and that becomes a threat to Japan, first, there is the nuclear umbrella of the United States upon which we can rely. But if it comes down to a crunch, possessing the will that 'we can do it' is important." Sam Jameson, "Foreign Minister Says Japan Will Need Nuclear Arms if N. Korea Threatens," *Los Angeles Times*, July 29, 1993, p. A-3.

71. Interview with Thomas Hubbard, June 27, 1996.

72. Interview with Robert Gallucci, March 1, 1996.

73. Interview with Thomas Hubbard, June 27, 1996.

74. U.S.-D.P.R.K. Agreed Statement of July 19, 1993.

75. Interview with Thomas Hubbard, June 27, 1996.

76. Unilateral U.S. Statement of July 19, 1995, U.S. Department of State, *Dispatch* IV, 30 (July 26, 1993), p. 535.

77. William Drozdiak, "U.S., N. Korea Reach Compromise on Nuclear-Arms Inspection Crisis," *Washington Post*, July 20, 1993, p. A-14.

78. Spurgeon M. Keeny, Jr., "Reprieve But Not a Pardon," *Arms Control Today*, July/August 1993, p. 2.

79. Michael J. Mazarr, "Lessons of the North Korean Crisis," *Arms Control Today*, July/August 1993, pp. 8–12.

80. Doug Bandow, "The Risks of Coercive Nonproliferation," *Freedom Review*, September–October 1993, p. 30.

81. Larry DiRita, "Clinton's Naivete on North Korea Could Be Deadly," *Wall Street Journal*, August 25, 1993, p. A-8.

82. Stephen J. Solarz, "Pyongyang's Nuclear Game," *Far Eastern Economic Review*, September 23, 1993, p. 23.

83. "When the Coaxing Has to Stop," *Economist*, October 9, 1993, pp. 18–19.

84. Anthony Lake, "From Containment to Enlargement," speech at the

School of Advanced International Studies, Johns Hopkins University, Washington, September 21, 1993.

85. Douglas Brinkley, "Democratic Enlargement: The Clinton Doctrine," *Foreign Policy* 106 (Spring 1997), p. 108.

86. Kim Tae-woo and Kim Min-seok, "The Nuclear Issue of the Korean Peninsula," *Korea Focus* III, 5 (September–October 1993), p. 55.

87. Steve Glain, "South Korea Takes Harder Position Toward the North," *Wall Street Journal*, August 12, 1993, p. A-7. On the right-wing attacks, see Sim Jae Hoon, "Embattled Profs," *Far Eastern Economic Review*, July 15, 1993, p. 17; Steve Glain, "South Korea's Reunification Minister Uses Soft Approach, Irks Conservatives," *Wall Street Journal*, August 16, 1993, p. A-10. But hawkish pressure was unrelenting, for instance, *Tong-A Ilbo* editorial, August 31, 1993.

88. Lally Weymouth, "Peninsula of Fear," *Washington Post*, August 24, 1993, p. C-1.

89. Daniel Williams, "Pyongyang Rebuffs New Inspections," *Washington Post*, August 17, 1993, p. A-15.

90. Nayan Chanda, "Seal of Disapproval," *Far Eastern Economic Review*, March 31, 1994, p. 14.

91. Interview with Defense Department official, May 20, 1996.

92. Interview with Daniel Poneman, March 30, 1997.

93. Reiss, *Bridled Ambition*, p. 256.

94. Yonhap dispatch, October 19, 1993.

95. Interview with Defense Department official, April 24, 1996.

96. Statement to the 37th Session of the I.A.E.A. General Conference, September 27, 1993.

97. Julia Preston, "I.A.E.A., U.N. Warn N. Korea," *Washington Post*, November 2, 1993, p. A-15.

98. Reuters, "U.N. Atomic Agency Urges North Korea to Cooperate," November 1, 1993.

99. David E. Sanger, "U.S. Presses Japan on Missile Project," *New York Times*, November 3, 1993, p. A-12. On the high-tech exports, see David E. Sanger, "Tokyo Raids Seek to Halt Aid for North Korea on Missiles," *New York Times*, January 15, 1994, p. 6; Jathon Sapsford and David P. Hamilton, "Japan Probes Illegal Exports to North Korea," *Wall Street Journal*, January 17, 1994, p. A-6.

100. Interview with General James Clapper, October 31, 1996. Other intelligence officials say the warning problem was the subject of an April 1993 conference in Hawaii chaired by Charles Allen, National Intelligence Officer for Warning. Alarmists in the Defense Intelligence Agency and the C.I.A. took the tripping of indicators as a sign that North Korea was preparing to launch a war. The dominant view was that it was a technical problem with the warning indicators themselves.

101. One study completed in the Reagan Administration called into question whether allied forces in South Korea could hold off a short-warning attack until U.S. reinforcements arrived, but that was a "team B exercise" intended to challenge intelligence community assumptions. By April 1993, analysts in the Korea command, seconded by CINCPAC, leaned toward the more tempered

outlook advanced by the State Department's Bureau of Intelligence and Research. The basic conclusion of the 1994 assessment was, as Luck later put it, "Well, I can win a war. I just can't do it right away." Barton Gellman, "Trepidation at Root of U.S. Korea Policy," *Washington Post*, December 12, 1993, p. A-1. While the likelihood of war was lower in their estimation, the armed services remained firm about the costs.

102. Interview with General James Clapper, October 31, 1996.

103. Interview with senior military officer, May 2, 1997.

104. Interview with Defense Department official, April 24, 1996.

105. Interview with Ashton Carter, March 3, 1997.

106. Gellman, "Trepidation at Root of U.S. Korea Policy," p. A-1, and Peter Grier, "On US Wish List: Ability to Detect Nuclear Arms," *Christian Science Monitor*, December 28, 1993, p. 1. Cf., Robert D. Novak, "Aborted Ultimatum," *Washington Post*, December 16, 1993, p. A-25.

107. Interview with a member of the Joint Staff, December 14, 1995.

108. Interview with Defense Department official, May 20, 1996.

109. R. Jeffrey Smith, "North Korea Deal Urged by State Dept." *Washington Post*, November 15, 1993, p. A-15. Cf., a paper by a former U.S. commander in Korea, General John H. Cushman, "Military Options in Korea's Endgame," Nautilus Institute, May 1994, p. 11.

110. David E. Sanger, "U.S. Delay Urged on Korea Sanction," *New York Times*, November 4, 1993, p. A-9, and "Seoul's Big Fear: Pushing North Koreans Too Far," November 7, 1993, p. 16.

111. Tim Weiner, "U.S. in Quiet Talks with North Korea," *New York Times*, October 27, 1993, p. A-7.

112. Interview with State Department official, April 9, 1996.

113. Interviews with State Department official, April 9, 1996, with Ackerman, November 1, 1993, and with a North Korean official, November 23, 1993. Cf. Gallucci talk at the Center for Strategic and International Studies, Washington, June 29, 1994, and James Sterngold, "North Korea Assails Atomic Unit, Asks U.S. Talks," *New York Times*, October 13, 1993, p. A-14.

114. Interview with State Department official, April 9, 1996.

115. Peter Hayes, "Kim Yong Sun Meeting: October 16/93."

116. Interview with State Department official, April 9, 1996.

117. Hayes spoke to Kim Yong Sun October 19 in Pyongyang, "Should the United States Supply Light-Water Reactors to Pyongyang?" Paper presented at the Carnegie Endowment Symposium on "The United States and North Korea: What Next?" Washington, November 16, 1993 (unpublished), pp. 36–37. Cf., Selig Harrison's symposium paper, "Breaking the Nuclear Impasse: How North Korea Views the Nuclear Problem," pp. 9, 19–20; and Kim Dae Jung's speech to the Council on Foreign Relations, excerpted in "Avenues to Korean stability?" *Washington Times*, October 13, 1993, p. 17.

118. Statement by Kang Sok Ju, "The Nuclear Problem of the Korean Peninsula Can Never Be Solved by Pressure, But Be Solved Only by Means of Dialogue and Negotiation," November 11, 1993.

119. Interview with Defense Department official, April 24, 1996.

120. Interview with Defense Department official, May 20, 1996.

121. Interview with Ashton Carter, March 3, 1997.

122. Interview with senior official, February 7, 1997.

123. Interviews with senior official, January 11, 1996, and with Department of Defense official, May 20, 1996.

124. Interview with Ashton Carter, March 3, 1997.

125. Interview with Robert Gallucci, March 1, 1996.

126. Interview with Defense Department official, May 20, 1996.

127. Interview with Ashton Carter, March 3, 1997.

128. Steven Holmes, "Clinton Warns North Korea Against Building Atom Bomb," *New York Times*, November 8, 1993, p. A-6.

129. Interview with senior administration official, March 30, 1997.

130. Charles Krauthammer, "North Korea's Coming Bomb," *Washington Post*, November 5, 1993, p. A-27.

131. Andrew Weinschenk, "North Korea's Actions Bring Protest Storm From Officials," *Defense Week*, November 8, 1993, p. 3.

132. "Eyeball to Eyeball with North Korea," *Economist*, November 13, 1993, pp. 16–17.

133. "Handle with Care," *Financial Times*, November 3, 1993, p. 15.

134. Dave McCurdy, "North Korea and the Bomb," *New York Times*, November 8, 1993, p. A-19. Michael Mazarr, on McCurdy's staff, helped draft the op-ed.

135. Interview with Defense Department official, May 20, 1996.

136. Ibid.

137. Ibid.

138. Interview with senior administration official, May 1, 1997.

139. R. Jeffrey Smith, "U.S. Weighs N. Korean Incentives, November 17, 1993, *Washington Post*, November 15, 1993, p. A-31. Cf., Smith, "North Korea Deal Urged by State Dept.," p. A-15; Steven A. Holmes, "A Compromise Seen with North Korea," *New York Times*, November 16, 1993, p. A-16. On Team Spirit, Reiss, *Bridled Ambition*, p. 308 n. 136.

140. Interview with State Department official, April 9, 1996.

141. Interview with Thomas Hubbard, June 27, 1996.

142. Mark Matthews and Charles Corddry, "U.S. Warns North Korea over Nukes," *Baltimore Sun*, November 18, 1993, p. 1.

143. Interview with Defense Department official, May 20, 1996.

144. Interview with State Department official, June 27, 1996.

145. Arnold Kanter, "Carrots and Sticks," Paper for the Carnegie Endowment Symposium on The United States and North Korea: What Next?" Washington, November 16, 1993 (unpublished). At the same time Kanter also called for diplomatic isolation of North Korea and for military actions that would demonstrate determination to enforce economic sanctions, specifically a multilateral naval exercise including South Korea, Japan, Russia, and China and a U.S.-R.O.K. exercise of ground-based air defenses like the Patriot antimissile.

146. Jim Mann, " 'Carrot' Offer to N. Korea Is a Victory for Doves," *Los Angeles Times*, November 24, 1993, p. A-2; Thomas W. Lippman, "North Korea Could Prove Sanction-Proof," *Washington Post*, December 25, 1993, p. A-30.

147. Charles Krauthammer, "Talk Loudly But Carry a Big Stick," *Washington Post*, November 26, 1993, p. A-31.

148. Thomas L. Friedman, "U.S. and Seoul Differ on Appeal to North Korea on Nuclear Sites," *New York Times*, November 24, 1993, p. A-16.

149. Mann, " 'Carrot' Offer to N. Korea Is a Victory for Doves."

150. Interview with Charles Kartman, December 3, 1996.

151. Jim Mann, "Seoul Is Said to Back U.S. Bid to N. Korea," *Los Angeles Times*, October 26, 1993, p. A-1.

152. "U.S.-N.K. Ties Should Help Inter-Korean Relations," *Newsreview*, October 30, 1993, p. 6.

153. Yonhap dispatch, November 13, 1993, in *FBIS*, November 15, 1993, p. 25.

154. *Korea Herald*, November 7, 1993, p. 1.

155. T. R. Reid, "Aspin Prods, Warns North Korea," *Washington Post*, November 5, 1993, p. A-29.

156. "Denuclearization Policy Under Fire," *Newsreview*, November 6, 1993, p. 5.

157. David E. Sanger, "U.S. Delay Urged on Korea Sanction," *New York Times*, November 4, 1993, p. A-9.

158. Interview with Robert Gallucci, March 1, 1996.

159. Interview with senior administration official, May 1, 1997.

160. Interview with Thomas Hubbard, June 27, 1996.

161. Text of the Clinton-Kim press conference, November 23, 1993. By untying Team Spirit from inspections, President Kim unintentionally opened up the possibility of cancellation in the absence of any North Korean quid pro quo.

162. Text of Foreign Minister Han Sung Joo's press conference, November 23, 1993.

163. Text of White House background briefing, November 23, 1993.

164. Interview with Defense Department official, May 20, 1996.

165. Steve Glain, "Korean Nuclear Puzzle Grows Complex," *Wall Street Journal*, March 7, 1994, p. A-7E.

166. Interview with Thomas Hubbard, June 27, 1996.

167. Interview with State Department official, June 27, 1996.

168. Interview with Thomas Hubbard, June 27, 1996.

169. Interview with State Department official, June 27, 1996.

170. D.P.R.K. Foreign Ministry Statement, "We Have No Idea of Having Dialogue Under Pressure," November 29, 1993.

171. Ministry of Atomic Energy of the D.P.R.K., "On Maintaining the Continuity of I.A.E.A. Safeguards in the D.P.R.K.," December 1, 1993.

172. "Try This Deal on North Korea," *New York Times*, December 7, 1993, p. A-26.

CHAPTER 4
A "BETTER THAN EVEN" CHANCE OF MISESTIMATION

1. *High on Foggy Bottom: An Outsider's Inside View of the Government* (New York: Harper & Row, 1968), p. 78.

2. Interview with senior administration official, May 1, 1997.

3. Interview with Defense Department official, May 20, 1996.

4. Interview with senior administration official, March 30, 1997.

5. R. Jeffrey Smith, "U.S. Analysts Are Pessimistic on Korean Nuclear Inspection," *Washington Post*, December 3, 1993, p. A-1.

6. Bill Gertz, "N. Korea Unlikely to Give Up Nukes," *Washington Times*, August 24, 1994, p. 4.

7. Correspondence with INR official, October 22, 1996.

8. Interview with Defense Department official, May 20, 1996.

9. "If North Korea Has Bombs," *New York Times*, December 7, 1993, p. A-26.

10. Bill Gertz, "U.S. Intelligence: North Korea Could Have Nukes," *Washington Times*, December 2, 1993, p. 3.

11. R. Jeffrey Smith, "West Watching Reactor for Sign of N. Korea's Nuclear Intentions," *Washington Post*, December 12, 1993, p. A-49.

12. Stephen Engelberg and Michael Gordon, "Intelligence Study Says North Korea Has Nuclear Bomb," *New York Times*, December 26, 1993, p. 1.

13. Director of Central Intelligence Robert Gates' prepared testimony, House Foreign Affairs Committee, February 25, 1992.

14. Robert Gates, "The Rogue Probably Has the Bomb; Now What Do We Do?" *Los Angeles Times* (June 17, 1994), p. A-11.

15. U.S. Institute of Peace, "North Korea's Nuclear Program," A Report of the North Korea Working Group, Washington, February 24, 1994, p. 10. The group's members included Richard Solomon, Morton Abramowitz, Richard Armitage, Donald Gregg, Stephen Hadley, Arnold Kanter, Zalmay Khalilzad, Robert Manning, Steve Pieczenik, Alan Romberg, and Helmut Sonnenfeldt, all but three of whom served in the Bush Administration.

16. Robin Wright, "China Opposes Sanctions for North Korea," *Los Angeles Times*, November 27, 1993, p. A-1.

17. Interview with INR analyst, February 27, 1996.

18. Interview with General James Clapper, October 31, 1996.

19. "If North Korea Has Bombs," *New York Times*, December 28, 1993, p. A-10.

20. Interview with Defense Department official, April 24, 1996.

21. Testimony of Robert Gallucci, U.S., Senate, Committee on Foreign Relations, December 1, 1994.

22. Interviews with intelligence and Defense Department officials.

23. David Albright, "North Korean Plutonium Production," *Science and Global Security* V, (1994), p. 83. For a considerably lower estimate for the amount of plutonium to make a bomb, *assuming advanced technology*, Thomas B. Cochran and Christopher E. Paine, "The Amount of Plutonium and Highly-Enriched Uranium for Pure Fission Nuclear Weapons," Natural Resource Defense Council, August 22, 1994. The worst of the worst-case estimates is Gregory S. Jones, "How Many Nuclear Weapons Does North Korea Have: Will We Ever Know?" RAND Project Memorandum (June 1994).

24. Jim Wolf, Reuters dispatch, February 8, 1994.

25. Interview with James Laney, June 4, 1996.

26. Interview with Defense Department official, May 20, 1996.

27. Michael R. Gordon, "Pentagon Studies Plans to Bolster U.S.-Korea Forces," *New York Times*, December 2, 1993, p. A-1.

28. Interview with senior administration official, May 1, 1997.

29. Interview with senior military officer, May 2, 1997.

30. Smith, "U.S. Analysts Are Pessimistic on Korean Nuclear Inspection."

31. I.A.E.A. Chronology, p. 39.

32. R. Jeffrey Smith, "North Korea Faces Inspection Deadline," *Washington Post*, February 7, 1994, p. A-1.

33. Interview with Robert Gallucci, March 1, 1996.

34. Michael R. Gordon, "North Korea Softens Nuclear Stance," *New York Times*, December 4, 1993, p. 3.

35. Interview with Defense Department official, May 20, 1996.

36. Interview with senior administration official, May 1, 1997.

37. William Claiborne, "N. Korea Is Not Trying to Build More Nuclear Bombs, Aspin Says," *Washington Post*, December 13, 1993, p. A-13.

38. Ruth Marcus and R. Jeffrey Smith, "Clinton, U.N. Agency Dismiss N. Korean Nuclear Inspection Offer," *Washington Post*, December 7, 1993, p. A-19.

39. Remarks to the Atlantic Council, Washington, July 22, 1994, paraphrased in Paul Leventhal and Steven Dolley, "The North Korean Nuclear Crisis," *Medicine and Global Survival* I, 3 (September 1994), p. 173.

40. Interview with Thomas Hubbard, June 27, 1996.

41. Memorandum of the D.P.R.K. Ministry of Foreign Affairs, April 20, 1994, in *FBIS*, April 20, 1994, p. 4.

42. Lally Weymouth, "North Korea: Talk Means Nothing to Gangsters," *Washington Post*, December 14, 1993, p. A-25. Alan Romberg, Senior Fellow for Asia at the Council on Foreign Relations, took exception to the column on December 21, "Back from the Brink," p. A-23.

43. Asian Studies Center Symposium, "The U.S. Response to Possible North Korean Aggression," The Heritage Foundation, Washington, December 15, 1993.

44. Zalmay M. Khalilzad, Paul K. Davis, and Abram N. Shulsky, "Stopping the North Korean Nuclear Program," *RAND Issue Paper*, December 1993, pp. 1, 4, 7.

45. Reuters, "U.S. Studies N. Korean Arms Response," *Washington Post*, December 5, 1993, p. A-39.

46. Nayan Chanda, "Fission Chips Down," *Far Eastern Economic Review*, December 2, 1993, p. 17.

47. David Sanger, "North Korea's Game Looks a Lot Like Nuclear Blackmail," *New York Times*, December 12, 1993, p. IV-6.

48. Interview with State Department official, June 27, 1996.

49. I.A.E.A. Chronology, pp. 40–41.

50. David E. Sanger, "Hint of Progress, and Warning, from North Korea," *New York Times*, January 2, 1994, p. A-3.

51. Interview with State Department official, April 9, 1996.

52. Interview with Defense Department official, May 20, 1996.

53. R. Jeffrey Smith, "North Korea Agrees to Nuclear Inspection," *Washington Post*, January 4, 1994, p. A-10; Steven Greenhouse, "U.S. Now Seeks Just One Survey of North Korea," *New York Times*, January 5, 1994, p. A-1.

54. "A New Opening in North Korea," *New York Times*, January 8, 1994, p. 22.

55. Greenhouse, "U.S. Now Seeks Just One Survey of North Korea."

56. R. Jeffrey Smith, "U.S. Aide Upbeat on North Korea Talks," January 6, 1994, p. A-22.

57. A. M. Rosenthal, "The Price of Korea," *New York Times*, January 21, 1994, p. A-27.

58. Interview with Defense Department official, May 20, 1996.

59. Richard K. Betts, "Outlaw with a Bomb," *New York Times*, December 31, 1993, p. A-29.

60. Brent Scowcroft and Richard Haass, "Foreign Policy Nears a Peril Point," *New York Times*, January 5, 1994, p. A-15.

61. Charles Krauthammer, "Capitulation in Korea," *Washington Post*, January 7, 1994, p. A-19.

62. Smith, "U.S. Aide Upbeat on North Korea Talks."

63. David E. Sanger, "U.S.-North Korean Atom Accord Expected to Yield Dubious Results," *New York Times*, January 9, 1994, p. 1.

64. Nayan Chanda, "Bombs and Bombast," *Far Eastern Economic Review*, February 10, 1994, p. 18.

65. Ibid., p. 17.

66. Lynn Davis, "No Capitulation," *Washington Post*, January 26, 1994, p. A-21.

67. Interview with State Department official, April 9, 1996.

68. I.A.E.A. Chronology, pp. 41–43.

69. David E. Sanger, "North Korea Reported to Balk at Inspection Terms," *New York Times*, January 21, 1994, p. A-5.

70. I.A.E.A. Chronology, p. 44.

71. Michael R. Gordon, "U.S. Said to Plan Patriot Missiles for South Korea," *New York Times*, January 26, 1994, p. A-1. "Looking favorably" were State Department spokesman Mike McCurry's words at the daily briefing that day.

72. Interview with State Department official, June 27, 1996.

73. Lee Su-wan (Reuters), "North Korea Denounces U.S. Missiles," *Washington Post*, January 29, 1994, p. A-20.

74. "Seoul Warns N. Korea of Military Exercises," *Washington Post*, February 1, 1994, p. A-17. (Emphasis added.)

75. I.A.E.A. Chronology, pp. 45–46.

76. Memorandum of the D.P.R.K. Foreign Ministry, April 20, 1994, in *FBIS*, April 20, 1994, p. 5.

77. R. Jeffrey Smith, "North Korea Faces Inspection Deadline," *Washington Post*, February 7, 1994, p. A-1.

78. "Who Is Running Our Korea Policy?" *New York Times*, February 11, 1994, p. A-34.

79. Michael R. Gordon, with David E. Sanger, "North Korea's Huge Military Spurs New Strategy in South," *New York Times*, February 6, 1994, p. 1.

80. Jim Wolf, Reuters dispatch, February 8, 1994.

81. Reuters dispatch, February 13, 1994.

82. U.S. Institute of Peace, "North Korea's Nuclear Program," pp. 1, 12, 14, 19, 22–23.

83. Interview with James Laney, June 4, 1996.

84. Interview with State Department official, June 27, 1996.

85. Kelly Smith Tunney, Associated Press dispatch, February 8, 1994; David E. Sanger, "South Korea Tries to Soothe North," *New York Times*, February 9, 1994, p. A-6. On Patriot, testimony of Joint Chiefs of Staff Chairman John Shalikashvili to the House Armed Services Committee, Reuters dispatch, February 22, 1994, and David E. Sanger, "South Korean Expects Atomic Backdown by North," *New York Times*, February 24, 1994, p. A-8.

86. Ed Paisley, "Prepared for the Worst," *Far Eastern Economic Review*, February 10, 1994, pp. 22–23.

87. Julia Preston, "China Breaks Ranks on N. Korean Nuclear Plants," *Washington Post*, February 10, 1994, p. A-24; Paul Lewis, "U.S. Urges China to Pressure North Koreans to Open Nuclear Sites," *New York Times*, February 5, 1994, p. 5.

88. I.A.E.A. Press Release 94/4, February 15, 1994.

89. D.P.R.K. Foreign Ministry Statement, February 21, 1994.

90. David E. Sanger, "North Koreans Agree to Survey of Atomic Sites," *New York Times*, February 16, 1994, p. A-1.

91. Carol J. Williams and Jim Mann, "North Korea Approves Review of Nuclear Sites," *Los Angeles Times*, February 16, 1994, p. A-1.

92. Interview with Thomas Hubbard, June 27, 1996.

93. Statement on Resumption of U.S.-D.P.R.K. Negotiations on Nuclear and Other Issues, March 3, 1994. (Emphasis added.)

94. Department of State daily briefing, March 3, 1993. (Emphasis added.)

95. Interview with Thomas Hubbard, June 27, 1996.

96. "North Korea Asserts U.S. Endangers Pact on Atom Inspections," *New York Times*, March 5, 1994, p. 5.

97. Department of State daily briefing, March 3, 1993. (Emphasis added.) The State Department's Office of Korean Affairs "did not promote the linkage," according to a Korea hand. Interview, April 9, 1996.

98. Interview with Charles Kartman, December 3, 1996.

99. Memorandum of the Ministry of Atomic Energy of the D.P.R.K., March 19, 1994.

100. Interview with Robert Gallucci, March 1, 1996.

101. Interview with State Department official, July 8, 1996.

102. R. Jeffrey Smith, "N. Korean Conduct in Inspection Draws Criticism of U.S. Officials," *Washington Post*, March 10, 1994, p. A-34.

103. John Burton, "N. Korea's 'Sea of Fire' Threat Shakes Seoul," *Financial Times*, March 22, 1994, p. 6.

104. Michael R. Gordon, "U.S. Will Urge U.N. to Plan Sanctions for North Korea," *New York Times*, March 20, 1994, p. 1. R. Jeffrey Smith and Ann Dev-

roy, "U.S. Backs Military Exercise in S. Korea," *Washington Post*, March 20, 1994, p. A-1. Team Spirit could not be held at that late date, but the Focus Lens exercise already scheduled for the summer could be renamed "Team Spirit."

105. Stephen Barr and Lena H. Sun, "China's Cooperation on N. Korea Seen," *Washington Post*, March 21, 1994, p. A-12.

106. Steven Greenhouse, "Christopher Says U.S. Stays Firm on Korea, but Pledges Diplomacy," *New York Times*, March 23, 1994, p. A-12.

107. Allison Smale, "I.A.E.A. Asks U.N. to Intervene on North Korea Nuclear Dispute," Associated Press, March 21, 1994.

108. Compare the text of the March 25 draft resolution with the Security Council President's statement of March 31, 1994. (Emphasis added.)

109. R. Jeffrey Smith, "N. Korea Enlarges Arms Effort," *Washington Post*, April 2, 1994, p. A-1.

110. Statement by Michael McCurry, State Department Spokesman, "North Korea: Senior Policy Steering Group," April 7, 1994.

111. Interview with Defense Department official, April 24, 1996.

112. Interview with Charles Kartman, December 3, 1996.

113. Interview with Robert Gallucci, March 1, 1996.

114. Interviews with senior Clinton Administration officials, May 1994 and February 5, 1996.

115. Michael Kramer, "Playing Nuclear Poker," *Time*, February 28, 1994, p. 45.

116. Jim Hoagland, "Containing North Korea," *Washington Post*, March 10, 1994, p. A-21.

117. Perry on *Meet the Press*, quoted in Don Phillips, "Sanctions a First Step, U.S. Warns North Korea," *Washington Post*, April 4, 1994, p. A-1.

118. Mark Thompson, "Well, Maybe a Nuke or Two," *Time*, April 11, 1994, p. 58.

119. Lena H. Sun, "North Korea Doesn't Have Nuclear Arms, Leader Says," *Washington Post*, April 17, 1994, p. A-29.

120. T. R. Reid, "N. Korea's Kim Says U.S. Blocks Progress," *Washington Post*, April 19, 1994, p. A-12.

121. R. Jeffrey Smith, "S. Korea Offers Gesture to North," *Washington Post*, April 16, 1994, p. A-13, and "U.S.-South Korean Exercise Put Off as Gesture to North, April 21, 1994, p. A-18.

122. David E. Sanger, "Defense Chief Says North Korea Could Soon Build 4 A-Bombs," *New York Times*, April 21, 1994, A-7.

123. Interviews with senior military officer, April 18 and May 2, 1997.

124. Interview with James Laney, June 4, 1996. Cf., Steve Coll and David B. Ottaway, "New Threats Create Doubt in U.S. Policy," *Washington Post*, April 13, 1995, p. A-1.

125. Interview with State Department official, April 9, 1996.

126. Ibid.

127. Interview with senior administration official, February 7, 1997.

128. Speech to the Asia Society, Washington, May 3, 1994.

129. I.A.E.A., Press Statement, "Inspections Requirements in North Korea," June 15, 1994.

130. Telex from Choe Jong Sun, Director of External Affairs, D.P.R.K. Ministry of Atomic Energy, to I.A.E.A. Deputy Director-General Bruno Pellaud, April 29, 1994.

131. R. Jeffrey Smith, "N. Korea Refuses Demand to Inspect Reactor Fuel," *Washington Post*, April 28, 1994, p. A-22.

132. Ibid.

133. Interview with State Department official, April 9, 1996.

134. Interview with Defense Department official, April 24, 1996.

135. Interview with State Department official, April 9, 1996.

136. Interview with State Department official, June 27, 1996.

137. Interview with senior administration official, February 5, 1996.

138. Interview with Defense Department official, May 20, 1996.

139. Text of Gallucci letter of May 2, 1994.

140. Interview with State Department official, April 9, 1996.

141. Interview with senior administration official, April 9, 1996.

142. Associated Press, "Mitchell and Dole Back Sanctions Against N. Korea," *Washington Post*, May 16, 1994, p. A-10.

143. William J. Taylor, Jr., "Will North Korea Get the Message in Time?" *Washington Post*, May 22, 1994, p. C-7.

144. Jim Hoagland, "Thinking About Korean War II," *Washington Post*, May 12, 1994, p. A-27.

145. Interview with Defense Department official, May 20, 1996.

146. Interview with senior administration official, May 24, 1994. Cf., Gallucci testimony, House Foreign Affairs Committee, June 9, 1994, in U.S. Department of State, *Dispatch*, June 27, 1994, p. 423. The White House daily briefing, March 31, 1994, garbled the conditions.

147. Michael R. Gordon, "Citing Progress, U.S. Plans New Talks with North Korea," *New York Times*, May 21, 1994, p. 1.

148. R. Jeffrey Smith, "North Koreans' Behavior Puzzling," *Washington Post*, May 24, 1994, p. A-13.

149. R. Jeffrey Smith and Julia Preston, "Nuclear Watchdog Says N. Korea Steps Up Fuel Rod Withdrawal," *Washington Post*, May 28, 1994, p. A-25.

150. U.N. Security Council, S/PRST/1994/28, May 30, 1994.

151. R. Jeffrey Smith, "U.S. Plans to Seek North Korea Sanctions," *Washington Post*, June 1, 1994, p. A-22.

152. Ibid.

153. R. Jeffrey Smith, "Inspectors Say N. Korea Broke Deal," *Washington Post*, May 30, 1994, p. A-1.

154. Keith Bradsher, "Bradley and Gingrich Back Trade Curbs on North Korea," *New York Times*, May 30, 1994, p. 5.

155. Michael R. Gordon, "U.S. Finds It Hard to Win Consensus Over North Korea," *New York Times*, June 10, 1994, p. A-1.

156. Daniel Williams, "U.S. Considers Gradual Path for North Korea Sanctions," *Washington Post*, June 2, 1994, p. A-1. Briefing by Madeleine Albright, Ambassador to the United Nations, Associated Press, June 15, 1994.

157. Interviews with Chinese and Japanese sources.

158. William Safire, "Reactor Roulette," *New York Times*, June 2, 1994, p. A-23.

159. Charles Krauthammer, "Get Ready for War," *Washington Post*, June 3, 1994, p. A-23.

160. "North Korea's Dangerous Lurch," *New York Times*, June 1, 1994, p. A-20.

161. Reuters, "Clinton: U.S. May Press for N. Korea Sanctions," June 2, 1994.

162. Reuters, "I.A.E.A. Says It Can't Tell If N. Korea Diverted Atom Fuel," June 2, 1994.

163. Interview with Defense Department official, April 24, 1996.

164. Ann Devroy and Julia Preston, "U.S. to Seek Sanctions on N. Korea," *Washington Post*, June 3, 1994, p. A-1.

165. Michael R. Gordon, "White House Asks Global Sanctions on North Koreans," *New York Times*, June 3, 1994, p. A-1.

166. John Burton, "U.N. Meeting on N. Korea Reactor Rods," *Financial Times*, June 2, 1994, p. 5.

167. Statement by the D.P.R.K. Foreign Ministry spokesman, June 2, 1994.

168. State Department regular briefing, June 3, 1994.

169. Interview with Defense Department official, May 20, 1996.

170. Reuters dispatch, June 2, 1994.

171. Interviews with Chinese official, March 2 and June 16, 1994. Cf., Patrick E. Tyler, "China's Balancing Act: Trying to Chastise an Old Ally," *New York Times*, April 3, 1994, p. 6.

172. Lena H. Sun, "North Korea Presents China with Dilemma," June 17, 1994, p. A-20. Cf., Patrick E. Tyler, "China Tells Why It Opposes Korea Sanctions," *New York Times*, June 13, 1994, p. A-5. On June 10 China conducted a nuclear test, which some saw as partly intended to reassure Pyongyang.

173. Interview with senior South Korean official, June 7, 1994.

174. Christopher W. Hughes, "The North Korean Nuclear Crisis and Japanese Security," *Survival* XXXVIII, 2 (Summer 1996), p. 90; William Dawkins, "Japan's SDP Opposes Korean Sanctions," *Financial Times*, June 6, 1994, p. 6.

175. T. R. Reid, "Accord Near on N. Korea Sanctions," *Washington Post*, June 12, 1994, p. A-1.

176. John Darnton, "Clinton Says That North Korea Can Still Avoid U.N. Sanctions," *New York Times*, June 5, 1994, p. 14.

177. R. Jeffrey Smith and William Drozdiak, "U.S. Aides Say Other Powers Are Leaning toward Tougher North Korean Sanctions," *Washington Post*, June 11, 1994, p. A-17.

178. Michael R. Gordon, "U.S. Is Considering Milder Sanctions for North Korea," *New York Times*, June 12, 1994, p. 1.

179. Statement by the D.P.R.K. Foreign Ministry spokesman, June 13, 1994.

180. Interview with James Laney, June 4, 1994.

181. Interview with senior administration official, March 30, 1997.

182. Ann Devroy, "'War Talk' by N. Korea Rejected," *Washington Post*, June 5, 1994, p. A-1.

183. For example, David Ignatius, "The Secret Korea Debate," *Washington Post*, June 12, 1994, p. C-1; Jill Smolowe, "What If . . . War Breaks Out in Korea?" *Time*, June 13, 1994, pp. 32–34.

184. William Safire, "Korean Conflict II?" *New York Times*, June 9, 1994, A-25.

185. Douglas Jehl, "U.S. Is Pressing Sanctions for North Korea," *New York Times*, June 11, 1994, p. 7.

186. Interview with senior military officer, May 2, 1997.

187. Interview with James Laney, June 4, 1994.

188. Interview with Charles Kartman, December 3, 1996.

189. Reiss, *Bridled Ambition*, p. 271.

CHAPTER 5
DEADLOCK

1. KCNA, "North Korea Threatens to Call Off Nuclear Activities," September 26, 1994.

2. Memorandum of conversation by a participant, October 19, 1993.

3. John Burton, "N. Korea's 'Sea of Fire' Threat Shakes Seoul," *Financial Times*, March 22, 1994, p. 6.

4. Memorandum of conversation by a participant, June 6, 1994.

5. Peter Hayes, Report on a Trip to Pyongyang, May 8–11, 1993, p. 6.

6. Robert Axelrod, *The Evolution of Cooperation* (New York: Basic Books, 1985).

7. Interview with U.S. official, February 16, 1996.

8. Jim Hoagland, "More Donald Trump than John Wayne," *Washington Post*, January 13, 1994, p. A-27.

CHAPTER 6
OPEN COVENANTS, PRIVATELY ARRIVED AT

1. H. H. Gerth and C. Wright Mills, tr. and ed., *From Max Weber: Essays in Sociology* (New York: Oxford University Press, 1958), pp. 245–46.

2. Interview with State Department official, April 9, 1996.

3. Interview with Thomas Hubbard, June 27, 1996.

4. Interview with State Department official, June 28, 1996.

5. "A Stooge or a Savior?" *Newsweek*, June 27, 1994, p. 38.

6. Interview with State Department official, April 9, 1996. Cf., Reuters, "U.S. Says Graham Carried Message to N. Korea," February 3, 1994.

7. Interview with senior administration official, May 1, 1997.

8. Interviews with Stephen Linton, November 29, 1993, December 20, 1993, and February 20, 1994, and with senior administration officials, December 9, 1993, and January 19, 1994.

9. White House background briefing, June 22, 1994, and interviews with State Department officials, April 9, 1996.

10. Testimony to the Committee on Foreign Relations, Subcommittee on East Asian and Pacific Affairs, January 14, 1992.

11. Interview with Selig Harrison, March 27, 1997.

12. Ibid.

13. Correspondence with INR analyst, October 22, 1996.

14. Interview with Charles Kartman, December 3, 1996.

15. Memorandum by K. A. Namkung, June 7, 1994.

16. Interviews with K. A. Namkung, January 25 and February 1, 1996. The reference to concrete proposals, Namkung says, was an allusion to North Korean acceptance of dual seating in the United Nations and a safeguards agreement with the I.A.E.A. Word of those steps was passed to the study group when it stopped in Moscow en route home from Pyongyang by Yevgeny Primakov, then the director of the Institute of World Economics and International Relations (IMEMO) later chief of Russia's Foreign Intelligence Service and then foreign minister.

17. Interview with K. A. Namkung, January 25, 1996.

18. *Divided Korea II*, Report of the Second Asia Society Study Mission (New York: Asia Society, 1993).

19. Memorandum by K. A. Namkung, July 1, 1994.

20. K. A. Namkung, handwritten notes of May 1993, "D.P.R.K. Initiatives/ Tactics." (Emphasis in original.)

21. Telex from K. A. Namkung to Charles Kartman, June 1, 1993. Interview with Namkung, January 25, 1996.

22. Interview with K. A. Namkung, February 1, 1996. He was also told that in December 1992 an inebriated I.A.E.A. official had approached a D.P.R.K. representative in Vienna and said that the I.A.E.A. had the goods on North Korea. To the North that meant the I.A.E.A. was interested in prosecuting, not dealing with it.

23. Interview with State Department official, April 9, 1996.

24. Memorandum by K. A. Namkung, June 7, 1994.

25. Memorandum from K. A. Namkung to Thomas W. Graham, "U.S.-North Korean Relations: Cultural, Linguistic, and Psychological Issues," July 7, 1994.

26. Memorandum by K. A. Namkung, June 7, 1994.

27. Correspondence with INR official, October 22, 1996.

28. Loren Renz and Steven Lawrence, *Foundation Giving* (New York: The Foundation Center, 1992), pp. 29, 53, 59. As of February 1997, the Rockefeller Foundation spent $2.3 million on its North Korea programs.

29. Interview with foundation officer, October 25, 1994.

30. Telephone conversation with the author, April 8, 1996.

31. Memorandum by Thomas Graham, October 27, 1994.

32. Peter Hayes, "Kim's Elusive Bomb," *Far Eastern Economic Review*, November 7, 1991, p. 10.

33. Peter Hayes, "Nuclear Inspections in Korea: Rough Waters Ahead?" Nautilus Pacific Research, Berkeley, November 17, 1992, p. 4.

34. Peter Hayes, "Light-Water Reactor Technology Transfer to North Korea: Does It Make Sense?" Nautilus Pacific Research, Berkeley, September 5, 1993, p. 2.

35. Peter Hayes, Report on a Trip to Pyongyang, May 8–11, 1993, p. 7.

36. Interview with Peter Hayes, October 9, 1996.

37. Peter Hayes, "Light-Water Reactor Technology Transfer to North Korea: Does It Make Sense?" Nautilus Pacific Research Working Paper, Berke-

ley, September 5, 1993; "The Transfer of L.W.R. Technology to the D.P.R.K." Nautilus Pacific Research Working Paper, Berkeley, October 29, 1993.

38. Interviews with State Department officials, April 9, 1996.

39. "Cooperation on Energy Sector Issues with the D.P.R.K." Nautilus Pacific Research Working Paper, Berkeley, October 29, 1993; "Cooperation on Environmental Issues with the D.P.R.K." Nautilus Pacific Research Working Paper, October 29, 1993.

40. Scott Snyder, "Possible Areas of Cooperation with the D.P.R.K.," An Asia Society Research Project for the Rockefeller Foundation (unpublished), October 1993.

41. Memorandum from Namkung to Graham, March 3, 1994.

42. Memoranda by K. A. Namkung, June 6 and 7, 1994.

43. Interviews with Robert Gallucci, June 23, 1995, and with State Department official, February 27, 1996.

44. Author's notes of the meeting, May 24, 1994.

45. Thomas Graham, Memorandum to President Carter, "Reflections on the North Korean Situation," June 9, 1994. (Emphasis in original.)

46. K. A. Namkung, Memorandum to Thomas Graham, "U.S.-North Korean Relations: Cultural, Linguistic and Psychological Issues," June 7, 1994.

47. Ibid.

48. Interview with CNN, June 22, 1994.

49. Tim Shorrock, "Ex-Leaders Go on Trial in Seoul, *Journal of Commerce*, February 27, 1996, p. 1-A. Although the redeployed units were not under joint command, U.S. policy was that "we should not oppose R.O.K. contingency plans to maintain law and order" by using the army in Kwangju.

50. Hayes, *Pacific Powderkeg*, chaps. 5, 13.

51. Statement to author, October 8, 1992.

52. Interview with Carter aide, August 22, 1996.

53. Interview with James Laney, June 4, 1996.

54. Interview with Defense Department official, May 20, 1996.

55. Interview with Robert Gallucci, March 1, 1996.

56. CNN interview with Carter, June 19, 1994.

57. Interview with senior administration official, May 1, 1997.

58. Ibid.

59. Carter, "Report of Our Trip to Korea, June 1994," p. 1.

60. Interview with Carter aide, August 22, 1996.

61. For a brief synopsis by an INR analyst of how Kim Jong Il had been groomed to succeed his father, Merrill, "Korean War: Questions of Leadership," pp. 21–22.

62. Interview with State Department official, June 27, 1996.

63. R. Jeffrey Smith and Ann Devroy, "One Small Concession Looms Large," *Washington Post*, June 26, 1994, p. A-1.

64. R. Jeffrey Smith, "U.S. to Propose Delay in N. Korea Sanctions," *Washington Post*, June 15, 1994, p. A-32.

65. Reuters, "Highlights of U.S. Draft Resolution on North Korea," June 15, 1994.

66. Reuters, "Clinton Hews to Carrot, Stick North Korea Policy," June 15, 1994.

67. Karen Elliott House, "Korea: Raise Another Desert Shield," *Wall Street Journal*, June 15, 1994, p. A-19. (Emphasis in original.)

68. Brent Scowcroft and Arnold Kanter, "Korea: Time for Action," *Washington Post*, June 15, 1994, p. A-25.

69. Kim Dae Jung, "The North Korean Nuclear Problem and the Reunification of Korea," Address to the Korea Society, May 18, 1994, and "'Timing of Carter's Visit to P'yang Not Good,'" *Newsreview*, June 18, 1994, p. 7.

70. "'Timing of Carter's Visit to P'yang Not Good.'" *Newsreview*.

71. Carter, "Report of Our Trip to Korea, June 1994," p. 1.

72. Ibid.

73. Interview with senior military officer, May 2, 1997.

74. Interview with Carter aide, August 22, 1996.

75. Interview with senior administration official, May 1, 1997.

76. Michael R. Gordon, "Clinton May Add G.I.'s in Korea While Remaining Open to Talks," *New York Times*, June 17, 1994, p. A-1. Cf., David E. Sanger, "Carter Optimistic after North Korea Talks," *New York Times*, June 17, 1994, p. A-10.

77. Interview with State Department official, June 28, 1996.

78. Carter, "Report of Our Trip to Korea, June 1994," p. 2.

79. Carter, CNN interview, June 22, 1994.

80. Carter, "Report of Our Trip to Korea, June 1994," p. 3.

81. Ibid.

82. Interview with James Laney, June 4, 1996.

83. Interview with State Department official, June 28, 1996.

84. Carter, "Report of Our Trip to Korea, June 1994," p. 4. Cf., CNN interview, June 22, 1994.

85. Interview with Defense Department official, May 20, 1996.

86. Interview with Carter aide, October 25, 1996.

87. Interview with State Department official, June 28, 1996.

88. Interview with State Department official, June 27, 1996.

89. Interview with senior administration official, May 1, 1997.

90. Interview with Robert Gallucci, March 1, 1996. The idea that Gallucci should try to talk Carter out of announcing the deal on CNN was naive. Not only would that needlessly affront the ex-president, but it also would look like the administration was spurning a chance to avert a confrontation, or keep from disclosing the deal to the American people. "The first question I was asked at the press conference," recalls Gallucci, "was whether I had told Carter not to go on television. I was relieved to be able to say no."

91. Carter, telephone interview, CNN, June 15, 1994.

92. Ibid.

93. Carter, "Report of Our Trip to Korea, June 1994," p. 2.

94. Interview with State Department official, June 28, 1996.

95. Lena H. Sun, "North Korea Presents China with Dilemma," *Washington Post*, June 17, 1994, p. A-20.

96. Alessandra Stanley, "Moscow Is Miffed by U.S. Draft on Sanctions," *New York Times*, June 17, 1994, p. A-10.

97. R. Jeffrey Smith and Ann Devroy, "One Small Concession Looms Large," *Washington Post*, June 26, 1994, p. A-1.

98. Interview with Robert Gallucci, March 1, 1996.

99. Interview with participant, April 9, 1996. Several of Trollope's female characters deliberately mistake a gesture of intimacy by a male friend as a proposal of marriage.

100. During the missile crisis, the back-channel message came in the form of a personal letter from Khrushchev to Kennedy and a meeting between Alexander Fomin, KGB station chief in Washington, with ABC newsman John Scali. Robert F. Kennedy, *Thirteen Days* (New York: W. W. Norton, 1969), pp. 86–110; Graham T. Allison, *Essence of Decision* (Boston: Little Brown, 1971), pp. 218–27; McGeorge Bundy and James G. Blight, "October 27, 1962: The Transcripts of the Meetings of the ExComm," *International Security* XII, 3 (Winter 1987–88), pp. 57–62, and James G. Blight and David A. Welch, *On the Brink* (New York: Noonday Press, 1989), pp. 336–37.

101. Smith and Devroy, "One Small Concession Looms Large."

102. Interview with participants, March 1 and April 9, 1996.

103. Interview with Robert Gallucci, March 1, 1996.

104. Interview with Marion Creekmore, October 8, 1996.

105. Interview with State Department official, June 28, 1996.

106. Interview with senior official, February 7, 1997.

107. President Clinton, opening statement, news conference, June 16, 1994, U.S., Department of State, *Dispatch* V, 26 (June 27, 1994), p. 421.

108. Interview with senior official, April 9, 1996.

109. Robert Gallucci, White House briefing, June 16, 1994.

110. Carter, "Report of Our Trip to Korea, June 1994," p. 5.

111. Interview with State Department official, June 28, 1996.

112. Interview with Carter aide, August 22, 1996.

113. Carter, "Report of Our Trip to Korea, June 1994," p. 5. Cf., Carter interview on CNN, June 19, 1994. Somehow Washington lost track of Kim's commitment to allow joint teams to search for the remains, which led to a dispute with the North a year later.

114. CNN interview with Carter, June 19, 1994. Asked about his statement, Carter said that he went on to say that the sanctions were "held in abeyance."

115. Interview with State Department official, June 28, 1996.

116. R. Jeffrey Smith and Bradley Graham, "Carter Faulted by White House on North Korea," *Washington Post*, June 18, 1994, p. A-1.

117. Interview with State Department official, April 9, 1996.

118. Interview with senior administration official, May 1, 1997.

119. Michael R. Gordon, "A Shift on North Korea," *New York Times*, June 18, 1994, p. A-1.

120. Gates, "The Rogue Probably Has the Bomb; Now What Do We Do?" p. A-11.

121. Richard Haass, "Keep the Heat on North Korea," *New York Times*, June 17, 1994, p. A-31.

122. R. Jeffrey Smith, "White House Hails Carter for Efforts," June 20, 1994, p. A-1.

123. Philip Zelikow, "Can Talks with North Korea Succeed?" *New York Times*, June 24, 1994, p. A-27.

124. Donald P. Gregg, "Korea: Toughness and Talk," *Washington Post*, June 17, 1994, p. A-25.

125. R. Jeffrey Smith and Ruth Marcus, "White House Hails Carter for Efforts," *Washington Post*, June 20, 1994, p. A-1.

126. Michael R. Gordon, "Back from Korea, Carter Declares the Crisis Is Over," *New York Times*, June 20, 1994, p. A-1.

127. Text of Gallucci letter to Kang.

128. Text of Kang reply to Gallucci letter.

129. Interview with State Department official, June 28, 1996.

130. Transcript of White House press conference, June 22, 1994.

131. White House briefing, June 22, 1994. When North Korea asked Carter to resume mediation, Secretary of State Christopher traveled to Plains, Georgia, to dissuade Carter. In an interview afterward, Christopher said that Carter's involvement posed "a complicated situation that has to be reviewed on a case-by-case basis," but he left little doubt about keeping him out of the nuclear issue, which he said, "needs to be worked on carefully and with as much precision and discipline as we can." Jack Nelson, "White House Worries Carter May Imperil N. Korea Talks," *Los Angeles Times*, October 2, 1994, p. 1.

132. Charles Krauthammer, "'Peace in Our Time,'" *Washington Post*, June 24, 1994, p. A-27.

133. Henry A. Kissinger, "No Compromise, but a Rollback," *Washington Post*, July 6, 1994, p. A-19.

134. Robert D. Novak, "Package Deal on Korea," *Washington Post*, June 20, 1994, p. A-17.

135. Jessica Mathews, "North Korea: A Path Not Taken," *Washington Post*, June 19, 1994, p. C-7.

136. R. Jeffrey Smith and Ann Devroy, "U.S. Debates Shift on North Korea," *Washington Post*, June 21, 1994, p. A-1. The other participants were Robert Scalapino, James Lilley, Arnold Kanter, Leonard Spector, Alan Romberg, Jessica Mathews, and Michel Oksenberg.

137. Reuters, "Americans Favor Resuming North Korea Talks—Poll," June 18, 1994.

138. David E. Sanger, "Carter Visit to North Korea: Whose Trip Was It Really?" *New York Times*, June 18, 1994, p. 6.

139. T. R. Reid, "2 Koreas' Leaders Seek First Summit," *Washington Post*, June 19, 1994, p. A-1.

140. Carter, CNN interview, June 22, 1994.

141. Correspondence with State Department official, October 22, 1996.

CHAPTER 7
GETTING TO YES

1. Cited by Ambassador Kim Jong Su, D.P.R.K. Mission to the United Nations, to K. A. Namkung, October 20, 1993, "Possible Areas of Cooperation with the Democratic People's Republic of Korea," An Asia Society Research Project for the Rockefeller Foundation, Appendix B.

2. Interview with Thomas Hubbard, June 27, 1996.

3. Interview with senior administration official, May 1, 1997.

4. Interview with State Department official, June 28, 1996.

5. John Steinbruner, "An Offer They Can't Refuse," *Washington Post*, July 10, 1994, p. C-5.

6. Mark Helprin, "My Brilliant Korea," *Wall Street Journal*, July 25, 1994, p. A-14.

7. T. R. Reid, "Carter: N. Korea Unlikely to Give Up A-Fuel Rods," *Washington Post*, July 7, 1994, p. A-14.

8. David Albright, "North Korea's Corroding Fuel: Summary," Institute for Science and International Security, Washington, August 2, 1994.

9. Interviews with Defense Department official, July 7, 1994, State Department official, July 8, 1994, and Department of Energy official, July 8, 1994.

10. Interview with Thomas Hubbard, July 27, 1996.

11. Interview with Defense Department official, July 14, 1994. Also, interview with K. A. Namkung, July 26, 1994.

12. *Korea Herald*, July 10, 1994, p. 2, in *FBIS*, July 11, 1994, p. 42.

13. T. R. Reid, "North Korea Summons Mass Meeting," *Washington Post*, July 11, 1994, p. A-1.

14. Andrew Pollack, "Kim's Funeral Is Delayed for Two Days," *New York Times*, July 16, 1994, p. 3.

15. Andrew Pollack, "A 'Dear Leader,' Not Very Well Known, but Trained for Years to Take Control," *New York Times*, July 9, 1994, p. 12.

16. Thomas E. Ricks and Steve Glain, "Death of Kim May Be Beginning of End for North Korea's Communist Regime," *Wall Street Journal*, July 11, 1994, p. A-3.

17. Jonathan D. Pollack, "The Nuclear Card Is Back in Play," *Los Angeles Times*, July 14, 1994, p. A-11.

18. Interview with State Department official, June 28, 1996.

19. R. Jeffrey Smith, U.S. Officials Admit Shortage of Leverage, Insights on N. Korea," *Washington Post*, July 10, 1994, p. A-29.

20. Alexandre Mansourov, "Comparison of Decision-Making on the Nuclear Issue Under Kim Il Sung and in the Post-Kim Il Sung Era," Nautilus Research, Berkeley, July 26, 1994, p. 2. Cf., "North Korean Decision-Making Processes Regarding the Nuclear Issue," Nautilus Research, Berkeley, May 1994.

21. R. Jeffrey Smith, "U.S. Reassured on North Korean Nuclear Policy," *Washington Post*, July 11, 1994, p. A-11; Reuters, "Inspectors Remain at N. Korea Nuclear Complex," July 13, 1994.

22. James Sterngold, "North Korea, Its Chief Dead, Leaves World Guessing," *New York Times*, July 9, 1994, p. 1.

23. Interview with State Department official, June 27, 1996.

24. Associated Press, July 9, 1994, 2:24 A.M. Naples time. Interview with State Department official, June 28, 1996.

25. "Dole Criticizes Clinton for Offering 'Condolences' to North Korea," *New York Times*, July 11, 1994, p. A-3.

26. Ju-Yeon Kim, "Korea—How Sorry?" Associated Press, July 14, 1994. Cf. "Debates Rage Over Sending Condolence on Kim's Death," *Newsreview*, July 16, 1994.

27. Interview with State Department official, June 28, 1996.

28. Moon Ihlwan, "S. Korea Offers Olive Branch to New N. Korean Leader," Reuters, July 11, 1994.

29. Interview with Charles Kartman, December 3, 1996.

30. T. R. Reid, "New Outburst Stokes Feud on Korean Peninsula," *Washington Post*, July 19, 1994, p. A-13.

31. Ibid.

32. Andrew Pollack, "South Renews Recrimination in Korea," *New York Times*, July 21, 1994, p. A-9.

33. Reuters, "N. Korea Says Talks with U.S. Set for August 5," July 22, 1994.

34. Reuters, "N. Korea Warns Against Setting Conditions for Talks," July 25, 1994.

35. James Sterngold, "Defector Says North Korea Already Has 5 A-Bombs and May Make More," *New York Times*, July 28, 1994, p. A-7.

36. Moon Ihlwan, "Seoul Dismisses Nuclear Claims Made by N. Korean Defector," *Washington Post*, July 30, 1994, p. A-13.

37. Carol Giacomo, "U.S. Faults S. Korea Rhetoric Ahead of N. Korea Talks," Reuters, August 2, 1994.

38. Interview with Thomas Hubbard, June 27, 1996.

39. Moon Ihlwan, "U.S., S. Korea Ready to Help N. Korea Better Ties," Reuters, July 21, 1994.

40. Interview with Thomas Hubbard, July 27, 1996.

41. "Seoul Seeks Initiative in Building N.K. N-Reactors," *Newsreview*, July 30, 1994, p. 5.

42. Interview with Thomas Hubbard, June 27, 1996.

43. R. Jeffrey Smith, "U.S. to Dangle Prospect of Reactor at N. Korea," *Washington Post*, July 7, 1994, p. A-1.

44. Associated Press, "Senate Votes to Ban Aid," *New York Times*, July 16, 1994, p. 3. Cf., Frank Murkowski, "Don't Bribe North Korea," *Washington Times*, August 11, 1994, p. 19.

45. Victor Gilinsky, "No Quick Fix on Korea," *Washington Post*, August 2, 1994, p. A-15. The op-ed summarized the argument he had made in a paper coauthored by William Manning, "A U.S.-Type Light-Water Reactor for North Korea? The Legal Realities," Nautilus Research, Berkeley, December 1993.

46. Robert A. Manning and James J. Przystup, "Korea's Political Dynamic," *Washington Post*, August 5, 1994, p. A-21.

47. Stephen J. Solarz, "Next of Kim," *New Republic*, August 8, 1994, pp. 26–27.

48. Interview with State Department official, June 28, 1996.

49. R. Jeffrey Smith, "North Korea Offers Plan on Reactors," *Washington Post*, August 9, 1994, p. A-14. The article wrongly concluded that the North was refusing to freeze construction until the new reactor was completed, "which could defer any freeze for years."

50. Interview with Thomas Hubbard, July 27, 1996.

51. Ibid.

52. Interview with Defense Department official, August 11, 1994.

53. Correspondence with INR analyst, October 22, 1996.

54. Text of the Agreed Statement, August 12, 1994.

55. Interview with senior State Department official, August 13, 1994. The June 1993 Joint Statement referred to "impartial application of full-scope safeguards." The word "impartial" was Pyongyang's way of accusing the I.A.E.A. of partiality and "full-scope," Washington's term of art for special inspections.

56. Jon B. Wolfsthal, "U.S., North Korea Sign Accord on 'Resolution' of Nuclear Crisis," *Arms Control Today*, September 1994, p. 31.

57. R. Jeffrey Smith, "Korean Diplomat Predicts New Era in U.S. Reactions," *Washington Post*, August 14, 1994, p. A-1.

58. Interview with Thomas Hubbard, June 27, 1996.

59. Andrew Pollack, "South Korea Sees North's Move as Helpful," *New York Times*, August 14, 1994, p. 18.

60. Andrew Pollack, "Seoul Offers Help on Nuclear Power to North Korea," *New York Times*, August 15, 1994, p. A-1.

61. Interview with Thomas Hubbard, July 27, 1996.

62. Pollack, "Seoul Offers Help on Nuclear Power to North Korea."

63. Steven Greenhouse, "Clinton Demanding North Korean Inspections," *New York Times*, August 18, 1994, p. A-6.

64. James Sterngold, "North Korea Turns Away from Nuclear Inspection Condition," *New York Times*, August 21, 1994, p. 25.

65. Andrew Pollack, "North Korea May Rebuff South's Reactor Offer," August 29, 1994, p. A-2.

66. Associated Press, "Leaflets by Dissidents Reported in North Korea," *New York Times*, August 24, 1994, p. A-9.

67. Jim Mann, "N. Korea Succession 'Not Falling into Place,'" *Los Angeles Times*, August 19, 1994, p. 7.

68. Paul Blustein, "Rumors Rule in N. Korea, and Apparently Kim Too," *Washington Post*, August 26, 1994, p. A-19.

69. James Sterngold, "New Wrinkle in Korea Issue: Who Is in Charge in North?" *New York Times*, August 25, 1994, p. A-1.

70. T. R. Reid, "U.S.-North Korea Ties Worry Seoul," *Washington Post*, September 6, 1994, p. A-12.

71. Michael R. Gordon, "U.S. Reassures Seoul on Nuclear Arms Talks with North Korea," *New York Times*, September 8, 1994, p. A-6.

72. R. Jeffrey Smith, "U.S. Soothes South Korea on Dialogue with North," *Washington Post*, September 8, 1994, p. A-33.

73. Steve Glain, "South Korea, Under Corporate Pressure, May Drop Its Ban on Trade with North," *Wall Street Journal*, September 12, 1994, p. A-13.

74. Jim Mann, "U.S. Ceding Upper Hand to North Korea, Critics Say," *Los Angeles Times*, September 19, 1994, p. 1.

75. Michael R. Gordon, "North Korea and the U.S. at an Impasse," *New York Times*, October 6, 1994, p. A-7.

76. Telephone interview with George Perkovich, April 8, 1996. Cf., Perkovich, "The Korea Precedent," *Washington Post*, September 28, 1994, p. A-23.

77. Mann, "U.S. Ceding Upper Hand to North Korea, Critics Say." For an

early version of the poisoned carrot argument, Paul Bracken, "Nuclear Weapons and State Survival in North Korea," *Survival* XXXV, 3 (Autumn 1993), pp. 137–53.

78. Robert Gallucci, State Department regular briefing, September 21, 1994. Cf., R. Jeffrey Smith, "North Korean Demands Puzzle U.S. Negotiators," *Washington Post*, September 23, 1994, p. A-32.

79. Interview with State Department official, June 27, 1996.

80. Robert Evans, "North Korea Reports Progress at U.S. Nuclear Talks," Reuters, September 12, 1994.

81. T. R. Reid, "Dispute Could Hurt U.S.-N. Korea Talks," *Washington Post*, September 15, 1994, p. A-28.

82. Interview with State Department official, June 27, 1994.

83. Rick Atkinson, "N. Korea Asks Cash for Nuclear Shift," *Washington Post*, September 16, 1994, p. A-34. Told by reporters that the North Koreans wanted the United States to pay for a reactor of their choice, Gallucci dismissed the idea as "ludicrous." Sang-hun Choe dispatch, Associated Press, September 16, 1994.

84. Robert Gallucci, Department of State regular briefing, October 25, 1994.

85. "Don't Feed Seoul's Hawks," *New York Times*, September 16, 1994, p. A-22.

86. Reuters, "S. Korea Asks to Be Key Player in Nuclear Deal," September 22, 1994.

87. Robert Gallucci, State Department regular briefing, September 21, 1994.

88. Interview with Thomas Hubbard, June 27, 1996.

89. Ibid.

90. Interview with State Department official, June 27, 1996.

91. Interview with Thomas Hubbard, June 27, 1996.

92. Joseph Owen, "Carrier Group Boosts U.S. in N. Korea Nuclear Talks," *Pacific Stars & Stripes*, September 21, 1994, p. 1.

93. Bruce Cumings, *Korea's Place in the Sun: A Modern History* (New York: W. W. Norton, 1997), pp. 96–98.

94. Reuters dispatch, September 23, 1994.

95. Paul Shin dispatch, Associated Press, September 27, 1994.

96. Bill Gertz, "U.S. Carrier Sails from Korea," *Washington Times*, October 6, 1994, p. 14.

97. Associated Press, "Seoul Warns North with a Military Display," *New York Times*, October 2, 1994, p. 12.

98. Reuters, "South Korea, U.S. to Hold Security Talks Next Week," September 28, 1994.

99. Moon Ihlwan, "S. Korea Ready to Take Tough Line against N. Korea," Reuters, October 11, 1994.

100. Foreign Minister Han Sung Joo, "Intra-Korean Relations and Diplomacy: A Gap between Perception and Reality," Speech to the Kwanhun Club, Seoul, September 24, 1994, *Korea Update*, October 3, 1994, p. 5.

101. "U.S. N-Arms Cut Plan Won't Affect Security Here," *Newsreview*, Oc-

tober 1, 1994, p. 6. Cf., T. R. Reid, "South Korean Moves Said to Undermine U.S.-N. Korea Talks," *Washington Post*, October 9, 1994, p. A-43.

102. James Sterngold, "South Korea President Lashes Out at U.S.," *New York Times*, October 8, 1994, p. 3. Sulzberger was in South Korea "primarily to drum up advertising," according to William L. Pollack, the *Times*'s executive vice president of sales, in an article in the *Times*'s in-house magazine, "In the Field Means Asia," pp. 4–5. Kim was more temperate in an interview three days later with Steve Glain and Karen Elliott House, "Kim, Moderating His Earlier Comments, Praises State of South Korea-U.S. Ties," *Wall Street Journal*, October 11, 1994, p. A-15.

103. Reuters, "Seoul Says U.S.-North Korea Talks May Fail," September 29, 1994.

104. R. Jeffrey Smith, "U.S.-N. Korea Talks Snag on Pyongyang Demands," *Washington Post*, September 30, 1994, p. A-36.

105. Robert Gallucci, State Department regular briefing, September 21, 1994.

106. Interview with Defense Department official, October 3, 1994.

107. Interviews with State Department officials, March 25 and June 27, 1996.

108. R. Jeffrey Smith, "Clinton Approves Pact with North Korea," *Washington Post*, October 19, 1994, p. A-1.

109. Interview with Thomas Hubbard, June 27, 1996.

110. Walter B. Slocombe, "Resolution of the North Korean Nuclear Issue," *Fighting Proliferation: New Concerns for the Nineties*, ed. Henry Sokolski (Maxwell Air Force Base, Ala.: Air University Press, 1996), pp. 192–93.

111. David E. Sanger, "Clinton Approves a Plan to Give Aid to North Koreans," *New York Times*, October 19, 1994, p. A-1. The subhead, "For Korean Vow to End Arms Program, U.S. Will Provide $4 Billion for Energy," was inaccurate and misleading.

112. Robert S. Greenburger, "U.S. Will Sign Pact with North Korea Amid Skepticism," *Wall Street Journal*, October 19, 1994, p. A-3.

113. "New Deal for Pyongyang," *Wall Street Journal*, October 21, 1994, p. A-14.

114. Jim Hoagland, "Facilitator-in-Chief," *Washington Post*, October 20, 1994, p. A-21.

115. Gerald F. Seib, "In North Korea, Trouble Starts in Credibility Gap," *Wall Street Journal*, October 21, 1994, p. A-20.

116. Elaine Sciolino, "Clinton Ups Atom Stakes," *New York Times*, October 20, 1994, p. A-7.

117. William Safire, "Clinton's Concessions," *New York Times*, October 24, 1994, p. A-17.

118. Transcript, *The McNeil-Lehrer NewsHour*, October 21, 1994.

119. Sciolino, "Clinton Ups Atom Stakes."

120. R. Jeffrey Smith, "N. Korea Accord: A Troubling Precedent?" *Washington Post*, October 20, 1994, p. A-32.

121. Jessica Mathews, "A Sound Beginning with North Korea," *Washington Post*, October 21, 1994, p. A-25.

122. Thomas Wagner dispatch, Associated Press, October 22, 1994.

123. Chon Shi-yong, "Kim Seen to Be Haunted by U.S.-N.K. Deal," *Newsreview*, October 22, 1994, p. 5.

124. Lee Man Woo, "The North Nuclear Issue: A South Korean Perspective," Seminar on Contemporary Korean Affairs, Columbia University, November 17, 1994.

125. Charles Aldinger dispatch, Reuters, October 21, 1994.

126. James Sterngold, "Japan Hints at Conditions on Aid for North Korea Atom Plants," *New York Times*, October 26, 1994, p. A-13.

127. T. R. Reid, "Policy Won't Change, Christopher Assures S. Korea," *Washington Post*, November 10, 1994, p. A-55.

128. Shim Jae Hoon and Nigel Holloway, "Hold the Champagne," *Far Eastern Economic Review*, October 27, 1994, p. 14.

129. Karen Elliott House, "A Dangerous Capitulation," *Wall Street Journal*, November 14, 1994, p. A-10.

130. James Sterngold, "North Korea Reports Fulfilling a Nuclear Promise," *New York Times*, November 21, 1994, p. A-3. First word of a halt in construction of two new reactors had come earlier. Cf., Thomas Wagner, "N. Korea Blasts Military Exercises," *Washington Times*, November 2, 1994, p. 11.

131. "Mr. McCain's Risky Korea Strategy," *New York Times*, October 27, 1994, p. A-28.

132. Ben Barber, "Senator Seeks to Change N. Korea Deal," *Washington Times*, December 1, 1994, p. 23.

133. U.S., Senate, Committee on Foreign Relations, Subcommittee on East Asian and Pacific Affairs, *Hearing: U.S.-North Korea Nuclear Agreement*, December 1, 1994.

134. Andrew Pollack, "G.O.P. Critic of Korea Pact Eases Stance," *New York Times*, December 13, 1994, p. A-11; T. R. Reid, "Visiting Senators Learn Little of N. Korean Leader," *Washington Post*, December 13, 1994, p. A-32.

135. Elaine Sciolino, "Both Sides Can Claim a Victory in Release," *New York Times*, December 30, 1994, p. A-8.

136. Interview with Thomas Hubbard, June 27, 1996.

137. Andrew Pollack, "North Korea Says U.S. Pilot Admits a 'Flagrant Violation,'" *New York Times*, December 29, 1994, p. A-1.

138. Bill Richardson, "Diary of a Reluctant Diplomat," *Washington Post*, January 15, 1995, p. C-1.

139. Alexandre Mansourov, "Seven Lessons of the U.S.-D.P.R.K. Helicopter Incident," Nautilus Institute Discussion Paper, January 4, 1995.

140. Testimony of James Woolsey, Director of Central Intelligence, and General James Clapper, Director of the Defense Intelligence Agency, to the Senate Intelligence Committee, January 10, 1995.

141. Transcript of press conference, January 6, 1995.

142. D.P.R.K. Permanent Mission to the United Nations, "Let Us Dynamically Advance in the New Year Under the Leadership of the Great Party," Press Release, January 1, 1995.

143. Art Pine, "North Korea Complying with Pact, U.S. Says," *Los Angeles Times*, January 6, 1995, p. 1.

144. Associated Press, "North Korea to Lift Ban on Trade Ties with U.S.," *New York Times*, January 9, 1995, p. A-6.
145. Steven Greenhouse, "U.S. Eases Trade Limits on North Korea for First Time Since 1950," *New York Times*, January 21, 1995, p. 3.
146. R. Jeffrey Smith, "Clinton Lifts Some Restrictions on U.S. Trade with North Korea," *Washington Post*, January 21, 1995, p. A-11.
147. Thomas W. Lippman, "Senate GOP Concedes Assault on N. Korea Pact Is Futile," *Washington Post*, January 20, 1995, p. A-25.
148. U.S., Congress, Senate, Armed Services Committee, *Security Implications of the Nuclear Non-Proliferation Agreement with North Korea*, 104th Cong., 1st Sess., January 26, 1995, p. 5.
149. Secretary of State Warren Christopher, testimony before the Senate Foreign Relations Committee, January 24, 1995. (Emphasis in original.) The line he took was urged on the administration by former Secretary of State James Baker when Robert Gallucci briefed him on the contents of the Agreed Framework, according to a State Department official. Interview, October 25, 1996.
150. Senate Concurrent Resolution 4, introduced January 24, 1995.
151. Reuters, "U.S.-Korean Ties Linked to South," *Washington Post*, January 28, 1995, p. A-21.
152. Andrew Steele dispatch, Reuters, February 28, 1995.
153. R. Jeffrey Smith, "North Korea Rejects Nuclear Deal," *Washington Post*, February 7, 1995, p. A-14.
154. Interview with Thomas Hubbard, June 27, 1996.
155. Reuters, "North Korea Diverted Oil to Army, General Says," *New York Times*, February 17, 1995, p. A-12.
156. Thomas W. Lippman, "McConnell Says Christopher Misled Senate on Korean Nuclear Pact," *Washington Post*, March 2, 1995, p. A-13.
157. R. Jeffrey Smith, "N. Korea Seeks More Aid Under Nuclear Agreement," *Washington Post*, February 8, 1995, p. A-24.
158. Steven Greenhouse, "North Balks, Threatening Korean Pact," *New York Times*, February 9, 1995, p. A-7.
159. Interview with Thomas Hubbard, June 27, 1996.
160. Steven Greenhouse, "U.S. Presses North Korea to Accept Reactors Made by South," *New York Times*, March 10, 1996, p. A-11.
161. Reuters, "N. Korea Says U.S. Bids to Quash Nuclear Deal," March 17, 1995.
162. Jim Mann, "N. Korea Threatens to Pull Out of U.S. Nuclear Deal," *Los Angeles Times*, March 23, 1995, p. A-1.
163. Han Dong-soo, "Seoul Won't Give Up Main Contractor Status in N. Korean Reactor Project," *Korea Times*, April 1, 1995, p. 2.
164. R. Jeffrey Smith, "N. Korea Breaks Off Talks on Seoul's Role in Nuclear Deal," *Washington Post*, April 21, 1996.
165. D.P.R.K. Foreign Ministry spokesman, "Comments on the Break-up of the Berlin Expert Meeting," April 22, 1995.
166. Interview with Thomas Hubbard, June 27, 1996.
167. Text of U.S.-D.P.R.K. Press Statement, Kuala Lumpur, June 13, 1996.

168. Text of Resolution 1995–12 of the KEDO Executive Board, June 13, 1995.

169. Interviews with a senior KEDO official, May 21, 1996.

170. Interview with Thomas Hubbard, June 27, 1996.

CHAPTER 8
NUCLEAR DIPLOMACY IN THE NEWS—AN UNTOLD STORY

1. Don Oberdorfer, "N. Korea Releases Extensive Data on Nuclear Effort," *Washington Post*, May 6, 1992, A-11.

2. Sheryl WuDunn, "North Korean Site Has A-Bomb Hints," *New York Times*, May 17, 1992, p. A-1.

3. "N. Korean Proposal," *Washington Post*, June 8, 1992, p. A-13.

4. Reuters, "N. Korea Seeks Deal on Nuclear Technology," *Washington Times*, June 12, 1992, p. 9.

5. David E. Sanger, "North Korea Plan on Fueling A-Bomb May Be Confirmed," *New York Times*, June 15, 1992, p. A-1. (Emphasis added.) The story was datelined "Washington—June 12."

6. R. Jeffrey Smith, "N. Korea May Consider Reducing Atom Program," *Washington Post*, June 20, 1992, p. A-17.

7. David E. Sanger, "U.S. Delay Urged On Korea Sanction," *New York Times*, November 4, 1993, p. A-9.

8. David E. Sanger, "Seoul's Big Fear: Pushing North Koreans Too Far," *New York Times*, November 7, 1993, p. 16.

9. T. R. Reid, "Aspin Prods, Warns North Korea," *Washington Post*, November 5, 1993, p. A-29.

10. Interview with Ashton Carter, March 3, 1997.

11. R. Jeffrey Smith, "North Korea Bolsters Border Force," *Washington Post*, November 6, 1993, p. A-19.

12. Sanger, "Seoul's Big Fear: Pushing North Koreans Too Far."

13. James Adams and Jon Swain, "U.S. Targets Cruise Missiles at Korea," *Times* (London), November 7, 1993, p. 1.

14. Kathleen DeLaski, Department of Defense briefing, November 9, 1993. Cf., Gen. Gary Luck's testimony to the Senate Foreign Relations Committee, January 25, 1995, contains some indications of the internal estimates.

15. R. Jeffrey Smith, "North Korea Deal Urged by State Dept.," *Washington Post*, November 15, 1993, p. A-15.

16. Michael R. Gordon, "U.S. Will Urge U.N. to Plan Sanctions for North Korea," *New York Times*, March 20, 1994, p. 1.

17. John Burton, "N. Korea's 'Sea of Fire' Threat Shakes Seoul," *Financial Times*, March 22, 1994, p. 6.

18. "The decision, which was made at President Kim Young Sam's Blue House, sharply increased public anger at North Korea and apprehension about a war," reported Don Oberdorfer, "The Remilitarized Zone," *Washington Post*, May 1, 1994. p. C-2.

19. Associated Press dispatches, April 17, 1994, and June 30, 1994; Reuters,

"North Korea Says U.S. Military Moves Threaten Talks on Nuclear Dispute," *Washington Times*, July 1, 1994, p. 16.

20. Michael R. Gordon, "North Korea Said to Have A-Bomb Fuel," *New York Times*, June 7, 1994, p. A-7.

21. David B. Ottaway, "N. Korea Forbids Inspections," *Washington Post*, June 8, 1994, p. A-25.

22. Joint Statement of June 11, 1993. It is worth noting two further clauses in the sentence, "mutual respect for each other's sovereignty and noninterference in each other's internal affairs," which were linked, at least for the North Koreans.

23. Statement by Kang Sok Ju of November 11, 1993, D.P.R.K. Foreign Ministry text.

24. Joint Statement of August 12. That passage had been the subject of a last-minute delay in issuing the joint statement.

25. James Sterngold, "North Korea Turns Away from Nuclear Inspection Condition," *New York Times*, August 21, 1994, p. 25.

26. Ambassador-at-Large Robert Gallucci, State Department regular briefing, September 21, 1994.

27. Joseph Owen, "Carrier Group Boosts U.S. in N. Korea Nuclear Talks," *Pacific Stars & Stripes*, September 21, 1994, p. 1.

28. Reuters dispatch, September 23, 1994. Cf., Frances Williams, "North Korea Digs in Heels over N-Talks," *Financial Times*, September 26, 1994, p. 6.

29. Paul Shinn dispatch, Associated Press, September 27, 1994.

30. Frances Williams, "N. Korea Threatens to Quit N-Talks," *Financial Times*, September 29, 1994, p. 4.

31. R. Jeffrey Smith, "U.S.-N. Korea Nuclear Talks at Stalemate As Pyongyang Takes Hard-Line Stance," *Washington Post*, September 28, 1994, p. A-1.

32. This way of thinking about newsmaking is elaborated in Leon V. Sigal, *Reporters and Officials: The Organization and Politics of Newsmaking* (Lexington, MA: Lexington Books, 1973).

33. The first of these editorials, "Help the Koreas in from the Cold," appeared June 25, 1990. The 60th, "A Korean Reactor by Another Name," ran on March 23, 1995.

34. Interview with State Department official, March 25, 1996.

35. Interview with senior Clinton Administration official, February 5, 1996.

36. A poll taken for the Chicago Council on Foreign Relations in October 7–21, 1994, just before the October U.S.-D.P.R.K. accord, showed the public much less enthusiastic than leaders in the foreign policy establishment, academic, media, and business community about military intervention in Korea and supportive of diplomatic contact. Asked if they would favor use of U.S. troops if North Korea invaded South Korea, just 39% of the general public said yes, compared to 82% of the leaders. (A Council poll taken in the fall of 1990 found 44% of the public and 57% of the leaders willing to commit U.S. troops.) Asked whether the United States should establish normal diplomatic relations with North Korea, 57% of the leaders said yes. So did 50% of the general public. John E. Reilly (ed.), *American Public Opinion and U.S. Foreign Policy 1995* (Chicago: The Chicago Council on Foreign Relations, 1995), pp. 21, 35. A

Yankelovich poll taken June 15–16 1994, at the height of the crisis just as the Carter visit began, found 78% of the public in favor of sanctions if North Korea did not allow inspections and 17% opposed. Asked if they favored U.S. military action along with the United Nations, 51% said yes and 37% no. Asked if it were worth risking war to keep North Korea from making nuclear arms, 48% said yes, 42% no. *American Enterprise*, July/August 1994, p. 83. A *Newsweek* poll taken at the same time found 68% in favor of resuming talks even if North Korea did not permit inspections, compared to 25% in favor of the American position at the time, no talks until inspections resumed. Asked what they would support if North Korea refused sanctions, 76% backed tighter economic sanctions, 40% backed sending more U.S. troops to the region, 44% backed airstrikes against suspected nuclear targets, and 28% backed an invasion of North Korea. "A Stooge or a Savior," *Newsweek*, June 27, 1994, p. 39; Reuters dispatch, June 18, 1994.

37. *Wall Street Journal*, October 19, 1994, p. A-3.

38. David E. Sanger, "Clinton Approves a Plan to Give Aid to North Koreans," *New York Times*, October 19, 1994, p. 1.

39. Bernard Gwertzman, "Memo to the *Times* Foreign Staff," *Media Studies Journal*, Fall 1993, pp. 33–35.

40. As of January 1, 1993, for instance, the *New York Times* had 32 foreign correspondents in 29 countries plus 55 stringers, the *Los Angeles Times* had 26 in 27 countries plus 17 stringers, ABC had 23 in 16 countries plus 49 stringers, and CNN had 30 in 25 countries plus 26 stringers. By comparison, *Yomiuri Shimbun* had 44 correspondents in 29 countries and just 16 stringers. The Freedom Forum Media Studies Center Research Group, *The Media and Foreign Policy in the Post-Cold War World*.

41. Gwertzman, "Memo to the *Times* Foreign Staff," p. 36.

CHAPTER 9
THE POLITICS OF DISCOURAGEMENT

1. The classic discussion of organizational interests is that of Morton H. Halperin, *Bureaucratic Politics and Foreign Policy* (Washington: Brookings, 1974), chaps. 3, 5.

2. This was often true in arms control negotiations with the Soviet Union during the Cold War, for instance, in 1946 when the Baruch Plan was proposed, in 1950 when the decision to build the hydrogen bomb was made, and in strategic arms limitation talks (SALT) where the Arms Control and Disarmament Agency took the lead.

3. Interview with senior official, February 7, 1997.

4. Reliance on liaison did pose problems in the past. "In the period 1952 to 1963," according to an official history of the C.I.A., "the Agency acquired most of its clandestine information through liaison arrangements with foreign governments. . . . The existence of close liaison relationships inhibited developing independent assets. First, it was . . . far easier to talk to colleagues who had numerous assets in place than to expend the time required merely to make contact with an individual whose potential might not be realized for years. Second,

maintenance of liaison became an end in itself, against which independent collection operations were judged." U.S., Senate, Select Committee to Study Governmental Operations with Respect to Intelligence Activities, *Final Report, Book IV: Supplementary Detailed Staff Reports on Foreign and Military Intelligence* (Washington: Government Printing Office, 1976), p. 49.

5. Interview with INR analyst, February 27, 1996.

6. Correspondence with INR analyst, October 22, 1996.

7. Interviews with senior INR analyst, February 27, 1996.

8. U.S. Congress, House, International Relations Committee, Hearings, January 12, 1995. His line of argument was anticipated in an editorial, "A Prudent Turnabout," *New York Times*, December 17, 1994, p. 22.

9. Henry D. Sokolski, deputy assistant secretary of defense for nonproliferation policy from 1983 to 1993 and director of the Nonproliferation Policy Education Center, testimony before the House Armed Services Committee, March 24, 1994.

CHAPTER 10
WHY WON'T AMERICA COOPERATE?

1. Anthony Lake, "Confront Backlash States," *Foreign Affairs* LXXIII, 2 (March/April 1994), p. 46. Michael Klare, *Rogue States and Nuclear Outlaws* (New York: Hill & Wang, 1995), chap. 1, traces the rise of the "rogue state" doctrine.

2. Address to the United Nations General Assembly, September 27, 1993.

3. Scott D. Sagan and Kenneth Waltz, *The Spread of Nuclear Weapons: A Debate* (New York: W. W. Norton, 1995), p. 37.

4. Ibid., p. 15.

5. Another leading realist theoretician, John Mearsheimer of the University of Chicago, argued in 1993 that American attempts to remove the nuclear arms left in Ukraine after the Soviet Union's disintegration were misguided. Mearsheimer favored a policy of "controlled proliferation" on the grounds that "nuclear proliferation sometimes promotes peace." He rested his case on two contentions: "Ukraine cannot defend itself against a nuclear-armed Russia with conventional weapons, and no state, including the United States, is going to extend to it a meaningful security guarantee" and "it is unlikely that Ukraine will transfer its remaining nuclear weapons to Russia, the state it fears most." Never mind that Ukraine had a nuclear arsenal in name only and would have had considerable difficulty retargeting it against Russia and keeping it operationally reliable, safe, and secure in the meantime. Never mind that Ukraine, like North Korea, would have antagonized its neighbors and alienated its potential allies by nuclear-arming. Never mind that, again like North Korea, Ukraine's most immediate sources of insecurity were economic and political, and that a nuclear arsenal was a major impediment to easing that insecurity. By realist logic, nuclear-arming makes states secure. John J. Mearsheimer, "The Case for a Ukrainian Nuclear Deterrent," *Foreign Affairs* LXXII (1993), pp. 50–51.

6. Sagan and Waltz, *The Spread of Nuclear Weapons*, p. 19.

7. Ibid., p. 98.

8. Kenneth Waltz, *Theory of International Politics* (Reading, MA: Addison-Wesley, 1979), p. 116.

9. Ibid., pp. 102–14. Cf. Edward Hallett Carr, *The Twenty Years' Crisis, 1919–1939* (New York: Harper & Row, 1964), chaps. 8, 13.

10. For examples of such arguments, see John G. Ruggie, "International Responses to Technology: Concepts and Trends," *International Organization* XXIX, 3 (Summer 1975), pp. 557–84; Stephen D. Krasner, ed., *International Regimes* (Ithaca: Cornell University Press, 1983); Robert Keohane, *After Hegemony* (Princeton: Princeton University Press, 1984), chaps. 5–6.

11. Peter Haas, *Saving the Mediterranean* (New York: Columbia University Press, 1990), pp. 52–56; and Ernst B. Haas, *When Knowledge Is Power* (Berkeley: University of California Press, 1990), pp. 40–49, 129–30, 163.

INDEX

Clapper, Gen. James R., Jr., x, 21, 74–75, 93–94

Clark, William, 57

Clinton, William Jefferson: and Agreed Framework, 190, 192, 198; and Carter's mission, 151–52, 159–62, 164–66; China policy of, 57; council of war convened by, 155, 157–58; criticism of, 98–100, 102–3, 127, 133, 154, 163, 170, 174, 184, 192–93, 223; and diplomatic give-and-take, 8–9, 169, 226; failed policy of, 10, 13–14, 38, 52–55, 108; and Kim's death, 174–75; letter to Kim from, 134, 264; and North Korea as threat, 50–51; and package deal, 78–81, 84–85, 87; priorities of, 108–9, 112–14, 170–71; on proliferation, 245; and replacement reactors, 194, 202–3; and sanctions, 95–96, 118–22, 132–33, 162; and Team Spirit, 47–48; and threats against North Korea, 71–77; and U.S.–North Korea talks, 56–59, 61–65, 67–68, 97

Clough, Ralph, 270n. 70

CNN, and Carter's mission, 148, 157–58, 166

coal (D.P.R.K.), 23, 178, 186

Cochran, Thomas B., 70, 281n. 23

coercion: cooperation combined with, 3; failure of, 5–10, 12, 33, 51, 104, 109, 162, 168–72; gradual campaign of, 75–77; pressure for, 153; realism on, 248; skepticism toward, 50–51, 70; support for, 33–35, 44, 107, 126–27, 237, 238–40, 245–46, 251. See also carrot-and-stick approach; crime-and-punishment approach; sanctions; step-by-step approach; Team Spirit

coercive diplomacy. See coercion

Cohen, William, 98

Cold War: arms control negotiations during, 304n. 2; foreign policy after, 3–5; foreign policy during, 230; and news coverage, 208–9, 226–27

Combustion Engineering Corporation, 201

communists: attitudes toward, 223; nuclear proliferation tied to, 85–86, 127, 182; and South's destabilization efforts, 172–73

conciliation. See cooperation

conditionality, 87

conditional reciprocity. See cooperation

conflict: emphasis on, 249; news coverage of, 221–22

conventions, journalistic, 219–20, 221–22

cooperation: Bush Administration consideration of, 27; conditional reciprocity, 4; costs of, 9–10; counterattack on, 33–38; emergence of, 126; feasibility of, 146–50; liberalism on, 244–45, 250–51; motives for, 249; news coverage of, 221–22; in nongovernmental areas, 147–48; opposition to, 6–7, 10, 12–13, 17, 62–63, 126–27, 183, 231, 237, 245–46, 251; realism on, 247–49; role of, 3–4, 252–53; success of, 4–5, 133, 254. See also diplomatic give-and-take

cooperative security. See cooperation

cooperative threat reduction. See cooperation; nonproliferation

counterproliferation, 236

Creekmore, Marion, x, 148, 156, 160

crime-and-punishment approach: adoption of, 17, 32–38, 51, 232, 240–41, 244, 251; concept of, 12–13; failure of, 66, 120–22, 124–27, 229; and intelligence estimates, 91; and liberalism, 245; and news coverage, 207, 226; opposition to, 133; rejection of, 157, 168; support for, 85, 165, 217, 223, 244. See also coercion; Team Spirit; war

Crowe, Adm. William, 269n. 29

Cuban missile crisis, 159, 252

cultural exchanges, 147–48

Cumings, Bruce, xi, 242

Czechoslovakia, and nuclear weapons, 27

Davis, Lynn, x, 54–55, 99

deadlines, role of, 219–20, 224

Defense Intelligence Agency (D.I.A.), 91, 93–94, 155, 236

Delaney, James, x

demilitarized zone (DMZ): Clinton's visit to, 68; North's buildup along, 77, 212–13; North's drawback from, 161; U.S. helicopter in, 195–97

democracies, and proliferation, 245

Democratic People's Republic of Korea (D.P.R.K.). See North Korea

Leon V. Sigal is a consultant at the Social Science Research Council in New York and Adjunct Professor in the School of International and Public Affairs, Columbia University. A frequent contributor to the New York Times editorial page, he is also the author of *Fighting to a Finish: The Politics of War Termination in the United States and Japan, 1945.*